Surviving Debt

Other National Consumer Law Center Publications

LEGAL PRACTICE MANUALS

Fair Debt Collection

Consumer Bankruptcy Law and Practice

Repossessions and Foreclosures

Fair Credit Reporting Act

Unfair and Deceptive Acts and Practices

Truth in Lending

Credit Discrimination

The Cost of Credit

Consumer Warranty Law

Access to Utility Service

Automobile Fraud

Consumer Class Actions

Consumer Law Pleadings

PERIODICALS

NCLC Reports

NCLC Energy & Utility Update

Surviving Debt

A GUIDE FOR CONSUMERS

Third Edition

From
THE NATIONAL CONSUMER LAW CENTER,
America's Consumer Law Experts

Principal Authors
Gary Klein
Deanne Loonin
Jonathan Sheldon

For reprint permissions or ordering information, contact
Publications, NCLC, 18 Tremont St., Boston MA 02108,
(617) 523-8089, Fax (617) 523-7398, E-mail: consumerlaw@nclc.org

Library of Congress Catalog No. 99-61226
ISBN 1-881793-76-1

This project was supported by AT&T Universal Card Services Partners in
Credit Education, the Public Welfare Foundation, the National Consumer
Law Center, the AFL-CIO, the United Auto Workers, and others.

10 9 8 7 6 5 4 3 2 1

This book is intended to provide accurate and authoritative information in
regard to the subject matter covered. This book cannot substitute for the independent judgment and skills of a competent attorney or other professional.
Non-attorneys are cautioned against using these materials in conducting litigation without advice or assistance from an attorney or other professional.
Non-attorneys are also cautioned against engaging in conduct which might be
considered the unauthorized practice of law.

Cover design and illustration by Lightbourne Images, copyright ©1999.

Printed in Canada

ABOUT THE AUTHORS

The National Consumer Law Center (NCLC) is the nation's expert on the rights of consumer borrowers. Since 1969, NCLC has been at the forefront in representing low income consumers before the courts, government agencies, Congress, and state legislatures.

NCLC has appeared before the United States Supreme Court and numerous federal and state courts and has successfully presented many of the most important cases affecting consumer borrowers. NCLC provides consultation and assistance to legal services, private, and government attorneys in all fifty states.

NCLC publishes a nationally acclaimed series of manuals on all major aspects of consumer credit and sales. (See Bibliography for a complete list of NCLC publications.) NCLC also conducts state and national training sessions on the rights of consumer borrowers for attorneys, paralegals, and other counselors.

This book draws on the expertise of sixteen present and former NCLC attorneys, each averaging about twenty years of consumer law specialization. Two of these attorneys, Gary Klein and Deanne Loonin, were the principal authors of this edition.

Gary Klein is an NCLC attorney specializing in sustainable homeownership, consumer credit, foreclosure prevention, and consumer bankruptcy. He directs NCLC's Sustainable Homeownership Initiative. He has served as an expert witness on a variety of consumer issues for Congress and administrative agencies. He has published numerous books and articles on consumer law topics and has conducted seminars on managing credit, foreclosure prevention, responses to high rate lending, and bankruptcy. Mr. Klein has also frequently represented clients in litigation establishing significant consumer rights.

Deanne Loonin is a staff attorney at National Consumer Law Center, focusing on consumer issues affecting low-income seniors and immigrants, as well as student loan, repossession and auto fraud issues. Ms. Loonin previously worked as a staff attorney at Bet Tzedek Legal Services in Los Angeles, directing Bet Tzedek's senior consumer fraud unit.

Jonathan Sheldon has been an NCLC staff attorney since 1976 specializing in repossessions, leasing, student loans, credit reporting, and deceptive practices. His many publications include *Unfair and Deceptive Acts and*

Practices (4th ed. 1997 and Supp.), *Repossessions and Foreclosures* (3d ed. 1995 and Supp.), *Automobile Fraud* (1998) and *Consumer Warranty Law* (1997 and Supp.).

ACKNOWLEDGMENTS

Surviving Debt is the culmination of years of work and numerous contributions from experts in the field. Along the way, we have received generous support from the AFL-CIO, the United Auto Workers, the Public Welfare Foundation, various church groups, and particularly NCEE/AT&T Consumer Credit Education Fund. The views in this book are NCLC's and should not be construed as those of any other entity contributing to the development of *Surviving Debt.*

Numerous individuals contributed to the writing and final production of this volume and the prior editions. Gary Klein and Deanne Loonin were the principal authors of this edition. Other NCLC staff contributing to this book include Jon Sheldon (for his work as a principal author of two prior editions of this book), Margot Saunders (particularly for the chapter on utility terminations), Richard DuBois, Robert Hobbs, Willard Ogburn, Jerry Oppenheim, Rita Gordon Pereira, Jon Rao, and Elizabeth Renuart. We would like to thank former NCLC attorneys and other experts in the field for their assistance in this project through three editions, including Kathleen Keest, Elizabeth Ryan, Nancy Brockway, Roger Colton, Deborah Harris, Carolyn Carter, Mark Budnitz, Elizabeth Imholz, Richard McManus, Susan Reif, and Henry Sommer. Thanks also to Christine Peterson, Mark Benson, Nika Elugardo, and Mary Kingsley for research.

Special thanks to Denise Lisio for editorial assistance, helpful recommendations, production work, and extraordinary patience with the principal authors.

Ani Tashjian designed and typeset this edition, Donna Wong provided advice on style, and Lightbourne Images designed the cover.

CONTENTS

Part VI Getting Back on Your Feet

Appendices

– Introduction –

How to Use
This Book

YOU HAVE
MANY IMPORTANT
CONSUMER RIGHTS

If you are having debt problems, you may feel overwhelmed and powerless. During periods of financial hardship, you may not have the resources to pay pressing debts, to meet family needs, and to get necessary legal help. You may feel helpless to fight debt collectors pressing you for payment or threatening to seize your home, car, or other possessions.

In writing this book, we hope to help you even the playing field, and to make the best choices possible despite difficult financial circumstances. We will explain which debts you can ignore for a period of time while you get back on your feet. When you cannot ignore a particular debt without serious consequences, such as foreclosure or repossession, this book sets out helpful options to deal with these problems, both in the short term and the long run.

This book also explains your *rights as a consumer.* You are not powerless. Many federal and state laws are designed to provide help to people facing financial problems. These include protection against abusive debt collectors, relief from unfair business practices, limits on wage garnishments and seizures of property, and the right to eliminate many obligations in bankruptcy. In most cases, however, you need to know about your rights in order to exercise them. This book attempts both to explain these rights and tell you when and how to utilize them.

HOW THIS BOOK
IS ORGANIZED

The process of dealing with financial problems is mostly about making the best available choices. This book is organized into six parts, each part dealing with different types of choices you may face. Each part of the book is further divided into chapters which cover more specific issues.

Part I (Understanding Debt, Chapters 1-5) covers the different choices you will face when you cannot keep current on your debts. Chapters One and Two help you reevaluate your budget and correctly prioritize your debts. The goal is to put you in a position to deal with your most pressing problems first and to have as much money as possible available to meet those needs. This book is not intended to second guess your choices about minor issues like what groceries to buy, but rather to point out some major areas in which you can increase your income or where savings may be possible. You can then use your available money to pay for pressing needs including your home and your car.

People can easily make poor choices about which debts to pay when there is not enough money to go around. It is common for consumers to use money to pay debts, like credit card bills, which do not urgently have to be paid, just because that creditor is employing the most obnoxious collection techniques. If you are having financial problems, you should instead be paying those creditors who can do the most to actually hurt you — especially those who can take your home or your car.

Chapters Three and Four warn you about a number of unwise choices you may be tempted to make to resolve your financial problems. Getting your financial house in order is as much about avoiding the wrong choices as it is about picking the right ones. If you cannot repay your debts, you may be tempted to refinance them. This will mean that you replace your old debts with new ones. Chapter Four provides advice as to when to and when not to refinance existing debt, including potential difficulties involved in refinancing, and ways to avoid the worst pitfalls.

Chapter Five suggests some options for financial management which may help you avoid costly problems in the market for financial services. Because we explain the types of financial choices which can increase your financial problems in Chapters Three and Four, Chapter Five is provided to recommend alternatives.

Part II (Debt Collection, Your Credit Rating, Collection Lawsuits and Credit Cards, Chapters 6-10) focuses on problems when you are delinquent on "unsecured debt," those debts for which you have not put up your home, car or other property as collateral. Common examples are credit cards, doctor and hospital bills, and charges with retailers.

Creditors' major techniques for collecting on such debt are debt collection contacts, threats about your credit record, and, less frequently, collection lawsuits. Part II provides strategies for dealing with all of these collection techniques. Chapter Ten then offers some advice to help you make wise decisions about credit cards.

Part III (Home Foreclosures, Chapters 11-14) deals in depth with one of the most severe consequences of financial distress — the potential loss of your home. If you have put up your home as collateral on a loan, that lender can seize your home if you fall behind on your payments. Part III explains the foreclosure process, tells you what steps you can take to avoid foreclosure, and what you should do if foreclosure cannot be avoided.

Part IV (Evictions, Shutoffs, Repossessions, Seizure of Tax Refunds, and Other Threats to Property, Chapters 15-19) covers your best choices, both in the short term and the long term, to deal with other debts that can threaten your property. In Part IV, we explain:

- How to determine whether or not a particular debt can be temporarily ignored;
- Options you may have for negotiating with that creditor;
- Rights you may have to repay the debt over time;
- Strategies to create delay and to gain time to get back on your feet;
- Legal protections and rights you have in the debt collection process;
- How to go about enforcing your rights; and
- Situations in which it makes sense to get help.

Each chapter covers a different type of debt problem that may lead to the immediate loss of property or essential services, such as evictions, utility terminations, car repossessions, or government seizure of a tax refund. The basic lesson of each chapter is that there are many things you can do for almost every common consumer debt. Giving up is almost always the wrong choice.

Part V (Your Bankruptcy Rights, Chapter 20) provides a brief overview of your bankruptcy options, which may make particular sense for dealing with your long term financial difficulties. Bankruptcy is your most basic protection against unmanageable debt. The information in Part V is intended to help you make the right choices about when bankruptcy relief makes sense.

Note that as this book is being written, Congress is evaluating major changes to the bankruptcy laws. If you are using this book after September of 1999, you may want to ask a bankruptcy professional if changes to the bankruptcy law affect your rights.

Part VI (Getting Back on Your Feet, Chapter 21) offers advice to help you reestablish your credit once your financial problems are under control. After you have addressed your current problems, you can begin to take steps to reestablish yourself for the future.

Glossary and Bibliography. A helpful glossary of terms appears at the back of the book. Terminology used by lenders and debt collectors can vary. We have attempted to give you simple definitions of relevant terms. It is important to understand the terms being used in order to understand your rights and options.

Finally, you may decide you need more information about a particular topic than we have included in this book. A bibliography at the back of the book suggests some sources for more information.

Budget Forms. Budget forms are provided at the back of the book with notes designed to help you fill them out. These forms are designed to help you get a clear picture of what resources you have available to meet your family's financial needs. Consider using these forms as you read through Chapters One and Two.

Business and Tax Debts. This book does *not* address business-related debts. Although some of the issues related to enforcement of business debts are the same as those discussed here, major business debts may create problems of special complexity. These can include the extent of your liability for debts of corporations and partnerships with which you have been affiliated, complicated tax issues, enforcement of personal guarantees, and special liabilities associated with employment relationships. We recommend that you consult a lawyer if you have significant business-related debts.

Income tax issues can also be very complicated. In this book, we do little more than alert you to the need to deal with those debts and to some issues in dealing with IRS income tax collection activity. We recommend that you consult a tax lawyer or an accountant if you have significant potential debts to the IRS or state taxing authorities.

WHAT YOU NEED TO READ

We recommend that everyone facing financial difficulties read this book's first three chapters. You cannot make good choices about specific debts until you understand the priorities about which debts to pay, as set out in Chapter One. You will also need to set up an appropriate budget so that you have a good idea of how much money you have for payment of your debts, as explained in Chapter Two. Chapter Two also provides advice on increasing your income, decreasing your expenses, dealing with medical care, and whether you should dip into your savings. Chapter Three warns against certain options you might be tempted to try to get yourself out of financial trouble. Choosing these options are likely to make matters worse for you.

After you read these three chapters, you can then pick and choose chapters from the rest of the book which cover specific issues. For example, if you are a homeowner, you should read the chapters on foreclosure (Chapters 11-14) rather than the chapter on your rights as a tenant (Chapter 15) and *vice versa*. Read Chapter Four if you are considering refinancing your debt, Chapter Six is you are concerned with debt collectors, and Chapter Seven if you are worried about your credit rating. Other chapters focus on collection lawsuits, credit cards, utility terminations, repossessions, and government collection of student loans and taxes.

Chapter Twenty on bankruptcy may be applicable to almost any consumer in financial trouble, and should at least be skimmed by all readers. This will help you decide whether to consider the bankruptcy option. Read the chapter in full if you want initial information about whether, when and how you should file for bankruptcy.

Chapter Twenty-one on rehabilitating your credit standing should be read after your financial problems are under control. As discussed throughout the book, it rarely makes sense to worry about your credit standing until you have dealt with more urgent problems related to your current financial needs.

OBTAINING PROFESSIONAL ASSISTANCE

This book outlines your rights and gives you basic information about enforcing them. In many cases, exercising your legal rights is difficult because the applicable law and court procedures are complicated. You may need a lawyer or a nonprofit counselor to help you with enforcing many of your rights. You may also need help to apply material in this book to your particular situation.

An additional factor is that state instead of federal law governs many of your rights. These laws can vary substantially from state to state. You may need to get more information of the laws applicable to your state. We have tried to point this out whenever possible.

Hiring a Lawyer. It can be difficult to get legal help when you do not have much money. A good place to start is any option in your area for free legal services. In most communities (or close by if you live in a rural area), there are organizations which provide free legal help to people whose income fall below certain amounts. Although Congress has unfortunately cut back on funding for these organizations, they continue to exist and should be sought out if you need help.

These organizations vary widely on the type of cases they handle. They also have strict income limits so that they are forced to turn away many cases. However, it can't hurt to ask. If they can't help you, they generally will make a referral to the appropriate legal organization (often called "bar association"), sometimes for free help from a private lawyer. They also may have special pamphlets or other helpful information on your state's laws.

If you need to pay for a lawyer, it is important to get competent help. All lawyers, like all doctors and all accountants, are not the same. You should try to find someone who has expertise in consumer rights. A first step is to try to get a referral from a friend or relative to a lawyer who has done good work in the past. If you cannot get a referral, try calling your state or county bar association. Most such organizations maintain a referral service that will give you names of lawyers who specialize in consumer credit problems.

You should always have an opportunity to talk to a lawyer before you agree to pay for that lawyer's services. Make sure you have a clear idea of what the lawyer will do for you and what you will be charged. You should know whether you are paying an hourly rate or if you are paying a flat fee for a particular service. If you pay a flat fee, you should be sure to get a written statement of what the fee covers.

After you have signed a "retainer" (a contract with the lawyer laying out the services to be provided and how much you will pay), if you are dissatisfied with the service you are getting, you can always cancel. You will only have to pay for services you have already received. If you are entitled to a refund that you do not receive, consider making a complaint to the local disciplinary agency for attorneys.

Unfortunately, the cheapest lawyer will not necessarily be the best. Price should not be the only consideration when hiring a lawyer — although it is always a factor. Be sure to get someone who you feel comfortable will help you with the specifics of your problem. Lawyers should be willing to provide a free initial consultation. They should also be willing to explain the potential consequences of doing nothing about your delinquent debt. You do not want to pay a lawyer if there are no negative consequences for you if you just ignore your debts.

Finally, lawyer advertising has become a problem in our society. Some lawyers review court lists to find out who is being sued or read published foreclosure notices, and then solicit these individuals. Some lawyers make outrageous claims in their advertisements. Although not all lawyers who advertise are bad, you should not take an advertisement at face value. Make sure you know what the lawyer will do for you and whether the advertised services meet your needs. An eye-catching advertisement alone is not a good reason to hire a particular lawyer.

Getting Help From a Counselor. If you cannot afford a lawyer or if you feel you don't want one, another place to get help is from a nonprofit counselor. Many communities have both nonprofit "debt" counselors and nonprofit "housing" counselors. If you have a housing related problem, a housing counselor is probably preferable.

Counselors cannot offer the full range of services which a good lawyer can provide, but they can often help with some specific issues. Counselors, like lawyers, may focus on some options rather than others. You should be sure you understand what the counselor can do for you and make sure you feel the options offered include the right choices for your circumstances.

Some nonprofit counselors charge a fee to cover their costs. Others are free. Make sure you know from the beginning if there is a charge for counseling and how much it will be. If the fee seems unreasonable, find other help.

Finding a nonprofit counselor can sometimes be difficult. Try calling city officials, legal services, a consumer help line, or a friend or relative who has had similar problems. Sometimes a helpful creditor will make a recommendation. No matter where the recommendation comes from, make sure you exercise care that you are dealing with a legitimate nonprofit counselor from a reputable organization with expertise in the area in which you need help.

Always avoid "for profit" debt counseling. This has become a significant consumer rip off. The charge for such counseling will almost always exceed the value of the counseling. Additionally, many such counselors are geared to funneling business to high-interest rate lenders and other disreputable businesses which take advantage of people with financial problems. These businesses will only make your problems worse.

NOTE TO COUNSELORS USING THIS BOOK

This book is a revision of a prior publication which was addressed directly to debt counselors. Although the book is now written to consumers directly, it is still very valuable to counselors. Most of your clients will need your help to exercise the basic rights and options discussed in this book. Although we have tried to write simply, many clients will need help to understand the discussion here. We have not shied away from discussing complicated issues when they are necessary to a complete understanding of rights and options.

Because you regularly see clients with financial problems, you will almost always have more expertise in addressing these problems than the particular individual who seeks your help. Although we encourage you to recommend this book to your clients, you can also use it to advise clients on specific issues. Your explanations and background as a counselor will frequently reinforce the discussion which this book provides.

We recognize that many of the strategies discussed in this book go beyond what you are accustomed to doing in the counseling process. Each counselor must make his or her own decision about how far to go in actively intervening in a clients' debt problems. At a minimum, however, we ask that you make every effort to give financially stressed consumers their full range of choices by counseling them on the availability of options which go beyond the scope of what your organization would be able to do.

For example, if you work for an organization which helps consumers make payment agreements with their creditors, you should nevertheless explain that bankruptcy is an alternative to some payment agreements and cover the circumstances in which bankruptcy may make sense. Similarly, if you are accustomed to dealing with credit card issues, we ask that you be sure that you do not recommend a strategy for dealing with credit cards which undermines a consumer's ability to deal with a mortgage, car or utility payment. Whenever possible, problems should be dealt with in the context of the consumer's financial situation rather than in isolation.

NOTE TO LAWYERS
USING THIS BOOK

For lawyers who do not specialize in consumer rights, this book is intended to be a useful introduction to strategies for dealing with debts. Although we have deleted many of the statutory references due to their inaccessibility to consumers, we have included a bibliography with references to treatises containing more detailed legal information.

The best source of information for lawyers on consumer claims related to credit and utility issues is the National Consumer Law Center's series of consumer law manuals. For more details, see the bibliography, call NCLC Publications at (617) 523-8089, FAX (617) 523-7398, or write: National Consumer Law Center, Publications Department, 18 Tremont Street, Suite 400, Boston, MA 02108. Our website can be found at www.consumerlaw.org.

Lawyers who do specialize in consumer credit problems may already own other NCLC publications. You should consider using *Surviving Debt* to educate your clients, paralegals, law students or others in your office. Bulk publication orders can be arranged at substantial discounts by contacting NCLC Publications at the phone number or address above.

SOME FINAL THOUGHTS

This book is not intended to be a treatise on the law related to consumer credit. Readers who want more information should refer to the bibliography and the sources mentioned in each chapter. As stated in an earlier disclaimer, the book is also not intended to substitute for the independent judgment and skills of a competent attorney or other professional. Please read the disclaimer on the reverse of the title page for related information.

The law often changes. In addition, state laws vary a great deal. You should always make sure that you have the most recent edition of this book, and that you get necessary information about issues described here as "state" law. If the law does change, consider getting additional help.

Finally, we are eager to have feedback on your use of this book. If you have other suggestions about how to deal with debts, experiences which are contrary to the advice given here, or other comments, please feel free to write the authors.

– 1 –

Choosing Which Debts To Pay First

- *Rules for Choosing Which Debts to Pay When You Can't Pay Everyone*
- *The Consequences of Not Paying Different Types of Debt*
- *What If You Cannot Pay All Your Important Debts?*

SIXTEEN RULES ABOUT WHICH DEBTS TO PAY FIRST

If you are having serious financial problems, you probably are having trouble keeping all of your debts up to date. You can only reduce some expenses, and available income can only be stretched so far. This leaves you with no choice but to delay or not pay some debts.

Once you determine that you can't afford to pay all of your debts as they come due, you will have to make hard choices about which bills to pay first. Your home or apartment, your utility service, your car, and even your household possessions may be at stake. Following the rules in this chapter may make the difference between keeping or losing important property.

Instead of delaying or eliminating certain debt repayments, you may be tempted to take on more debt to repay old debts. This is generally a bad idea. When you should and should not refinance, consolidate, or take out new loans is discussed in Chapter Four. Chapter Two describes ways to increase your income or decrease your expenses to help you to make ends meet.

However, your main strategy in dealing with too much debt is deciding which debts to pay first, which you can refuse to pay, and which you can put off until later. The most important creditor to pay is not necessarily the creditor that screams the loudest or the most often. Creditors who yell the loudest often do so only because they have no better way to get their money than to intimidate you into paying. Of more concern are creditors who not only threaten, but actually *can* take quick action against your residence, utility service, car, or other important assets.

Pay off creditors who can take

the quickest action to hurt you,

not those who are calling the most often.

Pay your mortgage or rent first;

worry about credit card or doctor bills later.

You should direct your limited resources to what is most necessary for your family — typically food, clothing, shelter and utility service. Unfortunately, there is no magic list of the order in which debts should be paid. Everyone's situation will be different. Instead, what follows are sixteen rules about how to set priorities, followed by more detailed information about the consequences of not paying certain types of debts.

1. Always Pay Family Necessities First. Usually this means food and unavoidable medical expenses. You may want to look at ways to keep these expenses to a minimum as discussed in Chapter Two.

2. Next Pay Your Housing-Related Bills. Keep up your mortgage or rent payments if at all possible. If you own your home, real estate taxes and insurance must also be paid unless they are included in the monthly mortgage payment. Similarly, any condo fees or mobile home lot payments should be considered a high priority. Failure to pay these debts can lead to loss of your home.

If you are having very serious unresolvable problems which require you to move to a cheaper residence, you might choose to stop paying the mortgage or rent. When you do so, you should not use that money to pay other debts, but rather save it as a fund to use for moving. Dealing with mortgage debts is discussed in more detail in Chapters Eleven through Fourteen. Rent payments and dealing with landlords are discussed in Chapter Fifteen.

3. Pay the Minimum Required to Keep Essential Utility Service. While this may not always require full and immediate payment of the entire amount of the bill, the minimum payment necessary to avoid disconnection should be made if at all possible. Working hard to keep your house or apartment makes little sense if you cannot live there because you have no utilities. Options for dealing with utility payments and disconnections are discussed in Chapter Sixteen.

4. Pay Car Loans or Leases Next If You Need to Keep Your Car. If you need your car to get to work or for other essential transportation, you will usually make your car loan or lease payments your next priority after food, housing costs, unavoidable medical expenses and utilities. You may even want to pay for the car first if the car is necessary to keep your job.

If you do keep the car, stay up to date on your insurance payments as well. Otherwise the creditor may buy costly insurance for you at *your* expense that gives you *less* protection. And in most states it is illegal not to have automobile liability coverage.

If you can give up your car or one of your cars, you not only save on car payments, but also on gasoline, repairs, insurance, and automobile taxes. Car loan debts are discussed in Chapter Seventeen.

5. You Must Pay Child Support Debts. These debts will not go away and can result in very serious problems, including prison, for nonpayment.

6. Income Tax Debts Are Also High Priority. You must pay any income taxes you owe that are not automatically deducted from your wages, and you certainly must file your federal income tax return even if you cannot afford to pay any balance due. The government has many collection rights which other creditors do not have, particularly if you do not file your tax return. Remember, though, if you have lost income due to a change of circumstances, your tax obligations will also be reduced. Pay only what is necessary.

7. Loans Without Collateral Are Low Priority. Most credit card debts, attorney, doctor and hospital bills, and other debts to professionals, open accounts with merchants, and similar debts are low priority. You have not pledged any collateral for these loans, and there is rarely anything that these creditors can do to hurt you in the short term. Many won't bother to try to collect in the long term.

8. Loans With Only Household Goods As Collateral Are Also Low Priority. Sometimes a creditor requires you to place some of your household goods as collateral on a loan. You should generally treat this loan the same as an unsecured debt — as a low priority. Creditors rarely seize household goods because they have little market value, it is hard to seize them without involving the courts, and it is time consuming and expensive to use the courts to seize them. Seizure and threats to seize household goods are discussed in more detail in Chapter Eighteen.

9. Do *Not* Move a Debt Up in Priority Because the Creditor Threatens Suit. Many threats to sue are not carried out. Even if the creditor does sue, it will take a while for the collector to be able to seize your property, and much of your property may be exempt from seizure. On the other hand, nonpayment of rent, mortgage and car debts may result in immediate loss of your home or car. Debt collection lawsuits and threats to sue are discussed in Chapters Six and Eight.

10. Do Not Pay When You Have Good Legal Defenses to Repayment. Some examples of legal defenses are that goods purchased were defective, or that the creditor is asking for more money than it is entitled to. If you have a legal defense, you should obtain legal advice to determine whether your defense will succeed. In evaluating these options, remember that it is especially dangerous to withhold mortgage or rent payments without legal advice. However, for all debts you should consider fighting back when you have a valid defense as discussed in Chapter Nine.

11. Court Judgments Against You Move Up in Priority, But Often Less Than You Think. After a collector obtains a court judgment, that debt often should move up in priority, because the creditor can enforce that judgment by asking the court to seize certain of your property, wages, and bank accounts. Nevertheless, how serious a threat this really is will depend on your state's law, the value of your property, and your income. It may be that all your property and wages are protected under state law. So, pay off your more pressing obligations first and then come back and pay this debt. For more detail, see Chapter Eight. This is also a good time to obtain professional advice if you have not done so already.

12. Student Loans Are Medium Priority Debts. They should generally be paid ahead of low-priority debts, but after top priority debts. Most delinquent student loans are backed by the United States. The law provides special collection remedies to the government which are not available to other creditors. These include seizure of your tax refunds, special wage garnishment rules, and denial of new student loans and grants. These issues are discussed in Chapter Nineteen.

13. Debt Collection Efforts Should *Never* Move Up a Debt's Priority. Be polite to the collector, but make your own choices about which debts to pay based on what is best for your family. Debt collectors are unlikely to give you good advice. Debt collectors may be most aggressive to get you to pay debts which you should actually pay last. You can easily stop debt collection contacts and you have legal remedies to deal with collection harassment. See Chapter Six.

14. Threats to Ruin Your Credit Record Should *Never* Move Up a Debt's Priority. In many cases, when a collector threatens to report your delinquency to a credit bureau, the creditor has already provided the credit bureau with the exact status of the account. And if the creditor has not done so, a collector hired by the creditor is very unlikely to do so. In fact, your mortgage lender, your car creditor, and other big creditors are *much* more likely to report your delinquency (without any threat) than is a debt collector that threatens you about your credit record. See Chapter Seven.

15. Cosigned Debts Should Be Treated Like Your Other Debts. If you have put up your home or car as collateral on a loan, that is a high-priority debt for you if the other cosigners are not keeping the debt current. If you have not put up such collateral, treat cosigned debts as a lower priority. If others have cosigned for you and you are unable to pay the debt, you should tell your cosigner about your financial problems so that he or she can decide what to do about that debt.

16. Refinancing Is Rarely the Answer. You should always be careful about refinancing. It can be very expensive and it can give creditors more opportunities to seize your important assets. A short term fix can lead to long term problems. Some simple refinancing rules and techniques to avoid scams are discussed in Chapter Four.

WHAT HAPPENS TO YOU IF YOU DO NOT
PAY DIFFERENT TYPES OF DEBTS

To better understand the basis for these sixteen rules and how to apply them in particular cases, you should learn the potential consequences of not paying different types of your debt. This section is a brief overview. More on specific types of debt is found in the rest of this book.

Unsecured vs. Secured Debt. The most important principle in setting priorities is understanding the concept of "collateral." Collateral is property which a creditor has the right to seize if you do not pay a particular debt. The most common forms of collateral are your home in the case of a mortgage (or deed of trust) and your car in the case of most car loans.

A creditor may also have collateral in your household goods, business property, bank account, or even wages. Collateral can take many forms. When a creditor has taken collateral for your loan, it has a "lien" on your property.

Determine which of your debts
are "secured" and which are "unsecured."
You should almost always pay secured debts first.

Creditors who have collateral are usually referred to as "secured" creditors. They have the security of knowing that they can take the collateral and sell it to get their money. Creditors without collateral are often referred to as "unsecured." It is usually hard for unsecured creditors to collect what they are owed unless you pay voluntarily.

Home Foreclosure. If you own a home and do not pay the mortgage, deed of trust, or land contract (we will refer to all of these as "mortgages"), the creditor can foreclose on your home. This means the lender can sell the home and you will have to move. You will also typically lose all your equity in the house. This is because foreclosure sales rarely are for full market value.

It is sometimes difficult to stop a foreclosure once you have fallen behind. Even filing for bankruptcy may not help you permanently prevent a foreclosure. This makes it critical to prioritize your bills and pay your home mortgage payments first.

Real estate taxes and property insurance are also high priorities if they are not paid with the mortgage, because failure to pay these obligations can result in defaults on your mortgage and loss of your home. Additionally, you can lose your home to fire or other catastrophe if your insurance is canceled.

If you own a condo, condo association fees need to be paid as well, although they will usually be a slightly lower priority than the mortgage. In most states condo associations can enforce a lien against your property for condo fees by foreclosure or another similar process.

If you own a mobile home, and you rent your lot, you will need to treat your lot rent as a priority. Failure to pay lot rent can result in eviction. In some states seizure of the home can also result. If you are evicted, even if you do not lose the mobile home, you are likely to have difficulties finding a new lot.

There are two important exceptions to the rule of always paying a mortgage and related debts first. Sometimes a fraudulent home improvement contractor, shady finance company, or other questionable company will obtain a second mortgage or lien on your home. In that case, you may have legal reasons why you do not have to repay the loan — e.g., the aluminum siding was never installed or the replacement windows are shoddy and overpriced. Before making a final decision about whether to pay a loan of this type, make sure to obtain legal representation.

The other exception arises when you know that you will not be able to afford the home for the long term. Further payments after that point will generally go to waste. Consider selling the home in that situation or using one or more of the other options discussed in Chapter Twelve.

Apartment Eviction. If you are a tenant and do not pay rent, your landlord can evict you unless you have a valid defense to payment. In most states, defenses may include your landlord's failure to keep the property in good condition or to provide essential services.

If you are jointly responsible on a lease with a roommate or cosigner, their failure to pay can also result in your eviction. You cannot be evicted for failing to pay your other bills (except that under some leases a utility termination may lead to eviction). While a bankruptcy may offer short term relief from an eviction, the only way to stay in an apartment for the long term is to keep rent payments up to date, and, in most cases, to pay any back rent.

Utility Termination. Every household is hooked up to a series of utilities — telephone, water, gas, and/or electric service. Nonpayment of the utility bill may result in disconnection of service, although in many instances this can be delayed or avoided even though the bulk of the bill is outstanding. If service is turned off, you will usually be required to pay some or all of the back bill plus a reconnection fee to get the service turned back on. The essential nature of utility service means that these debts usually should be given very high priority.

Each utility bill must be dealt with independently. Failure to pay a telephone bill will have no impact on the continuation of your electric service and vice versa. In fact, the only bill that can lead to utility termination is the bill for that particular utility. A bankruptcy can wipe out old utility bills, and can allow service to be reconnected as long as you stay current on new bills and pay any required deposit.

Car Repossession. When you take out a loan to purchase a car, you typically put up the car as collateral for the loan. You may have also put up your car as collateral on other loans. You may also be leasing the car. Whenever a car is collateral on a loan, the lender can seize the car if you get behind on that loan. The same can happen if you get behind on lease payments. In almost all states, no court procedure is required; the creditor just drives away with the car, unless you are present and object. This is called "repossession."

Not only will you lose the car if it is repossessed, but the creditor will usually sell the car for less than it is worth and then seek a "deficiency" — the amount owed on the debt less the amount for which the car is sold.

As a consequence, whenever a car is essential transportation, auto loan and lease payments should be treated as high-priority debts. Related insurance payments must be made as well.

Seizure of Household Goods. Sometimes creditors who have taken your household goods as collateral threaten to repossess those goods. The reality is that repossession of property inside your home is much more difficult and less profitable to the creditor than the seizure of an automobile. Creditors cannot enter your home to seize property without your permission. Unless you are presented with a court order, you have no legal obligation to grant a creditor permission to enter your home and you should not do so. If you do not grant permission, the creditor will have to go to court in order to take the items.

Goods the creditor does repossess rarely have any market value. From a purely financial point of view, it is generally not worth it for creditors to seize household goods. For these reasons debts which involve household goods as collateral should usually be a relatively low priority. Nevertheless, you should probably pay them if you can, before debts with no collateral at all.

Lawsuits to Collect a Debt. You may be worried by a threat that a particular creditor will go to court to collect a debt. These threats almost always occur when the creditor has little or no collateral for the loan. Many such threats are never carried out.

You should also understand that a creditor's filing a lawsuit does not immediately harm you. First of all, you may win the lawsuit. Second, your decision to contest the lawsuit may be enough to convince the creditor to drop the case.

If the court eventually rules in the creditor's favor, then the court will order you to pay the debt. Even this court order to pay should not be viewed as especially threatening — failure to pay does not place you in contempt of court. Instead, the judgment allows the creditor to take certain actions to garnish wages, seize property, or examine you about your assets. It is these actions, and not the filing of a lawsuit by itself, which can cause special concern.

This is not to say that you should ignore lawsuits entirely — only that lawsuits and threats of lawsuits should not by themselves change your financial priorities. If you are sued, you should try to obtain immediate assistance from a lawyer or counselor to understand your risks, to determine whether you have defenses, and to evaluate the consequences if you don't respond.

Wage Garnishment and Seizure of Bank Accounts. Before the creditor can seize your wages or bank accounts, you almost always have a right to a court hearing to determine whether you owe the money. Only after the court orders you to pay can the creditor get an order to garnish, i.e., seize your wages or bank account.

The probability of wage garnishment or seizure of a bank account varies a great deal depending on which state you are in. In some states garnishment is not possible, while in others garnishment is rarely, or never, used because the procedure is difficult. However, in a few states garnishment is very common.

Depending on state procedure, a garnishment order can come from the court, a court clerk, or a sheriff. The order for garnishment is presented to your employer or bank, but even then state and federal law limit what can be taken.

Under federal law, the first $154.50 a week of take home pay is exempt from garnishment. In addition, no more than 25% of your wages can be seized (with the exception of certain child support obligations). State law may give you even greater protections. In some states, wage garnishment is not allowed at all, while in others the amount that can be garnished is less than the federal standard.

Additionally, many forms of government benefits, such as social security payments, veterans benefits, and similar income cannot be garnished. If these government benefits are placed in a bank account, particularly if no other funds are in the same account, the account may also be exempt from garnishment.

Filing bankruptcy is another method of dealing with garnishments. A bankruptcy filing generally eliminates garnishment as a threat.

Wage garnishments, bank account seizures, and judgment liens are not nearly as imminent or dangerous to you as home foreclosures, car repossessions, or evictions.

Judgment Liens. Creditors' rights to seize your property are significantly limited when you have not put up property as collateral for a loan. Where property is not collateral, the lenders must first obtain a court order that you owe them money before they can seize your property. You can contest the debt in court. Court permission or a final decision on the debt is required before the creditor can put a "judgment lien" on your home or other property. Once the lien is in place, a further request to the court or a sheriff is required to sell or seize your property.

In many cases creditors with judgment liens will not ask for permission to seize your property, or will not do so for many years. This is because seizing and forcing the sale of property may be expensive and once seized, the property may not have enough value to satisfy the creditor's claim after a sale. Instead of forcing a sale, some creditors may be willing to wait until you voluntarily sell the property and then collect from the proceeds of the sale.

If a creditor does seek to seize and sell your property, state law protects certain family possessions from seizure. Household goods of little economic value are generally exempt from seizure. This usually includes most of your furniture and appliances. Even a home or a car may be exempt from seizure, particularly if your equity in the property is not very much. In some states, there are additional protections against seizure of property (including homes) which are owned jointly by husband and wife, if only one of the spouses is responsible for the underlying debt.

Filing bankruptcy will postpone the threat of seizure of real estate and personal property, at least for a period of time, and sometimes permanently. In bankruptcy many judgment liens can be eliminated entirely.

Creditors may be willing to work out payment schedules even shortly before a threatened seizure. They often prefer to receive cash rather than deal with the costs of seizing and selling property.

Debt Collection. Debt collectors are companies or individuals who are hired by creditors to collect money. Debt collectors cannot take steps against your property other than those discussed in this book. Most debt collectors are not even allowed by the creditor who employs them to take those steps themselves. Usually, debt collection agencies can only recommend that the creditor take further action against you.

It is usually not difficult to stop a debt collector from contacting you or others with respect to a debt. The federal debt collection law, for example, gives you the right to stop all collection contacts simply by requesting the collection agency to stop. (A written request is best.) The creditor or the collector then may only use other means to collect, including lawsuits and attempts to seize collateral if they are allowed.

Many creditors and collectors, however, will go away entirely when told to stop making collection calls. This is because they have no real remedies other than to bother you for payment on the telephone. For these and other reasons, a particular collection agency's aggressiveness in collecting a debt should have *no* bearing on whether you pay that debt.

Credit Record. If you are having financial problems, you are likely to have negative information listed on your credit record. There is no way to avoid this. Deciding to pay one creditor instead of another usually will not help your credit record. Just because one creditor says it will report the default to a credit bureau does not mean it will. On the other hand, creditors who do not make threats may in fact report you to credit bureaus — without notice to you. Sadly, even if you make an effort to work with a particular creditor, a negative report may already have been made or it may still be made in the future despite your efforts.

If you are having financial problems, you should make sensible choices about which debts to pay which have nothing to do with your credit record. Always focus your resources on dealing with your highest priority debts. It is often better to try to improve your credit in the long term by rehabilitating it, rather than to worry about one more negative reference today.

One exception is that if you have a credit source with a small balance or no balance, you may choose to keep up with payments to that creditor only. Although this does not really improve your long term prospect for new credit, it is unlikely that your credit with that one creditor will be canceled as long as you are up to date on that obligation. Of course, this does not mean that you should make heroic efforts to pay one debt when thousands of dollars are due. If you do so, you may jeopardize more important priorities and lose your credit anyway.

Taxes, Student Loans, and Other Debts Owed to the Government. The government has special powers not available to other creditors to collect tax obligations, student loans and other debts owed to a government agency. The I.R.S., after a series of warning letters that may take a number of months, will start putting liens on your property and may begin to seize your property. While certain minimal possessions are exempt from seizure, most of a family's property can be seized by the I.R.S. A court procedure is not required.

The consequences of nonpayment of student loans and other obligations to government agencies are not so serious. But be prepared for the government to intercept income tax refunds and earned income tax credits and garnish wages without a court judgment. The government will also utilize debt collection agencies and may seek large collection costs. Up to ten percent of your wages can be garnished to pay student loan claims if you have been working continuously for a year, but you can avoid this, after receiving the garnishment notice, by agreeing to a payment plan. Student loan defaults will definitely be reported to credit reporting agencies. Student loan defaulters may also be ineligible for future student loans and grants.

Cosigned Debts. You have to be very careful of not only your own debts, but those you incur as a cosigner. If your property serves as collateral, you can lose the property if the debt is not paid, even if you are not responsible for the failure to pay. You can also be sued. In that case, your liability is the same as if you had incurred the debt alone. If you have cosigned any debts, it is a good idea to make sure that the debt is being paid.

If others have cosigned for you on your debts, you should let your cosigners know if you are not able to pay, so that they can get independent advice and decide what to do to protect themselves.

IF YOU CAN'T PAY ALL
YOUR HIGH-PRIORITY DEBTS

Although everyone has slightly different priorities, most people will want to pay debts required to maintain essential shelter and transportation before worrying about other debts. In some cases, you may find that your financial situation is so bad that you cannot even maintain required payments on those high-priority debts. Your income, for example, may not be enough to pay the mortgage and the car loan.

One serious mistake that some people make in this situation is to pay smaller, low-priority debts if they cannot keep up with their high-priority debts — "If I can't pay my mortgage, at least I will keep up with my credit cards."

This is a bad idea. Almost any long term plan for saving your home and your car will require that you start making payments again at some point. In the short term, if you don't have enough to make full payments, you can try to negotiate with the creditor to accept partial payments. If you are unsuccessful, save the money. You can use it later to make a lump sum down payment to get caught up or to cover the costs of moving to a new residence or buying a new car.

Another pitfall to avoid is making desperate choices. Although it is hard to accept that you will lose a home or a car or other valuable property, the alternatives can sometimes be worse. For example, refinancing a low-rate mortgage with a high-rate mortgage may buy you a few months, but in the long term the situation is likely to be hopeless. You have a better chance of working out a solution with the existing lender, than you do of avoiding foreclosure by taking out a loan with an aggressive finance company that makes high-rate loans.

There are many strategies for dealing with debt problems discussed throughout this book. Occasionally, though, it is best to step back and accept the inevitable change which money problems sometimes require. You may be living in a home you can't afford or you may need to substitute a cheaper auto to fit a new lifestyle.

Once that point is reached, you can do things which make the transition easier. These may include selling the property at a good retail price to avoid a low foreclosure sale price or giving up the property in exchange for a promise that the creditor will not make you pay any deficiency.

These choices are difficult and have to be made based on your individual evaluation of your long term prospects. Once the choice is made however, it is a good idea to stop making payments on that debt in favor of other pressing items. Continuing to pay a debt on property which you will lose in the long term anyway is expensive. You do not want to "throw good money after bad."

USING BANKRUPTCY
TO GET A FRESH START

When you file for bankruptcy, most of your *unsecured* debts will be "discharged." This means that your legal obligation to pay those debts will end even if you can't pay. On the other hand, despite your bankruptcy, a *secured* creditor usually will eventually be able to seize its collateral unless you make a plan to pay that debt.

**Even if do not plan on filing bankruptcy,
you should understand how bankruptcy
would affect your debts and your creditors.**

This difference in bankruptcy between unsecured and secured debts is another reason to make unsecured debts a lower priority. In general, you don't want to pay debts which bankruptcy can eliminate, instead of debts for which the creditor has collateral.

Bankruptcy can also be used to get a creditor to back off of aggressive collection efforts. If a creditor refuses to give you some time to get things together, or if a creditor refuses to accept small but affordable payments, filing bankruptcy can take care of the problem. Sometimes just telling a creditor that you are considering bankruptcy will make that creditor more reasonable.

Making a choice about whether to file bankruptcy can be difficult. Complicated issues in this area usually require legal assistance. However, necessary background for making a good choice about bankruptcy is provided in Chapter Twenty. Since there are situations in which rights in bankruptcy can be lost by delay, you should consider bankruptcy as an option from the start of your planning process for surviving your financial problems.

FEELINGS OF MORAL OBLIGATION TO PARTICULAR CREDITORS

In deciding your priorities, you may feel that some creditors are more entitled to repayment than others. You may have good feelings toward some creditors, but bad feelings toward others. These feelings should rarely be a factor in deciding which debts to pay first. Giving up the family home to pay off a creditor for whom you have good feelings is too big a sacrifice. If a creditor is sympathetic or has done you favors in the past, they are more likely to be patient as you work out your financial problems.

A related issue comes up in small communities where there may only be one store or one doctor or one pharmacist with whom you can do business. You may not want to lose your ability to obtain services from that particular creditor and you may feel you have no choice other than to pay that debt first. This may be true, but only in limited situations.

You should not assume that a business or a doctor will cut you off from future service right away if you don't pay. Explain the situation and ask for tolerance. Similarly, before assuming that you need to use a particular creditor, look around. There may be others in or near your community who are available in a pinch.

Everyone has financial problems at one time or another. It is nothing to be embarrassed about. Ask for help from creditors with whom you have a good relationship if you need it, and explain that you will make every effort to pay when you can get back on your feet.

Establishing a Budget Which Addresses Financial Problems

- *How to Develop an Income and Expense Budget*
- *Increasing Your Income and Lowering Your Expenses*
- *Making Choices About Your Savings and Your Assets*
- *Dealing With Pressures Caused By a Tight Budget*

THE INCOME AND EXPENSE BUDGET

It Is Essential That You Set Up (and Try to Stay on) An Income and Expense Budget. The first step in deciding your best strategy for dealing with your financial problems is to set up a budget based on your expected income and expenses. This budget will help you decide your best options. Most importantly, your budget will tell you what you can and cannot afford to pay.

There are three primary reasons to set up a budget as soon as you recognize that you are likely to be facing financial problems. These are:

1. The budget will help you determine how much money you have to cover your necessities and how much is left over to pay your bills. This will help establish your range of choices to deal with your debts.
2. The budget will help guide your spending habits. Your budget is likely to be based on your best planning about what you need. If you can live within the budget, you can be assured that you are not overspending and making your problems worse.

3. In some cases you will want to work with creditors that offer options for payment plans and modification of debts. These options will be particularly important if you wish to save your home and your car. Your ability to qualify for these programs will be based on your budget. If you have already done the work to develop a budget, you will have a sense of what you can afford to offer your creditors and you will be able to provide basic information which will make the process move more smoothly.

How to Set Up a Budget. Your budget is nothing more than a list of your anticipated income and a list of your expected expenses. Setting up a budget for the future involves making predictions based on your best information about what your income and expenses are likely to be.

A good place to start is with your existing income and expenses, without trying to adjust for future changes. Usually this is easiest to do on a monthly basis, using the most recent calendar month. What were your sources of income? How did you spend your money?

You then need to subtract your expenses from your income. When you do so, you should not be surprised if you find out that your expenses exceed your income. This is why you are having financial problems.

Once you have your current income and expenses on paper, you will need to begin the difficult work of evaluating what you expect for the future. Is your income likely to go up or down over the next few months? Can you change your spending patterns to reduce your expenses? Do you anticipate new expenses which were not included in the current budget?

Throughout the budgeting process, your goal should be to minimize any shortfall between your income and expenses. This means on one side, that you should be evaluating whether you have ways to increase your income. On the other side, you should look at whether there are ways to reduce expenses to make things more manageable.

In making these choices, it is essential to be realistic about what is possible. For example, you may feel that you can reduce your family food expenses by cutting out restaurant meals, but it is unrealistic to say that you can cut your food expenses to zero. Everyone has to eat. Unrealistic budgeting will lead to wrong choices about which debts to pay and potentially to a sense of hopelessness when your chosen strategies do not work out.

After completing the process of setting up a realistic budget for the future, subtract your expenses from your income again. Can you afford the future budget you have set out? If not, don't despair. Much of the rest of this book is about options for reducing or eliminating your obligations on various debts. You can come up with a combination of strategies which will address your shortfall.

Once you have a budget in place, try to live with it for a month to get a sense of whether it works. At the end of the month, go back and put in your actual income and expenses. Afterwards you can make adjustments based on your experience to make your budget more realistic for future months.

Try photocopying the budget forms at the back of this book.
They come with instructions to help you create an accurate budget.

To help you write up a budget, we have included, as an appendix at the back of this book, a sample budget form with some notes about how to use it. The form includes many potential sources of income and common expenses. However, don't assume we have thought of everything. Your budget should be based on your personal experience.

Income Budget. Your income budget should include all sources of income which you presently have. Employment income is a good place to start. If you are not working on salary, you should try to use the best realistic estimate of what you will earn. Overtime should be included if it is guaranteed, but it is a bad idea to budget based on hopes for extra work.

Your income budget should also include any other money that you receive on a regular basis, including child support and alimony, trust payments, dividends, royalties, insurance, pensions and public benefits.

One problem which sometimes occurs is how to deal with expected future increases or decreases in your income. If you know of an expected change and that change is certain, you can use it in planning your budget. If you then share your budget forms with a creditor from whom you are seeking a modification of loan terms, the expected change should be fully explained. Most creditors will want documentation.

When you prepare your income budget, you should carefully evaluate whether you are maximizing your income. Do you have opportunities for overtime? Can you begin drawing on your pension? Is there a manageable part-time job which will help you get through a tough period? Can you permanently or temporarily cancel wage deductions which you have been making voluntarily?

Does it make sense to draw down money you have been saving for the future and then to rebuild your savings plan after your financial problems are resolved? There are no easy answers to these questions, and you will have to make a decision which is right for you.

A later section in this chapter provides some ideas for increasing your income, including availability of the earned income tax credit and a variety of public benefit and entitlement programs. Many people overlook these options. You have a right to use these income sources to help you manage your financial problems, and you should not hesitate to do so.

Expense Budget. Your expense budget should include all of your expected monthly expenses, including food, shelter costs, utilities, clothing, transportation and medical expenses. It is often difficult to figure out exactly where all of your money goes. A review of your check book and your credit card bills may serve as a reminder.

Computing the true cost of various expense categories can also be difficult. Food expenses, for example, consist of your costs at the grocery store, plus (most likely) a few trips to the convenience store for special needs each week, plus the costs of occasionally dining out. If you look at your grocery store bills alone, you may underestimate your food expenses. You should do your best to estimate the real total. Then, think about ways you can minimize unnecessary food expenses, by, for example, regularly taking your lunch to work.

On the other hand, you need to be realistic about the real costs of feeding your family. For example, if the kids aren't going to drink powdered milk, it makes little sense to budget as if they will.

Other expenses can be more tightly controlled. New clothing purchases, for example, can usually be minimized until you get back on your feet. Later in this chapter, we list ways to reduce your expenses which you might not think of on your own. A frank family discussion about establishing new priorities may be necessary to get through a tough period.

Finally, you need to exercise care to budget enough to deal with the real costs of essentials. Home maintenance, for example, can be minimized but not eliminated. If you need your car, insurance and repairs are essential related costs. It may also be a good idea to reserve a small percentage of your budget for inevitable but unknown emergency needs.

How to Treat Credit Card Bills and Other Unsecured Debts in Your Expense Budget. Unless you can afford to meet all of your obligations, you should generally not include credit card and other unsecured debts in your expense budget. If you do not have enough income in your budget to pay all of your debts, Chapter One discusses the best ways to prioritize among your various bills. Credit card and other unsecured debts are low priorities.

You should always budget to pay for necessities, including shelter costs and necessary transportation costs, before paying anything on your credit cards and other debts for which the creditor has no collateral. This means you should not even budget to make minimum payments on your credit cards, if the result will be that you cannot pay for your home and car. For reasons discussed throughout this book, you should always protect important property by making plans to prevent foreclosure or repossession before you worry about your credit rating and your ability to borrow again in the future.

How to Include Your Savings and Other Assets in Your Budget. You will have to decide how to treat your savings and other assets in your budget plan. Are you better off spending your retirement money now, or toughing it out now so you have money when you retire? Should you take a little money out of your savings account each month to help balance your budget or should you take all your savings and pay it in one lump sum toward getting your mortgage current? Should you sell off stocks or other property to make ends meet? Later in this chapter, there are tips about how to deal with your savings and other assets. Read that section carefully, make smart choices, and then incorporate your decision in your budget plan.

How to Budget Lump Sums You Are Expecting But Have Not Received. Many people have money which they expect in the future, but which is not yet in hand. Sometimes the expectation is no more than a possibility, while in other cases it is guaranteed. Examples include:

- Money or property which has been left to you by a deceased relative, but which is tied up in probate;
- Social security or other public benefit lump sums;

- Money from a lawsuit which has not yet been heard in court or settled;
- Money for sale of property when the sale has not yet closed;
- Retirement funds or workers compensation which are owed but unpaid;
- Money promised by a friend or relative to help you out in tough times; and
- Insurance money which has not yet been paid.

It is possible to include this money in your financial plan, but you need to be realistic about when the money may come and how much it will be.

If you are waiting for a lawyer to settle a lawsuit or an estate in probate, it may be a good idea to call to let the lawyer know about the nature and urgency of your financial difficulties. There may be things which can be done to speed up legal processes, although in some cases there will be costs in the form of a decreased recovery. For example, the need for urgent settlement of a personal injury case can reduce the amount you are paid, particularly if the other side senses your situation.

Some money is certain to come in on a particular date. For example, if your social security payments are due to start on a particular date, you can use this knowledge in making your financial plan. You may be able to supplement your income from savings for a few months while you wait for the permanent change to kick in. Similarly, if a lump sum is guaranteed, you can plan to use that lump sum in a way which will cure your defaults on urgent debts.

On the other hand, it can be a poor choice to count on money which is no more than a hope either in timing or amount. Payment that is too uncertain should probably not enter into your plans at all.

Finally, some mortgage and car loan creditors will negotiate with you about a temporary delay in payments if you can show them that you have long-term prospects for getting caught up. (This is not a negotiation which makes sense on your lower priority debts.) If you do want to use an expected change in income or a lump sum in negotiating with a particular creditor, you will need to gather the best documentation possible of the availability of the money including a letter from the person who is handling the matter for you or who has oversight of the funds. Sometimes an affidavit will be required.

Balancing Your Budget With New Credit Card or Other Debt. If your expenses are more than your income, you may feel tempted to incur further debts to make up the difference. This is normally a bad choice. New debt will just put you further in the hole with bigger problems for the future, unless your situation turns around quickly.

While we can never recommend your borrowing money to make your budget work if you are already in financial distress, some types of new loans will be worse than others in this situation. Incurring new unsecured credit, such as adding to your credit card debt, is better than incurring new secured debts. As described in Chapter One, the consequences of not paying credit card or other unsecured debt are unlikely to be as severe as if you do not pay a mortgage, car loan or utility bill.

Nevertheless, use of credit card debt to balance your budget can make your situation worse. Credit card debt is high-interest debt with potential penalties for nonpayment. If you intend to make only the minimum payments each month on the bill, your debt will quickly compound — making it unlikely that you will ever get back on track.

Although credit card debt can usually be eliminated in bankruptcy, this may not be so if you run up big bills or cash advances just before filing. Creditors argue, with some success, that if you use a credit card at a time when you did not have the ability to repay, you have committed a fraud which prevents the debt from being eliminated in the bankruptcy process.

Of course, there may be situations where you have to take out new debt. For example, you may need to buy a car to get to work. See Chapters Four and Seven for advice on obtaining new credit and refinancing old loans while you are experiencing financial problems. If you do seek new debt, it is always a bad idea to misrepresent your situation in your application. This can lead to claims of fraud giving rise to lawsuits and even, on occasion, criminal prosecutions.

Generally, Refinancing Will Not Help Make Your Budget Balance.
You may be tempted, as a way to make ends meet, to consolidate many small loans into one larger loan, to refinance your home mortgage, or to take other steps to turn old loans into new loans. Chapter Four evaluates refinancing as a strategy to deal with your financial problems. In general, it is a bad option when you are already facing financial problems. It is always a bad idea to refinance unsecured debt into secured debt and to trade low-interest rate credit for higher rate loans.

Balancing Your Budget By Borrowing From Friends and Relatives.
Friends and relatives may offer to help out when you have financial prob-

lems. There is nothing wrong with accepting this help to get you through a tough period. Occasional problems arise, however, if you count on this help. Your friends and relatives may face their own financial difficulties and may withdraw their assistance — sometimes when you need it most. It is usually not a good idea to make help from others a cornerstone of your financial plan or to ask others to help you pay back debts which you would not otherwise need to pay.

When assistance from a friend or family member is part of your budget plan and you need to verify this income for the purpose of getting a payment agreement on your mortgage or car loan, you may need to ask for a formal statement of some type. If possible, use a signed letter for this purpose so that you don't put anyone in the uncomfortable position of contracting to loan you money.

Some creditors will push you to get a friend or relative to cosign with you when you are facing financial problems. You should avoid this whenever possible. The person who cosigns will be on the hook with you. Your financial problems may become their's as well, if you cannot afford to pay. You don't want your friendships and family relationships to be on the line if your financial circumstances do not improve.

SOME OPTIONS FOR
INCREASING YOUR INCOME

This section points out ways to increase your income, the next section deals with medical and dental care, and a third section provides ideas about reducing your expenses. In reading through these sections, particularly the section on increasing your income through the Earned Income Tax Credit and certain public benefit programs, keep in mind that the law on these issues often changes. We try to point out some programs which are likely to be available for the foreseeable future, but you will need to get more detailed information to pursue these options.

You should take advantage of these programs when they are available. Each program was created to help people with financial problems and there is no reason to be ashamed of using them. It is likely that you contributed financially to funding the programs either through tax payments or by payroll deductions.

You should also remember that most of the programs discussed here have appeal rights and procedures. If you are denied assistance which you think you are owed, consider filing an appeal. Professional help may be useful, but it is not required.

The Earned Income Tax Credit. The Earned Income Tax Credit is a frequently overlooked means of increasing your income if you are employed. If you have not qualified for this credit in the past, a change in your income or a lay-off may make you eligible during a year in which you have financial problems.

The amount of your tax credit is based on the amount of your income and your family's size. If you are employed and your total income falls below a threshold amount, you qualify for the credit even if you do not owe the government any money. Thus it is not a "credit" in the conventional sense of the word. You can get money back even if you owe little or nothing.

You should check with an accountant or other tax professional to determine if you qualify. Obtaining the credit will require that you file the necessary tax returns.

Unemployment Compensation. You should always think about unemployment compensation when you have lost your job for any reason or when your hours have been significantly reduced. You should apply as quickly as possible after your employment is terminated or reduced.

Unemployment benefits are most commonly available after a lay-off. You may not be eligible for benefits if you have been fired for cause or if you voluntarily quit. However, in some cases, you may still qualify for benefits even if your employer told you that you were fired rather than laid off. Similarly, you may qualify in some circumstances even if you quit your job. In general, it can't hurt to apply, although if you were fired or if you quit, you may first want to learn more about your state's benefit program.

Some lawyers and other professionals specialize in this area. In addition, there are several books and pamphlets available which discuss unemployment compensation. Call the personnel office of your former company, the state labor department, or your state's unemployment office. If you are a union member, ask the union if it provides help with unemployment compensation applications.

Applying for Unemployment Compensation: The First Appointment. To expedite the award and receipt of unemployment benefits, you should assemble and bring all relevant documents to the first appointment, including *at least:* a Social Security card, a driver's license and other identification, a lay-off notice if you received one, and your four most recent pay-stubs. At the first appointment, you should be prepared to describe accurately the nature and cause of job termination or reduction.

To speed up receipt of your unemployment benefits, assemble and bring all relevant documents to the *first* appointment.

This description should be worded carefully. Stating that the reason for leaving employment was voluntary will lead to denial of benefits. If you left work in anticipation of layoff or discharge, you should carefully set out the reasons why the lay-off or discharge was not voluntary.

Unemployment compensation applications can be denied if the state employee taking down the information misinterprets the reasons given for the discharge, and if you sign the statement as true without carefully reading and correcting it. For example, your statement that a supervisor began to verbally harass you and finally told you to leave and not return might be recorded incorrectly as: "The worker was verbally abusive and fired for cause." You should not sign this statement.

Steps to Take When Unemployment Compensation Benefits Are Denied. Unemployment compensation can be denied for a variety of reasons, including that your employer is not covered by unemployment insurance laws, you were discharged for misconduct, or that you quit without a good reason. You can contest denial of unemployment benefits by requesting an administrative hearing. You should do so as soon as you receive a denial, because there are tight and strictly enforced deadlines.

After a hearing, if the claim is still denied, additional appeals are possible. Always make sure you meet the required deadlines. It may be wise to consult someone with experience in the unemployment compensation process after you file the papers, but before any hearing on appeal.

Food Stamps. If you are experiencing severe financial problems, food stamps can supplement your monthly food budget. To qualify, your income must be below program limits which vary by family size. Emergency food stamps may be available in certain circumstances.

You apply for foodstamps by filing an application form. You can get an application form by contacting any food stamp office. Often food stamp offices are located with welfare offices in your community. You can call and have an application mailed to you or you can visit the office in person.

Food stamp offices may require the following documents to support your application:

1. Identity of the person applying;
2. Social security number of household members;
3. Income of household members;
4. Where you live (unless you are homeless, a migrant farm worker, or recently relocated);
5. Proof of age;
6. Proof of the amount of your utility, rent, mortgage and other shelter expenses;
7. Dependent care expenses;
8. Medical expenses; and
9. Receipt of disability benefits.

Sometimes agency personnel improperly deny a food stamps application because of their confusion about eligibility requirements or because of arithmetic mistakes. Do not take a denied application as final. Consider taking an appeal before the required time deadline expires.

Program requirements are subject to change. For more detailed information on the program, you may want to review program manuals and regulations, pamphlets available from the welfare office, or seek help from an advocate who specializes in food stamps.

Other Food Programs. Other programs for assistance with food may be available in your community. If your family includes a pregnant woman or a child under five, you should inquire about assistance from the Women, Infants and Children (WIC) program. Typically, WIC is administered by local public health departments and provides vouchers for supplemental foods important to the health of mothers and to the early development of their children. Eligibility for this program is based on family income and on whether the women, infants or children in the family are at nutritional risk. Welfare offices or health departments can provide information about WIC.

Many unions, churches and community groups have community cupboards or food pantries that distribute food for home preparation. Churches and social service organizations such as the Salvation Army maintain cafeterias to which families can turn. These programs can be located by contacting local church offices, United Way offices, or other social service agencies.

Other Welfare Programs. Although Congress eliminated the Aid to Families with Dependent Children (AFDC) program in 1996, all states administer some form of cash and other assistance to families with children. States have great flexibility in setting eligibility requirements and benefit levels. A universal requirement is that the family includes a minor child or a pregnant woman.

Applications for this assistance can be made at a local welfare office, sometimes called a department of public assistance, department of social services, or department of human services. As with other programs, you need to provide proof that you are eligible.

If you qualify for the program, the amount of your benefits will be based on your other income and family size as well as certain other factors in some states. Job training, work requirements and time limits may also apply.

Some states have other emergency assistance or other welfare programs. Many states also have local General Assistance or General Relief programs. Benefits and eligibility requirements vary tremendously among states, but the programs are usually available only to people who are ineligible for any other form of assistance, and who have few or no resources.

Some general assistance programs cover only certain categories, such as children or the disabled. Some programs provide benefits for only a limited number of months each year. Most programs require that employable people participate in a work or job search program. Local legal services offices can provide more information about these programs.

Other Emergency Programs. Some states and communities have other emergency funds available to help with basic needs, such as food, shelter, medical care, clothing, or transportation. Often, these programs provide vouchers rather than direct cash.

Private social service groups and charitable and religious organizations sometimes have small funds available that provide limited grants or short-term loans to families lacking other available resources. The Salvation Army is a valuable resource in many communities, as are shelters, food banks, and crisis centers. Your church, synagogue or mosque may also provide help.

Public and private funds are often difficult to locate. Some are listed in the social services section of the phone book. In many communities, one agency serves as an information clearinghouse or referral service for various sources of assistance.

Social Security and SSI Benefits Based on Age. If you are age 62 or over, you may be eligible for Social Security benefits. The survivors of an insured worker may also be eligible for Social Security benefits upon the worker's death.

Social Security benefits are available only for those who have been employed a sufficient number of years in covered jobs, that is jobs contributing to the Social Security fund. Those aged 65 or over not eligible for Social Security may still be eligible for Supplemental Security Income (SSI). This is a federal program open to those whose income and assets are under established guidelines.

Sometimes people who are eligible to receive Social Security benefits at age 62 postpone receipt of these benefits because they will be eligible for larger monthly payments at a later date. While this strategy may make sense when the family's financial resources are adequate, it is not a good choice in a time of financial distress.

Disability Benefits. You may also be eligible for Social Security or Supplemental Security Income (SSI) disability benefits. Disabilities take many forms. Illnesses, physical and mental limitations, extreme pain, and depression or anxiety all qualify as disabilities. To qualify, the impairment or combination of impairments has to have lasted or be expected to last a year or more, and has to prevent you from engaging in substantial gainful activity in light of your age, education, and work experience.

Federal disability benefits are paid by the Social Security Administration. Social Security is a federally administered program, separate from the other public assistance programs discussed here. Applications are made at local Social Security offices.

If your past employment record does not qualify you for Social Security disability benefits, you can apply for SSI disability benefits. SSI is the federal Supplemental Security Income program for individuals whose income and assets fall below established guidelines.

Many applicants who are initially denied disability benefits succeed on appeal. Make sure to file an appeal at each stage and consider contacting a lawyer or other advocate who specializes in disability benefit cases.

Workers Compensation. If you were seriously injured on the job, or if you suffer from serious job related medical conditions, it is likely that you are entitled to workers compensation benefits. These may include medical benefits and monthly income payments until you are able to go back to work. If you are a union member, the union may help you qualify. Otherwise contact the worker's compensation board in your state directly. Your doctor's assistance in this process will be helpful. If you are having difficulties qualifying, you may wish to contact a lawyer specializing in workers compensation cases.

Child Support. You may be owed current or back child support. If you cannot obtain an attorney to press your claim for child support, a state agency should help you to collect. Contact the local welfare office to see which state agency assists families in the collection of child support and what type of assistance they can offer.

Other Family Support Issues. If a family relationship is terminated or terminating, you may be entitled to alimony, property distribution, debt payment assistance, or other remedies in addition to child support. These options should be explored with a lawyer or family counselor who understands your financial problems. The nature of your financial difficulties are relevant to the family court process, so you should be sure to explain where things stand to the person who assists you.

Other Ways to Increase Income. Other ways to increase the family income may be obvious, such as taking a second job temporarily, increasing overtime, or collecting debts owed to you by others. Consider also whether you have space in your home which you can rent, or a marketable skill which you are not using. For those who have made a voluntary decision not to work, such as a potential breadwinner caring for children, financial difficulties create an opportunity for reevaluation. Of course, any choice to return to the workforce in this circumstance must be evaluated in light of the potential increased costs of child care, taxes, and other expense.

MEDICAL AND DENTAL CARE

Paying for medical and dental care may be a significant problem when you are experiencing financial problems. This section provides advice on obtaining low-cost and free care. How to handle back-due medical and dental bills is explored in other chapters, particularly Chapters One and Six.

**Unpaid doctor and hospital bills
should not prevent you from getting free
or low-cost medical and dental care.**

Keeping Your Health Insurance After Losing Your Job. Ordinary preventive medical care, particularly dental care, tends to be postponed during times of crisis. Nevertheless, families sometimes suddenly confront large, unplanned medical expenses, and are caught with no medical insurance. Such nightmares can sometimes be prevented, particularly if you have just been laid off.

Within thirty days of being laid-off (unless the union or employment contract provides different terms), you should receive a notice from your former employer's health insurance company stating that your insurance has been terminated. The notice should specify a time period during which you can convert to an individual policy without any lapse in coverage.

If you can afford to pay the premium to convert to an individual family policy, you should do so, particularly if someone in your family has an existing medical condition requiring care. Often the only way to avoid restrictions on coverage of a pre-existing condition is to maintain coverage with the existing insurer.

Medicaid. If it is not possible to maintain private health insurance coverage, consider applying for a state or federally funded medical assistance program, known in many states as Medicaid. Eligibility for Medicaid varies from state to state, but hinges on available family income and resources.

If services are covered, Medicaid pays the physician, the pharmacist, and any other service provider directly. Many states have co-payment systems, in which the Medicaid patient pays a small amount, usually only a few dollars, toward the service. Under current federal law, states must provide certain mandatory services, including inpatient hospital care, physician services, and skilled nursing services. States cannot deny service because of an individual's condition, although they can deny services that are not medically necessary. A determination that a service is not medically necessary can be appealed.

States must also pay for transportation to necessary medical care. Optional services, which some states choose to cover, include prescription drugs, eyeglasses, dental care, psychiatric services, and private nursing. If you are a low-income senior, Medicaid generally also covers long-term care such as nursing facilities. Most states provide lists of the services they cover.

As with other assistance programs, applications and information about medical assistance are available at local welfare offices. If benefits are initially denied, remember to exercise your appeal rights.

Medicare. If you are elderly or disabled, make sure you are getting available Medicare benefits. If payment of a claim is denied, make sure you know why. If you have a reason to disagree, contact your local Medicare office and take available appeals. You may be able to save money by joining a Medicare health maintenance organization (HMO). Be advised that most HMOs require you to use only those medical providers affiliated with the HMO. This may mean you can no longer get coverage to see your family doctor. HMOs may deny coverage for certain types of medical procedures that you think you need. You have the right to appeal these denials and should pursue appeals, if possible, with professional help.

Other Medical Care Options. For applicants not qualified for Medicaid or for state medical assistance, Catastrophic Medical Assistance is available in some states to assist with major medical expenses. When medical bills exceed a certain percentage of an applicant's household income, the balance of the bill above that percentage is reimbursed.

Some hospitals have an obligation to provide free care to certain patients under either state or federal law. And all hospitals and doctors have an ethical obligation to deal with medical emergencies. In a crisis, you should use the emergency room of your local hospital and worry about the bill later.

Local service clubs also sometimes have programs designed to meet particular needs. The best known is the Lions Club, which helps to purchase eyeglasses for children.

Medical Prescriptions. Several options are available for families unable to obtain prescription drugs through Medicaid. Any patient receiving a prescription should ask whether or not a less expensive generic drug can be substituted. Doctors may have free sample supplies of medication available if you explain your hardship.

Additionally, most drug companies run programs which provide free medication for those in need. Find out the name of the company which makes the drug you need, and call telephone information for that company's "800" phone number. Call the company to ask whether there is a program for reduced cost or free supply of prescribed medication. Emergency one-time grants or small loans for drug prescriptions also can sometimes be obtained from private social service agencies or church organizations.

Low Cost Dental Care. Dental care often takes a back seat to more pressing financial obligations. However, there are several ways that families can obtain free emergency dental care or low-cost preventive care. First, some types of dental care are covered by health or dental insurance. Some dental coverage is included in Medicaid. Second, if neither insurance nor Medicaid is available, many community college dental hygiene programs and university dental schools provide services for free or at negligible cost as part of their teaching programs. Some hospitals have low-cost oral surgery clinics.

SOME OPTIONS FOR REDUCING YOUR EXPENSES

Everyone's expense needs are different. We are not going to attempt to suggest all of the ways you might consider economizing. However, we will list a dozen tips about possible expense reductions which are often overlooked by consumers. A combination of these savings can reduce your expense budget by several hundred dollars a month.

1. Real Estate Tax Reductions. If you own a home, many communities have a variety of real estate tax abatements, deferrals and hardship repayment plans. Most states have an abatement for older homeowners and many have a deferral process for people facing financial hardship. Less than half of those eligible take advantage of available real estate tax reductions.

2. Utility Conservation Measures. If you pay for your own utilities, you may be paying too much. Look into utility conservation assistance programs, many of which are offered free by utility companies. In addition, many books and pamphlets offer valuable tips. These can lower your utility costs by one half to one third. A variety of options to reduce your utility costs are discussed in Chapter Sixteen.

3. Reduce Your Telephone Expenses. Look into your telephone calling plan. You may want to change your local billing method or comparison shop among competing companies for long distance service. The types of calls you make and times you are likely to use the phone can greatly affect what type of calling plan works best for you. These issues are discussed in more detail below in Chapter Sixteen.

4. Reevaluate Your Homeowner's Insurance Needs. Many people pay more than necessary for their homeowner's insurance. If your property value has decreased, or if you are insuring for a value which includes the cost of the land your home is on, you are paying too much for homeowner's insurance. You also can consider eliminating unnecessary coverages or applying for special rate programs (such as reductions for using a smoke detector). Check with your agent; you may be able to cut your annual bill by hundreds of dollars. (More on this topic can be found in Chapter Five.)

5. Reevaluate Your Other Insurance Needs. Look into your life insurance and other coverages with the help of a trustworthy insurance agent. It helps for the agent to understand the nature of your financial problems. You may consider dropping optional coverages until your financial problems are solved. You might also consider converting a whole life policy to a term life policy in order to save money. Some policies may be "capped" or may include an option for deferring payments for a temporary period. Your auto insurance coverage is another area where it may be possible to save. Are all your coverages required in order to operate your car? Do you qualify for any savings plans? (More on this topic can be found in Chapter Five.)

6. Eliminate Discretionary Purchases. Although you will have to continue to pay for necessities, discretionary items can be eliminated from your monthly budget temporarily. Each purchase has to be evaluated to determine if it is more important to you than saving your home or car.

7. School-Related Expenses. If you have children in private school, you may have to consider a change during a period when you are experiencing financial problems. Private schools are expensive and public schools are free. If you decide to switch, you can tell your children that you had to choose between changing schools or loss of the family home. Family counseling may help with these difficult transitions. If you feel your children must stay in private school, you may want to speak with a school official or a financial aid officer. Special assistance programs may be available for families having temporary financial difficulties.

8. Religious Expenses and Charitable Contributions. If you are having financial problems and religious expenses are stretching your budget, consider talking to your priest, minister, rabbi, or imam. More often than not, special efforts will be made to help you through a tough financial time without affecting your membership or standing in the community.

9. Sliding Scale Community Services. Many community-based social service programs offer assistance for free or on a sliding scale. Low-cost counseling on a variety of issues is widely available if you are persistent in looking for it. These programs are designed to help people in your situation in a confidential and effective way. You should not be embarrassed to get help.

10. Public Transportation vs. Driving. Automobiles can be very expensive. Between car payments, gas, repairs, and insurance, an automobile is some communities can be as expensive as a home. If you can find a way to get by without a car temporarily or permanently, you may find that you save many hundreds of dollars a month. Similarly, if you have two cars, consider whether your family can manage with one.

11. Unnecessary Payroll Deductions. If your income has gone down, you may be having excessive amounts deducted from your pay for income taxes. Check with your employer, or with an accountant if necessary.

Similarly, you may have agreed to a payroll deduction for any one of a variety of reasons when things were going well. These might include savings plans, voluntary pension contributions, vacation clubs, credit union deductions, optional but inessential health coverages, charitable contributions, or voluntary wage assignments to creditors that you have decided are not a high priority. Check to see if these deductions can be temporarily reduced or eliminated.

12. Adult Children Living at Home. You may feel a great deal of obligation to adult family members or friends who share your home with you. However, if that person has income, it is certainly fair to ask for a contribution to the household expenses. Alternatively, it may be time to politely ask that person to find somewhere else to live permanently or temporarily. If you continue to pay the expenses of persons who can manage on their own, this may stretch your budget to the point that everyone loses their home.

DIPPING INTO SAVINGS
AND SELLING YOUR ASSETS

You may have a lump sum of money in a savings account, a mutual fund account, a certificate of deposit, or a retirement account which you feel you can use to get you through a tough financial time. Similarly, you may have stocks, bonds, or other valuable property that you could sell to raise cash. It may be a good idea to sell assets which are easy to liquidate, like stocks and bonds, in order to give yourself more flexibility for meeting urgent financial needs. Sale of other nonessential valuable assets, like vacation homes and extra cars or even antique furniture and heirlooms, should be considered. It is sometimes better to make a difficult choice in order to raise cash, rather than to lose everything.

There are several things you should keep in mind about using savings or selling off assets when you are having financial problems:

1. Think Carefully Before Spending Your Retirement Money. You may be tempted to dip into your retirement savings to get you through temporary financial difficulties. The most important consideration is whether you will have time to rebuild these savings before you retire. If you are close to retirement age, you should look carefully at whether there are other ways to manage your financial difficulties which will allow you get over a difficult period with your retirement plan intact. On the other hand, if you are young and likely to have many productive years before retirement, use of retirement funds may make sense, if it helps you avoid loss of property or other hardship.

2. Using Your Savings or Selling Off Assets Should Be Part of an Overall Plan, Not Your Only Plan. If your income does not cover your expenses, you will need to use your savings or proceeds of an asset sale carefully. You should not use this money to finance an unreasonable lifestyle. For this reason, do not spend savings or other assets before evaluating your budget and cutting back on expenses. Your savings will go much farther if they are applied to the pared down expenses which you find essential to prevent true hardship.

3. Usually You Should Not Use Savings or Other Assets to Pay Low-Priority Debts. You may have more pressing needs before your financial circumstances get better. If your income does not meet basic expenses, your savings are a valuable resource which you should use only to protect important property or to pay for other necessities. You should not be pressured into using essential savings or your remaining assets to pay off your credit card bills or to get involved in a "get rich quick scam." Priority of debts is discussed in Chapter One.

4. Taking Loans Against Savings May Be a Bad Idea. Unless you can borrow money at a very low interest rate, borrowing against savings will be a losing proposition because you will be paying higher interest charges on the loan than you earn on your savings. This will eat into your budget (or your savings) more quickly then just spending down the savings account.

5. Spending Savings or Other Assets in a Lump Sum Versus Spending Down Part Each Month to Meet Ongoing Expenses. One difficult question you will face is how best to use your savings or the proceeds of an asset sale, in making your plan to manage your financial problems. You should consider two choices.

Some people use a set amount of their savings each month in their monthly budget to meet essential expenses. This can be the right choice if you have good discipline and if the savings will make the difference between meeting your essential expenses and falling hopelessly behind. As discussed above, you should not fall into the trap of using your savings to finance an unrealistic lifestyle. You will only postpone the day of reckoning.

The other choice about savings or other assets is to spend them in a lump sum for a particular purpose, like paying down a mortgage default. This choice may be necessary in order to postpone a catastrophic loss of property to foreclosure or repossession. However, you should be careful not to make this choice unless you have a longer term plan to get back on your feet. Paying many thousands of dollars on a mortgage to keep a home you cannot afford in the long term may be a waste of money.

In addition, if you plan to use savings on a mortgage or a car loan, you should probably avoid paying ahead. Use the saving to get caught up, and then keep any extra money to make future payments as they come due. This will give you more flexibility for the future.

If you feel you must pay ahead, make sure to make clear to the creditor in writing that you are paying future payments rather than a lump sum toward the principal. (This will also help to make sure you are not being charged prepayment penalties.) Although in good financial times it may be a good idea to pay down principal due on a debt in order to reduce total interest payments, the opposite is true if you are having financial difficulties. A lump sum paid on the principal will not excuse you from future payments unless the loan is fully paid off. That is, even after you pay a lump sum as an advance on the principal, the next monthly or weekly payment will be due as scheduled. You will be in default if you do not pay it.

Never tell those collecting on credit card or other unsecured debt that you have savings, and don't use such savings to pay them.

---

6. Do Not Talk About Your Savings with Bill Collectors. You should not tell bill collectors that you have savings. (That is, you should not tell those collecting on credit cards or other unsecured debts. On the other hand, you may need to let the bank which holds your mortgage or car loan know about your savings as part of a workout plan, as discussed in Chapters Twelve and Seventeen.) Your choice about how to deal with your financial problems is personal. Bill collectors may use knowledge about your savings accounts in order to garnish the accounts or to pressure you into making wrong choices. More about dealing with bill collectors and protecting your savings from garnishment is included in Chapters Six and Eight.

7. How Best to Sell Off Assets. If there is an established market to sell certain of your assets, such as most stocks and bonds, you can delay selling this type of property until you need money urgently. For other types of property that are harder to sell, it is usually best to avoid panic sales at the last minute. Urgency will usually reduce the sale price. Plan ahead and try to get the best price possible by using the most common means that similar property is sold.

As discussed in Chapter Three, you should avoid pawn shops and other fringe businesses which buy or make loans on property. These companies are in the business of making money off your emergency need for cash.

DEALING WITH PRESSURES CAUSED BY A TIGHT BUDGET

Financial difficulties can be emotionally draining. It is not uncommon for pressures to build up within families, which cause quarrels, temporary separations, or even divorce. Some studies document increases in physical abuse associated with money problems. As you make the difficult choices associated with your financial problems, you should be aware of the emotional pressures which may be building.

Mental health counseling, family therapy, and marriage counseling may be useful for managing the stress of financial problems. If you have health insurance, your policy may include free or low-cost mental health assistance. It can't hurt to ask your doctor. This type of assistance is also usually available from a variety of organizations on a sliding scale fee basis or for free. Call a local credit counseling agency or family services for a reference. You can also call and ask a therapist about low-cost or free mental health counseling options available in the community.

Everyone has financial problems at one time or another. You should not be embarrassed to talk about your difficulties, either to seek help from a friend, or in the more formal process of therapy. Whatever course you choose, it is important that you remain aware of the additional stress you may be feeling and that you try to deal with it in the healthiest possible way.

As you struggle to get past your financial difficulties, keep in mind that better days will come. With careful planning to minimize short-term hardship and some patience, you can put yourself in the best possible position to get a fresh start and to recover good financial health.

– 3 –

Choices That Could Get You Into Trouble

- *Mistaken Choices Some People Make Under Financial Pressure*
- *Ways That Businesses May Try to Take Advantage of You*
- *Bogus Debt Counseling and Credit Repair Scams*

It can be very difficult to make good consumer decisions in times of financial trouble. Earlier chapters have described various techniques to help you make ends meet. Chapter Five will give you additional tips on better financial alternatives.

This chapter assumes that you are already in financial trouble. Recognizing how hard it is to spend your money wisely under these circumstances, this chapter lists bad choices you should avoid at all costs.

Be particularly wary of anyone advertising or soliciting with easy ways to reduce your financial problems. These are usually scams or bad deals.

Some of these mistakes are steps you might be tempted to take out of a sense of desperation, but many will not be your idea. An entire industry of unscrupulous businesses exists to pressure you into making these mistakes. These businesses know that people in financial distress often make desperate or poorly informed choices. They also know that people who feel that their options are limited are likely to be willing to overpay for credit and other services.

Unfortunately, even reputable companies have gotten into businesses which take advantage of consumers in financial trouble. You cannot assume that because a company is well known or because it advertises on TV that it will give you a fair deal. Also be suspicious of companies that use names which are designed to create confusion about their identity, such as using the name "United States." Other companies use names very similar to legitimate organizations, such as calling themselves the AARI, instead of AARP.

In the following list, we recommend avoiding a number of practices which may increase your financial problems. This is not a complete list of scams. New scams constantly arise and old ones change form. The main message is that services aimed at people with bad credit or other financial problems are often rip-offs. If they seem too good to be true, they probably are. When in doubt, just say no.

1. Bouncing Checks. It may be tempting to write a check when you know that you have insufficient funds in your account to cover it. At best, you may hope to make a deposit before the check is cashed. At worst, you may be deliberately using the check as a way to make the creditor temporarily happy.

You should avoid this temptation. Bouncing checks is never the answer. Not only will you be charged a fee by the bank and by the creditor which will put you in a deeper hole, but you could also face criminal prosecution for fraud. You may be able to defend yourself successfully if you are prosecuted, but it is far better not to have to deal with this problem at all.

Whenever you are in doubt, find out your balance with the bank before writing a check. Remember that your balance may seem higher than it really is because of other checks you have written that have not yet been deducted from your account. If you have a joint account, coordinate your check writing carefully with any other person who has power to write checks and make withdrawals.

2. Postdated Checks. A postdated check is one dated later than the date on which the check was written, with the expectation that it will not be cashed until that later date. Usually this is done with the hope there will be sufficient funds in the account by the time the check is cashed.

Never give a creditor a postdated check. Even if you believe that you will have the money in your account to pay the check by that date, you may be wrong because something unexpected could happen. If that happens, you will bounce the check or you will not have the money for something else that is more important. Also keep in mind that creditors occasionally deposit checks before their due date. Even though this may be improper, it does happen and can cause you substantial problems. Finally, if you give a postdated check and later change your mind about paying that debt, it may be difficult and expensive to stop payment on the check.

Creditors often encourage you to write postdated checks as a collection tactic. They want your check in hand as a way to get their money. You should resist the urge to give in to this pressure. You can offer instead to deliver the check on the day you write it — a day on which you have sufficient funds in your account. This allows you to decide not to deliver the check if your priorities change or if you end up not having enough money in the account.

3. "Payday" Lenders. Some collectors, check cashers or small lenders exploit financial emergencies by making short-term loans until "payday." They will offer to take a personal check dated for some time in the future from you or from someone you know. The lender will hold that check and not cash it until the date on the check. (In some cases, lenders hold the check until your payday. This is why they are called "payday" loans. The same types of loans are also called "postdated check," "deferred presentment," or "cash advance" loans.)

After you give the check, the lender will give you an amount of cash that is less than the amount written on your check. At the end of the agreed time period, you must either pay back the full amount of the check (more than what the lender gave you), or the lender will cash the check.

The difference between the amount of your check and the amount of cash you get in return is interest or a loan fee that the lender is charging you. These types of short-term loans are always very expensive.

For example:

Five Days Work for Four Days Pay? The High Cost of Borrowing Against Your Pay Check.	
You write a check dated in two weeks for	$256
You get back today	$200
Interest and charges	$56
The interest rate for a loan of two weeks is	728%

Compare this 728% interest rate loan to annual interest rates as low as 10-15% that bank, credit unions and finance companies charge. The $56 you spend on this short-term loan means that you will have that much less money in your monthly budget.

Some lenders making this type of loan will encourage you to keep refinancing for short periods of time by writing larger and larger checks. Each refinancing will allow the lender to charge more interest and fees. This just makes a bad situation worse by compounding the expense.

4. Selling or Giving Away a Creditor's Collateral. You may have property which serves as collateral for a loan from one of your creditors. A common example is a car which serves as collateral for your car loan.

It is a bad idea to give away or sell a creditor's collateral. This practice is usually called "conversion" of collateral.

If you have already lost, given away, or sold collateral, you may be prosecuted by a state official or sued by the creditor. There are many defenses to these types of suits. The most important defense is that your conduct was not intentional. In most cases, this means that you did not understand that the property was collateral or that you did know the consequences to the creditor of disposing of the property. In addition, most such prosecutions and lawsuits can be ended by payment of the value of the collateral either in installments or in a lump sum if you have it. Given overcrowding in most prisons and the technical nature of the supposed crime, jail time is rarely or never imposed. Still, this is not a risk worth taking.

5. Transferring Property to Protect It From Creditors. If you are in debt and you have valuable property to protect from your creditors, it may occur to you to give it away to a friend or relative, or to sell it for a small percentage of its real value to someone who will later return it. Some people believe that this will protect the property from judgment liens and other creditor collection.

There are many problems with these types of property transfers. When the transfer of some of your assets leaves you with insufficient assets to pay your debts, creditors can have the transfer canceled under your state's law covering "fraudulent transfers" or "fraudulent conveyances."

A transfer of this type may delay the inevitable because the creditor will have to bring a legal action in order to cancel the transfer. However, this extra time now could cost you a lot of money later by increasing the amount you owe to a creditor, including attorneys fees and costs. You also may have to pay additional damages and you can lose your right to bankruptcy protection. In rare cases, you could be criminally prosecuted. It is also possible that the creditor will sue the person to whom you have transferred the property.

An improper transfer is different from exemption planning. Exemption planning is less likely to cause you problems. The idea of exemption planning is that you keep the total value of all of your property, but trade one type of property that is not exempt from seizure under your state laws for another type that is.

For example, the money in your bank account may not be exempt from seizure. However, state law may allow you to take that money and purchase a life insurance policy which is exempt from seizure. Small transfers of this type are usually acceptable, but state laws on these issues vary a great deal. You may wish to obtain expert advice before engaging in exemption planning.

6. Misleading Your Creditors. It is a bad idea to lie or mislead your creditors. However, you have no obligation to tell a debt collector anything, and in general it is a bad idea to give a debt collector too much information about your circumstances. The best rule of thumb is to refuse to answer any prying questions. For example, if you tell a debt collector too much about a new job, the collector may use that information to harass you at work. If you tell a debt collector about your bank account, it may use that information to seize money in the account after the collector obtains a judgment against you.

An exception to the rule of not volunteering information to creditors applies when you try to work out a deal with a creditor for a temporary change in loan terms, for installment payments instead of the creditor seizing your property, or for similar purposes. In those instances, the creditor will want and is entitled to information about your circumstances. When you are asking for help from a creditor, providing that creditor with accurate information is essential.

Lying or misleading that creditor cannot only get you into serious trouble for fraud, but also undermine the creditor's confidence in working with you to reach a mutually acceptable solution. Since much of the information you give to a creditor can be independently verified, your lie will be caught.

Occasionally, you may feel that a creditor wants you to lie in a written statement to qualify for a particular repayment option or refinancing. This usually means that the creditor is unscrupulous. The creditor may want a signed statement from you which misrepresents your financial situation for use in a later lawsuit against you if you fail to pay. These types of misstatements can also be used in some cases to prevent you from getting relief in bankruptcy.

7. Pressure-Related Spending Sprees. Some consumers respond to financial pressures by spending money in irrational ways. Not only does this dig you deeper into debt but some types of spending for unnecessary items or through cash advances on credit cards can also cause problems if you later choose to file bankruptcy. You may lose your right to erase these debts in bankruptcy if the creditor can prove that you ran up your credit cards knowing that you could not pay them back.

There are counseling groups in many communities which can help you address uncontrollable spending habits. A credit counselor can usually point you in the right direction.

8. Unscrupulous Trade Schools. It may seem like a responsible road to financial recovery to try to go to school, learn a new skill, and get a job where you make more money. Although this can be a good idea, it may backfire if you enroll in the wrong type of school.

Many trade schools advertise aggressively that they can teach you a trade which will help you increase your income. Some even guarantee that you will make a certain amount of money. They will often claim you do not have to pay for the tuition until you obtain your high-paying job, or that you never have to pay because of a government grant.

Many of these schools are rip-offs. The fact that the school is accredited or approved by a government agency is *no* protection against the school being a fraud. Thousands of sham trade and vocational schools have received accreditation and government approval over the years.

The only sure-fire way of knowing whether a school's training is any good, and whether the training will actually lead to a job, is to talk to employers in your area. Make sure you talk to employers you find on your own rather than to people recommended by the school. Ask them whether they would hire a graduate of that school, and, if not, what type of training they would recommend.

You should also ask employers whether they prefer to train their own people rather than hire graduates of vocational and other schools. Even though education is usually a good idea, keep in mind that in many cases, the types of short-term courses offered by many trade schools will not lead to employment because either there are no jobs available or because entry qualification requirements are much higher.

If you find out that additional education is likely to lead to employment in a particular field, it is a good idea to check out your local community colleges which often offer the same courses as trade schools at a fraction of the cost. If you do decide to go to a trade school, you should first find out what percentage of the school's students graduate. Steer away from schools with a high dropout rate.

**Too often a trade school,
even one with government approval,
is a dead end,
just getting you deeper into debt.**

In all cases, make sure you know what the tuition is, because you will eventually have to repay it with interest. How does that tuition stack up with other alternatives? Also, find out also what you will have to pay if you dropout after a few weeks — you often have to repay almost all of the tuition.

Making the wrong choice on a vocational school is much more serious than you think. Not only have you wasted valuable time, but you have incurred a loan that must be repaid. As described in Chapter Nineteen, failure to repay student loans can lead to tax refund intercepts, wage garnishment, large collection fees, and more. Perhaps most important, failure to repay the loan can make it difficult to obtain additional job training that may really be worthwhile.

9. Rent-to-Own. The rent-to-own industry makes huge profits renting property such as furniture, electronics or appliances mostly to people facing financial hardship. In a rent-to-own deal, you are supposedly renting property for a period of time until you qualify for ownership. It is marketed as a way for people who do not qualify for credit to have use of an item while it is being purchased.

There are two major problems with rent-to-own. First, items purchased in this way are very expensive, often costing you more than three times the cash price.

For example:

The High Cost of Renting to Own
You rent a 19-inch color TV ($300 value)
You pay $16 per week for 52 weeks...$832
Value of property you bought..$300
Interest you pay (254% on an annual basis)...$532

On top of that, you may have purchased a *used* T.V. that is only worth $150.

The second problem with rent-to-own occurs when you can't keep up the payments. If you miss even one payment, the item can be repossessed. You will then lose the benefit of any payments you have made toward owning the property. The more you have paid, the more you have to lose if at some point you end up missing a payment. Many people have paid more than $1000 for property worth less then $500 only to lose that property for missing one payment.

If you need to buy furniture, appliances or electronic goods, and you can't immediately afford them, you should look at options besides rent-to-own. The best option may be to save money if at all possible and then to pay cash. Consider selling something you don't need to buy something you do. Also don't assume that you cannot qualify for more conventional credit. Stores may grant credit even to people with a bad credit record or they may have other ways for you to purchase at a reasonable rate of interest. Shop for the best possible cash price and the best possible interest rate. Chapter Six includes other ideas on how to make purchases without paying for rent-to-own and other high-cost services.

10. Pawn Shops and Auto Title Pawn. For hundreds of years, pawn shops have made small loans in exchange for property. Pawnbrokers take property from you in exchange for an amount of money that is always less than what the property is worth. If you cannot repay the loan, the pawn shop keeps the property. Usually a pawnbroker will lend only one-half of the value of your property so that they can be sure to get their money back if you don't pay. They also charge very high-interest rates.

If you have valuable property you can live without, consider selling it in a more conventional way for its full value. When you get your financial circumstances back on track, you can buy a replacement.

A new type of "pawn" cropping up in some states is called an "auto pawn" where you borrow money at very high-interest rates (for example, 240% or 360%) and put up your car title as collateral for the loan. This is also a bad idea. An auto pawn is not as simple and hassle free as the title lenders advertise it to be. You can borrow money elsewhere at lower interest rates without endangering your car.

For example:

The Auto Title Pawn Scam

Your car is worth $1,000.
You give up your car title ($1,000 value) for a $500 loan.
You pay weekly installments of $103.30 for 10 weeks.
Your total payments are $1,033.
You pay $1,033
You receive $500
Interest and charges total $533
This is an interest rate of ....826%.

In addition to the extremely high-interest rate charged, if you ever fall behind on your monthly payments, your car will be at risk no matter how much you have already paid. For example, if you borrow $500 and make $110 monthly payments for 10 months and miss the eleventh month, your car can be repossessed. Once your car is repossessed, you are unlikely to get fair credit for payments you have made.

11. Sale and Lease Back. Another way that some companies and individuals make money is to buy your property from you at a low price, and then to lease that property back to you at a high rental rate. These deals often are targeted at people facing foreclosure or repossession. Some companies get their leads by reading published foreclosure notices.

These businesses are rip-offs. Once you have sold your property to them, you no longer have the rights of an owner. You are likely to be overpaying in rent for something you formerly owned. You will have no certain way of getting it back. Additionally, there are many reported cases of fraud involving promises made in connection with these contracts. People have been talked into transferring title to property without getting anything in return.

12. Auto Brokerage and Subleases. Another practice to avoid involves hiring a broker to sell or sublease your car to another person who will make your loan or lease payments for you. Often the broker arranges the transfer without the permission of your car lender or leasing company, making the deal illegal. In addition, the broker may not pass on the payments to your lender or leasing company. If the new car owner skips with the car, you will be left holding the bag. This form of auto brokerage is illegal in many states.

13. "Hard Money" Lenders. A variety of companies advertise loans supposedly designed for people with bad credit or by promising no credit check. Other loan companies rely instead on a network of loan brokers to bring them business. These companies make money by lending to people in difficult financial situations on hard terms (usually meaning bad terms) including very high interest rates.

There is a whole industry of lenders
preying on those in financial trouble,
overcharging them and taking unfair advantage.

When you deal with such a lender, expect the lender to engage in some of the following shady practices:

- Misrepresenting the loan terms—a 10% loan will turn into a 20% loan at the time of closing;
- Making loans which the lender knows you cannot repay in order to seize valuable collateral such as your home or car;
- Charging unacceptably high interest rates;
- Refinancing debts which are better off left alone;
- Charging high hidden costs;
- Paying loan brokers, car dealers and contractors incentives to mislead you about your credit options or to make inappropriate referrals;
- Hiding ties to loan brokers in order to charge you illegal commissions;

- Making loans on complicated terms, including negative amortization or balloon payments, in order to make an unaffordable loan look temporarily affordable;
- Forming alliances with other sleazy businesses to finance shoddy work or inferior goods, and then to share the profits from doing so; and
- High pressure sales tactics designed to get you to agree to buy credit insurance or other unnecessary "tie-in" products.

Don't be suckered by hard money lenders. They have many techniques designed to draw you into deals, only to make it almost impossible for you to back away. You should never agree to refinance a low-priority debt, as discussed in Chapter Four. Ways to avoid refinancing scams are discussed in more detail in that chapter.

14. Tax Refund Anticipation Loans. Another major scam aimed at those in financial distress involves loans which are based on your expected tax refund. The lender may even be the company preparing your tax return. The loan is for a very short period of time between when your return is filed with the government and when you would expect to get your tax refund.

For example, you might file a return with the government on March 15. You would normally expect a refund, if you are entitled to one, within thirty days. In a tax refund anticipation loan, a company will give you the amount of the refund less a fee on March 15, so that you don't have to wait until April 15 for your refund check. The fees can be very high.

The fee you are charged is effectively interest on what amounts to a very short-term loan. Looked at in this way, you may be charged interest at an annual rate of 200% or more. Some companies may try to fool you about the annual interest rate by telling you the rate assuming that the company will not be repaid for two or three months. Since the company is actually getting the money back in one month, the real interest rate is two or three times the number you are told. The best advice is to avoid tax refund antic-ipation loans. Be patient and wait for your full refund if at all possible. You may be able to get a refund more quickly by filing electronically.

15. Voluntary Wage Assignments. In some states you can voluntarily assign some of your wages to a particular creditor, meaning your employer automatically sends some of your paycheck to that creditor. A voluntary wage assignment is different from a wage garnishment or an assignment ordered by a court because it is something you do by agreement, rather than something which is forced on you after a court judgment against you.

Creditors that have no other way to get payment will often pressure you to agree to a voluntary wage assignment. This is almost always a very bad choice. The wage assignment gives these creditors priority ahead of your more pressing debts, such as your rent or mortgage.

If you do want to pay that creditor ahead of other creditors, go ahead and do so, but pay by cash, check or money order. The voluntary assignment will reduce your flexibility, because you will not be able to make other choices for use of that money if the need arises.

16. "For-Profit" Debt Counseling. While debt counseling may be a good idea, it is rarely smart to pay a "for-profit" counselor for this service. Many companies and individuals charge high fees for counseling which are not justified by the help they can offer.

If you choose a debt counseling option, try to find a qualified nonprofit counselor. Although some nonprofits charge a small fee, the fee is almost always less than what a for-profit business charges. Get a recommendation if possible. If you cannot get a recommendation from a friend or relative, try calling your state attorney general, a local legal services program, or a consumer help hotline.

It is not always easy to distinguish between nonprofit and profit-making credit counselors, because profit-making entities may adopt "nonprofit" type names, such as "foundation" or "service." A United Way logo on the counselor's letterhead is usually a reliable indication that a counselor is a nonprofit, although not all nonprofit credit counselors are affiliated with the United Way.

It is also very important not to pay anything other than a small fee to people who claim they will be able to help you. Some unscrupulous debt counselors will tell you they can make an arrangement on a debt for you if you bring them cash for the creditor, or if you write a check to the counselor which will be passed on to the creditor. There are many reports of counselors keeping this money rather than paying your debts.

17. Credit Repair Scams. Credit repair businesses can now be found all over the country. They sometimes call themselves credit clinics or credit service organizations. These businesses charge unreasonable fees for services which they claim will help you improve your credit. At best, these businesses are charging you for work you can do yourself for free. More often, they are making promises to improve your credit which they cannot hope to keep. At worst, they will get you involved with rip-off businesses or even, in some cases, in schemes which can later cause you serious legal problems. More discussion of credit repair is included in Chapter Seven, including some simple steps you can take on your own behalf.

18. Get Rich Quick Schemes. Many products and jobs are advertised with the promise that you will make a lot of money quickly. These are almost always scams.

For example, real estate investment seminars are sold with the promise that you can make a bundle by buying and selling investment property. The reality is that the only one making a bundle is the person selling you the seminar. When seminars of this type are offered for free, usually there will be an aggressive effort to sell you something which is very expensive or very profitable for the person giving the seminar.

A similar problem involves jobs which are offered with the promise of making quick financial returns. A common example is an advertisement with a bold heading such as **"Make up to $1,000 a week immediately — working at home."** The vast majority of these offers require payment of substantial "set up" or "one-time start-up" fees to a person or company that promises you a money making plan in return. The company keeps these fees and you wind up with no real way of making money.

Once again follow the rule: if it seems too good to be true, it probably is. An advertisement which implies that you can make easy money almost always signals a rip-off.

19. Telemarketing Scams. Many products, services, investments, and loans are advertised over the telephone. Every consumer thinks that he or she recognizes telephone rip-off schemes, but nevertheless every year millions of people are victimized. Telemarketers use very sophisticated techniques to get consumers to sign up for things they don't need, products that don't work, services which are too expensive, or outright rip-offs. Elderly individuals, in particular, are often targeted for investment scams and other telemarketing abuses.

Most telemarketers are highly trained in aggressive sales techniques. For example, they may tell you that you have already won a prize, that you can participate in a sweepstakes, that they are only taking a survey, that they are offering a free product, or that they are selling something which has been endorsed by celebrities. Telemarketers are usually offered large commissions by their employers based on the number of sales they make—increasing their incentive to be aggressive on the phone or to deliberately mislead you.

For these reasons, it is a good idea never to agree to buy anything over the phone. The best choice is not to listen to the sales pitch in the first place to avoid the waste of time.

However, if you do listen, or if you are interested, do not invite the telemarketer to call again or to come to your home. This will make you a target. Instead ask that detailed follow up information be sent in the mail, before you agree to anything. Doing so will give you an opportunity to think clearly about whether you are being cheated and to see the terms of the offer in writing. Pressure to sign up right away without receiving detailed written information on what you are buying is always the sign of a scam.

20. The Truth About the Lottery and Prize Sweepstakes. People facing financial difficulties sometimes look to the lottery as a way to improve their financial situation. This is an expensive long shot at best. Spending substantial money on the lottery or other gambling can greatly compound your financial problems.

The lottery pays out only a percentage of the money it takes in. The percentage in some states is one half or less. This means that for every two dollars spent on lottery tickets, you are likely to win back only one.

Very few people win big prizes. The chance of winning a million dollars is far less than one in a million. While you are experiencing financial difficulties, it is best to reduce or eliminate your expenses on the lottery, rather than to look at it as a way to solve your problems.

Similarly, most sweepstake offers, including those you receive by mail, are usually longshots, meant to convince you that your odds of winning prizes are greater if you buy products you don't need, such as magazines. Others advertise prizes or "free" gifts as a come-on to get you interested in buying things you don't need.

Refinancing
Do's and Don'ts

- *Twelve Simple Refinancing Rules*
- *Deciding When and When Not to Refinance*
- *Reverse Mortgages*
- *Refinancing Scams to Avoid*

Refinancing is a process in which you pay off one or more debts by borrowing new money from an existing creditor or a new creditor. It is sometimes suggested as a good way for people with financial problems to address their difficulties.

We recommend that you be very careful when refinancing debts. Refinancing an unaffordable amount of debt is one of the most tempting but risky steps you can take when you have financial problems. Many refinancing loans will hurt you more than they help.

Refinancing's attraction is that it seems to resolve your financial problems even though your income and your expenses do not change. The stroke of a pen pays off creditors who have been threatening action against you. After refinancing, you only have to make one monthly payment to a new creditor who is not (yet) threatening anything.

The disadvantages of refinancing are often hidden. Problems occur because of the complex mathematics which sometimes govern the refinancing process, including hidden fees and costs, and because the new loan may give the creditor ways to force payment and seize your property that were not available under the prior loan. There are even times when a refinancing deal is nothing more than a scam to steal your home or other property. Each potential refinancing deal must be reviewed carefully on its merits based on the principles discussed in this chapter.

TWELVE SIMPLE
REFINANCING RULES

1. When in Doubt, Do Not Refinance or Consolidate Debts. Refinancing deals almost always come with significant costs. These costs will usually just make matters worse in the long term.

2. Do Not Let Debt Collectors Pressure You Into Refinancing. Debt collectors may try to scare you into refinancing because they have no other way to get their money. Better ways to address debt collection problems are discussed in Chapter Six.

3. Never (or Almost Never) Refinance Unsecured Debt Into Secured Debt. For example, do not take out a mortgage on your home to pay off credit card or medical bills. Unsecured creditors rarely can do anything to seriously hurt you if you fail to pay. By trading in unsecured debt for a mortgage loan, you face loss of your home if you continue to have financial problems. Do not refinance unsecured debt into secured debt even if this allows you to lower the interest rate you are paying.

4. Do Not Refinance Utility Debts. Most utility companies have flexible repayment plans and you can usually work something out with them instead of paying off utility debts through refinancing. Even if you cannot work out a payment plan, it will almost always be cheaper to get the utility turned back on then it will be to pay the refinanced debt. For more information on utility bills, see Chapter Sixteen.

5. If You Have an Existing Debt With a Finance Company or High-Rate Second Mortgage Company, Do Not Refinance that Debt With the Same Company. Ask the company to agree to lower payments on the existing loan, but do not allow the creditor to refinance that loan, which may involve prepayment penalties, new closing costs, and perhaps even a higher interest rate. Never allow the company to add new security — such as your home.

6. Do Not Turn Your Car Loan Into a Second Mortgage Unless You Would Rather Lose Your Home Than Your Car. If you are in danger of losing your car, you may be tempted to pay off your car loan by taking out a second mortgage on your home. You may save your car temporarily this way, but you are putting your home in danger. Although repossession is bad, foreclosure is worse.

7. Do Not Refinance a Loan With Household Goods Collateral into a Second Mortgage Loan. Not only is your home worth more than your household goods, but it is very hard for a lender to repossess your household goods. See Chapter Eighteen.

8. Do Not Refinance Low-Interest Debts With Higher Interest Loans. You should always evaluate the interest rate on the new debt and look for a lower rate than on the old debts. Furthermore, the "APR" (Annual Percentage Rate) of the new loan must be lower than the *stated interest rate* of the old loan, or you will be losing money. You have already paid for certain up-front fees in the old loan, and you must make sure that a new lower rate is actually lower after both the old and new fees are accounted for.

Also remember that the interest rate is not the only consideration when evaluating a loan. Other fees, charges, and expenses which are not considered interest may make a loan which looks cheaper into one which is actually more expensive. In particular you may want to look at the material in Chapter Two discussing "hard-money" lending.

9. Do Not Include Your Long-Term First Mortgage in a Refinancing Package. Do not let second mortgage lenders pay off your first mortgage and give you a new mortgage equal to the first mortgage plus the new loan amount. The only exception is if the new mortgage is for the equivalent length of time and the interest rate is significantly *lower* than the old first mortgage — to offset prepayment penalties and fees and charges.

10. Do Not Refinance Loans When You Have Valid Legal Reasons Not to Pay That Debt. If you have a legal defense to repayment of a debt, you can raise that defense in court. If you refinance with a new lender, the defense will not be available against the new creditor. You should get legal help to see if you have a valid defense *before* entering the refinancing deal.

11. Watch Out for Scam Refinancing Companies. Refinancing involves great potential for hidden costs, fees, and other unfair loan terms. Even some reputable lenders make unfair refinancing deals. When in doubt, get help in reviewing the loan *before* you sign anything. You can walk away from a bad deal even at the last minute. A lender that is unwilling to let you get outside help should not be trusted. Another way to avoid scams is never to let a contractor or salesperson arrange financing for you and be wary of mortgage brokers. Unfortunately many brokers find refinancing deals which involve big commissions for them rather than good loans in your best interest.

12. You Can Cancel Any Refinancing Deal That Involves a Mortgage on Your Home. In most refinancings in which you give the lender a mortgage, federal law gives you the right to cancel for any reason for three days from the date you sign the papers. Make sure you cancel in writing before the deadline. You can, but need not, use the cancellation form provided by the lender.

DECIDING WHEN
TO REFINANCE

As summarized by the twelve rules described above, many refinancings are bad deals that will make matters worse for you. This section goes into more detail about the factors you must consider before deciding to refinance your debt. The rule of thumb is that when in doubt, do not *refinance even if you are behind on a debt.*

Unsecured and Secured Debts. Most debts are called "unsecured." This means that a home, car, or other property is *not* collateral for the loan. Good examples of unsecured debt are hospital and doctors' bills, lawyers' bills, and most credit card debt. Utility debt is also unsecured. As described in Chapters One and Seven, you have relatively little to fear if you are not able to pay your unsecured debts. To recover anything, the creditor will have to go to court, and even then may have difficulty collecting.

It is almost always a bad idea to refinance unsecured debt into secured debt, such as happens when you use a home equity line of credit or a second mortgage to refinance your debt. When you put up your home, car, or other property as collateral on a loan, this is a secured loan and the creditor has a "security interest" in your property. Secured debt will pose serious problems for you if you get behind in payments because the creditor has the right to quickly seize the collateral.

Also, do not "trade up" on security. For example, do not refinance a lower priority secured loan such as a car loan into a second mortgage, or turn a loan secured by household items (which creditors rarely if ever seize) into a home mortgage loan.

**If you are having trouble making ends meet,
never refinance low-interest or unsecured debt
into high-interest debt
or debt that requires a mortgage on your home.**

Be sure to look at the loan documents and disclosure statements in any refinancing to see what property you are putting up as collateral. These documents will describe whether you are giving the creditor a "security interest" in any of your property.

Utility Bills. Utility debts should not be refinanced. While you do not want your heat or electricity shut off, there are many preferable ways to prevent a utility termination or to get service turned back on (see Chapter Sixteen) than to refinance your utility debt with a new lender.

Refinancing a utility debt can begin a downward spiral. If you are having trouble paying the utility bills, refinancing these low or no interest debts will not improve matters. Instead, you will have to pay both the *old* bills now refinanced with interest and your current monthly utility bills. It is particularly unwise to fold a utility debt into a home mortgage debt. Not only are you paying more in interest, but the risk in the event of default is much more serious. Even if you are facing shut-off, there are always better ways to deal with the back debt than to refinance.

Low-Cost vs. High-Cost Credit. Refinancings or loan consolidation often converts low-cost loans into high-cost loans. This makes things more unaffordable for you. Many of your existing bills charge you *no* interest or charge only minimal late charges. A mortgage loan you took out to purchase your home also usually has a relatively low-interest rate.

Refinanced loans, on the other hand, will often be high-cost loans. Not only will the stated interest rate be high, but the creditor will assess points, closing costs, insurance charges, maybe even brokers' fees or hidden charges. In addition, the loans you are paying off may include penalties for early payment (prepayment penalties).

One way of determining the real cost of the new loan is to look at the "disclosure statement" explaining all the terms for the new loan. The federal Truth-in-Lending law requires that creditors provide this statement before you sign the loan papers. You should look at the APR (annual percentage rate) of the new loan rather than the amount of the payments.

Lenders have numerous ways to make payments look artificially low, even when the loan is at a very high cost to you. For example, in some variable rate loans, your monthly payments will climb after the first several months. Monthly payments can also be artificially low if there is a large, lump sum "balloon" payment at the end of the loan. Similarly, some loans require monthly payments that are less than the monthly interest due so that the principal amount keeps going up even though you keep on making payments (this is called negative amortization). Other times you will pay high closing costs and up front fees, but not realize this because they are deducted from your loan amount.

You should examine all of the loan terms before you sign any papers. Do not look at the monthly payment as the only issue. If loan terms are not favorable, shop around for another loan. You can always walk away from signing loan papers, even at the last minute. Definitely walk away if the lender tries to change loan terms from what you had been originally offered. Remember also that if you have to put up your primary residence as collateral for a refinancing, federal law allows you to cancel the loan *for any reason* up to three days *after* signing the loan.

Here are some questions to ask when looking at the loan's disclosure statement:

- What is the Annual Percentage Rate or "APR?" This will give you an idea of the interest rate with many of the costs and fees on the loan included. Be sure you understand any variable rate provisions since this may later change the amount of your monthly payment.
- What is "the finance charge" (the total cost of the credit over the life of the loan)? This is how much you are paying the lender for use of its money over the term of the loan.

- How much is the "amount financed?" This is supposed to be the money the creditor is giving you. Sometimes, much of the amount financed never goes to you or to pay off your obligations, but instead goes to purchase insurance or to pay various fees and charges. Request an itemization of the amount financed which will explain where your money is going and why. If this statement is different from what you expected, walk away from the loan. Most important, ask questions or seek professional help to review the paperwork if the loan terms are unclear to you.
- Can you permanently afford the "payment schedule" for the loan? The payment schedule shows not only the amount of your first payment, but also describes the ways that your monthly payments may change. Make sure all of the payments on the loan will be affordable. Do not rely on an oral promise to refinance when scheduled payments go up.

You can compare your answers to these questions about a new loan to your current debts as well as to alternative loans.

Bank Loans vs. Finance Company Loans. In general, do *not* refinance a bank loan with a finance company loan. (In fact, try to avoid finance companies entirely.) Finance companies tend to make loans at higher interest rates and may include unnecessary insurance, fees, and hidden charges.

Many consumers think only finance companies will make loans to them, that banks will not make a loan because of a bad credit history. Do not make assumptions — ask a few banks. Also, beware of finance company loan "flipping." Many finance companies encourage frequent refinancings, each time making the loan more expensive to you and increasing the total amount you must repay. For this reason, some finance companies encourage you to refinance when you get behind on your payments rather than offer a repayment plan.

There may also be alternatives to banks and finance companies, such as credit unions, that can, in some cases, offer you better terms. See Chapter Five for more information.

Long-Term vs. Short-Term Credit. Always look at the length of a loan and whether there is a balloon payment (that is, a very large payment that is due as the last payment). You should not refinance a loan you are paying out over fifteen years with a loan you have to pay off in four years.

Particularly watch out if the monthly payments for the shorter loan are the same or lower than the longer term loan. This almost always means the shorter term loan has a large balloon at the end. You may not be able to pay the balloon payment when it comes due. You will be in a very weak position if you are later forced to refinance the balloon and will likely be stuck with whatever loan terms the creditor wants to offer. If the creditor will not refinance the balloon, and you cannot find another way to pay off the balloon, the lender may seize any collateral it has taken, including your home.

Variable vs. Fixed Rates. You will be offered either a fixed or variable rate loan if you refinance. In a variable rate loan, the interest rate you pay can go up or down during the life of the loan. The interest rate in a fixed rate loan stays the same for the full term of your loan.

Whether your variable rate interest goes up or down will usually depend on whether other interest rates in the economy are going up or down. For example, your rate may be set at five percentage points above the current interest rate for one year United States Treasury Bills. Your rate then changes in the same direction as the rate on one year treasury bills.

You need to exercise care when refinancing from fixed rate loans to variable rate and sometimes *vice versa*, because it is difficult to compare loans of the two types. A good rule of thumb is never to refinance from a fixed rate into a variable rate, because of the risk of increased payments with variable rate loans.

Occasionally, a variable rate option is the right choice, but you must first make sure you know what you are doing. Getting help from an expert is good advice. Check the loan documents. The lender is required to tell you the maximum rate which could ever apply to your variable rate loan. Make sure you can afford the loan even if the rate increases to the maximum.

One other problem to watch out for in variable rate loans is low "teaser rates." These are rates designed to be low for the first months of the loan, but which often increase dramatically later. Pay less attention to the stated teaser rate then to the Annual Percentage Rate (APR) disclosed for the whole term of the loan. If you are not good at understanding interest rates, it is best to avoid teaser rates and variable rate loans entirely. The more a particular lender pushes variable rate loans as an only option over your objection, the stronger you should resist the deal.

Another trick of unscrupulous lenders is to change an offered loan from fixed rate to variable rate at the last minute. This is a sure sign of a bad loan. If any term of the loan is changed at the last minute, do not sign the loan papers. You should either have a professional review the papers to make sure they don't include unfair terms, or walk away from that lender entirely.

> **Beware of lenders trying to change**
> **the loan terms at the last minute.**
> **Whenever you have doubts about loan terms,**
> **your best course is to walk away.**

Points, Broker's Fees and Other Up-Front Charges. When you refinance one or more loans into a new loan, you often have to pay points, a broker's fees, or other up-front charges. Since you have already paid for any such charges on your old loans, these charges are an extra cost of the new loan. Even if the new loan's interest rate appears lower, these added charges may make the new loan more costly.

Make sure the "APR" (Annual Percentage Rate) on the new loan is lower than the *interest* rate stated on the old loans. The "interest rate" (as opposed to the APR) on the old loan will not reflect points, brokers' fees, closing costs, and other up-front fees. The APR is a measure of the total cost of a loan with all of these up-front costs factored in. For example:

Comparing the Costs of Loans
Amount borrowed in new loan $25,000
Interest rate 10%
Origination Fee (3 percent of loan amount).. $750
Brokers' fees. $500
APR for new loan... 12.23%
You should not use this loan to refinance an older loan which was at a 12% interest rate or lower. The origination fee of $750 and brokers' fee of $500 are additional costs of getting the new loan which are not included in the interest rate on the new loan. Factoring them in to the APR makes clear that the total cost of the new loan is actually higher than the rate you have been paying, even though the interest rate is lower.

Insurance and Other Extras. Consumer debt frequently is loaded up with a lot of extras. Just as some auto dealers make their real profits selling expensive rustproofing and service contracts, so, too, lenders sell overpriced extras or tack on fees and charges to their loans in order to make money. Unless you have a special reason for wanting these extras, you should not purchase them. That sounds easy, but you often do not know what extras you are buying and lenders have sophisticated techniques to sell unnecessary products.

One of the biggest problems is credit life and credit accident and health insurance. These policies are supposed to pay off your loan if you cannot. To sell this coverage to you, the lender will need you to initial a statement that you want this coverage. You should not do so. Only a small percentage of these insurance premiums are ever paid out as losses to policyholders.

Additionally, many such policies are designed so that companies can deny coverage to you even when it appears that you have a valid claim. For example, the insurance may not cover many types of accidents which you would expect it would cover. Any benefits that are paid out are limited to the amount left on the loan, so that you never actually receive much if anything. You will always be better off buying insurance from other sources.

While you have the legal right to turn down credit insurance and many other extras, you are likely to be compelled to pay for certain other charges if you want a loan from a particular lender. Examples are property insurance on the collateral and title examination fees. However, you may be able to negotiate and lower the amount of these fees.

If mandatory charges seem overpriced to you and the lender is unwilling to negotiate, shop around for another lender. You will find a lot of differences among lenders as to closing costs and other charges. In addition, you should always factor in the cost of all extra charges when you are trying to decide whether you are saving or losing money by refinancing existing loans with a new loan.

Prepayment Penalties. When you pay off old loans through refinancing, there are almost always significant prepayment penalties on the existing debt. These penalties should be treated like extra charges on the *new* loan. Add them to the finance charge on the new loan and consider that they increase the interest rate on the new loan accordingly.

You will find it difficult to measure the size of these penalties, but they frequently exist. Even if the creditor does not have an explicit prepayment penalty, some states allow creditors to compute payoff figures to their own advantage. Additionally, if you purchased credit-related insurance on the old loan, that insurance will be canceled and you will receive less than a full rebate. (The creditor may then try to sell a new insurance policy with the new loan.) If you have difficulty computing the prepayment penalties, assume that they exist and that they are a significant disadvantage to refinancing.

Borrowing More than Your Home is Worth. Some lenders are now offering to provide refinancing to consumers in amounts far more than their homes are worth. These loans are sometimes called "125%" loans, "high-LTV" loans, or "no-equity" loans. These loans can be quite large and very expensive. Some lenders provide misleading information about the tax consequences of such loans. They claim that you will be able to fully deduct interest charges in a way which the IRS may not allow.

These loans can be very expensive and very risky. Mortgage lenders willing to lend you more than your home is worth typically charge rates about 5% higher than more traditional loans. In addition, your home will be at risk of foreclosure if you fail to pay the new higher loan amount. Finally, remember that taking a loan of this type will prevent you from building up equity in the home for a long time. The loan will make it very difficult to sell or refinance until you have paid the loan down below your property's market value. This can greatly reduce your flexibility if you need to move.

Lenders making these loans are reporting very high default and foreclosure rates. We recommend that you avoid these loan products despite their aggressive advertising campaign on television and through the mail.

Consumer Defenses. You may have legal grounds not to pay a debt. These include, for example, that the goods were never delivered or that repair work was shoddy. If this is the case, never refinance such a loan with a different creditor, because you may lose the ability to raise these defenses against the new creditor. The more removed a creditor is from the original seller, the harder it is to raise defenses.

Backing Out of a Refinancing. If you change your mind about a refinancing deal in which your home is collateral, federal law allows you to cancel the loan within three days of signing the loan papers. If you decide to cancel, you will need to fill in and mail the cancellation form that the creditor is required to provide you at the time you signed the contract. It is important that you do so by the three-day deadline. Federal law also provides other grounds for canceling refinancings if your home is put up as security. See Chapter Fourteen for more details.

Of course, any time you are considering refinancing, whether or not your home is collateral, you can always back out before the papers are signed. You should never feel embarrassed to walk away from a bad deal even if you are being pressured. Some lenders will threaten penalties or legal action if you do not sign papers which have already been prepared. These threats are false, because you have no responsibility to pay if there is no binding agreement. There is no binding agreement until you sign the papers.

REVERSE MORTGAGES

Reverse mortgages are increasingly available as a refinancing option for older homeowners who have built up substantial equity in their property. (Equity equals the value of your home minus what you owe. The longer you have lived in the house and paid off your mortgage, the less you owe and therefore the more equity you have).

The rules of reverse mortgages are different from those of traditional mortgages. In a traditional mortgage the lender gives cash to the borrower and, in return, takes a mortgage. As the borrower repays, the amount of the debt decreases. The amount of equity, therefore, increases.

In a reverse mortgage the lender gives the homeowner cash based on the value of the property without an immediate repayment obligation because the lender expects repayment through the sale of the property at some point in the future. In contrast to a traditional mortgage, the amount of the debt in a reverse mortgage increases over time, while the homeowner's equity decreases.

For most reverse mortgages, you can draw down your home equity without having to repay that loan for quite some time. Some reverse mortgages have no repayment obligation as long as you remain in the property — no matter how long you stay.

In most reverse mortgages, the lender will look at your age, the amount of equity you have in your home, and the prevailing interest rates in order to determine the amount it will lend you. You will then be able to receive your loan amount in one of the following ways:

- One large payment that is given to you in cash or is used to pay off other debt or both.
- Fixed monthly installments that will be paid to you for a set period of time. This is called a "term" plan.

- Fixed monthly installments (smaller ones) that will be paid to you for as long as you live in the home (this is usually called a "tenure" plan).
- As a line of credit to be drawn at your convenience. This may also be combined with a term or tenure plan.

A reverse mortgage may be a good way to get some money now based on the value of your house whether or not you are having financial problems. If you are interested, look for a bank or mortgage company in your community who offers this product. However, a good deal of caution is required for a number of reasons.

Most important, you can only borrow against your equity once. If you have taken a reverse mortgage and spent the money, you will not have the financial resource of home equity available again to you in the future. For example, if you use your home equity as a resource for a reverse mortgage or another loan at age 65, the equity will not be available to help pay for home health care later if you should need it.

Other potential drawbacks to a reverse mortgage include:

- The costs involved in getting a reverse mortgage can be very high. Some reverse mortgages include up-front fees as high as $5,000 or more. You should shop around for the loan product with the smallest total fees.
- The amount of cash you get may not really meet your needs. For example, a 65-year old with $50,000 in home equity may get as little as $100 per month on a term mortgage. (This calculation varies for different lenders and it depends on a variety of factors, including regional loan limits, interest rates, and the amount of the closing costs.)
- A reverse mortgage can affect your eligibility to receive certain government benefits such as SSI and Medicaid. (Social Security payments are not affected.)
- Some shady lenders offer very unfair reverse mortgages or conventional mortgages that look like reverse mortgages. You should only work with a reputable lender in an established program.
- A reverse mortgage makes it difficult to pass your home on to your heirs after your death, and instead the home usually will

go to the lender when you move or if you die. Because you need to use the equity in your home, you will not be able to pass the home on to your heirs. This is not necessarily a bad decision if you need money now, but it is important to make the decision fully aware of what it may mean for the future.

Reverse mortgages provide an orderly way to spend whatever equity you have in your home. But there are expenses, pitfalls to avoid, and disadvantages.

Reverse mortgages are not for everyone. You should work with a knowledgeable counselor if you are at all in doubt, especially since free counseling is an element of most reputable reverse mortgage programs. If you do take out a reverse mortgage, set up a plan to use the money wisely. You will not be able to tap your home equity again.

REFINANCING SCAMS

Tips to Avoid Refinancing Scams. Many unscrupulous companies prey on people in distress. Here are twelve tips to help you steer clear of frauds:

1. *Be wary of anyone who contacts you about refinancing or loan consolidation,* particularly if the solicitation does not come from an established financial institution in your community. Be skeptical of any solicitation from a finance company, even if the company has helped you out before. Well-known finance companies have engaged in serious frauds.
2. *Definitely avoid anyone who solicits loans via a "door to door" visit of your home.* It is very expensive to market anything door to door, and odds are someone coming to the house to help bail

you out of trouble is really coming to get you in deeper.

3. *When in doubt, check out the lender.* If you have any reason to suspect someone you are considering doing business with, check with your state's attorney general, banking commission or consumer complaint hotline. You definitely want to know if there are complaints on file from other consumers. Check both the business's name and the names of any individual you are dealing with, because some individuals change their company names on a repeated basis to avoid becoming well-known in the community. (If you do check on a business, remember that the absence of complaints does not necessarily mean that the business is reputable. You still need to pay attention to the other scam avoidance techniques discussed here.)

4. *Never sign documents without knowing what is in them.* If you own a home, you should be especially wary, because odds are any deal to "help" you will involve a mortgage or other rights to your home.

5. *Avoid any offer that you sell your home, with an option to buy it back.* This will always be the quickest way to lose your home and any equity you have built up. Any sale of your home means that you no longer have the rights of an owner.

6. *Be careful of advertised schemes to save homes from foreclosure or personal solicitations to help you avoid foreclosure.* "For profit" foreclosure assistance has a very poor track record. Many financially strapped consumers pay money for short-term help or no help at all. Nonprofit counseling or bankruptcy assistance is usually a better alternative.

7. *If your regular banker or credit union cannot help you, odds are lenders and brokers who advertise cannot get you a good deal either.* Most loan brokers and some lenders advertise as offering help to people who are credit risks. These advertisements will usually get you involved with people who are known as "hard money lenders" and who will almost always make your situation worse. Brokers are often expensive to use. Many will shop for a loan which includes a big commission to them, rather than the best terms for you.

8. *Beware of anyone who wants to consolidate all of your debts into one loan.* This *never* makes sense. The solicitation shows that the

person suggesting the loan consolidation is not out to help you, but to fleece you.

9. *Do not send an "application" or "processing" fee to a lender who advertises "Bad Credit, No Problem" and then asks you to call an 800 or 900 number.* This may just be a scam to make off with the fee. Any "900" number call will also cost you money which is very hard to get back.

10. *Do not refinance repeatedly with the same lender.* Encouragements to refinance regularly can only mean that the lender is looking to make a large profit at your expense by taking advantage of hidden costs of frequent refinancing.

11. *Do not refinance to take advantage of offers of small amounts of cash or to get a gift.* These deals are almost always designed by lenders to be very costly to you. Cash or a gift is offered in order to convince you to make a deal which has no real financial advantages for you.

12. *If it is too good to be true, it is not true.*

Other Steps to Take If You Are Victimized by a Refinancing Scam. It is much easier to avoid a refinancing scam than to get your money back. Do not expect a business which is ripping you off to easily agree to return money or to be responsive to your complaints. However, you should always take action if you are ripped off, both to try to get your money back and to help prevent the same thing from happening to other honest consumers.

Your first step should always be to ask for return of any money you have lost in a refinancing scam. There is some hope that the lender does not want to alert law enforcement officials and is willing to "buy off" one victim so that they can keep victimizing others. For this reason, threats to go to a state attorney general's office or district attorney or the local press may help.

A second step is to not just threaten, but to actually complain to your attorney general, your state commission overseeing banks, and to your local better business bureau. Consumer complaint hotlines, the press, and neighborhood nonprofits can also be useful. You may find that other people have made similar complaints and that legal action is pending or can be brought. At a minimum, a complaint to a public official or complaint hotline will be on record and will help prevent others from being ripped-off. You should keep all paperwork and make records of all conversations with whoever you think is working a scam.

Your best course is usually to enlist the aid of an attorney who will represent your interests. Although some lawyers will not want to handle a consumer fraud issue, they may tell you if you have a good claim and may make a referral to someone who does handle consumer law cases. You will want an attorney who is willing to pursue your case aggressively. As discussed briefly above, there may be grounds to cancel the mortgage which has been placed on your home and to undo the whole agreement. The lawyer may be able to take other action as well that reduces your obligation on the loan.

Filing bankruptcy is another strategy. It will stop a scam operation's attempt to foreclose your home. To be effective in the long run, though, your bankruptcy attorney must aggressively challenge the scam operator in the bankruptcy proceeding, something not all bankruptcy attorneys are prepared to do.

– 5 –

Obtaining Financial Services on Fair Terms

- *Affordable Banking Services*
- *Way to Save on Insurance*
- *Alternatives to High-Rate Lenders*

Despite your financial problems, it is important to continue to try to find appropriate and reasonably priced financial services in the marketplace. This chapter gives you some ideas about how to avoid expensive checking services, insurance policies, and high-rate loans which will only get you deeper in debt.

Checking Accounts. You can avoid the high cost of cashing checks and buying money orders by opening a bank checking account. It is important to shop around and make sure you find an account that won't end up costing you a lot of extra money.

In exploring the costs of different checking accounts, find out whether the bank offers any free checking and under what terms. For example, is there a minimum balance you must keep in the account at all times to get free checking? If not, how much is the monthly fee? Will you be charged per check?

It is especially important to find out about automated teller machine (ATM) fees. These may be charged not only by your own bank, but also by the bank that owns the machine where you withdraw money. These are unnecessary charges you should avoid as much as possible.

Generally, there will be no charge if you use your card at your own bank. However, some banks put limits on the number of times each month you can use even the bank's own ATM machines. This means that every withdrawal you make past the limit will cost you extra money.

You also may be charged fees for withdrawing money from an ATM that is not owned by your bank. These fees will show up on your monthly bank statement and can add up quickly.

Another important factor is whether the bank has branches that are conveniently located to your home or work. If not, are there ATM machines located throughout your area that you can use at no charge?

There are other ways that the bank might charge you fees. For example, banks charge large fees if you write a check with insufficient funds in your account ("bounced check" or "NSF" fees). You can try to avoid this problem by asking about the bank's overdraft protection and whether this will cost you extra. If you do use the overdraft protection, remember that it is like a loan. The bank will charge you interest.

Of course, the best way to avoid bounced check charges is to avoid bouncing checks entirely. When in doubt about whether you have enough to cover a check you plan to write, stop to look at your records or ask the bank.

You should also find out about the bank's check clearing policy. All banks require that you wait a certain amount of time until a deposited check clears. Knowing how long it will take for your money to be available to you after you deposit a check will help you avoid bounced checks.

If you are having trouble getting an account. If you are turned down for a checking account by one bank, you should find out why. Some banks deny accounts to people that have bounced checks in the past. Ask if the bank pulled a credit report and made a decision on that basis. You are entitled to a free copy of your report within sixty days of a credit denial. (For information about how to order a credit report, see Chapter Seven).

**You can avoid expensive check cashing fees
by exploring your alternatives
for a free or low-cost checking account.**

At some banks, you can explain problems with your credit report or past bounced checks or ask a manager to reconsider. With a reasonable explanation, you may get the account you need. But be careful not to let the bank sell you an account that requires a minimum balance way above your means, or too many extra fees. This will not be worth it in the long run. Instead try shopping around. Find out more about the account services at other banks, or about alternatives to bank accounts discussed below that might work better for you.

Not all banks follow the same practices. Denial of an account at one bank does not mean that you will be denied by all.

Alternatives to Bank Checking Accounts. Just because it is expensive or inconvenient to open a bank account does not mean that you have to keep your money at home and risk theft, or go to expensive check cashers who will charge you high fees just to cash your checks.

Low-Cost Electronic Bank Accounts. Many banks now offer no or low-cost electronic accounts as alternatives to checking and savings accounts. In many cases, you can arrange with your employer to have your paycheck automatically deposited at a bank. You can then ask that bank to open an electronic account for you. Some banks also provide electronic accounts to anyone who receives federal benefits payments. These accounts are called ETAs (electronic transfer accounts).

Electronic accounts require you to withdraw money using only bank ATM machines or point-of-sale (POS) cash withdrawal machines usually located at grocery and other stores. Generally as long as you use the ATM machines owned by the banks, there will be no extra charges. You should also check to be sure that stores do not charge you to use the POS machines.

There are institutions other than mainstream banks that might better suit your financial needs. A few of these options are listed here.

Credit Unions. Credit unions are nonprofit cooperative financial institutions. Some, but not all, are connected to a particular employer. All credit unions are owned by their members and deposits are insured by a federal agency. Most offer a wide range of financial services.

There may be credit unions in your area that will allow you to open a checking or saving account at little or no cost. Most credit unions also make small loans to their members which can be used to purchase necessities, pay medical bills or car repair bills.

Community Development Credit Unions. Community Development Credit Unions (CDCUs) are a special kind of credit union. CDCUs serve low- and moderate-income communities throughout the country. They provide a full range of credit and financial services to communities that are underserved by conventional financial institutions, including personal loans, mortgages, small business loans, savings clubs and accounts, check cashing, checking accounts and ATM access. To get a list of CDCU's in your area, contact the National Federation of Community Development Credit Unions, 120 Wall St., 10th Floor, New York, NY 10005-3902. (212) 809-1850.

Just as with banks, you should shop around if you are considering opening an account with a credit union. Do not assume that you will automatically get a better deal just because an institution has "community" in its name or seems to be friendlier or more helpful.

Other Ways to Cash Checks. If you are unable to open an account at a bank or credit union, you still might be able to cash payroll checks without going to expensive check cashers. If you are employed, your employer might agree to cash your check for you, or help you cash checks for free at the bank where the employer has its account. Some grocery stores will cash your checks if you shop there. Many banks will also cash government checks for free. Finally, checks may always be cashed for free by non-depositors at the bank whose name is on the check.

Saving. A good way to prevent future financial problems is to put aside money each week, if possible in a bank savings account, so that you can avoid expensive borrowing later. Budget counselors can help you figure out how to allocate your resources so that there is something left over each month for savings.

Your employer might have a plan where you can automatically contribute a certain amount each month to a retirement plan. Chapter Two has a more detailed discussion about when to dip into savings and retirement money. In general, you should try to avoid the temptation to use up retirement savings to get through temporary financial difficulties. This is particularly true if you are close to retirement age.

It is sometimes difficult to think about saving in a society that bombards you with advertisements and encourages you to spend, spend, spend. However, in making your budget (see Chapter Two), you should carefully consider whether you can set aside, even a very small amount, each week or month for savings, as a cushion against future problems.

Insurance. You should also plan ahead by taking a close look at your insurance policies and look for ways to lower your insurance costs. Here are ten practical suggestions to lower insurance costs:

1. Comparison shop. Prices for the same coverage can vary widely by company, so it is essential to shop around for the lowest premium. Consumer buying guides are especially helpful — *Consumer Reports* has an Internet website that compares auto insurance rates at www.consumerinsure.org. Life insurance quotes can be obtained at www.quoteswith.com.

You may be paying too much for your basic insurance needs. Hidden costs of insurance can drain hundreds of dollars from your monthly budget.

---

2. Take advantage of discounts. Insurers offer discounts for safety measures that can save you a significant amount on premiums. Most companies offer auto insurance discounts for driver's education courses, mature drivers (over 50), good students, good drivers, nonsmokers, group plans, anti-theft devices, automatic seat belts and/or air bags, low annual mileage, and multiple cars with one company.

Potential homeowner insurance discounts include multiple-policy (both auto and homeowners with same company), fire-resistant material, smoke detector/dead-bolt locks, nonsmokers, mature homeowner, loyal customer and group plans. Unless you ask, the discounts may not be offered or provided.

3. Insure the home, not the real estate. You should insure for an amount necessary to rebuild your home—not for the amount equal to the entire value of the property. This is because the land itself cannot burn down.

4. Consider raising the deductibles. Deductibles are the amount of money you pay toward a loss before the insurance company starts to pay.

Asking the insurance company to raise the deductibles will lower the premiums, although it increases your risk. Sometimes the extra cost of a low deductible amount is much greater than the potential benefit you will get if you need to make a claim. Consider whether you can raise the deductibles temporarily in order to save money until you can back on your financial feet.

5. Drop coverages on older cars. It makes sense to drop collision premiums for older cars worth less than a few thousand dollars. These premiums may cost as much as the car is worth. You can find out the cash or "blue book" value of the car from a local library, through the internet (try the Kelly Blue Book site at www.kbb.com), or by asking the insurance company.

6. Consider cashing in life insurance policies. You should consider surrendering cash value life insurance policies to generate funds to pay pressing debts such as the home mortgage. The home may be more important to your family's long-term security than an insurance policy. You can replace the whole life policy with less expensive term coverage.

7. Buy annual renewable level term life insurance, but only for the amount necessary for dependents to maintain their standard of living. Under level term insurance, you pay the same amount on an annual basis for a period of ten, twenty or thirty years. However, switching from whole life to variable term after many years of paying for whole life may not be a good move because variable term policies become more expensive as you get older.

8. Stay current on car and home insurance policies if possible. Lenders require you to buy insurance for their collateral. If you don't purchase this insurance or you allow it to lapse, lenders "force-place" substitute insurance (meaning they buy it for you) and bill the premium to your account. Forced-placed insurance premiums are several times higher than for policies you select yourself. You should replace a forced-placed policy with one of your own choosing as quickly as possible to save money. You might also have legal challenges to forced-placed policies.

9. Do not purchase credit insurance. Many lenders sell a variety of credit insurance policies including credit life, credit disability, and loss of income insurance. These policies supposedly cover the lender's claims if the loan can't be repaid due to death, disability, or unemployment of the borrower. They are sold to many consumers who take out installment loans, and to an increasing number of consumers who acquire credit cards. Research shows that most credit life insurance is extremely overpriced. The lender ends up making a large commission for the sale of a policy which will never do more than pay off the lender's existing claim.

10. Avoid service contracts on cars and household appliances. These contracts are very similar in content and appearance to a written warranty, but differ from a warranty because you must pay for the service contract on top of the price of the product. Before entering into a service contract, you should compare the costs of the contract to the benefits of repairing the particular item and its replacement cost. Most consumers in financial crisis should cancel their present service contracts.

Education. Education and job skills training may help you get a higher paying job so that you can better meet your expenses. As was noted in Chapter Three, education is often a good idea, but unfortunately there are schools that will try to take advantage of your attempts to better yourself.

If you find out that education is likely to lead to employment in a particular field, it is a good idea to shop around, check out community colleges which often offer the same courses as trade schools at a fraction of the cost. Student loan borrowing should be kept to a minimum to avoid future problems.

Borrowing Money. Even if you follow some of the measures discussed in this chapter, you may still face financial problems at some point. It is simply impossible to plan ahead for everything. These are the times that consumers are most vulnerable to high-cost services that claim to offer quick cash regardless of credit history. Chapter Three listed some of these types of business and why you should avoid them.

Avoiding these exploitative services will save you money, but won't necessarily help you get back on your feet. There are other options available in most communities where you can borrow money at reasonable rates, rather than paying the exorbitant rates charged by pawnbrokers, rent-to-own stores and payday lenders.

Many credit unions and community development credit unions discussed above have various types of lending programs with more flexible criteria than most banks. There are also community development banks and loan funds which receive loans made at below-market rates by depositories and then reinvest the money in businesses and distressed communities that conventional lenders have written off as bad risks. But, as noted above, don't assume that you are getting a better deal just because it is a credit union or community fund.

Job Access Loans. Some communities have started job access loan programs specifically to help people getting back to work with work-related expenses such as buying cars and clothes. Some of these programs are limited to current or former public assistance recipients.

Discrimination. If you are denied credit by banks and credit unions, or offered credit only at high rates, it is possible that you are being illegally discriminated against. It is against the law for creditors to base decisions to extend or deny credit on sex, age, race, color, religion, national origin, marital status, or the receipt of public income or assistance. You also cannot be denied credit for exercising your rights under consumer protection laws. You should consult a lawyer or legal services office if you think this applies to your situation.

Responding to Debt Collectors

- *What Debt Collectors Can and* Cannot *Do To You*
- *Seven Ways to Stop Debt Harassment*
- *Illegal Debt Collection Practices and What to Do About Them*

DO NOT LET COLLECTORS PRESSURE YOU

Do not let debt collectors push you around. Chapters One and Four showed you which bills to pay first and when to refinance. It is the job of some bill collectors to persuade you to pay the wrong bills first and to refinance bills that should not be refinanced.

Do not let debt collection harassment force you into making wrong decisions that will hurt you later. If a certain bill is less important, explain to a creditor why you are not paying and when you propose to pay:

> *"I have to pay my rent and utility bills first. I just got laid off, but when I get a new job I will do my best to meet my credit card debt. I understand that you will want to cancel my card, and I will pay you when I can."*

If the creditor or a bill collector still calls at all hours and writes threatening letters, use the tips in this chapter to stop debt collection harassment.

COLLECTORS CANNOT
LEGALLY DO MUCH
TO HARM YOU

Debt collectors are experts at making threats about the dire consequences of nonpayment. It is important to know what a debt collector can and cannot legally do when you get behind on a particular debt. Most debts, such as virtually all credit card obligations, doctor bills, small amounts owed merchants, and many small loans are "unsecured." This means you have not put up any collateral, such as the family home or car, to secure the loan's repayment. An *unsecured* creditor can legally do only the following three things:

1. Stop Doing Business With You. For example, a credit card issuer can cancel your card or a dentist to whom you owe money might refuse to let you continue as a patient. Usually, though, there are other merchants or professionals who will offer the same goods or services on a cash basis or even on credit. The threat of stopping business with you is only serious where a particular creditor has a monopoly in your community, such as the only doctor in a rural area. Utilities also usually have a monopoly, and dealing with utility bills involves special issues discussed in detail in Chapter Sixteen.

2. Report the Default to a Credit Reporting Agency. The fact that you are behind on your bills almost certainly will end up on your credit record. You cannot stop this, short of always being current on all of your bills. While this is unfortunate, you only make matters worse by paying a particular bill first just because that collector is threatening to ruin your credit record.

The reason you make matters worse is that the collection agency threatening to ruin your credit is almost always bluffing. If a creditor routinely reports delinquent debts to a credit bureau, your delinquency is already noted in your credit record even before the collector starts making threats. If the creditor does not normally report information to a credit bureau, collectors who threaten you almost never go to the bother of doing so themselves.

Many creditors never threaten to ruin your credit record. However, they automatically report to a credit bureau by computer every payment and delinquency *on a monthly basis.* So if you pay a creditor that threatens you rather than one that does not, you may end up with a problem on your credit record anyway. The reasons why threats to ruin your credit record should not be taken too seriously are explained in more detail in Chapter Seven.

3. Begin a Lawsuit to Collect the Debt. This is the threat that may worry you the most. But there are four reasons why the threat of a lawsuit is far less serious than you imagine. First, it is hard to predict whether a particular creditor will actually sue on a past due debt. It is expensive to take you to court. Many creditors will not do so for small debts, say under $1000, although some creditors do take even small debts to court. Still other creditors do not take even large debts to court. How aggressively a collection agency threatens suit is no indication whether the creditor will actually sue, even if the threat appears to come from an attorney.

Second, if the creditor does decide to sue you, you have a right to respond and explain why the money is not owed. Do not let the creditor win by default. You do not have to hire an attorney to respond to the lawsuit. Often when a creditor sees that you will contest the action, it will stop pursuing the lawsuit. How to respond to a lawsuit is detailed in Chapters Six and Eight.

Third, even if the creditor does pursue the lawsuit and eventually wins, the worst that can happen is that a court judgment will be entered against you. You will *not* automatically be in contempt of court for failure to pay the judgment. The judgment only gives the creditor the legal right to *try* to seize your property, to garnish your wages or to seek a court order requiring payment.

Fourth, if you are "judgment proof," you have nothing to fear from even these special collection techniques. You are "judgment proof" if all your assets and income are protected by law from a creditor trying to enforce a court judgment.

State exemption laws usually protect a certain amount of your property from seizure pursuant to a court judgment. A local legal services program, an attorney, or a credit counseling agency can provide a list of exempt property in your state and advise whether your state's laws allows your home or any other valuable property to be taken and sold by a creditor with a judgment against you. Often the information is also available in pamphlet form.

To be judgment-proof, your wages or other income must also be exempt from seizure. Federal law limits the amount of wages that a creditor can seize. The first $154.50 a week of take home pay is protected, and only a portion of the amount over $154.50 can be seized.

Your state's law may supplement this protection. In certain states no wages can be garnished at all. In other states more than the first $154.50 is protected.

Finally, social security and other government benefits cannot be seized at all. More information on state exemption laws and protections from wage garnishment can be found at Chapter Eight.

For these reasons, the threat of a court action on an unsecured debt is not nearly as real or dangerous as the threat of a landlord's eviction action, a bank's foreclosure on a mortgage, a car's repossession, or a utility's termination of gas or electricity service. These latter four actions usually happen quickly with a minimum of legal process and expense to the creditor.

Debt Collectors Cannot Legally Take Other Actions to Collect on Unsecured Debts. A creditor, if it chooses to, can stop doing business with you, report a default to a credit bureau, or sue on the past due debt. Threats to do anything else on an unsecured debt are deceptive and violate federal law. The collector cannot seize your wages or property before the creditor has obtained a court judgment, nor can it send you to jail or send your children to foster care. Additionally, collectors cannot publish your name in a newspaper, report a debt to your neighbors, or seek to collect from other family members, unless they cosigned the debt or a court order is entered which makes the family member responsible.

Remember the cardinal rule about debt collectors —
unless they work for your landlord, utility,
mortgage holder, or other secured creditor,
they often have no bite behind their bark.

Creditors who growl the loudest should not drive you into the teeth of a creditor with real bite.

DEALING WITH GUILT FEELINGS

You are not a deadbeat when circumstances outside your control prevent you from paying your debts. If you have excess debt burdens, you must repay your most important debts first, and postpone payment of other debts.

Believe it or not, the collector knows this even better than you. Creditors know from long experience that most people pay their bills and, when they do not, it is because of job loss, illness, divorce, or other unexpected events. Creditors take this risk of default into account when they set the interest rate—creditors make enough money off you and others in good times so that when you default, the creditor is covered.

Do not be fooled by collector statements to the contrary. Debt collectors are *instructed* to ignore your reasons for falling behind on your debts, to show no sympathy, and not to listen to reason.

You have no moral obligation to pay one debt before you pay another debt, particularly where the debt you pay is more central to your family's survival. Creditors know this. They should not be rewarded for trying to pressure you to pay them off at the expense of another creditor or more importantly at the expense of your family.

SEVEN DIFFERENT WAYS
TO STOP DEBT COLLECTION
HARASSMENT

Because bill collectors have no bite behind their bark, they will bark very loudly, hoping to intimidate you. Do not let them. This section lists *seven different approaches* to stop debt harassment.

Keep in mind that the effectiveness of any of these approaches may depend on whether the creditor is doing its own collection (for example, the doctor's office is calling you up) or whether the creditor has hired a debt collection agency or attorney. You have more rights if you are dealing with a debt collection agency or an attorney.

The key federal law regulating debt collection, the Fair Debt Collection Practices Act (FDCPA), applies only to debt collection agencies and attorneys, and generally does *not* apply to creditors collecting their own debts. Nevertheless, most states have laws which regulate creditors collecting their own debts, and the seven approaches listed here generally will work with creditors collecting their own debt, and not just with collection agencies.

1. Head Off Harassment Before It Happens. When you have more bills than you can afford to pay, you obviously cannot pay all of them. While you should pay your most important bills first, you should not totally ignore any of your bills, such as by tossing a series of warning letters in the trash. Instead, there are steps you can take short of payment which will make it clear to the creditor that you are not ignoring the bill.

Creditors will not forget about a bill just because you fail to respond. The creditor will hire a collection agency or turn the matter over to an in-house collection bureau. The job of these collectors is to get you to notice the bill, and sometimes they are not very nice in the methods they choose to attract your attention.

To avoid this result, before the creditor refers the debt to a collection agency, call up the creditor and explain your situation. Promptly contacting the creditor is most important with hospitals, doctors, dentists and similar creditors who would otherwise quickly turn a debt over to a collection agency. Although retailers, banks and finance companies are more likely to have an in-house collection section, it still pays to try to avoid the transfer of the debt to that office.

You can explain that you have to pay the landlord or mortgage, utilities and certain other bills first. You have not forgotten the creditor and will pay when you can. Make it clear that you cannot afford to pay the bill, and will not pay a collection agency either. Do not over-promise, but be polite and honest.

Make sure the creditor understands you will pay as soon as you can so that there is no need to go to the expense of hiring a collection agency. You will not pay a collection agency any sooner than the creditor.

The creditor then has a financial interest *not* to turn the matter over to a collector. Collection agencies usually charge the creditor a fee of approximately one third of what they collect, or sometimes charge the creditor a flat fee per debtor. The creditor can avoid this fee by sitting tight.

You also have a financial interest in heading off referral of a debt to a collection agency. Creditors are generally more flexible than debt collection agencies, and are more willing to work out payment plans. You may waste a lot of time trying to negotiate with debt collectors, where you would have been more successful dealing directly with the creditor. In addition, the costs of collection can, in some cases, be added to your debt.

One danger of calling the creditor is that the creditor might convince you to start making reduced payments that you cannot afford to make. For this reason, you might ask a counselor or friend to help you in talking to the creditor.

2. The Cease Letter. Assuming you fail in explaining the situation to the creditor, and you are being harassed for the debt, the simplest strategy to stop collection harassment is to write the collector a cease letter. Federal law requires collection agencies to stop their collection efforts (sometimes referred to as dunning) after they receive a written request to stop. The federal law does not apply to creditors collecting their own debts, but even these creditors will often honor such requests.

The letter need not give any special explanation why the collector should cease contacts. Nevertheless, it is generally a good idea to explain why you cannot pay and your hopes for the future. The letter might also describe prior abusive tactics of the collector's employees and your resulting distress. It is very important to keep a copy of the written request.

Here is an example of such a letter (delete references to billing errors, debt harassment, or any other statements that do not apply to you. A simple request to stop collection contacts is sufficient):

"Cease" Letter Sample

Sam Consumer
10 Cherry Lane
Flint, MI 10886

January 1, 1999

NBC Collection Agency
1 Main Street
Flint, MI 10887

Dear Sir or Madam:

I am writing to request that you stop communications to me about my account number 000723 with Amy's Department Store as required by the Fair Debt Collection Practices Act, 15 USCA 1692c(c). [*NOTE: Delete reference to the Fair Debt Collection Act where the letter is to a creditor instead of to a collection agency* .]

I was laid off from work two months ago and cannot pay this bill at this time. I am enrolled in a training program which I will complete in March and hope to find work that will allow me to resume payments soon after that.Please note that your letters mistakenly list the balance on the account as $245. My records indicate that the balance is less than that.

You should be aware that your employees have engaged in illegal collection practices. For example, I received a phone call at 6:30 a.m. from one of them last week. Later that day I was called by the same person at my training program which does not permit personal phone calls except for emergencies. My family and I were very upset by these tactics.

I will take care of this matter when I can. Your cooperation will be appreciated.

Very truly yours,

Sam Consumer

3. The Lawyer's Letter. You do not need a lawyer to send a cease letter. Believing that they have serious legal problems, people often go to lawyers, when all they actually need is relief from a few abusive bill collectors. When such relief is all that is needed, you can send a simple cease letter without the cost of legal assistance.

However, if a cease letter does not stop collection calls, a letter from a lawyer usually will. In addition, the lawyer may be able to raise legal claims on your behalf for violations of the FDCPA.

Collection agencies must stop contacting a consumer known to be represented by a lawyer, as long as the lawyer responds to the collection agency's inquiries. Even though the FDCPA requirement does not apply to creditors collecting their own debts, these creditors also will generally honor requests from a lawyer. A collector's lawyer also is generally bound by legal ethics not to contact debtors represented by a lawyer.

4. The Work-Out Agreement. Probably the most common consumer strategy, though not the best, to deal with debt harassment is to work out a deal with the collector. Collectors will generally stop collection efforts after you work out a payment plan with the collector.

Many collection agencies and creditors claim initially that they must receive payment of the balance in full. They will urge you to borrow from a loan company or from relatives to pay off the debt. As described in Chapter Four, this is almost always a bad idea.

If you resist this suggestion, eventually most collectors will agree to an installment plan. Again collectors initially will ask for payments beyond your financial capability. If you stick to your guns, the collector will agree to a realistic plan, one that often greatly reduces the amount of the debt.

In some locations, credit counseling agencies offer help in obtaining workout agreements on unsecured debts. Although these agencies can be helpful if you can afford to pay some but not all that you owe, you should not use a consumer counseling plan if it requires payments which are more than you can pay or if you have better options for dealing with your creditors, as discussed elsewhere throughout this book. You should be especially careful not to agree to a credit counseling plan if it requires that you pay low-priority debts at the expense of not meeting your high-priority obligations.

While you may feel good about negotiating a large debt down to small monthly payments, even this may be offering too much to the collector. As described in Chapter One, you must prioritize your debts. Even a small payment to an unsecured creditor is unwise if this prevents payment of your mortgage or rent. There are other, better ways to stop debt harassment.

5. Complaints About Billing Errors. Collection letters are sometimes in error, mistaking the amount due or the account number, or billing the consumer instead of his or her insurance company. Occasionally, you may even receive collection letters aimed at someone with the same or a similar name. When a collection letter contains a mistake, write to request a correction. Collection agencies, by law, must inform you of your right to dispute the debt. If you then dispute the debt in writing within the next thirty days, the collection agency must stop collection efforts while it investigates.

If the dispute involves a line of credit, a credit card, or an electronic transfer of money, you have the additional legal right under the Federal Fair Credit Billing Act *to require* the creditor *to investigate* the bill. You must write a letter pointing out the mistake within sixty days of receipt of the disputed bill. Your rights to correct billing errors are periodically included with credit card statements. A sample letter for this purpose is contained in Chapter Ten.

Although other creditors are *not required* to *investigate* errors, they usually do so as well. Even after deadlines have passed, most collectors will stop their collection efforts and investigate.

6. Complaining to a Government Agency. Another strategy is to write to government agencies responsible for enforcing laws that prohibit debt collection abuse, like the Federal Trade Commission or your state's attorney general's office. A government agency is not likely to investigate immediately unless it has other complaints against the same collector, a fact that probably cannot be known ahead of time. Even so, sending a copy of your letter to the collector often produces good results.

Your letter of complaint should be sent to the Federal Trade Commission, Bureau of Consumer Protection, Washington, D.C. 20580. Copies of the letter should be sent to the consumer protection division within the state attorney general's office, usually in the state capitol, and also to any local office of consumer protection listed in the local telephone book. Addresses can be obtained from a local better business bureau or office of consumer affairs. An example of such a letter follows:

Sample Complaint Letter

Sam Consumer
10 Cherry Lane
Flint, MI 10886

January 25, 1999

Federal Trade Commission
Bureau of Consumer Protection
Washington, DC 20580

Dear Sir or Madam:

I am writing to complain of abusive debt collection tactics used by ABC Collection Agency, 1 Main Street, Flint, MI 10887 which I request that you investigate.

I was laid off by U.S. Steel two months ago and have not been able to maintain all payments on all my bills. ABC began contacting me in December about my account with Amy's Department Store in Flint. ABC's abusive collection tactics have included:

1. Telephoning my sister asking her to lend me the balance when she does not have anything to do with this account.
2. Calling me at 6:30 a.m. at home.
3. Using offensive language, calling me a "God damned deadbeat."
4. Writing that they would sue me if they did not receive payment in ten days (this was a month and a half ago) whereas all they have done since then is to call and to write. (A copy of that letter is enclosed).

5. Continuing to contact me after I sent them a letter asking them to stop. (Enclosed is my letter to them and a later letter from them).

6. Billing me for $245 when no more than $185 is owed on the account.

My family and I are doing our best to get back on our feet, and this abuse is very distressful. Your assistance will be appreciated.

Very truly yours,

Sam Consumer

cc: Attorney General's Office
Bureau of Consumer Protection
Lansing, MI 10826

Flint Office of Consumer Affairs
14 Main Street
Flint, MI 10887

ABC Collection Agency
1 Main Street
Flint, MI 10887

7. Bankruptcy. When you file your initial papers for personal bankruptcy, this instantly triggers the automatic stay. This stay automatically stops all collection activity against you, from collectors, creditors, or even government officials. No further collection activity can proceed unless a particular collector obtains permission from the bankruptcy court, and the bankruptcy court will not grant this permission to collectors seeking to contact you about unsecured debts. Filing for bankruptcy is thus a very effective means of stopping debt harassment.

Nevertheless, as a general rule, a bankruptcy filing is not your best strategy where your only concern is debt harassment. Bankruptcy should be saved for when you have serious financial problems. Debt collection harassment is usually easily stopped without having to resort to bankruptcy. In fact, be wary of any attorney offering to file bankruptcy for you where the only problem is debt harassment.

ILLEGAL DEBT
COLLECTION CONDUCT

This section lists many types of illegal debt collection harassment. This will help you to demand that the collector stop its harassment. If you suffered financial, physical, or even emotional harm from the illegal collection harassment, you might consider suing the collector. In a successful debt collection suit, you can recover all your damages, no matter how large they are. Even if you are not damaged by the illegal collection activity, you can also sue the collector for up to $1000 plus all of your attorney fees.

It is illegal for a collector to contact

your employer or neighbors about your debt,

call you late at night, call you at work,

call you repeatedly, make false threats,

or engage in any other form of

deceptive conduct or unfair harassment.

The major law listing illegal debt collection conduct is the federal Fair Debt Collection Practices Act (known as the "FDCPA"). The FDCPA requires collection agencies to take certain actions:

- The collection agency must stop contacting you if you so request in writing or if you dispute the debt in writing.
- The collection agency, in its initial communication or within five days of that communication, must send you a written notice. That notice identifies the debt and the creditor, and gives you the right to dispute the debt or to request the name and

address of the original creditor, if different from the current one. If you raise a dispute, the collector must suspend collection efforts on the disputed portion of the debt until the collector responds to the request. (Note that your failure to dispute a debt is not an admission of liability. The collector would still have the burden of proof in any court action to collect the debt.)

- Any lawsuit by a collector must usually be brought in the same county or other judicial district where you reside or signed the contract.

The following collection agency conduct also violates the FDCPA:

- Communicating with third parties, such as your relatives, employers, friends, or neighbors, about a debt unless you or a court has given the collector permission to do so. Several narrow exceptions to this prohibition apply. Collectors may contact creditors, attorneys, credit reporting agencies, cosigners, your spouse, and your parents if you are a minor. Third-party contacts are also permitted if the contacts are solely for the purpose of locating you and do not reveal in any way the contact's underlying purpose.
- Communicating with you at unusual or inconvenient times or places. The times 8:00 a.m. to 9:00 p.m. (in the time zone where you live) are generally considered convenient, but daytime contacts with a consumer known to work a night shift may be inconvenient.
- Contacting you at work if the collector should know that the employer prohibits personal calls, or contacting you at other inconvenient places, such as a friend's house or the hospital.
- Contacting you if you are represented by a lawyer, unless the lawyer gives permission for the communication or fails to respond to the collector's communications.
- Contacting you when you write a letter asking the collector to cease communications. The collector is allowed to acknowledge the letter and to notify you about actions the creditor or collector may take.
- Using obscene, derogatory or insulting remarks.
- Publishing your name.

- Telephoning repeatedly and frequently.
- Telephoning without disclosing the collector's identity.
- Making communications that intimidate, harass or abuse you, such as a threat to conduct a neighborhood investigation of you, or telling you that you should not have children if you cannot afford them.
- Making false, misleading or deceptive representations in collecting debts, such as pretending that letters carry legal authority.
- Falsely representing the character, amount or legal status of a debt, or of services rendered or compensation owed.
- Falsely stating or implying a lawyer's involvement, such as where form letters written on an attorney's letterhead and bearing an attorney's signature in fact came from a collection agency and were not reviewed by a lawyer.
- Threatening arrest or loss of child custody or welfare benefits.
- Stating that nonpayment will result in arrest, garnishment or seizure of property or wages, unless such actions are lawful, and unless the creditor or the collector fully intends to take such action.
- Threatening to take actions that are illegal or that are not intended. To verify a collector's intention to file suit, you could ask the local court clerk to help you check the plaintiff's index to see whether the company making the threat has a history of filing similar suits. Suit is less likely the smaller the debt (e.g., less than $500), the more distant the collector, and the stronger the consumer's dispute of the debt. Other common threats that the creditor may have no intention of pursuing are that the collector will refer the action to a lawyer, harm your credit rating, or repossess household goods.
- Using any false representation or other deception to collect or to attempt to collect any debt or to obtain information about you.
- Failing to disclose in communications that the collector is attempting to collect a debt.
- Using unfair or unconscionable means to collect debts.
- Collecting fees or charges unless expressly authorized by the agreement creating the debt and permitted by law.
- Depositing post-dated checks before their date. The collector also must give at least three days but not more than ten days

notice before depositing the postdated check, or using the
check for the purpose of threatening or filing criminal charges.

- Causing expense to another party while concealing the purpose of the communication, for example, by making collect
  telephone calls and sending collect telegrams.
- Threatening self-help repossession without the legal right to
  do so, or if the collector has no present intent to do so.
- Creating the false impression that the collector is an affiliate or
  agent of the government.
- Using any communication, language, or symbols on envelopes
  or postcards that indicate that the sender is in the debt collection business.

SUING DEBT COLLECTORS
FOR THEIR ILLEGAL CONDUCT

Why Sue the Debt Collector? If a debt collector is engaged in illegal conduct, you have a legal right to sue. Debt collection harassment is illegal and
you can be compensated for any injury suffered. Obviously, any money
awarded in a successful suit or settlement — or any amounts written off
existing debts in settlement of a harassment charge — will be particularly
welcome. At the same time, any money awarded will deter future misconduct by debt collectors.

**Suits for Up to $1000 and Your Attorney's Fees For Collector
Misconduct.** Even when you are subjected to only minor forms of illegal
collection action, you can sue the collector and recover up to $1000 and all
of your attorney's fees for any violation of the FDCPA. You can recover up
to $1000 whether or not the conduct caused you any injury.

On top of the $1000, you can recover for any injuries that were caused
by the illegal conduct. Courts may award damages for such emotional
injuries as loss of happiness, loss of energy, loss of sleep, tension headaches,
crying spells, and marital problems. Consumers have been awarded as much
as $6,000 for emotional distress when the stress aggravated pre-existing med-
ical problems.

Where the collector's conduct is seriously improper, you may also be able
to recover additional punitive damages on top of your actual damages.

Examples of such conduct are threats to throw you in jail, to deport you, or have your children taken away. The punitive damages are intended to punish the collector and prevent future misconduct.

If you win an FDCPA case, the collector must pay your attorney fees, which may encourage a private attorney to take the case without charging you, particularly where the claim appears strong. In fact, the collector may end up paying more in attorney fees than in damages.

Even though many debt collectors are small operations, you can usually recover your judgments against the collectors. Many collectors carry professional liability insurance to protect themselves against consumer claims. The existence of such insurance is often important in settling claims. You thus have a lot of leverage in dealing with a collector that violates the FDCPA.

Finding an Attorney to Sue a Debt Collector. It is not always easy to find an attorney to handle an FDCPA claim. Families with low incomes and limited assets may be eligible to obtain free legal services from a neighborhood legal services office, and those offices may pursue such claims. Other consumers can contact local bar associations for pro bono attorneys who might handle the case. Some cities have lawyers who regularly handle debt collection harassment cases. In other areas, you can find a personal injury lawyer willing to pursue the case on a contingent fee basis. The key to convincing a private attorney to take the case will be the availability of an attorney fee award paid by the collector if you win the lawsuit.

Private attorneys unfamiliar with the FDCPA can find everything they need to pursue an FDCPA claim with a minimum of expenditure in the National Consumer Law Center's book *Fair Debt Collection* (3d ed. 1996 & Supp.). This book is a thorough resource for bringing cases under the FDCPA as well as under other debt collection laws. The manual analyzes and reprints the law and agency interpretations, discusses cases and includes sample court documents, interview checklists, and other important practice aids. Most of the materials are on a computer disk, allowing the attorney to quickly edit all documents which must be filed. Information on how to obtain NCLC's books is contained in the bibliography.

What You Should Tell Your Attorney. Once you find an attorney, your job is to document the extent of collector misconduct and the impact on your family. Although you may not want to discuss your feelings about the harassment, it is key to determining what kind of legal case you have. All symptoms of emotional distress should be discussed including: anxiety, embarrassment, headaches, nausea, indignation, irritability, loss of sleep, and interference with family or work relationships. Did you consult a doctor? Were there illnesses brought on by the harassment?

Out-of-pocket losses should also be listed, ranging from loss of employment to loss of wages because of time taken off from work to try to resolve the dispute. In addition, telephone charges, transportation, medical bills, and counseling services could all be part of your actual damages.

Keep a record of all expenses related to the collection effort. Prepare a statement describing your physical and emotional response to the collection efforts, and list all costs incurred as a consequence of that response. If you consulted a doctor or counselor, include that expense. Consider whether you can obtain supporting statements from family members, relatives, friends or coworkers.

A verbatim telephone log of collection contacts is also helpful. Pen and paper should be kept near the telephone to record all telephone contacts. Abusive messages left on an answering machine should be kept if possible.

What if the FDCPA Does Not Apply? The FDCPA applies to collection agencies and lawyers. It does not generally cover creditors or their employees collecting their own debts. That is, the FDCPA only applies to an independent debt collection agency hired by a creditor to collect its debts and when a creditor hires an attorney to collect its debts.

If the FDCPA does not apply to collection efforts, you still have legal remedies for debt collection harassment. These remedies will mostly involve state law, not federal law. While there will be variations from state to state, in every state there will always be at least some remedy for debt collection harassment. For more detail on these other state remedies, see the National Consumer Law Center's *Fair Debt Collection* (3d ed. 1996).

What You Need to Know About Your Credit Rating

- *Addressing Threats to Damage Your Credit Rating*
- *How to Get a Copy of Your Own Credit Report*
- *Coping With a Bad Credit Record*
- *Cleaning Up Your Credit Record*

If you are experiencing financial problems that make it impossible to pay all of your bills on time, it is unavoidable that your credit record will indicate these problems. Despite the claims of many credit repair companies that they can "fix bad credit," the truth is that there is often nothing you can do about a bad credit history other than get back on your feet and try to rebuild your credit. Even so, a negative credit report may not be as important as you think. This chapter explains what a bad credit record does and does not mean for you, and how you should deal with it. It also covers several strategies to improve your credit record.

What is a Credit Rating? Your credit rating is a record of how you have borrowed and repaid debts. Almost every adult American has a credit file with the three major national credit bureaus, Experian (formerly TRW), Equifax and Trans Union.

Your file has basic personal information about you — social security number, birth date, current and former addresses and employers, etc. The report will also list individually, for many of your debts, basic account information, including the latest activity on the account, the current balance, and the amount past due. Most importantly, each account includes a code which explains whether the account is current, thirty days past due, sixty days past due, ninety days past due, or if the account involves a repossession, charge off or other collection activity.

The report will also include a summary of your past credit experience, such as the number of times that any account was thirty, sixty, or ninety days delinquent, the date of the most recent delinquencies, and the date of the most severe delinquency. The report will list any accounts that have been turned over to a collection agency, any court judgments against you, tax liens, foreclosures, and bankruptcies.

Your credit report is an up-to-date, reasonably objective description of the status of many of your credit accounts. It does *not* include personal comments or opinions about you from creditors or debt collection agencies, such as a notation that you are a deadbeat or a lousy credit risk.

How Do Credit Bureaus Collect Information? Most major creditors subscribe to one or more credit bureaus. Subscribing to a credit bureau is a two way street — the creditor agrees to continuously supply the credit bureau with current account information on the creditor's customers in exchange for the right to find out information about other credit applicants. Usually creditors supply information to credit bureaus by computer. Each month the creditor gives the credit bureau access to a computer tape of the status of thousands of accounts. The relevant information from this computer tape automatically updates each borrower's credit file.

Threats to Damage Your Credit Rating. Creditors and debt collectors often threaten to ruin your credit rating if you do not pay them. However, they will rarely take action on these threats.

Creditors may threaten to report more information if you don't pay a debt, but this is just meant to pressure you to pay. The reality is that they *automatically* report to credit bureaus the exact number of days your account is delinquent. There is nothing else for them to report other than this status of your account. They do not report comments or subjective opinions about you. And creditors will not withhold information from a credit bureau to give you another chance to pay.

Doctors, local stores, and other smaller creditors are also unlikely to report information about you to a credit bureau. Most of these smaller creditors do not supply monthly information to credit bureaus. It would be most unusual for one of these creditors that does not regularly report account information to supply information on you individually. Moreover, the credit bureau may not accept information from a non-subscriber.

**Creditors may threaten to report
negative information to a credit bureau,
but the threat is only meant to pressure you to pay.
The reality is that they *automatically* report
information about your account every month
whether they threaten to do so or not.**

It is even more unlikely that a collection agency hired by a creditor will report information on you to a credit bureau just because you do not respond to the agency's collection attempts.

It is a big mistake to stop paying one creditor with whom you are current to pay another who is threatening damage to your credit record. The delinquent debt that is the subject of the threat either has already been reported to a credit bureau or is not likely to be reported at all. On the other hand, it is very likely if you stop making payments to another creditor, a new delinquency on your credit record will result. You will have just made things worse.

Debt collection agency threats concerning your credit record should not just be ignored. The threats are probably illegal under the federal Fair Debt Collection Practices Act (FDCPA). You can sue the collection agency under that statute and receive as much as $1000 even if you are not injured by the threat. Furthermore, if your suit is successful, the debt collector will have to pay your attorney's fees. Such suits against debt collectors are described in Chapter Six. If a creditor itself is doing the threatening (not an independent agency hired by the creditor), then the FDCPA does not apply, but you may have other legal ways of challenging the creditor's conduct, as discussed in Chapter Six.

Don't Worry If the Collector and Credit Bureau Seem to Be the Same Company. Sometimes a threat to ruin your credit rating (or even just an inquiry about a debt) takes on an added bite because it appears that a credit bureau is doing the threatening. Do not give any special notice to such threats.

Credit bureaus do not collect debts and do not threaten to ruin your credit record. An entity doing so is a debt collector or a creditor, *not* a credit bureau. A debt collector or creditor misrepresenting itself as a credit bureau is violating federal law, and you can sue for up to $1000 plus any injury caused to you plus your attorney's fees. (See Chapter Six.)

Getting a Copy of Your Report. The first step in deciding how to deal with problems with your credit history is to order your credit report and read it carefully. This will allow you to see if bad information you think is listed in the report is really there. As noted above, not all creditors actually report information to credit bureaus and so some delinquent accounts might not even be in the report. You should also look for any mistakes or old information that should be deleted.

Because there can be differences in the reports kept by each of the three major national credit bureaus, you should order your report from all three. Each company requires that you give them certain information to order a report and each has a toll-free number that you can call for more information.

Experian's telephone number to order reports is **1-888-EXPERIAN (1-888-397-3742)**.
Written requests should be sent to **Experian National Consumer Assistance Center P.O. Box 2104, Allen, TX 75013-2104.**
You can also order on-line at **www.experian.com.**
You will need to give them your full name, date of birth, social security number, spouse's first name, current address, addresses for the last five years (with apartment numbers and zip codes) and a copy of the notice of denial if you are requesting a report in response to a denial of credit.

Equifax's number is **1-800-997-2493**.
Written requests should be sent to **Equifax Customer Information Service Center P.O. Box 740241, Atlanta, GA 30374-0241.**
Reports can also be ordered on-line at **www.equifax.com.**
Equifax requires that you give them your full name, date of birth, social security number, current and former addresses, daytime and nighttime telephone number, and copy of driver's license or utility bill to confirm current address. You also need to supply a copy of the notice of denial or the name of the creditor if you are requesting a report in response to a denial of credit.

TransUnion Corporation's phone number is **1-800-916-8800**.
Written requests should be sent to: **TransUnion Corporation, P.O. Box 390, Springfield, PA 19064-0390.**
Reports can be ordered on-line at www.transunion.com.
TransUnion requires the following information: full name and spouse's full name if a joint request, date of birth, social security number, current address and addresses for the last five years, current employer and telephone number.

The credit bureaus are required to give you a copy of your report for free if you have been denied credit within the past sixty days.

Even if you haven't been denied credit, there are other situations in which you can get reports for free.

You can get one free report in any twelve month period if you:

- Are unemployed and will be applying for a job within the next sixty days; or
- Are receiving public welfare assistance; or
- You have reason to believe that the file at the credit bureau contains inaccurate information due to fraud.

If these circumstances do not apply, credit bureaus can charge you no more than $8 per report. This is a maximum charge, not a required charge. Some states have passed laws limiting the amount credit bureaus can charge consumers in those states. In some states, consumers can get one free report each year. You should check with your state consumer affairs department or legal services office to see what the limits are, if any, in your state.

CORRECTING ERRORS AND DELETING OLD INFORMATION

Take a careful look at your report and check to see if there are any mistakes. For example, there might be information from another person's account that has been reported on your account by mistake.

Correcting Errors. It is common to find that there is incorrect information in your credit file. You have the legal right to correct this information and should do so. Accurate damaging information is bad enough. You do not also need inaccurate damaging entries. You should send a written dispute to each credit bureau that has reported incorrect information. The credit bureau by law must reinvestigate the entry and correct erroneous information. In most circumstances, the agency is required to get back to you with the results of the investigation within thirty days.

The creditor who initially supplied the information to the bureau also has a duty to correct and update the information. If you can show the creditor that reported information was not accurate or complete, they must provide the bureau with the information necessary to make your report correct or complete.

Even after the entry is corrected, periodically check to make sure that this incorrect information has been deleted permanently. Inaccurate items have a habit of popping up again even after they are corrected.

Deleting Old Information. Information about your accounts can only be reported for seven years from the date of delinquency. If there is information older than that on your report, you should follow the steps outlined above to request that the credit bureau investigate and delete the information. Information about bankruptcies can appear on your report for ten years.

CREDIT SCORING

Many lenders now rely on a "credit score" when they analyze your credit record. A credit score is a number which summarizes your credit history. Your score may differ depending on which credit bureau (Equifax, Experian, or TransUnion) is making a report.

Credit scores can range from 350 to 900. They are based on items in your credit record including:

- The number and amount of debts you owe now;
- Your history of defaults, if any;
- Prior problems such as bankruptcy, court judgments, foreclosure or a criminal record;
- The length of time since your most recent credit problem;
- How long you have kept your existing accounts; and
- Certain other aspects of your use of credit over time.

The purpose of the score is to help lenders evaluate whether you are a risky borrower. A credit score of 620 or above is usually considered a good risk. Below 620, some creditors may deny you credit or insist that you pay a higher interest rate.

Improving Your Credit Score. If you are denied credit, or if you are offered credit at rates that are higher than the best rate offered by your lender, you should inquire whether the decision is based on your credit score. If you are told you have a low score, there are some things you can do to improve it:

- **Correct all errors on your report.** Your credit score can be based on erroneous information in your credit record. For example, if your credit record includes a default you dispute, having the record corrected can improve your score. (Correcting your credit record has been discussed earlier in this chapter.)
- **Wait for a period and pay all of your debts on time.** If you are able to pay all of your debts on time, your credit score will start to improve. The older the negative factor on the report, the less it lowers your score.
- **Cancel open lines of credit you do not need.** If you have too many open lines of credit (such as unnecessary credit cards,) these affect your credit score even if you do not use them. Consider canceling these cards to improve your score.
- **Concentrate on paying your existing debts rather than dealing with old unpaid debts which have been charged off.** It is more important for your credit score that you deal with recent debts, than that you go back and pay off the older debts to resolve old defaults.

Remember, though, that is never a good idea to worry about improving your credit score if you have high-priority debts that need to be paid. A foreclosure or auto repossession may be worse for your family *and your credit score* than a good history of payments on open credit cards.

Explaining a Bad Score. Your credit score is not the only thing that a creditor is likely to look at when deciding about making you a loan. Your reasons for problems on a credit record are still relevant. Although the creditor probably can do little to change your score with the credit bureau, it can override the score as an important factor in deciding to grant you credit.

This flexibility makes it important that you explain in detail your reasons for problems on your credit record. For example, loss of a job due to an illness may explain an old default. If you have returned to work, the creditor may grant you a loan on good terms even if your credit score is low.

If a creditor does not respond well to your explanation, shop around. Other creditors may have more flexibility.

Credit Shopping and Its Impact on Credit Scoring. You may have been told at some point in the past that it is a bad idea to shop around for credit at low rates by contacting several lenders when you need a loan. The advice was based on a concern that if you apply for too many loans, you may take on too much credit and be a bad credit risk. However, based on changes in credit scoring practices, this advice is not correct.

Whenever you apply for credit and the lender requests a copy of your report, this fact goes on your credit record. In the past, too many requests by lenders wishing to see your credit record had a negative impact on your credit score.

More recently, however, this problem has been fixed, so that a number of inquiries over a short period of time will not spoil your credit score. This means that there is no negative impact to shopping for loans in order to find the lowest interest rate and the best terms possible.

COPING WITH
A BAD CREDIT RECORD

Once you have corrected any errors and gotten rid of old information on your report, you are still likely to have problems with your credit report during times of financial hardship. This is unavoidable but as explained below not necessarily as important as you might think.

Not Everyone Can See Your Credit Report. There is a federal law that regulates who can and can't see your credit file. Keep in mind that not everyone is allowed to look at your report and that not everyone who is allowed to look at your report will do so.

Who Can See Your Report?
- **Creditors** can look at your report whenever you apply for credit or for a loan. This includes mortgages and car loans as well as credit cards and other loans.
- **Employers** can look at your report, but only under certain circumstances and only if you give them written authorization. Employers are allowed to look at your report to evaluate you for hire, promotions and other employment purposes. Employers are more and more using credit reports in making

employment decisions. However, not all employers will look at your report and not all who do will be concerned about problems. Most employers are generally less interested in your credit history than in public record information, such as your arrests, convictions, or any court judgments against you.

- **Government agencies** including those trying to collect child support can look at your report. Those considering you for eligibility for public assistance may review your credit report as well. But their reason for doing this is not to see if you have unpaid bills, only to see if you have hidden income or assets.
- **Insurance companies** can look at your credit report, although they are generally not interested in your credit history. They may, however, ask a reporting agency for information on your medical history and about any insurance claims you have filed.
- **Landlords** can look at your credit record when they are deciding whether to rent an apartment to you. Although your credit record can be important when you are leasing a residence, it is certainly more important when you take out a mortgage to buy a home. (See Below.) Larger landlords, landlords specializing in low-income housing, and larger-city landlords are most likely to pull your credit record. If a landlord turns down your rental application because of bad credit, you may still be able to rent the apartment if you can explain some of the problems. If the landlord doesn't accept your explanations, don't give up. You may have better luck with another landlord.

When Is A Bad Credit Report Less Important? In some cases, your concerns about the impact of a negative credit rating are likely to be exaggerated. For example:

- **Utility Service.** Your credit record will have no impact on your ability to obtain utility service, and generally does not affect the size of the security deposit you must offer. The only important precondition to your obtaining utility service is that you do not owe that particular utility company any money. For more information, see Chapter Sixteen.
- **Student Loans and Grants.** For most student loans and grants, your credit record is irrelevant. (The one exception is Unsubsidized Stafford Loans which require students with bad

credit records to have a creditworthy cosigner.) The key
issue instead is whether you are in default on a prior student
loan. How to obtain new loans and grants even when you
are in default on earlier student loans is explained at
Chapter Nineteen.

- **Your Credit Record Will Not Damage Your Friends,
  Relations, and Need Not Even Affect Your Spouse.**
  Your credit report has no impact on the ability of your friends,
  associates, or even family members to obtain credit or employment. A creditor is not allowed to look at your credit record
  if, for example, your spouse, child, or parent applies for credit,
  and they are not relying on your income or assets in the
  credit application.

- **Your Credit Record Will Not Damage Your Reputation
  in the Community.** No one can obtain your credit record
  for curiosity, gossip, or to determine your reputation. Your
  credit record can only be used to consider your application
  for insurance, credit, employment, and certain benefits and
  other business transactions. Federal law prohibits both credit
  bureaus and collection agencies from placing your name on
  a bad debt list that is circulated to the public.

Your credit record is just between you and creditors —
your neighbors and friends should never see it.

- **Your Credit Record Cannot Be Used in Divorce, Child
  Custody, Immigration, and Other Legal Proceedings.**
  Normally, no one can use your credit record in a divorce or
  in a proceeding to determine child custody or child support.
  Credit reports generally also cannot be used in other legal
  proceedings, such as immigration proceedings, applications
  for citizenship, or as a basis to deny your ability to register to
  vote. Government agencies can only receive a credit report on
  you if they are permitted by a court order.

CLEANING UP
YOUR CREDIT RECORD

The last section reviewed when a negative credit report is likely to cause you problems. This section provides tips on how to, and how *not* to, improve your credit record. It is important to understand that your credit rating is not your most important concern in times of financial hardship. More important is trying to save your home, utility service, car, and other essential possessions. You can go forward with your life even if you have credit card and hospital bill delinquencies on your credit history.

There are times, however, when you will want to try to rebuild or clean up your credit report. For example, you might want to take out a new home mortgage in times of financial distress.

Home Mortgages. Unfortunately, a bad credit report will make it more difficult to obtain a home mortgage at a reasonable rate, unless you can obtain a creditworthy cosigner.

Many conventional mortgages follow Fannie Mae or Freddie Mac guidelines. Under these guidelines, a foreclosure on your credit record will make it extremely difficult to obtain a mortgage for about the next three years, and will impact your ability for seven years. You should try to establish at least a year of on-time mortgage payments and pretty close to on-time payments for your other loans before applying for a new mortgage. Furthermore, it is difficult to obtain a mortgage for at least two years after you receive a bankruptcy discharge.

VA, FHA, and FmHA mortgages have looser guidelines than Fannie Mae or Freddie Mac. Even then, you should have no current defaults and a one or two year period since any bankruptcy discharge. You may also find other mortgage lenders with more flexible guidelines than those for Fannie Mae or Freddie Mac. Nevertheless, it is important to avoid con artists and unscrupulous lenders that charge outrageous interest rates for people with credit problems. As discussed throughout this book, desperate choices are likely to make your situation worse.

If you want to take out a home mortgage despite problems with your credit record, several steps should be taken. First, obtain a copy of your own credit report from several of the major credit bureaus several months before you apply for the mortgage. (How to obtain copies of your own report was described earlier in this chapter.) In many home sales, time is of the essence, and you should already be dealing with your credit report problems before you apply for the mortgage.

Try to clean up the report as much as possible, by correcting and notifying the credit bureaus of any inaccurate information, by establishing a good payment record on your current debts for a period of time. Paying down current balances is more important than addressing old ("charged-off") debts with creditors that you no longer do business with.

When the mortgage company questions an aspect of your credit record, try to explain any extenuating circumstances. You can also provide favorable information not present on your credit record, such as an excellent history of rent and utility payments.

Shop around for a mortgage company that says it can accept your credit history. Sometimes you may have to pay a slightly higher rate. For example, some legitimate lenders are now rating their applicants as A, B, C, or D, and then charging a slightly higher rate for each step in the scale. But definitely avoid extraordinarily high-rate lenders that prey on those in financial distress. They charge unaffordable interest rates as high as 13% to 30%, plus hidden fees, brokerage charges and points. A good rule of thumb is to avoid any lender that solicits you, particularly door-to-door or over the telephone. Also be mindful of the rules about refinancing discussed in Chapter Four.

If a husband and wife are seeking a loan or lease, and only one spouse has a bad credit record, you can apply in the name of the other spouse, relying exclusively on that spouse's income and assets. In that case, the creditor is not allowed to look at the other spouse's bad credit record. However, remember that any *joint debts* (debts owed by both spouses) will appear on both records no matter who had the primary responsibility to pay. This is true even after divorce, and even if there is a court order requiring one spouse to pay.

OTHER ADVICE ON CLEANING UP OR REBUILDING YOUR CREDIT RECORD

If you look at your report and see problems, don't panic. There are some things you can do on your own to clean up or bolster a bad report. These are steps you can take on your own. You do not need to go to a credit repair company to fix these problems.

The strategies included in this section are summarized from the National Consumer Law Center's *Fair Credit Reporting Act* (3d ed. 1994 and Supp.). Refer to that volume for more detailed information.

Avoid Credit Repair Agencies. Avoid companies that promise to fix your credit record for a fee. They usually call themselves credit repair, credit service, credit clinic or similar names. These agencies usually cannot deliver what they promise, and you can generally do a better job cleaning up your credit record at no cost, just by following the advice in this book. And in some cases, credit repair strategies recommended by these companies may make matters worse for you or occasionally may even cause you other legal problems.

Some of these companies will suggest file segregation as a solution. We strongly recommend against this. Under this approach, credit repair agencies will encourage you to try to confuse the credit bureaus about your identity so that a new, clean file is created for you. You would then put as much positive credit history as possible in the new file and apply for credit under the new identity. If the intent is to defraud creditors, and it almost always is, this approach is illegal. In addition, the credit bureaus have instituted new programs that may catch you, and this will reflect very poorly in your credit file.

Recognizing the many problems with credit repair agencies, federal law, and some states, now require most credit repair companies to give you certain information before you sign up. They are not allowed to provide any services until three days after you sign a written and dated contract. You have the right to cancel the contract for any reason during this three day period. You should contact a lawyer if you believe you have been ripped off by one of these companies. Remember you can achieve the same or better results than credit repair agencies on your own.

Cleaning Up Your Report On Your Own. Here are some steps you can take on your own or with the help of a reliable counselor or attorney to clean up problems with your credit report.

Stabilize Your Situation. In the long run, the most important thing for you to do to reestablish a good credit rating is stabilize your employment, income, and debts. This will prevent new delinquencies from being reported. While your past delinquencies can stay on you record as long as seven years, creditors are likely to ignore older debt problems if your situation becomes stable, and if you start paying your present obligations.

For example, continuous employment for the last two years may be a better indicator of your ability to repay a loan than a debt that was once delinquent for several months four years ago. Similarly, a creditor may be more likely to extend credit to you if you have a reasonable debt level, even if one or two accounts are delinquent than to someone with excessive debt, even if that individual has not yet defaulted on any loan.

Once you get back on track, each year your older debt problems will have less of an impact on your ability to obtain credit. Seven years will come around sooner than you might think, and then there will be no record of those past problems at all.

This means that you might be able to get new credit and credit cards even though you have a negative credit history. Getting a new credit card and paying it back on time can help you rebuild credit, but can also lead you down the same path that got you into trouble in the first place. For tips on what types of credit card arrangements are likely to work best for you, see Chapter Ten.

Supplying Positive, But Unreported Payment History. Your credit record may not indicate your regular payments to your landlord, utility, doctor, a local merchant, or others. These creditors may not subscribe or furnish information to any credit bureau. If you have a good payment record with these creditors, you may feel your credit record would be improved by getting credit bureaus to include this information.

This is generally difficult to do. Credit bureaus are not legally required to include this information, and may not accept your statement. Sometimes a credit bureau will allow you to include this information for a fee. You can also try to have the landlord, utility, or other creditor supply information on your payment history. A better strategy may be to supply this information yourself to the creditor from whom you have applied for credit rather than to the credit bureau.

Explaining Damaging Items. Credit bureaus are not required to include in your file your explanation of why you were delinquent, although they may agree to do so. However, they are required to accept at no charge your explanation why their entry is inaccurate. For example, they may not have to include your letter that explains that you were sick or lost your job. But they must include a letter that states that you were not delinquent because the creditor agreed to postpone payments until you could return to work from your illness.

A better approach may be to explain the delinquency to the lender from whom you are applying for credit rather than to the credit bureau. Federal law requires that creditors at least consider your explanation. Similarly, Fannie Mae requires its mortgage lenders to review any letter you provide explaining your credit blemishes.

Cleaning Up the Current Status of Accounts. Probably the most important aspect of your credit record is the current status of your credit accounts. You can clean up this part of your record, even though it will be more difficult to deal with the historical portion of your report that lists every time you were delinquent in the past.

While you are still experiencing financial difficulty, the wrong way to clean up your current account listing is to pay up everything you owe on all of your accounts. You should instead make sure you pay your high-priority debts first, such as your rent or mortgage, and let other debts stay delinquent if necessary.

Nevertheless, there may be a way to bring your accounts more current without a significant expenditure of money that you cannot afford. Since this information is replaced each month by more current data from your creditors, all you need to do is have certain of your creditors report to the credit bureau that the debt is no longer delinquent.

Having seen your own credit report, you will know which creditors supply information to credit bureaus and which do not. If your goal is to clean up your current account status on your credit record, you should only worry about those creditors that supply account information on you.

Some creditors will agree to report your account as current even when you have not brought that account current in full. Try to negotiate a repayment plan with the creditor for amounts less than the scheduled payments. It may be that the creditor will accept one half or less of the amount due, paid out over a series of months, rather than receive nothing.

It is critical though that you only agree to modified payment schedules that you can meet, while still being able to keep current on your other loans and financial obligations. In addition, a creditor may be less likely to agree to a second repayment agreement if you fail to make payments as negotiated.

The negotiated repayment agreement should require the creditor to supply updated account information to all relevant credit bureaus indicating the account is now current. This should occur either right away or after a few months of timely payments under the agreement. Only when you miss a payment pursuant to the repayment agreement should the creditor report the account as delinquent. Sometimes, it may be simplest for the creditor to mark the old account paid in full, and set up a new account with you under a new number, and report that new account status to the credit bureau on a monthly basis.

In negotiating with a creditor, you may want to ask someone you trust to provide moral support and to help you make sure the creditor does not talk you into a bad deal. It helps to have a maximum repayment figure you can afford written down in advance. Do not agree to a repayment plan which exceeds that figure. When negotiating, be sure to raise any reasons why you do not owe the amount in full. See Chapter Eight for more information on defenses to paying a debt.

Alternatively, contact a nonprofit consumer credit counselor, whose job is to negotiate repayment agreements with creditors. Consumers should never contact *for-profit* credit counselors, who are often scam operators. Even nonprofit consumer credit counselors may receive funding from creditors and cannot be expected to advocate too aggressively for you or point out legal defenses you may have. To locate a nonprofit consumer counselor, call your state's consumer affairs or attorney general's office or your local legal services office for a referral.

In any negotiation, do not be affected by threats to turn accounts over to a debt collector for collection. Collectors cannot do anything to you that the creditor could not. Similarly, the threat to furnish a negative credit report should not influence you because the creditor has most likely already done so. The issue in the negotiation is what type of payment will the lender accept in return for cleaning up the credit record.

Disputing Negative Entries Concerning Your Credit History. While your current account status is an important part of your credit file, creditors will also look at historical information to determine how often in the past you were delinquent or had a foreclosure or repossession. Working out a repayment agreement will not alter this credit history portion of your file. This is more difficult to clean up than your current account status.

An important method of clearing up your credit history is to dispute negative items appearing in your file. As discussed earlier in this chapter, you should dispute all items that are inaccurate or that do not show the whole picture. For example, you could dispute a debt being listed as delinquent if the creditor orally permitted you to make late payments. Or you may have paid late because you refused to pay until problems with the item purchased were resolved.

Do not dispute everything in the file, unless you have a valid basis to do so, but specify certain items with clear reasons why the items themselves are inaccurate or incomplete.

If a dispute is not frivolous or irrelevant, the agency must reinvestigate, at least by asking the original sources of the information what they think of your dispute. If the source cannot or does not verify the original item, your view must prevail. In fact, the older a debt, the greater the difficulty the credit bureau is going to have in confirming the information with the original source. The creditor may be out of business or not have saved files going back four or five years.

Cleaning Up Your File With the Help of the Creditor. As described above, your dispute can delete unverified information that a particular debt was ever owed. Of course, this will not work if the creditor insists you owed the money and verifies that fact to the credit bureau. In that situation, you can try to obtain the creditor's help in deleting this information.

In trying to persuade the creditor that its information was inaccurate, you should supply whatever proof you have. If your proof is not enough to resolve the matter, you may have to agree to pay part or all of the debt, either immediately or in installments. You may have a chance (particularly if you are persistent and talk to supervisors) to make an agreement with certain creditors for installment payments amounting to much less than the full amount owed. Other creditors though may refuse to change what they have already told a credit bureau.

If a creditor does agree to delete information, it can contact the credit bureau to request the deletion. For example, the creditor could tell the credit bureau that there was good reason for your late payment and the payment had not in fact been delinquent. Second best, the creditor can agree not to verify its original information if asked by the credit bureau. Then, when you dispute the item, the information will not be verified on reinvestigation, and it will have to be deleted.

Be sure that any agreement with the creditor to remove historical information is clear and in writing. Otherwise, creditors may not, in fact, follow through in deleting the information.

Student Loan Defaults. If one of your more troubling delinquencies on your credit record is a student loan default, there are certain special steps you can take, as described in more detail in the Chapter Nineteen. If you qualify for a closed school or false certification discharge (described in that chapter), the fact that you were ever in default on the student loan is deleted from your credit record.

You can also consolidate or rehabilitate a defaulted student loan (as described in Chapter Nineteen), so that you are no longer delinquent. Nevertheless, the fact that you were in default on that loan at one time will remain on your credit record.

Public Record Information. The most damaging information on your credit record is sometimes found from public records, such as arrests, convictions, judgments, foreclosures, tax takings, and liens. The best way to remove this information from your file is to do so at the source, and then make sure the corrected information is updated in the credit bureau's files.

For example, you may be able to come to an agreement with a creditor to remove a default judgment against you in return for a promise to enter into a repayment plan. You can then dispute the information in your file, and the credit bureau will have to remove the entry because it can no longer verify the accuracy of its entry of a default judgment.

Filing Bankruptcy. Filing bankruptcy sometimes may actually improve your credit record. A bankruptcy discharge gets you off to a fresh start and should reduce your debt burden. It should also enhance the stability of your employment and income. Wage garnishments, continuous collection calls, car repossessions, telephone disconnections, and other consequences of an unaffordable debt burden are eliminated, and this should help you find and hold steady employment.

The resulting stability of your income and lowered debt burden may be more important to a potential creditor than the fact that certain older debts were discharged in bankruptcy. Another advantage of bankruptcy is that it will clear up the current account status of most entries in your file. The credit bureau will have to list the outstanding balance as "0" for each item. While the bankruptcy will be listed in your file, and while the historical summary will list that certain debts had been delinquent at one time, the current account information should be much improved. This is a key part of any lender's review of a credit report, and the deletion of numerous outstanding balances should be an improvement.

The listing of a bankruptcy may mean that certain creditors will refuse to extend you credit or will offer credit only at higher rates. But other creditors look at the fact that you cannot file a second chapter 7 (straight) bankruptcy for another six years, and that fewer debts are now competing for your stream of income. In addition, certain government agencies will not provide a government-backed mortgage if you have outstanding defaults, but will do so if you have discharged your debts in bankruptcy. Usually you will only have to wait a year or two after the bankruptcy to become eligible for the mortgage loan.

Bankruptcies stay on your credit record for ten years from the bankruptcy filing, while the underlying debts are usually only reported for seven years from the delinquency. This means that if your delinquencies are five or six years old, bankruptcy may not be the best option to deal with the credit record issues. The debts will have to be deleted from credit reports within another year or two, while the bankruptcy will stay on your record for a full ten years from the date of the bankruptcy. For a more detailed discussion of bankruptcy, see Chapter Twenty.

Once You Have Resolved Your Financial Problems. If your financial problems are behind you, your credit record problems will not go away immediately. Be patient, your credit profile will improve over time. More information about getting back on your feet over the long-haul is contained in Chapter Twenty-one.

8

Collection Lawsuits

- *Will the Creditor Actually Sue You?*
- *How to Respond to the Collector's Lawsuit*
- *What a Court Judgment Against You Really Means*

Threats by a creditor or collection agency to sue on a debt can be very frightening. However, most threats of lawsuits are just that — threats. Threats should not lead you to make special efforts to pay a debt unless there is some way in which a lawsuit can hurt you. This chapter provides advice on how to respond if you are sued and explains what can and cannot happen to you if you lose the lawsuit. Here are the basic rules for dealing with lawsuits and threats of lawsuits:

1. *Not all threats of lawsuits will be carried out.* Many creditors and collection agencies threaten to sue as a way to scare you into paying back money which they could not otherwise collect. A threat is used because that collector has no good way of getting paid unless you *choose* to send in payments. A threatened lawsuit should not cause you to change your priorities about dealing with your debts.

2. *If you are sued, it is critical that you respond to court deadlines. You may want professional help to evaluate whether you are at risk of losing property in the legal process.* Ignoring a lawsuit can have unintended consequences. You might lose your right to argue that you do not owe some or all of the money. Failing to respond to a lawsuit might also result in a lien on your property. Generally, it is safe to ignore a lawsuit only if you have no defenses and if there is no possibility of being forced to pay a court judgment. You may want professional help to figure this out.

3. *The best way to deal with a lawsuit is to win it. You may have a defense to a lawsuit which can be raised in court.* You may have a good argument that you don't owe money which a creditor is trying to collect. This can offset, in whole or in part, the amount which the creditor is claiming due. Sometimes just raising a defense will lead the creditor to drop the case. More information about possible defenses to a lawsuit is in Chapter Nine.

4. *If you lose a lawsuit, there are a variety of ways the creditor can try to use the court judgment to force you to pay. You must remain alert to these tactics and deal with them as they come up.* Tools that can be used to enforce a judgment include garnishment of your wages or attempts to sell your property. You have exemptions which will prevent this from occurring in many cases. You may need to raise those exemptions in order to benefit from them.

Courts also may have special procedures to require you to make payments when there is a judgment against you. You need to comply with orders to appear in court or to make payments. However, you can raise defenses to payment in court if you cannot afford to pay. You can also consider using the bankruptcy process, because you may have more rights to deal with judgments in bankruptcy than in state court. These rights may include eliminating the judgment entirely in many situations.

WILL THE CREDITOR
ACTUALLY SUE YOU?

Creditors frequently threaten to sue to collect on overdue debts. These threats are likely to cause you a great deal of anxiety. Usually it is clear that these creditors *can* sue you, but the more important question is whether they *will* sue you. More often than not the answer is "no," even in cases where the creditor repeatedly threatens to sue.

Creditors do not always make rational decisions. However, the following are good indications that a creditor will *not* sue:

- Creditors typically will not file a lawsuit if they have a more effective remedy available. The lawsuit process is slow, somewhat expensive, and, as will be detailed later in this chapter, often unprofitable as a way to recover money from people who have few assets. If the creditor can do something else more effective, it will. For example, a creditor will generally not choose to go to court if, instead, it can repossess your car, foreclose on your house, or terminate your utility service.

- Creditors are unlikely to file a collection suit when the amount of the debt is small. Most creditors rarely sue on debts under $1,000 and some don't sue unless a debt is much higher than that.

- Creditors are unlikely to sue if you dispute the debt and threaten to raise a reasonable defense.

- Creditors are unlikely to sue when you are making small payments even if they are less than the creditor demands.

- Creditors are not likely to sue when that creditor has no history of filing suit. You can check with the local court clerk to see if certain common creditors in the area—for example large retailers or finance companies—file a lot of lawsuits to collect money.

- When a creditor is out-of-state, it is even more unlikely that it will sue over a small amount, particularly if you have informally raised a defense. It is simply too expensive for most out-of-state creditors to sue you in your home state to try to collect relatively small amounts.

Collectors often threaten other actions instead of or in addition to lawsuits against you. They are unlikely to carry out these threats. For example, a collection agency may threaten to garnish your wages. The truth is that except for a few special circumstances, collection agencies cannot garnish wages unless they first obtain a court judgment. Frequent threats are often a signal that the creditor or collection agency has no real remedy and is trying to intimidate you into voluntarily paying an otherwise uncollectible debt.

HOW TO RESPOND TO
A COLLECTOR'S LAWSUIT

Always Pick Up Your Certified Mail and Accept Notices About Court Actions. You will not escape the consequences of a lawsuit by hiding from notice about that action. Court judgments can be entered against you, even if you don't pick up your mail from the post office or accept delivery when it is brought to your home. You will also need a copy of the notice in order to respond appropriately.

Get Professional Advice If You Think You Do Not Owe the Money Or If You May Have A Defense. It is important not to ignore a lawsuit. Professional advisors may be able to make suggestions about the best way to respond. In many cases, a lawyer can take steps that will significantly improve the outcome for you. Doing nothing usually is the worst tactic.

If you cannot get the needed advice from a lawyer or counselor, see if a self-help manual has been written for your state on how to defend a lawsuit. It is likely that someone has published a pamphlet about how you can represent yourself in court, particularly in small claims court. Make sure you get a manual for *your* state. Check with the clerk of your local court, local library or bookstore.

Be careful who you consult about a lawsuit. There are some unlicensed counselors (some pretend to be lawyers) who claim that they can help defend your lawsuit. Many will take your money and do nothing. Others will file bogus responses to your lawsuit which in some cases may cause you to lose valuable rights and defenses. You should contact your local bar association if you are unsure whether someone who claims to be a lawyer is really a lawyer. Even if the person who is trying to help you is a lawyer, you may want to find out from the bar association whether there are complaints on file against him/her.

In addition to professional advisors and self-help manuals, you also may be able to get help by contacting the clerk of the court. Court offices are not just for lawyers — you have as much right to ask questions as someone with a law degree. Don't be intimidated. If you have been sued, you need to know the necessary response requirements and deadlines. It is the job of the court clerk to provide help on these issues.

In some busy courts, clerks may not be very helpful. In others, the advice they give may not be accurate. You may find that the officers in the individual courtrooms are more accurate than the employees in the clerk's office. It certainly cannot hurt to ask several clerks the same question and compare their answers. Whenever relying on information from a court clerk, write down the clerk's name and the answer you received.

Carefully Read All Court Documents You Receive. The creditor must file a document with the court in order to start a lawsuit. Usually this is called the petition or the complaint. In this chapter, we will use the word "complaint" to refer to the document which a creditor uses to begin a case. The complaint asks the court to enter an order or judgment that you owe the creditor a certain amount of money.

Along with the complaint filed with the court, the creditor usually must prepare another document, to be delivered to you. This document informs you that a lawsuit has been filed against you. It is often called a "summons" or "original notice." We will use the word "summons" here. The summons usually tells you what type of lawsuit it is, what the creditor wants, and the actions you must take to respond to the lawsuit, including the deadline for responding.

The summons must be delivered to you according to state procedure. Sometimes a sheriff or constable must personally deliver the summons to you or an adult member of your household. Sometimes mail is sufficient. Dropping the summons on your doorstep is not sufficient.

Never hide from a court summons, always read it carefully, follow the instructions, meet all deadlines, and attend all hearings.

Each court has its own procedures for responding to a summons. The summons should tell you what steps are proper to respond to a lawsuit *for that particular court.* Do not assume that a response appropriate for one type of court will be correct for another court or another type of case. Instead, read the instructions on the summons or seek help from the clerk's office. Be especially careful to meet the deadline. Responses received after the deadline might not be accepted by the court.

Summonses are sometimes written in legal jargon that is difficult to understand. Carefully read all the documents, noting any deadlines. If something is unclear, ask a lawyer or someone familiar with legal documents to explain what the document means. As described above, a court clerk may or may not be helpful in explaining the documents. In using a publication to understand the notice, make sure the publication is current, deals with your state, and with the particular court at issue.

Check Which Court Is Hearing the Case. You will want to read which court issued the summons, so that you can direct all questions and your responsive documents to the correct court. The rules are very different in different courts.

Knowing about the court where the case will be heard will also be critical in determining if you can handle your own case and how much legal help you need.

The most common court used by creditors to sue is "small claims court," a court designed to decide claims for relatively small amounts of money. For example, in some states the small claims court can only handle cases seeking $5,000 or less. Other states have higher limits. If the creditor is seeking more money than the small claims court limit, the suit must be filed in the state's general, all-purpose court. These courts have different names in different states.

Because small claims courts are set up to handle claims for small amounts of money, the procedure is usually simple and less formal. In many small claims courts a lawyer is not required. In fact, in a few states, lawyers are not permitted. If a creditor can sue in small claims court, it will often do so without hiring a lawyer. You should also feel confident appearing in that court without a lawyer.

A state's other courts usually follow more formal procedures. Creditors are represented by lawyers, and formal legal rules apply. Although you can represent yourself in this type of court (this is sometimes called appearing "*pro se*" or "*pro per*"), your wisest course may be to find a lawyer to represent you.

How to Answer the Summons. To avoid the creditor winning the lawsuit without you having a chance to defend it (this is called winning by "default"), you *must* follow the instructions on the summons. If those instructions are unclear, you should consult a lawyer (not the creditor's lawyer) or other reliable professional. Another alternative is to contact the clerk of the court where the suit was filed. The summons will tell you to appear at a hearing, to file a written response, or to file an appearance at the clerk's office. If a written response is required, there will also be a deadline in the summons. If the summons has both a deadline for a written response and a date to appear in court, you must file your written response by the deadline or you may risk losing by default and having your court date canceled.

If the summons requests you to appear at the hearing, it usually specifies a time, a date, and a place at which the hearing will be held. In more formal courts, it is unusual for a hearing to be scheduled immediately, without allowing time for you to file an answer. In some states hearings are scheduled right away for small claims courts cases. Whatever the court, eviction cases and demands for the immediate possession of property are also usually handled very quickly.

A summons often will tell you to file a written "answer" to the summons, also sometimes called an "appearance," within a certain number of days, usually less than thirty. Although the summons may say "appear and defend," this may not mean that you must physically appear on the date mentioned, but only that a written document must be filed with the court by that date.

Many small claims courts that require written answers provide prepared answer forms, which only need to be signed and returned to the court clerk. The answer form states that the defendant (you) deny the plaintiff's (the creditor's) claim. You should return these by the appropriate deadline if you wish to dispute the case. Other small claims courts require no written answer.

In more formal courts, there are usually no prepared answer forms. For these courts, the answer should usually be written by a lawyer, and should include reasons why you deny that you are required to pay all of the creditor's claim. If you do not wish to hire a lawyer, you may draft an answer on your own, but you should do your best to follow the court's procedural requirements. Although answers not written by lawyers are accepted by courts, they may be found insufficient on technical grounds.

If you need more time to find a lawyer or to prepare an answer, a time extension is usually allowed, either by written agreement with the creditor's attorney or by a court order. If you reach an agreement for an extension of time (or any other type of agreement) with the creditor or the creditor's attorney, you should confirm the agreement in writing.

Most courts require that you send a copy of the answer and any other document you file with the court to the creditor or the creditor's lawyer, if the creditor is represented by a lawyer. You should indicate on the original court document filed with the court clerk that a copy was mailed to the creditor or its lawyer. You should also keep a copy of what you file, stamped and dated by the clerk.

Respond to the Court Summons in a Timely Manner. It is important that you carefully meet all time deadlines set out in the summons, whether the deadline is to appear at a hearing, to file an answer or to file an appearance. (In many states there is no distinction between filing an answer and an appearance.)

If the deadline is missed, the creditor can win by default. This means that the court will order you to pay the money, plus court costs and any attorney's fees in some cases, even though there was no hearing on the lawsuit. You will have no opportunity to raise any defenses or explain why you should not have to pay. Instead, the creditor will be granted whatever it requested.

If you informally reach an agreement with the creditor, it is still important to file an appearance and answer. Creditors have been known to proceed with a case and take a default judgment despite having previously reached an agreement with you. Any agreed-upon payment plan or other settlement should be in writing and there should be a clear written statement that the creditor will drop its lawsuit.

An oral agreement with the creditor is *not* a substitute for filing an answer to the summons and cannot alone prevent a default judgment. In fact, the safest course is to file a copy of the written agreement with the court clerk to be entered into the court record.

Submit Defenses and Counterclaims to the Court. You can tell the court why the creditor should not collect on a debt by presenting a defense, a counterclaim, or both. A defense is a reason why you need not pay the creditor, in whole or in part. A counterclaim is a claim that the creditor owes money to you, regardless of whether you owe the creditor on the debt.

Sometimes the difference between the two is only technical. For example, where a dealer finances the sale of a car that turns out to be a lemon, you might use the car's defects both as a defense and as a counterclaim against the dealer.

It is extremely effective to raise defenses and counterclaims in debt collection lawsuits, particularly if the amount at stake is small. Frequently, creditors do not want to be bothered with a case and will let it drop just because you raise a defense.

Fewer than ten percent of consumers who are sued file answers, even though fifty percent or more have good reasons why an entire claim should not be granted. The creditor is most likely counting on your case being among the over ninety percent that result in a quick default judgment in the creditor's favor. Simply by answering, you change the creditor's evaluation of the case. The cost of actually trying the case and the possibility of losing may persuade the creditor to drop the case or to settle for less than the full amount claimed.

Many creditors' attorneys take debt collection cases on a contingent fee basis, meaning they keep about a third of the debts they collect. When the attorney takes the case on this basis, often it will be the attorney who will not want to pursue a lawsuit if you can raise valid defenses. Since the attorney's recovery is limited to one-third of the debt, it will not pay to put several hours into a small case.

The creditor is counting on you to give up; creditors often drop lawsuits if you put up a contest.

Each state and each type of court will have its own procedures as to how you present a defense or counterclaim. Some courts require a written statement filed at the beginning of the case specifying your defenses and counterclaims. Some small claims courts require only that you raise the defenses and counterclaims in your statements at the trial.

A wide variety of defenses are possible, for example:

- Failure to deliver the item purchased or to provide proper services under a contract;
- Defects in the item or services;
- Misrepresentation or duress (meaning you were unfairly pressured) in the creation of the debt;
- That money was paid by you but not credited to the account;
- That the debt is not owed or that you are current on your payments;
- That the creditor is collecting more than you agreed to pay;
- That you never agreed to pay the debt (if, for example someone fraudulently used your name);
- That the debt has been discharged in bankruptcy;

- That the debt was incurred so long ago that under state law the creditor has waited too long to bring the lawsuit;
- That the creditor has violated other laws in making or collecting the debt.

An important type of defense involves challenging the creditor's calculation of the amount due. The creditor may be seeking attorney fees or collection costs that are either excessive or not allowed by law. For example, the loan contract may not require that you pay fees and costs. The creditor may also have improperly computed the loan's payoff figure. For example, they may have applied incorrect rates of interest in calculating how much you owe.

You can raise not only defenses, but also counterclaims that the creditor owes you money. Counterclaims in consumer cases are often based on creditor or debt collector violations of consumer protection laws. Claims can also be related to a seller or creditor's unfair or deceptive conduct. Remember to look at all stages of the transaction, from the original sales solicitation all the way through to the creditor's debt collection procedures. Chapter Nine details many different consumer claims and defenses.

Attend All Court Proceedings and Respond to All Papers You Receive.
In small claims court, you generally only have to go to court once to resolve the case (unless the hearing is rescheduled). When a case is rescheduled, you need to return to court on the rescheduled date.

In more formal courts, a case could be more complicated. The creditor could, but rarely does, take your deposition or send you other paperwork (called "discovery"). A deposition requires you to appear, usually in the creditor's attorney's office to answer questions under oath without a judge present. Your answers are written down by a court reporter and can be used against you later if the case goes to trial and you give different answers. If you get requests for documents or questions about the case (usually called "interrogatories"), you will need to respond to the best of your ability, in writing. Keep copies of any responses you provide. As a participant in the case, you also have a right to hold a deposition or to send discovery to the other side. Because the requirements for doing so are technical, usually you will need a lawyer to set this up for you.

In more formal courts, either side can ask for a judgment before the trial if there are no important facts in dispute. This is usually called a "motion for summary judgment." If you receive a copy of a motion for summary judgment, you will need to respond to it. Otherwise, it may be granted automatically by the court. When you do file a response, always send a copy to the creditor or to the creditor's lawyer if they have one.

When any type of a hearing or deposition is scheduled, you should attend. You cannot avoid having a default judgment taken against you by not showing up, even if you filed an answer or appearance earlier. If you cannot attend, you should send someone else to ask for a delay (usually called a "continuance"), explaining the reasons why you could not attend the hearing that day. This will usually be allowed if you had a good reason for not attending (such as illness, family emergency, preexisting and unavoidable work conflict, or unusual transportation problems).

Whenever possible you should let the creditor or the creditor's attorney know in advance if you have a good reason for not attending the hearing. Often they will agree to a delay in the case. If a delay is agreed, you should put it in writing in the form of a letter confirming the agreement.

The hearing is the opportunity for both parties to tell their story to a judge or magistrate. In many small claims courts, the hearing is informal. Usually, the creditor first explains why it is suing. In most cases, the creditor gives the judge a copy of the purchase contract and the accounting records that shows any missed payments.

Next, you will present your response. To be most effective, you should consider consulting a lawyer for advice about presentation of your case. You should not hesitate to ask for a delay in the court date if needed to find an attorney.

Since court can be frightening, you should make notes about what you plan to say, so that you do not forget an important issue at the last minute. Assume that you will be nervous and prepare ahead of time as much as possible.

How to Prepare for a Court Hearing. Here are some tips to help you prepare for a court hearing:

- *Bring all relevant documents.* It is unlikely that you will have another chance to present documents except at the hearing. Remember that courts generally pay a lot of attention to written documents. Examples of written documents include complaint letters you have written to the creditor or cancelled checks showing you paid money on the account that wasn't credited. It will be helpful to have extra copies available, because the court and the creditor will keep copies of the documents you present.

- *Bring witnesses if there are any.* Witness testimony may be important, especially if the witnesses are not friends or relatives. For example, if the dispute is about an item which does not work properly, a mechanic or another witness can testify from their own experience in using that item.
- *Do not rely on written statements of your witnesses,* because the court usually will not allow them into evidence. Have the witnesses attend the trial.
- *Consider going to court beforehand to orient yourself* as to where the courtroom is, how the court works, how people dress, when to stand, how to tell when your case is called, where you sit during the hearing, whether a microphone is used and how to use it, the judge's personality, whether an interpreter is available, etc.
- *Take a companion to the actual hearing* to offer emotional support, to give you feedback and other help, to keep track of your documents, and to offer a second opinion if you must respond on the spot to a settlement offer.
- *Prepare a written chronological report of events in advance,* together with a checklist of points to make, and a checklist of documents to be given to the court, and take the checklist with you. Many judges will be impatient if you are disorganized. The more organized you are, the more likely the judge will be able to follow what you are saying.
- *Assume that the judge has not read any of the documents* already presented to the court and knows none of the facts of the case. Start at the beginning and tell your story in a clear and organized fashion in the order it happened.
- *Do not be afraid to be forceful, but do not make personal attacks on individuals,* including lawyers, witnesses, or the judge. A display of anger will usually hurt you more than it helps.

DEALING WITH
A DEFAULT JUDGMENT

As explained earlier, by not filing a written answer or appearance within the specified time, or by failing to attend the hearing, or by missing other deadlines, you may lose the opportunity to raise your defenses. This is usually called a "default." It is important that you not lose by default unless a lawyer has evaluated your case for you and determined that you will lose nothing by allowing a default to be entered.

Nevertheless, if a default has been entered against you, you may still be able to get another chance to be heard. This is called setting aside a default. Usually, a default can be set aside only for specific reasons and within a short time after the judgment has been entered into the court records.

Reasons for setting aside a default commonly include not having proper notice of the case or other unavoidable circumstances that made you unable to answer within the required time. In some courts, you will also have to tell the court briefly about your defense or counterclaim so that it will know that you have a chance to get a different result if the default is lifted. Usually, a request to "remove," "lift," or "set aside" a default has to be made to the court in writing. A copy of your request should always be mailed to the creditor or to its lawyer.

It may be very difficult to set aside a default. You should not assume you will be able to do this. You can avoid this problem by responding on time to all deadlines.

THE JUDGMENT AND
YOUR APPEAL RIGHTS

The judgment is what the court orders after hearing the case. If the creditor wins, the judgment gives the creditor the right to force you to pay by a variety of methods. You cannot be forced to pay unsecured debts until a judgment is entered.

Once the judgment is entered, if you do not pay, the creditor has special rights to seize your property or income, unless this property or income is protected by federal or state law. However, you may have certain rights to prevent payment of a judgment even after it is entered. This is discussed in more detail below.

A party that loses a lawsuit at the first court level can appeal to a higher level. For cases heard in small claims court, that usually means appealing to the state's trial court. This may be the only appeal that is allowed from a small claims court decision. Further appeal can be granted only if a higher court specifically says that it wishes to hear the case.

If a case starts in a more formal trial court, the losing party can appeal to another court which has power to hear appeals. In some states, more than one appeal is possible because there are several layers of courts. Deadlines for filing an appeal are generally short and strictly enforced. Procedures for what papers to file in an appeal may be quite technical and may also be strictly enforced. You may need professional assistance in bringing an appeal.

The costs of an appeal vary widely, but can be significant. Typical costs include a filing fee, fees for a transcript of the trial, and posting a bond to cover the judgment being appealed. In some circumstances, a party unable to afford these fees can request that some of them be waived.

Appeals rarely involve a completely new presentation of the case. Usually, an appeal court will review the case only on the facts presented in the court below.

CREDITORS' ATTEMPTS
TO COLLECT COURT JUDGMENTS

Significance of a Court Judgment Against You. Even if you lose a lawsuit, this does *not* mean you must repay the debt. If your family is in financial distress and cannot afford to repay its debts, a court order to pay may not really change anything. If you do not have the money to pay, the court's decision that you owe the debt will not make payment any more possible.

What the court order does do is let creditors use several special collection tools to try to squeeze money from you. How effective these tools are will depend not only on how much income and property you have, but also on the *types* of income and property involved. In some cases these tools are effective in recovering money and may even result in loss of your home. In other cases, these special tools will have *no* impact on you. In still others, the creditor will not spend the money to take further action against you even if they have a judgment.

Where losing a lawsuit has no adverse effects for you, you are called "judgment proof." This means that your assets and income are small enough and are of a type that federal and state law fully protects them from seizure by creditors. In that case, you do not really have to worry about the judgment unless your financial situation substantially improves.

**Even a court order cannot make you
pay a debt if all your income
and property is exempt from seizure.**

Being "judgment proof" is not a permanent condition. If your financial situation improves, the creditor may still be able to collect its money from you in the future. But it is important to assess your current situation and if you are judgment proof, you should ignore the judgment and save your income to pay your highest priority bills, such as a mortgage, rent, or utility payment.

If you are faced with a collection lawsuit, you should know in advance whether you are judgment proof. If you can be hurt by a judgment, that creates even more incentive to defend against the lawsuit.

If you do not know whether you are judgment proof under the laws of your state, you can consider consulting a lawyer on this limited issue. The most important consideration in determining whether you are judgment proof is whether the creditor can force you to pay with one or more of the special creditor remedies discussed below.

Creditors may be able to use any of four different types of special remedies to force you to pay if they obtain a court judgment against you. These remedies are very different in different states. If the creditor only collects some of the money you owe using any of these remedies, it can continue to use that same remedy or use a different one to try to recover the full amount. The remainder of this chapter discusses these special remedies in general terms. You will need to get specific information about practices in your state.

Attachment and Execution. A creditor with a court judgment can arrange for the sheriff to seize certain of your property. Because the creditor is armed with a court judgment and is asking the sheriff to do the seizure, the creditor can seize your property even though the creditor had not taken that property as collateral for its loan.

You shouldn't panic that your most important property will be seized in this process. The right of a creditor to take your property is limited. State law specifically protects certain types of your property and/or certain amounts of your property. Protected property is called "exempt." You can prevent the seizure of exempt property by filing a notice of exempt property, or by taking similar steps specified by your state law. In some states, you will need to file papers with the sheriff or a public official by a certain deadline in order to get the benefit of an exemption. In other states, the sheriff gives you permission to set aside exempt items at the time of seizure or sale.

Additionally, the sheriff cannot seize property in your possession which does not belong to you. To stop its seizure, the property's rightful owner may have to file a declaration of ownership with the appropriate office. More discussion on your rights to protect property from seizure are discussed later in this chapter under "Exemptions May Prevent Creditor From Seizing Property."

If the sheriff is able to seize your property, it will then be sold at public auction, and apply the proceeds to the judgment by paying the creditor.

These auctions are usually poorly attended and bring low bids. For this reason, creditors rarely seize used household goods, which will have minimal resale value. If property is sold at auction, you or your friends can attend the auction and purchase back the possessions at a bargain price.

Judgment Liens. Any unpaid judgment generally becomes a lien on real estate owned by you in the county where the judgment is entered (or statewide in some states). Creditors also may have the right to transfer judgments to make them applicable to your real estate in other locations.

Unless the real estate is legally exempt from execution, creditors can force its sale in much the same manner as they can force the sale of other property. Later in this chapter, there is a discussion as to when real estate is exempt from execution.

Even if the real estate is exempt from execution, the creditor's lien on your property usually remains in effect until you sell it. In most states, when you sell the property, mortgages are paid off first. Then you get to keep what is left up to your state's maximum exemption amount. Anything over that amount goes to satisfy all or some of the creditor's judgment against you. Even if your property is exempt from seizure today, if the property's value increases enough in the future, there may be enough money left over after sale to allow the creditor to recover its judgment.

One possible way of getting rid of judgment liens is to file for bankruptcy. To the extent the property is exempt when you file for bankruptcy, the lien can be permanently removed.

Garnishment. A creditor with a court judgment against you has the right to "garnish" money belonging or owed to you that is in the hands of a third party. In this context, to "garnish" means to take. Most often, garnishment takes money from your wages or bank account.

Garnishment usually can only take place *after* the creditor obtains a judgment against you. (One exception is for collection of student loans where garnishment is allowed even without a judgment). For more information, see Chapter Nineteen. After obtaining a judgment, the creditor can file a request for garnishment with the court clerk, sheriff or another local official depending on state practice. A notice is then issued to the "garnishee" (a bank, an employer, or another third party holding your property), directing that party to turn over the property at a specified time.

You must be given notice of the garnishment. You can then request a hearing to prove that state or federal law protects your money from garnishment. Federal and state law protect you from garnishment in two ways:

1. *A portion of your wages is protected from seizure.* Current federal law provides that the first $154.50 from weekly take-home pay, after taxes and Social Security are deducted, cannot be garnished at all. If the weekly take-home pay is more than $154.50, an employer, in response to a garnishment order, must pay the *smaller* of the following amounts to a sheriff:

- The weekly take-home pay (after withholding) minus $154.50; or
- Twenty-five percent of that take-home pay.

For example, if your weekly income after deductions are taken out is $200, your employer would be required to calculate the amount due under the two formulas: 1) ($200-154.50= $45.50) or 2) (25% of $200 = $50) and pay the creditor the smaller amount. In this case, the creditor would pay your creditor $45.50 from your take-home pay. A higher amount can be garnished if the debt is for child support or alimony.

The standard described above is based on federal law and sets out minimum wage protections for debtors in all fifty states. In some states, you have even greater protections against wage garnishment. Some states prohibit all wage garnishment or allow a smaller amount of wages to be garnished than the federal standard. Federal law and some state laws forbid employers from firing employees solely because their wages are being garnished.

**Usually, your first $154.50 a week
in take home pay and all your Social Security
or other government benefits
are completely exempt from seizure.**

---

2. *Certain types of income, primarily government payments, are completely exempt from garnishment.* Even if your income is large enough so that a portion may be garnished, certain sources of income are *completely* protected under federal or state law. For example, federal law completely exempts Social Security payments, Supplemental Security Income, and veterans' benefits. States with TANF (Temporary Assistance for Needy Families) and unemployment insurance programs usually exempt those benefits from garnishment as well.

Funds such as Social Security are also exempt from seizure if you keep them in a bank account. However, problems sometimes arise when your bank account contains both exempt and nonexempt money because it is hard to trace which part of the funds is exempt. In many cases, creditors will improperly seize money, such as Social Security payments, that should be exempt. You will then need to fight back and show that the seizure was illegal and that those funds were protected. If you are threatened with a court judgment, you must weigh the benefits of opening or keeping a bank account against the risk of having the money seized.

If a significant amount of your income or cash in a bank account is subject to garnishment, you may wish to work out a deal with the creditor rather than allow your money to be taken. The creditor may be just as happy to accept a certain amount a month instead of going through the garnishment procedures.

More information on garnishments and available defenses is contained in National Consumer Law Center, *Fair Debt Collection*, Ch. 9 (3d ed. 1996 and Supp.).

Debtor's Examination. After obtaining a judgment, a creditor can ask a judge to order you to appear in court to answer questions about your income and assets. The purpose is to find income or property that is not protected by law and which the creditor may seize.

In some states this procedure is called a debtor's examination, but the procedure goes by other names in other states. Some creditors routinely request a debtor's examination. Others never do. Three important things to remember about a debtor's examination are:

- It is a court-ordered appearance. Failure to show up can result in arrest, citation for contempt, and a jail sentence. A notice to appear for a court examination should *never* be ignored. Even if it's a bad time for you. You should appear anyway or make a written request to the court for a postponement. The court will usually grant a postponement if the creditor agrees to the request or if you have a good reason.
- Your answers are made under oath, and often are recorded by a court reporter. Lying under oath is perjury, a crime punishable by jail.
- If the creditor which holds a judgment does find assets or income not protected by law, the creditor can obtain a court order requiring you to turn over those assets to the creditor. Failure to comply with the order could be considered contempt, and could result in jail.

Because of all the various ways a debtor's examination can get you into trouble, it is a good idea to promptly find legal representation.

The first step in responding to notice of a debtor's examination is to review your assets *well before the examination*. Determine if all your property is protected by law and if all your income is exempt from garnishment. If so, immediately tell the creditor. This may be sufficient to get the creditor to drop the request for an examination since it will just be a waste of everyone's time. If the examination is canceled, be sure to get this in writing. Do not rely on the creditor's oral promise that it will drop the examination.

If there is property that legally can be seized, you may want to do some "exemption planning." Exemption planning is a way of maximizing the protection of existing laws by converting property that could be seized (for example, cash) into property that cannot be seized (for example, household goods or equity in the home).

For example, suppose you are a homeowner with $10,000 in cash and $10,000 equity in your home (your equity is the amount of cash you would keep if you sold your home and paid off all the liens on it). Assume the homestead exemption is $20,000 and other property exemptions allow you to exempt only $3,000 in cash. In this example, the $10,000 equity in your home is completely protected from seizure. In fact the homestead exemption ($20,000) would allow you to protect another $10,000 in equity. The other property exemptions protect only $3,000 of the $10,000 you have in cash, meaning that at least $7,000 in cash can be seized. Instead of losing the $7,000 to the creditor, you can use the cash to prepay the mortgage in part. If you prepay the mortgage, you will owe less on your home which will increase your equity. This increased equity in the home (up to $20,000) will be fully protected by the homestead exemption.

This type of planning is a better approach than giving nonexempt property to relatives or friends. Giving away assets in this way will be frowned upon and can be set aside by a court. If you cannot account to the court for transfers of large amounts of your property, you may be accused of fraud. This would make your legal problems even worse.

If there is property important to you that a creditor can seize, you can approach the creditor about a "workout" agreement. You can offer to pay all or a portion of the amount due over a period of months or even years. The amount you offer to pay should be directly related to what the creditor could seize after the debtor's examination. Do not offer to pay $3000 over twelve months when the only items the creditor could seize have a market value of $500.

There are two important points about workout agreements. First, always get the agreement in writing. The writing should excuse you from attending the debtor's examination if it has not already been held, and contain the creditor's promise not to use wage garnishment or execution on your property as long as you continue to make payments. (You can also ask for an agreement to waive the remainder of the debt if part is paid. Some creditors will accept partial payment if they know they can't get payment in full. From the creditor's perspective, some payment is better than none.)

A final option to avoid loss of property after a debtor's examination is to file for bankruptcy. The bankruptcy will immediately stop any seizure and may allow you to keep your property permanently. Since bankruptcy is a right under federal (national) law, your rights in the bankruptcy process will take precedence over the state court collection process. Chapter Twenty discusses consumer bankruptcy filings.

EXEMPTIONS MAY PROTECT YOUR PROPERTY FROM SEIZURE

State exemption laws protect certain types of your property from seizure after a court judgment and permit you to keep the basic necessities of life. However, exemption statutes provide little or no protection from a creditor seizing *collateral*. For example, if you agreed to put up a home or car as collateral on a loan, exemption laws do not prevent the creditor from seizing the home or car if you get behind in your loan payments. Exemption statutes give you important rights if you have not put up any collateral when taking out a loan, but where, *after a court judgment*, the creditor seeks an order to seize your property.

Some exemption statutes specify dollar amounts of property that are exempt from seizure. For example, the statute may specify that $8,000 worth of your personal property is exempt from seizure. Such a statute would allow you to choose which items of your personal property you want to keep, as long as what you keep is worth $8000 or less. Such a statute will apply to your personal property, and not your home, which is considered real estate. What types of property are considered your personal property will be specified by your state statute.

Homestead exemptions protect your residence, and can be as high as $100,000 or more in some states, but can also be significantly less in others. Texas and Florida also totally exempt a principal residence on a certain size plot of land. Under some state's laws if husband and wife own property jointly, that property may be entitled to special protection from the debts of one spouse or the other, but not from joint debts. Joint owners, whether married or not, usually may each obtain a separate exemption which covers their share of the property to double the amount of protection.

To benefit from the homestead exemption in some states, a declaration of the homestead must be filed with the property registry in your community.

In a few states this paper must have been filed before the credit was granted. You should always file your declaration as early as possible if you live in a state where a declaration is required. In other states protection is automatic.

Exemption amounts stretch a long way because they apply only to your equity in property, not to the property's value.

A homestead or other exemption usually allows you to exempt only a certain portion of your equity in the property. However, a relatively small exemption amount may be sufficient to protect property worth significantly more. If you have equity above the exemption limit, the creditor can force a sale and you would only be able to keep the amount of the exemption from the sale proceeds. Consider the following examples:

First, a state homestead exemption of $30,000 and a home worth $150,000. If you have a $100,000 first mortgage and a $20,000 home equity loan, you have $30,000 in equity. (Equity roughly equals the full value of the home, $150,000, minus the amount you owe for mortgages plus other liens, $120,000 = $30,000). Since the homestead exemption is $30,000, your home is fully protected from execution by a judgment creditor.

If the home's value increases to $200,000, a creditor with a court judgment could force a sale. (This is because your equity would now equal $200,000 - $120,000 = $80,000, of which only $30,000 would be exempted from seizure). The first $100,000 from the sale would go to the mortgage holder, the next $20,000 to pay off the home equity loan. The next $30,000 of sale proceeds would be kept by you. Only the last $50,000 of sale proceeds could be used to pay the creditor initiating the sale. If the creditor is owed less than $50,000, you get the balance.

Many creditors would not force a sale in the last example even though there is nonexempt equity. They will avoid the expense of forcing a sale, and instead wait to collect on their lien until you sell the property. They will then expect to be paid from the proceeds of the sale.

Some states specify that certain of your property is totally exempt from seizure, no matter how much money it is worth. The list of totally exempt property typically includes such items as tools and supplies required for your occupation, clothing, a car (usually with a value under a specified amount), a bible and household goods.

If you file for bankruptcy, in some states the property that can be exempted from seizure is increased because you can choose the federal bankruptcy exemptions. These may or may not be better than your state's exemptions. But some states have "opted out" of the federal exemptions, meaning that even in a bankruptcy, you must rely on your state exemptions.

Some creditors try to force you to turn over property that is exempt under law from seizure. The creditor will point to small print in the contract in which you agreed to waive rights under state exemption laws. These types of waivers are now illegal under federal law.

Even if exemption laws fully protect your property at one point in time, you may be at risk if your equity in your property increases. Court judgments remain on the books for many years. If your equity in a home or other property increases beyond the exemption limit or if you acquire nonexempt income or property, creditors may be able to reach it at some point in the future. At that point, if the judgment is still unpaid, you will have to work out a payment plan with the creditor or reconsider a bankruptcy filing.

State exemption laws can be very complicated. This is an issue where you may want to get professional help. At a minimum, you should try to find a publication which addresses your state's laws. This type of publication may be available from the local bar association, a legal services office, or a consumer credit counselor. Make sure anything you read is up to date.

9

Fighting Back

- *Reasons You Should Raise Your Defenses*
- *Identifying Your Legal Claims*
- *How to Pursue Your Legal Claims*

You may not have to repay all of your debt. Complaints you may have concerning the conduct of lenders, salespersons, collectors, contractors or service providers may reduce the amount you owe.

Misconduct and errors by creditors and sellers can contribute to your financial problems. Many examples are discussed below. Your legitimate complaints about this conduct create important legal rights for you, in the form of legal claims against your creditors. These claims can be used to eliminate the obligation to pay some or all of your debts. The fact that you have fallen behind on your payments doesn't prevent you from raising your defenses to repayment. Fight back whenever you have a chance. The best defense is usually a good offense.

WHY FIGHT BACK?

You should take the offensive and raise all your legitimate claims in the debt collection process for four reasons:

1. There May Never Be Another Chance. If you do not raise your claims in response to a debt collection lawsuit or other collection action, you may never have another chance to do so. If you wait to begin a case on your own behalf, the court may say that the action was brought too late and is barred under court rules. Similarly, a court may throw out your lawsuit, saying that you should have raised the issue at the same time the collector brought its case — that it is a waste of the court's time to hear the same case twice. Also, it is hard to find time and resources to begin a lawsuit. You may lose the drive and initiative to sue over a consumer problem if you wait to file a separate suit.

Raising claims immediately in response to a debt collection action will avoid these problems. You will be highly motivated — no one likes to pay a debt after being treated unfairly. It is cheaper and easier to respond to a lawsuit than to initiate your own suit. (Usually there are no fees for defending an action. In states where there are fees, you may be able to get them waived if you cannot afford to pay.) Additionally, courts may allow you to raise even very old claims if they are raised as a defense to a collection action, as opposed to a separate lawsuit.

2. You Should Not Have To Repay Money You Do Not Owe. Defenses to repayment can greatly reduce the amount you are expected to pay back. If the creditor has misallocated or lost a payment, overcharged you based on the contract, or seeks reimbursement for services which were not provided, you have a defense.

3. You Should Be Compensated If You Have Been Hurt. If you have a good claim, you are entitled to recover for any injury suffered. Many consumer laws also allow you extra compensation to discourage sellers or creditors from engaging in misconduct. In some cases this may include punitive damages, which are special damages designed to punish a party which is responsible for serious misconduct. If you pursue these claims aggressively, rather than pay the creditor, it may turn out that the creditor owes you money.

When your injury is very small, some consumer statutes still award you $100 or even as much as $2000 as a way of encouraging you to pursue the problem. If you cannot afford to pay a debt, raising even small claims against the creditor may help cut down the debt. If you have large claims, you may find that you are actually owed a significant amount of money.

4. Raising Claims Helps to Get Good Settlements. Creditors collecting on relatively small consumer debts expect that you will not fight back. This allows them to collect their money quickly and inexpensively. When you raise claims in response to a collection action, collectors' business calculations change dramatically. Not only does the collector have to factor in the value of your claim, but also the time and expense it will take to finally resolve the case.

Often collectors will drop cases when you present strong claims. Other times they will agree to settlements that are very much to your advantage. Of course, not every creditor will cave in at the merest mention of your claim. Some creditors are more willing to face a court trial than others.

IDENTIFYING CLAIMS
YOU MAY HAVE

Consumers are not always aware of the different claims they can raise relating to a debt. You may want to see a lawyer or nonprofit counselor to find out if you have a defense. In doing so, you should bring any documents you have concerning the debt or the transaction underlying the debt. Sometimes the documents will provide a good basis to reconstruct any problems you had with that creditor or seller.

Nevertheless, it is not only the documents which are important. Oral promises and other statements made to you can also be the basis for a claim. You should explore *all* of the following six stages related to a transaction.

1. The Original Sale of Goods or Services. Most debts arise from the purchase of goods or services. In the case of loans, the money often is earmarked for the purchase of particular goods or services. Additionally the loan itself should be thought of as a service which the creditor provides.

A first question is always what statements (and written advertisements) were made to encourage you to buy the goods or to clinch the deal. Were the seller's statements false? Did the written documents differ from than the seller's oral statements? Were high-pressure tactics used? Did the seller hide key information?

You may feel that you will lose in a contest with the seller and that a court will always believe an established business person over an individual who is fighting a debt. Actually, the opposite is usually true. Judges and juries may be more willing to believe what you say than what a used car dealer, aluminum siding or other disreputable salesperson says. Without getting into legal technicalities, anything that you find to be outrageous, unfair, unjust, or fraudulent is likely to form the basis of a case.

Pay special attention to door-to-door sales. High-pressure tactics and oral misrepresentations are common in those transactions. In addition, door-to-door salespersons have to give you written notice of your right to cancel the sale for any reason within the first three days. Were you given such a notice?

The National Consumer Law Center's *Unfair and Deceptive Acts and Practices* (4th ed. 1997 and Supp.) provides the best description of the many types of claims and legal theories available to consumers relating to sales abuses. The book lists thousands of practices, categorized by type of sale, that have been found to be deceptive or unfair.

2. Warranties. After receipt, goods or services often do not turn out as expected. The goods are later discovered to be defective, work is not completed, or the work is found to be substandard. These problems provide a strong basis for claims.

A common mistake consumers make is to assume that, when a product is sold "as is" or "without warranties," that they cannot complain about problems with the product. In fact, "as is" disclaimers often do not prevent you from winning court awards from sellers.

You should always raise claims when goods or services are not delivered, the wrong services are performed, or the work is not completed. Similarly, when goods or services come with a warranty, you should have a claim if the seller fails to comply with the warranty. For more detail on consumer claims based on the performance of the goods or services, see two National Consumer Law Center publications, *Consumer Warranty Law* (1997 and Supp.) and *Unfair and Deceptive Acts and Practices* (4th ed. 1997 and Supp.).

3. Loan Terms. Most debts begin with a loan contract—often called a "note." Anything that you find to be outrageous, unfair, unjust, or deceptive about the terms of the loan agreement may form the basis of a valid claim. Oral misrepresentations made to encourage you to enter into an agreement also may be a basis for claims, as should a lender's attempt to confuse you or hide important terms. High-pressure tactics should also be challenged.

You may also have a claim if a creditor made a loan to you that you could not afford from the outset, or if a refinanced loan will be worse for you than sticking with the original debt. Abusive practices such as bogus charges, double-charging and the sale of useless insurance may also form the basis of legal claims.

A common problem arises when two or more businesses team up to mislead you. For example, a home improvement contractor may have set up a high-rate loan for you to pay for home improvements because that contractor gets a commission from the loan company. Similarly, some loan brokers will arrange bad deals in order to take advantage of a high commission. In these types of cases, claims can be made based on the relationship between the parties. In many cases both parties can be sued based on the actions of either one. This is especially important when one of the companies you dealt with goes out of business. You should not assume that you have no claim when the party who took advantage of you is no longer in the picture.

In addition, the federal Truth in Lending Act, state installment sales laws, and other state credit legislation create various requirements as to what the creditor must tell you about a loan. These statutes are technical and you may need the assistance of a lawyer. The National Consumer Law Center's *Truth in Lending* (3d ed. 1995 and Supp.) is the best volume available about your rights under the federal Truth in Lending statute.

Many states have usury laws that set maximum interest rates and limits on certain types of credit charges. Creditors violating these "usury" statutes will have to pay significant damages, but again a lawyer is usually necessary to press such claims. National Consumer Law Center's *The Cost of Credit: Regulation and Legal Challenges* (1995 and Supp.) fully discusses a variety of types of credit overcharges.

4. Creditor's Subsequent Conduct. You can also raise claims and defenses based on a creditor's conduct after a loan is made. You should check whether payments have been properly applied, whether escrow amounts are handled correctly, and whether late charges are appropriate.

Car loan creditors and home mortgage lenders often purchase property insurance for you if your coverage lapses. Make sure this substitute coverage was not purchased for periods when you had your own insurance in place, did not contain unnecessary coverages, and was not sold at an inflated price. These problems are especially common now because many big companies which loan money also have interests in insurance businesses.

If the creditor's employees made false promises that the creditor would not repossess the collateral if certain payments were made, you can hold the creditor to these promises. If the creditor assigned the right to collect from you to a different creditor, were you clearly notified of a new address to send payments?

5. Debt Collection Tactics. Chapter Six discusses what types of debt collection practices are illegal. Even when your primary concern is a repossession, a debt collection lawsuit, or a foreclosure, do not forget to consider *earlier* debt collection contacts. If these earlier contacts were illegal, they will form the basis for legitimate claims against the creditor or collector. You may be able to obtain $1,000 in damages for collection agency misconduct even if your actual injury from the harassment is hard to determine.

6. Attempts to Enforce a Court Order or Security Interest. You may have problems with the way a creditor attempts to collect on a judgment, repossess a car, seize household property, foreclose on a home, evict you, or terminate utility service. Creditors often are sloppy in the way they sue, garnish wages, repossess or seize property. Their failure to follow proper procedures may lead to legal claims. In most states, these claims give rise to damage awards. Your rights in these areas are spelled out in Chapter Eight and Chapters Thirteen through Eighteen.

Sometimes raising all your defenses
and counterclaims to a collection lawsuit
will both cancel your debt and result in
a cash recovery for you and your attorney.

An Example. Ms. P was sued for the balance owed on a car loan after her car had been repossessed and sold. When she took out the loan, she was told the interest rate would be 8%, but the actual rate from a finance company was 15%. Also, the car never worked properly.

Ms. P received no notice prior to repossession and she was sued, not where she lives, but in the next county.

In defending the lawsuit, Ms. P should raise all of her available claims. These might include the seller's misrepresentations about the car and the credit terms, problems with the car's performance, and the seller's failure to repair the defects. The creditor may also be responsible for illegal repossession and for failure to give required notices. Finally, the lawsuit itself may violate federal law by not being brought where Ms. P resides.

All of these claims may be used to offset the amount Ms. P owes the creditor on the debt. In fact, it is not uncommon for an aggressive attorney to be able to settle a case like this one so that Ms. P owes the creditor nothing. Instead the creditor might be made to pay her several thousand dollars together with her attorney fees and court costs. On the other hand, if these defenses and counterclaims are not raised, the creditor might get a judgment against Ms. P which it could enforce by garnishing her wages or selling other property. (See Chapter Eight.)

HOW TO RAISE
YOUR CLAIMS

When to Raise Your Claims. Usually you will want to raise all available complaints as early as possible in the debt collection process. Waiting too long may make you less believable later. Warning a collector at an early stage that you have significant claims to offset a debt may be sufficient to get the creditor to drop collection activity. If you wait to raise the claims until after the creditor sues you, the creditor may be less likely to drop the case because it has already invested time and money in the lawsuit.

Consequently, you should mention your claims every time a creditor contacts you about payment. If the creditor still pursues a lawsuit on the debt, raise the claims at that point also. Chapter Eight explains how to raise counterclaims and defenses to the creditor's lawsuit.

After a seizure of property, a creditor may seek the remainder due on a debt, if the sale price is insufficient to cover the amount owed. This is called an action to collect the "deficiency." You may also raise all your claims in response to such a deficiency claim.

Put Your Complaints in Writing. If you believe you have claims against a creditor, you may want to put the basis for your claims in writing and mail them to the creditor and to its attorney, if any. This is especially important if you believe that you have warranty or similar claims. Don't forget to keep a copy of anything you mail. You might also want to send these letters by registered or certified mail so you have proof that they were received. This will prevent the creditor from later claiming that it did not know you were dissatisfied. You generally should try to put your complaint in writing as early as possible. However a letter to the creditor does not substitute for the formal process of raising your claims in a court action. You will need to file the appropriate court papers as well.

Complaints About the Sale Should Be Directed to the Collector as Well as the Seller. The creditor collecting a debt may not be the same person or company that provided goods or services to you. Many debts are passed along from one creditor to another over a period of time. Debt collectors usually do not want to hear about problems you had with the provider of goods or services or about previous collectors. The collector may tell you to go talk to the seller or that prior creditor.

Although the collector might not want to hear your complaints, you should tell the collector anyway. The very fact that the collector does not want to hear about these problems is a good indication of how important it is to press these claims.

There are several reasons why it is critical that you press available claims against the collector instead of just tracking down the original seller or creditor. By the time you get a court order against the original seller, the seller may be bankrupt or may have skipped town. Also, a court order against a seller may take years to obtain, and involve costly filing fees and legal bills. Finally, an award against the seller will not by itself stop a collection action brought by someone else. You can win against the seller, but lose in a separate case brought by the collector.

Despite their protests to the contrary, lenders are often liable for the problems you have with a seller of goods or a contractor that was paid from the proceeds of the loan.

On the other hand, when you raise defenses against the creditor collecting on the debt, it is the collection action that may take years to resolve. Raising your claims as a defense to a collection suit is also usually less expensive because the party bringing the lawsuit, not the person being sued, pays the court fees.

If you obtain legal representation, your attorney may decide to sue not only the creditor bringing the action, but also the seller, the original creditor, or even the debt collection agency. But the key thing to remember is that it is always better to defend the creditor's attempt to collect a debt than to give the creditor the money and try to get it back from someone else. When the creditor tells you to go talk to the seller, firmly answer "no thank you, I am raising my claims against you."

Settlement of Disputed Claims. Your claims against a creditor give you the opportunity to obtain a formal or informal settlement of the debt. Most commonly, a settlement involves cancellation of some or all of the debt in exchange for your agreement to drop your claims. However, you may also want to think about other settlement terms which could benefit you. You might ask for some or all of these terms together with a reduction in amount:

- **Agreement by the creditor to cancel the delinquency.**
  Even if the total amount you owe does not change, you benefit if the creditor agrees to ignore a delinquency and treat your debt as if it is current. This would protect you, at least temporarily, from debt collection actions such as foreclosure, repossession, or lawsuits.
- **Restructuring of payments.** Reduction or other restructuring of monthly payments may give you an opportunity to get back on your feet. An agreement to accept partial monthly payments for a period of time may also fall into this category. If you are settling your claims against the creditor, you should resist any creditor effort to charge you new fees for restructuring your debt.
- **Reduction of interest rate.** To settle a dispute, some creditors will agree to a reduction of the interest rate for future payments. It is always easier for a creditor to agree to collect less interest, than it is for that creditor to reduce the principal amount owed on the debt.
- **Return of property.** If a creditor has improperly seized property and has not resold it, you should ask that the property be returned. If it has been resold or damaged you are entitled to the replacement cost or the cost of repairs.
- **Credit record corrections.** You can ask the creditor to

change, correct or delete, the information it has provided to credit reporting companies as part of a settlement. At a minimum, you can ask the creditor to report your debt as "current" or fully paid.

Any type of agreement you reach with a creditor should be documented in writing. If you are not represented by an attorney, you may need help to determine if a settlement of a disputed debt is fair and reasonable. Depending on the amounts involved, it may make sense to hire someone to help you evaluate the settlement. If the amounts are small, advice from an objective but trusted friend or relative may be helpful.

Never agree to anything you do not understand or which you think is unfair. Whenever possible, wait until you see the terms of the settlement in writing before you agree. If a creditor has cheated you once, it may be possible that you are being cheated again.

Warning About Coupon Settlements. If you are owed money by a creditor, one type of settlement you may want to resist is a store coupon or additional extension of credit from that creditor. Coupons or new credit from a lender will only get you back into a relationship with a company that has given you problems. It is usually better to take a smaller amount of cash than to accept a store coupon, because you can spend it as you like.

Accord and Satisfaction. One final tactic in seeking to arrange a settlement on favorable terms is based on a legal doctrine known as "accord and satisfaction." The most common use of accord and satisfaction for consumers arises when you write "payment in full of a disputed debt" on the back of a check and a creditor endorses and cashes that check. Providing that there was a valid basis for the dispute, the law treats your check as final payment.

In order to protect yourself if you wish to try to settle a dispute by "accord and satisfaction," you should follow all of these steps:

- Make clear to the creditor that you have a dispute by sending a letter to the creditor and keeping a copy;
- The letter you send should clearly set out the basis of your dispute (for example, "you were hired to paint three rooms and you only painted two");
- The letter should make clear that the amount you are enclos-

ing is the total amount you believe you actually owe, and state the basis on which you calculate that amount;
- Carefully mark your check on the reverse in big block print: "payment in full of a disputed debt;"
- Keep a copy of the front and back of the check you send in case the creditor alters it in any way before cashing it; and
- Keep a copy of the canceled check when it is returned by the bank, together with the letter you sent accompanying the check.

Your letter and copy of the canceled check is your record that the creditor accepted the check as payment in full.

– 10 –

Credit Cards:
A Blessing or a Curse?

- *Choosing the Right Credit Card Options*
- *Ways to Prevent Out of Control Credit Card Debts*
- *Your Rights to Dispute a Credit Card Bill*
- *What to Do If You Get Behind on Payments*

As discussed throughout this book, when you are prioritizing your debts, credit cards generally should come near the bottom of the list. Nevertheless, you may find that credit card obligations are your biggest headache due to collection calls, concern about future credit, or because you can afford to pay everything but unmanageable credit card debts.

This chapter discusses strategies to avoid getting overwhelmed with credit cards, how to put-off credit card collectors when your budget is limited to more pressing needs, and finally ways to manage credit card debt after you have a solid plan for managing all of your higher priority debts. Because credit cards are generally one of several types of unsecured credit, much of the material in this chapter is a summary of material found in other chapters of this book. In particular you may want to review Chapters One, Five, Six and Seven.

PREVENTING
OVER-EXTENSION
ON CREDIT CARDS

There has been an enormous expansion of consumer credit card spending in recent years. A big part of this is due to lenders' increased marketing efforts. More than three billion credit card offers are mailed to consumers each year. Most of us get several offers for new credit cards every week. In addition, credit cards are advertised everywhere. We see advertisements on television, the Internet, at sporting events, in restaurants, and increasingly on college campuses and even in high schools.

In the past, consumers facing money problems rarely got new credit card offers. Lenders individually reviewed credit reports and chose not to offer credit to consumers they considered bad risks. More recently, however, lenders buy huge mailing lists and offer credit to everyone on the list without further evaluation. Many news stories have documented that credit cards are offered by mistake to children in kindergarten, family pets, people who have died, and to prisoners while in jail. In this environment, it is not surprising that people experiencing financial problems, including debtors in bankruptcy, continue to get offers for new credit cards.

Credit card offers can be very enticing. Nearly every offer promises some special benefit to a new card. In some cases, the offer is for a low rate. In others, no annual fee is promised. Still others advertise free goods or services, low minimum payments, frequent flyer miles, cash back, special member privileges, and contributions to schools or favorite charities. These offers, however, never discuss the downside of a new card or the potential risks.

The terms offered may also be confusing, misleading, or downright deceptive. Many cards fail to provide understandable information concerning late payment fees, penalty interest rates if you miss a payment, the nature of a temporary or variable interest rate, billing methods, and the consequences of making minimum payments. Often the relevant information is provided only after you apply for the card and then only in small print. And most lenders retain the right to change credit card terms, including the interest rate, at their discretion.

THINGS TO THINK ABOUT
BEFORE YOU TAKE
A NEW CARD

It is difficult to get by in our society without a credit card. Most people need some access to credit when they travel, for transacting business electronically, or to place orders by telephone. Here are some suggestions to keep in mind when reviewing credit card offers.

1. **Avoid accepting too many offers.** There is rarely a good reason to carry more than one or two credit cards. You should be very selective about choosing cards which are best for you. Having too much credit can lead to bad decisions and unmanageable debts.

2. **Remember that lenders are looking for people who will run up big balances, because those consumers pay the most interest.** You may find that credit companies are pursuing you aggressively by mail and phone. You should not view this as a sign that you can afford more credit. The lender may have a marketing profile based on your spending patterns, your credit record, your use of certain services such as home shopping, your magazine subscriptions, or even your zip code, which indicates to them that you are someone who is likely to carry a big credit card balance and pay a good deal of interest.

3. **Interest rate is important, but not the only consideration.** You should always know the interest rate on your cards and should try to keep the rate as low as possible. However, it is rarely a good idea to take a new card solely because of a low rate. The rate only matters if you carry a balance from one month to the next, and a temporarily low rate may encourage you to spend more than you can afford. In addition, the rate can easily change, with or without a reason. Remember that even the best credit card interest rates are relatively high rate credit.

   Additionally, other terms of credit may add to the cost, so that a credit card which appears cheaper is actually more expensive. Annual fees, late charges, membership fees, and the method by which balances accrue can add to the cost of credit.

4. **Beware of temporary "teaser" rates.** A teaser rate is an artificially low initial rate which applies only for a limited time. Most teaser rates are good only for six months or less. After that, the rate automatically goes up. Remember that if you build up a balance over the period of a temporary rate, the much higher permanent rate will apply to your repayment plan. This means that the permanent long term rate on the card is much more important than the temporary rate.

5. **If your rate is variable, understand the basis on which it may change.** Variable interest rates can be very confusing. Some variable rates conceal terms which ensure that your rate will go up steeply over time. Read the credit contract to understand how and when your rate may change.

6. **Be careful about juggling cards to take advantage of teaser rates and balance transfer options.** It takes a great deal of time and effort to juggle cards to take advantage of terms designed to be temporary. Remember that all teaser rate offers are designed to get you locked into the higher rate for the long term, because that is how the lender makes the most money. Even people who do successfully juggle many cards complain that use of numerous cards has a long-term negative impact on their credit record.

7. **Investigate terms related to late payment charges and penalty rates of interest.** Many credit card contracts, including those which advertise low permanent rates have provisions in the small print to increase your rate of interest if you make even a single late payment. This may be on top of late charges or other penalties. You should review your contract to see if such terms apply. If you are having financial problems, these terms are very important in deciding whether the card makes sense, because late charges and penalty interest rates can get you in further over your head. Even if you are not having financial problems, these terms may become important, because they apply equally to accidental late payments.

8. **Learn your credit card's billing method.** It is important to understand how you will be billed. If interest will apply from the date of your purchase without a grace period, a low rate may actually be higher than it looks. If you intend to pay off the balance in full each month, terms of the grace period are important. You need to understand how the grace period works and remember that many lenders do not mail bills until late in the grace period. Your payment may be due quite soon after you receive the bill in order to avoid additional accumulation of interest.

9. **Always read both the disclosures and the credit contract.** You will find disclosures about the terms of a credit card offer, usually in small print on the reverse or at the bottom of the offer. Review these carefully. However, the law does not require that all

relevant information be disclosed. For this reason, you must also read your credit contract, which comes with the card. This will include terms such as late payment fees, default rates of interest, and a description of the billing method. Since it may take a business or accounting degree to understand some of the terms, you have several choices if you do not understand. You can call the lender for an explanation. Or better yet, refuse credit with too many complex provisions, because those terms are likely to be designed to work to your disadvantage.

Avoid accepting too many credit card offers. The interest due when you carry big credit card balances can create an ever expanding hole in your budget.

UNDERSTANDING ALTERNATIVE TYPES OF CREDIT CARDS

Secured vs. Unsecured Credit Cards. Most credit cards are unsecured. However, there are three ways in which some credit card lenders take collateral. In general, all things being equal, you should seek and use credit cards which are unsecured in preference to those that are secured. Since interest rates on secured cards are typically just as high as those on unsecured cards, the choice in favor of unsecured cards should be clear.

Some credit card lenders, usually store credit such as Sears, claim to take collateral in items purchased with their card. This means that if you have problems making payments, those lenders may threaten to repossess property bought with the card. (In addition, personal property collateral may affect your rights if you later need to file bankruptcy.) As discussed in Chapter Eighteen, most threats to repossess personal property are not carried out. Nevertheless, it is a good idea to know whether the security interest exists. If it does, use an unsecured card in preference to the secured card whenever possible.

Another type of secured credit card involves card balances secured by a bank deposit. The card allows you a credit limit up to the amount you have on deposit in a particular bank account. If you can't make the payments, you lose the money in the account.

These cards are usually marketed as a good way to reestablish credit if you have had financial problems. They may be useful to establish that you can make regular monthly payments on a credit card after you have had trouble in the past. However, since almost everyone now gets unsecured credit card offers even after previous financial problems, there is less reason to consider allowing a creditor to use your bank deposits as collateral. It is preferable not to tie up your bank account, or to pay interest to a lender for the privilege of establishing that you can afford to make payments.

Finally, there are increasing opportunities to obtain credit cards in connection with a home equity line of credit. Each time you use the card, the balance is secured against your home. In many cases these are sold by home improvement contractors as a good way to pay for home improvements. Sometimes the initial amount advanced on such a card is as much or more than your credit limit.

Home secured credit cards are almost always a bad idea. You should always seek to avoid using high rate credit secured by your home, because the potential consequence of nonpayment if you have financial problems is loss of your family's shelter by foreclosure. And always beware of home improvement contractors offering credit. Often, they do not act in your best interest. You will likely do better if you seek a more traditional home equity credit line from a bank at a lower rate of interest. Review Chapters Three and Four of this book for more information on lending schemes which can get you into trouble and the pitfalls of home equity credit.

Cashed Check Loans. Another credit offer to avoid takes the form of a check mailed to your home. Cashing the check results in acceptance of high interest rate credit. Use of such a check reduces your flexibility and saddles you with a big balance on a new account right from the start. You are better served by finding a reasonable credit card offer and using the new card carefully. If you need a large lump sum, try to get a bank loan in preference to cashing a check on your credit card.

Credit Cards vs. Debit Cards. Many banks have begun issuing cards which allow consumers to have money taken directly from their accounts to pay charges made with the card. These cards are known as "debit cards." Often, these cards look similar to a more traditional ATM machine card (and use as an ATM card continues to be one of the important functions a debit card fills). However, merchants accept these cards, like credit cards, to pay for goods or services. Instead of sending you a bill, the bank instead takes the money to pay the merchant directly from your account.

There are advantages and disadvantages to these cards which you should evaluate in making your decision about whether and how to use them. For some people it is an advantage to have money to pay debts taken directly from their account, because they do not have to write checks. Automatic debiting from a bank account reduces the risk of running up a big unpaid balance on a credit card.

However, there are also a number of reasons not to use debit cards except at ATMs. For one, the payment flexibility available on a credit card is lost when using debit cards. The option of slower repayment with interest is not available with a debit card. This option may be necessary on a tight budget to make sure that your most pressing debts are paid first.

Second, the right you have to dispute a charge on your credit card bill (as discussed below) is not available on a debit card. For example, if you purchased a vacuum cleaner from a nearby store with your credit card and it breaks during the first week of use and the merchant refuses to fix it, you may dispute the charge for the vacuum on your credit card bill. There are NO similar rights available when you use your debit card to purchase goods or services.

Third, your responsibility for losses that may result if the card is lost or stolen is generally much greater for a debit card than for a credit card. As discussed below, your responsibility for unauthorized credit card charges is limited to $50. If money is taken from your bank account through your debit card, you could be responsible for as much as $500 of the losses unless you notify the bank within two days from the time the card is taken, and even then you have to be able to show that the losses were a result of an "unauthorized transfer." This may be a subject of some dispute with the bank. For example, it is NOT considered an unauthorized transfer if the money was withdrawn from your account by someone you know, to whom you had previously lent your card and provided them with your PIN (Personal Identification Number), even if this time this person took your card and used it without your permission.

Both VISA and MasterCard have policies that should limit your debit card losses in most situations to $50. However, many banks are not familiar with these policies, and as they are not formal laws, they are difficult to enforce.

Finally, the consequences of an unauthorized withdrawal from your bank account through your debit card may be worse than an unauthorized charge on your credit card. Since the money to pay the debit comes directly out of your bank account, you may temporarily or permanently lose use of that money — effective immediately. Even if the money is later restored to your account, temporary loss may mean that you cannot pay your bills, or meet other pressing needs. Banks may advance funds from a line of credit to cover withdrawals or debits through your debit card, which you will owe unless you can show the withdrawals or debits they were the result of an unauthorized transfer.

AVOIDING
CREDIT CARD PROBLEMS

Credit card debts can spiral out of control. If you have accepted a credit card and are using it, here are some ways to protect yourself from getting in over your head.

1. **It is important not to use credit cards to finance an unaffordable lifestyle.** If you find that you are constantly using your card without the ability to pay the resulting bill in full each month, you need to consider whether you are using your cards to make an unreasonable budget plan work. No one can live forever by borrowing without a plan to pay off the resulting debts.

2. **If you get into financial trouble, do not make it worse by using credit cards to make ends meet.** If you find that you are using credit cards to get through a period of financial difficulty, consider the likelihood that additional credit will only make things worse. For example, if you use cash advances on your credit card to pay bills, the interest due will only add to your debt burden sooner rather than later. Rather than use credit cards in periods of financial trouble, consider other options discussed throughout this book.

3. **Don't get hooked on minimum payments.** In most cases, the

credit card lender will offer an optional "minimum payment" in their monthly billing. If you pay only the minimum, chances are that you will not be paying down your debt, or that you will be paying it off very slowly. Especially if you are also making new purchases every month, the consequence of making minimum payments is that your debt will grow. This means that your monthly interest obligations will increase and lower the amount of money you have in the monthly budget for necessities.

In addition, lenders reserve the right to increase the minimum payment at their option. This means that you can budget for a $50 minimum payment only to find out that the new minimum payment of $100 applies.

Making the minimum allowable payments on your credit cards will barely pay down the balance even if you make no new purchases. If you get in over your head, the credit card lender may increase the minimum payment and create a spiral of financial problems.

---

4. **Don't run up the balance in reliance on a temporary "teaser" interest rate.** As discussed above, money borrowed during a temporary rate period of six percent, is likely to be paid back at a much higher permanent rate of fifteen percent or more.
5. **If you can afford to do so consistently with your budget plan, make your credit card payments on time.** Be careful to avoid late payment charges and penalty rates if you can do so without endangering your ability to keep up with higher priority debts. Bad problems get worse fast when you have a new higher interest rate and late charge to pay during a time of financial difficulty.

Most lenders will waive a late payment charge or default rates of interest one time only. It is worth calling to ask for a waiver if you make a late payment accidentally or with a good excuse.

6. **Avoid the special services, programs, and goods which credit card lenders offer to bill to their cards.** You are likely to receive numerous advertisements from your credit card lender. Most of the special services such as credit card fraud protection plans, credit record protection, travel clubs, life insurance, and other similar offers are a bad deal. Products offered are generally overpriced. It is best to throw out advertisements, or at a minimum, to read them with a high degree of caution.

7. **Beware of unsolicited increases by a credit card lender to your credit card limit.** Some lenders increase your credit limit even when you have not asked for more credit. It is easy to assume that this means that the lender thinks you can afford more credit. In fact, the opposite may be true. Lenders generally increase the limit for consumers that they think will carry a bigger balance and pay more interest. You need to evaluate whether you can afford more credit based on your individual circumstances.

CREDIT CARD DISPUTES

There are two types of credit card disputes which commonly arise. The first involves unauthorized use of your card. When someone steals, borrows or otherwise uses your card or card number without permission. These problems have increased in frequency as many more businesses accept credit card transactions by telephone and on the Internet.

Under the law, your liability for unauthorized use of your credit card is limited to $50. This means that if someone steals your card, for example, your credit card lender can charge you a maximum of $50 no matter how much the thief has charged on your card. (As discussed above, this limit may not apply to a "debit" card.)

As soon as you know of the unauthorized use of your credit card, you should call the lender to make a report. If you call before unauthorized charges are incurred, you cannot be charged even $50, since the lender can take steps to cancel your card and send you a new one. If a charge unexpectedly appears on your bill for something you did not authorize, you can also use your right to dispute the charge which is discussed below.

The second type of billing dispute which arises involves disputes about how much you owe. A merchant may have overcharged you on the card, charged you for products or work you did not receive, or may process a transaction in error.

The law provides a basis to dispute these incorrect bills. Information about how to raise a dispute appears on the back of each bill — including the mailing address to use. In summary, you must raise a dispute in writing within sixty days of the first bill with the improper charge. You must include the following information:

- Your name and account number;
- The dollar amount you dispute;
- A statement of the reason for your dispute.

Some examples of reasons for dispute are:

- I did not authorize this charge;
- I did not receive the goods I ordered;
- I returned the goods I ordered because they were defective, but did not get a credit;
- The merchant sent me the wrong goods;
- The merchant did not complete the services I contracted for or performed them incompletely;
- The merchant billed me for $100 when I agreed to pay $10;
- I canceled the contract with the merchant or contractor, before work was performed;
- Although I agreed to buy something from this merchant, I did not authorize her to bill my account.

Your dispute rights also apply to certain purchases on credit card, if you have problems with the quality of the goods or services you purchased. These apply whenever the credit card lender owns the business from which you made the purchase, or advertises the goods or services you purchased. In addition, this special right applies when the goods cost more than $50 and are purchased in your home state or within 100 miles of your mailing address. In order to dispute a charge for goods or services based on quality, you must have first made a good faith effort to resolve the issue with the merchant directly. Written evidence of your good faith efforts is helpful in this circumstance. For example, enclose a letter which you wrote directly to the merchant to outline your problem with the quality of the goods.

An example of a dispute letter appears below. If appropriate, send backup documentation such as a cancellation letter or a letter explaining the problem to the merchant.

Once you have raised a dispute, the credit card company is required to investigate and report back to you in writing. In many cases, the charge will be canceled. Often a merchant whose billing is challenged will back off rather than risk losing the privilege of accepting business by credit card. Interest associated with a successfully disputed debt must also be canceled.

Until the dispute is resolved, you need not pay the disputed portion of your bill. However, you must make a payment to cover any undisputed amount. Of course, the credit card company cannot report you as delinquent with respect to the disputed amount, but may do so if part of your debt is undisputed and you do not make necessary payments.

When you raise a written dispute with a credit card lender about a charge, the lender is required to investigate. You need not pay the disputed portion of the bill during the investigation.

If your dispute is not resolved favorably to you, you may nevertheless have legal rights. Refer to Chapter Nine for more information.

Sample Credit Card Dispute Letter

Joe Consumer
111 Park Street
Fairfield, CT 08341

DNC Credit Co.
P.O. Box 2400
Tulsa Oklahoma 74121
[the actual address you need to use appears on the back of the credit card bill you are disputing in a section called "Billing Rights Summary"]

Dear DNC Credit Co.:

My name is Joe Consumer. My account number is 272222272. I am disputing a charge on the bill you mailed on June 5, 1999. That bill includes a charge in the amount of $272.00 to Main Street Jewelers. This amount is in error.

In April of this year I took a watch to Main Street Jewelers to be repaired. They estimated that the work would cost $40. I told them since the watch was only worth $100 not to do any work in excess of $40. When they called to say the repairs were completed, they told me that the bill was $272.00. I did not agree to pay this amount and they have charged my account without my authorization. In addition, they have not returned the watch to me.

I have contacted Main Street Jewelers by telephone, in person, and by the enclosed letter in order to try to resolve the dispute. They have not agreed to withdraw the charge.

Please investigate this dispute and provide me with a written statement of the outcome. Thank you for your time and attention to this matter.

Very truly yours,

Joe Consumer

WHAT TO DO IF YOU GET BEHIND ON CREDIT CARD DEBTS

Unmanageable credit card debts can be the first sign of serious financial problems. If you have been scraping by and making minimum payments for several months, a lender's decision to raise your monthly minimum payment can precipitate a financial crisis. If you find that you cannot afford to make payments on your credit cards within your monthly budget, it is time to reevaluate your plan for managing debts as set out in the first five chapters of this book. A brief review of some key strategies is included here.

If you cannot pay your higher priority debts. If your inability to pay your credit card debts is part of a larger financial problem which affects your home, your car, and your high-priority debts, remember that it is necessary to deal with the other problems first. Don't let yourself be pressured into keeping up with credit card payments at the risk of losing a home or a car.

Credit card lenders are notorious for using aggressive debt collection agencies to collect from consumers with high pressure tactics. More recently, some debt collectors have discovered that they catch more flies with honey, and have tried to convince people to repay unaffordable debts by sweet talking them. Whether a collectors' strategy is abusive or polite (or a mix of both), don't let them convince you to use money set aside in your budget for more pressing debts to make credit card payments.

There are many more threats of lawsuits by credit card lenders than there are actual cases filed. Don't assume that a credit card lender will file a lawsuit because of a threat. As discussed in Chapters Six and Eight, even if a case is filed, there may be little that the lender can do to hurt you.

Rather than jeopardize your ability to pay higher priority debts, consider sending your credit card lenders a "cease" letter as discussed in Chapter Six. You can use the letter as an opportunity to explain why you cannot afford to pay and to promise to contact them as soon as your situation changes.

If a credit card lender does pursue a lawsuit. You cannot prevent a credit card lender from pursuing a lawsuit if it so chooses. If a lawsuit is commenced and you have a legal defense, you should consider raising it in court as discussed in Chapter Nine. (If you have no defense, if may make little sense to appear in court to contest the case.)

Don't assume that a credit card lender

will pursue a lawsuit.

But if you are sued, you need to be aware

of the ways a court judgment can be used

to seize property or garnish your wages.

If you fail to appear (or if you do appear and lose) a judgment will normally be entered by the court. You should determine whether the judgment can be used against you by the creditor to seize property or garnish your wages. Since the answer to this question depends on your state's law, this may be a good time to see a lawyer. If you are left with no other choice and cannot make affordable arrangements to pay the debt, you may need to consider bankruptcy. More about bankruptcy is found in Chapter Twenty.

If you get behind, but can afford to pay something less than the full amount of your credit card debts. You may find that with careful budgeting in a time of financial problems, you can afford to pay all of your higher priority debts and still have something left over to pay your credit cards. If the amount left over is enough to pay some, but not all, of your monthly credit card obligations, try one or more of the following approaches:

- **Contact each credit card lender and try to make a payment arrangement which fits your budget.** Explain your circumstances, but do not let the lender persuade you to pay more than you can afford. An unworkable payment plan is worse than no payment plan at all. It is doomed to fail, and it may be the only chance the lender will give you.
- **Make a decision about whether to focus your efforts on one card to maintain good credit with that lender, or whether to spread your resources to try to stay current on all of your cards.** Unless you see a big financial turnaround in your future, it is probably better to accept the fact that you will have some defaults, than to spread your resources too thin and to risk failing with every credit card lender.
- **Don't throw good money after bad.** You won't be doing your family any favors if you are unrealistic about your budget and try to juggle too many debts. An unworkable plan is bound to go down the drain in the long term. A default on an $800 balance in three months is not significantly better for your credit record than a default on $1000 today. What you will have lost is several hundred dollars which might otherwise have been used for more pressing needs.
- **Refinancing deals offering lower total monthly payments should be approached with caution.** Some refinancing and debt consolidation deals which seem like they will lower your total monthly debt payments are actually quite costly. If you secure your credit card debts with a home mortgage, you may lose your home. Refinancing options are discussed in Chapter Four.

- **Don't let history repeat itself.** If you get your credit card problems under control, don't let the problem crop up again. Be careful that you do not finance an unaffordable lifestyle with credit. And if you do choose to refinance your credit card debt, don't run up your balances all over again. The problem will only be worse the next time around.

Saving Your Home: An Overview

- *Twelve Tips for Dealing with Mortgage Problems and Foreclosure*
- *How to Use This Book to Defend Your Home*
- *How Foreclosures Work*

TWELVE TIPS FOR DEALING WITH MORTGAGE PROBLEMS AND FORECLOSURE

Potential loss of your home is the single most urgent problem you may face if you are having financial difficulties. For many people, foreclosure means not only loss of shelter, but also loss of many years investment to create home equity and a livable family environment. For this reason, you will almost always want to deal with a foreclosure problem as your highest priority if you are having financial problems and you own a home. (Evictions from a rented home or apartment are discussed in Chapter Fifteen.)

Here are twelve important tips for preventing foreclosures:

1. Reexamine Your Budget. Can You Cut Expenses or Increase Income If It Means Saving Your Home? If you are facing foreclosure, make a special effort to eliminate unnecessary expenses. Food, mortgage payments, utilities, essential transportation and unavoidable health related expenses should be your highest priorities, but even these essential expenses can be examined to see if reductions are possible. On the other side of the budget, look at whether there are ways to increase your income, including loans from pension plans, food stamps, fuel assistance, property tax abatements and unemployment or disability income. See Chapter Two.

2. Make Timely Home Mortgage Payments, If Possible. If you cannot pay all of your bills, you should make mortgage payments first after food and utilities. Mortgage payments are high-priority debts because the mortgage company has the right to foreclose and take your home while other creditors generally do not.

3. If You Fall Behind on Your Mortgage and the Creditor Returns Your Partial Payments, Save As Much Of This Money As Possible Each Month Toward Your Mortgage. When you fall behind on payments, the mortgage company has the right to refuse partial payment. If you can afford partial payments, but the mortgage company refuses to take them, the money should be put aside and not used to pay other bills. The money that is set aside will help you negotiate with the mortgage company later, and even if nothing can be done to save your home, you will have some money saved for moving expenses.

4. Resolve Any Disputes You Have Concerning the Amount Due. Use Legal Assistance If Necessary. Some foreclosures occur because of mistakes made by the mortgage company. When you disagree with the amount the mortgage company says you owe, you should immediately try to address the problem by contacting the mortgage company. Provide the documentation they request and keep copies for yourself. If you are not satisfied with the result (or if there is an unreasonable delay), you may want to get legal assistance. If you do so, you may be surprised to find that you have significant legal defenses to repayment of your mortgage, especially if you have a mortgage with high interest rates or unusual terms. See Chapter Fourteen.

5. Ask the Mortgage Company Whether It Will Agree to a Temporary or Permanent Change to Your Mortgage Terms (Called a "Workout"). A workout is often the best solution to your financial difficulties because it allows you to resume your mortgage payments. There are many different types of workouts, including repayment agreements (getting caught up over time) and loan modifications (changes to loan terms which do not change the total debt, but which reduce monthly payments). The mortgage company will ask you to send them documents which set out your monthly income and expenses. They will also request supporting information like recent tax returns. Not all workout proposals will be accepted. For a discussion of how to arrange a workout, see Chapter Twelve.

6. Evaluate Your Refinancing Options. Particularly if you have equity in your home, refinancing may be an option to avoid foreclosure. There are some loan programs, including reverse mortgages for older homeowners, which will reduce or eliminate your monthly payments. Refinancing options should be evaluated carefully, possibly with professional assistance. Avoid high rate refinancing loans and do not consolidate other substantial debts with your existing mortgage. These choices will only make your problems worse in the long-term. See Chapter Four.

7. Consider Selling Your House Before Foreclosure. It is a good idea to list your home for sale if you are behind on your mortgage. This is true even when you are pursuing other options. The reason to consider a sale is that the foreclosure process is not likely to bring the best possible price for your home. You will almost always get a better price if you sell your home on the open market instead of letting it go to foreclosure. If you owe more to the mortgage company than you can get from a buyer, you will need to get the mortgage company's permission to sell at that lower price.

8. Keep Track of Foreclosure Deadlines. If there is a court case, you will want to take steps to prevent the foreclosure before the court takes final action. You will *always* want to take steps to prevent foreclosure before a foreclosure sale is held. Once the sale is held, you will no longer own the property and in most states, it is impossible to keep your home. If you have applied to the mortgage company for a workout, do not let them wait until the last minute to give you an answer. Waiting too long prevents you from examining your other options. If you are considering getting help from a lawyer or nonprofit counselor, do so as far in advance of the sale as possible so that you can get complete advice.

9. If You Are Unable to Arrange a Workout or Other Satisfactory Solution, Consider Getting Legal Help to

Prevent the Foreclosure. Chapter 13 bankruptcy is one of several legal options you have which may solve a foreclosure problem. (Chapter 7 bankruptcy will delay but not prevent a foreclosure.) If you decide to obtain legal help, do it early so that the lawyer will have enough time to advise you properly. When selecting an attorney, be careful to find someone you trust even if the fee is slightly higher. The best way to do this is through recommendations from friends or family. If no recommendation is available, contact the Lawyer Referral Service of your local bar association and ask for a list of attorneys who handle foreclosure defense and bankruptcy.

10. Be Realistic About What Is Possible. If you are unable to afford your home over the long-term, your best option may be to sell it. If you have no equity in the house, you may choose to walk away from it by giving it back to the mortgage company. You should not waste money which you can use to move by trying to salvage an impossible situation.

Avoid anyone who reads advertising
about your foreclosure sale and offers
to help you with your foreclosure problem.

---

11. Avoid Foreclosure Scams. By law, foreclosure of your home will be advertised to the public. Unfortunately, there are many people who offer help to people facing foreclosure in order to rip them off. You should avoid sale/leaseback schemes and high rate loans which are offered as a way out of foreclosure. They will make things worse. Requests for high fees or for money to pay the mortgage (payable to someone other than the mortgage company) are also indications of scams. In addition, offers of new mortgages as a way out of foreclosure can lead to disastrous deals which will make your situation impossible to resolve. If you do sign a mortgage under pressure of foreclosure, remember that you have three business days to cancel.

12. Get Counseling Help. The foreclosure process can be very complicated. In most communities, there are *nonprofit* counselors who may be able to help you avoid foreclosure. If you cannot afford or cannot find a lawyer, nonprofit counseling may be a good alternative. However, nonprofit foreclosure counselors are not always easy to find. You can call a local nonprofit housing organization and ask if they do foreclosure counseling. You can also try to get a referral from your mortgage company or local officials. If someone offers to help, make sure you are dealing with a legitimate nonprofit with experience in default and delinquency counseling.

HOW TO USE THIS BOOK
TO PROTECT YOUR HOME

The next three chapters provide a variety of strategies you can use to protect your home from foreclosure. In cases where foreclosure prevention is not possible, the chapters also list some steps you can take to recover your equity, or to minimize the amount still owed to the lender after the foreclosure.

This chapter provides an overview of what is in those other chapters and gives you some general information about how foreclosures work. You should first read this chapter, and then read the relevant portions of the other three chapters.

Chapter Twelve: Workouts. Most foreclosures are straightforward. They occur because homeowners sometimes can't keep up payments on their mortgage loans when they are facing financial problems. In most cases, the homeowners agree that they owe the money. What they need is a short-term strategy to prevent a foreclosure sale of the property and a long-term strategy for paying the debt. Chapter Twelve discusses ways to establish a voluntary agreement to repay your mortgage company. This is called a workout. When you agree that you owe money and that you have no defenses to repayment, a workout is usually the first choice for addressing a foreclosure problem.

Chapter Thirteen: The Legal Process of Foreclosure. Foreclosure is a legal process with a variety of laws governing the rights of homeowners and lenders. Chapter Thirteen discusses your rights in the legal process of foreclosure, including the right to use bankruptcy to force a lender to accept payments over time and in some case to reduce or restructure the amount you owe.

Chapter Fourteen: Defenses to Foreclosures In Special Situations. There are some mortgages which involve special circumstances which create special issues in the foreclosure process. Chapter Fourteen provides an overview of special consumer issues in ten situations:

1. FHA and HUD guaranteed mortgages;
2. VA guaranteed mortgages;
3. Farmers Home (FmHA) mortgages;
4. Special state mortgage assistance programs and moratoriums on foreclosures;
5. Mortgages not used to purchase the home;
6. Mortgages resulting from a home improvement contract (where the seller's misconduct can be raised as a defense on the loan);
7. Mortgages on terms that are unfair or oppressive;
8. Foreclosures involving condominiums;
9. Mobile home foreclosures; and
10. Where the loan was not secured by a mortgage, but where the creditor is foreclosing based on a court judgment or other lien.

If a home foreclosure involves one or more of those ten situations, there are specific rights and foreclosure prevention strategies which apply. The "special" strategies should be considered first, before considering the general strategies for dealing with straightforward foreclosures which are described in Chapters Twelve and Thirteen.

Using Multiple Strategies. You will often want to think about more than one strategy to prevent foreclosure of your home. Sometimes, several strategies can be used together at the same time. In other cases you may want to try one course of action and switch to another only if the first strategy does not work.

Foreclosure can be very complicated. It is usually a good idea to get some help from a lawyer or a nonprofit counselor when deciding on the best foreclosure prevention strategy.

HOW FORECLOSURES WORK

When reviewing any of the next three chapters, it is useful to have a general understanding of how the foreclosure process works and to know how imminent a foreclosure is for your home. For more information, see National Consumer Law Center, *Repossessions and Foreclosures* Ch. 13 (3d ed. 1995 and Supp.).

Notice of Foreclosure. In every state, you will be entitled to some notice of a pending foreclosure on your home. However, the type, amount and timing of required notices varies considerably. You cannot necessarily rely on the lender to send notices, and, because of problems with mail delivery, you may not receive them. For this reason, if you know you are behind on your mortgage payments, you will need to stay on top of things by reading any notices you do receive carefully, by keeping track of deadlines, and by contacting the lender or the lender's attorney at regular intervals, if necessary, to get information about what is going on.

In addition, since many foreclosure notices are sent by certified or registered mail, you should make sure to pick up these notices from the post office. Not knowing what is in a notice does *not* protect you. You can only be hurt by not knowing what is going on.

Some of the typical types of notices which may be received if foreclosure is pending are discussed here. However, remember that each state has different procedures.

Notice of Default. You will almost always get a notice from the lender which says that you have fallen behind on your payments. This is usually called "notice of default" or "notice of delinquency." It may look like any other collection letter.

This notice will usually tell you how many payments you are behind, and it will sometimes include the exact amount of money you need to catch up. This amount is often called "the arrears." In some states, if you offer to pay the total amount of the arrears at this stage, the lender must accept the payment. Even if the law does not require it, almost all lenders will be very happy to take your full payment at this point if you have it. Partial payments are often rejected.

You should treat the notice of default as an important warning that there is a problem. It will be easier to address the problem if you begin looking for a solution at this early point.

Notice of Acceleration. When your mortgage is behind, lenders in most states must take a legal step known as "acceleration" before they can foreclose on your home. Acceleration means that you are far enough behind on your mortgage that the law allows the lender to treat the whole loan balance as due right away. In many states, and under some mortgage contracts, the lender must give you notice when this occurs. The notice will typically say that the whole balance (sometimes with the actual amount written into the notice) is due and payable immediately.

Receipt of a notice of acceleration is a good indication that the foreclosure process is moving quickly. This letter, if you receive it, should therefore serve as an important warning that you must put a strategy in place to prevent foreclosure or give up your home.

Court Notices. As discussed below, not every state requires a court action to foreclose a mortgage. However, if you are in a state which requires a court action, you will receive a summons or a similar notice (usually brought to the house by a sheriff, constable, marshal or process server).

This notice gives you a certain period of time to respond to the foreclosure lawsuit and to raise your defenses if you have any. You should take this deadline seriously. If you do not respond, the court will enter a foreclosure judgment against you. Although this is not the end of the process, you lose important legal protections once a court judgment is entered. Most important, you lose the right to raise defenses in most cases. For this reason, receipt of a summons or other court papers is always a good time to review your legal options and to see a lawyer if possible.

Notice of sale is generally sent *very late*
in the foreclosure process.
It usually represents your last
chance to do something about foreclosure.

Notice of Sale. In all states, lenders are required to send you a notice of the date and time intended for sale of your property. The sale date is the most important deadline in the foreclosure process because the sale will cut off all of your rights as owner. Sale of the property will also generally cut off your opportunity to obtain a workout or to use the bankruptcy process to help prevent foreclosure.

Notices After Foreclosure. Once a foreclosure sale is completed, you may receive a variety of different types of notices. These may include notice of the outcome of sale (who bought the property and for how much), eviction notices and court papers related to eviction.

If the property was sold for more than the lender was owed, you may be entitled to receive some money back. In this situation, when you move, you should let the mortgage company know your new address, since they will need to find you to pay you your share of the foreclosure sale receipts.

On the other hand, if the property was sold for less than the lender was owed, you may remain responsible for the balance. This is usually called the "deficiency." You may also receive a variety of notices about the deficiency including collection letters and court papers.

It is important to remember that after a foreclosure sale, it is rare that you can do much to recover your home. However, in a few states you retain the right to redeem the property from foreclosure (discussed below). In addition, occasionally you can challenge the procedures under which the sale was held and, in extreme circumstances, have the sale declared invalid. Finally, you can protect your right to your fair share of the sale proceeds, if the sale was for more than the amount owed on any liens on the property.

How Long Does Foreclosure Take? The length of time you have before your property is sold varies a great deal from state to state. The amount of time also varies because some lenders move more quickly than others. Depending on these factors, together with any response you put in place, foreclosure can be as quick as three months from the time you default to as long as a full year or more. You should check local practice and stay on top of any information you receive in foreclosure-related notices, as discussed above.

Whatever the length of time for foreclosure in your situation, your rule for action should always be the same. That is — *it is always better to act sooner rather than later.*

Delays can lead to a serious loss of legal rights. This will reduce your options for preventing foreclosure. Although delaying a sale will always help you, delay in taking action to prevent the sale will not. You will need both a short-term strategy to evaluate your options and a long-term strategy to prevent the foreclosure.

How a Lender Gets Permission to Foreclose. Foreclosure procedures vary from state to state. The procedures are established by state laws and by local practice. In some states, foreclosures involve court proceedings. In these states, the lender first files suit in a court — usually in the county where the property is located. Unless you successfully contest the foreclosure in court, a judgment is entered for the lender. This gives the lender permission to hold a foreclosure sale unless you can work out an agreement or take some other action (such as bankruptcy) to prevent it.

Other states have "nonjudicial foreclosures." In those states, lenders foreclose without a court action and without official permission to go forward. They advertise the home for sale, using a legal notice in a newspaper. If you want to contest this type of foreclosure, you must file a lawsuit and ask the court to stop the sale. You may have to file a bond to protect the lender.

Some states allow both types of foreclosure. Practicality and local custom usually dictate a lender's choice of one type over the other.

The Right to Cure and the Right to Redeem. Many states allow you a second chance. In these states you can avoid foreclosure by "curing" the default. Usually this means getting caught up on the arrears (missed payments together with foreclosure fees and costs). Occasionally, lenders claim that you breached your obligations in some other way, such as failing to keep the property insured. These defaults can also be "cured" by taking care of the problem.

You are also allowed to "redeem" the home up to the time of a foreclosure sale. To redeem, you must pay off the full amount of the loan in one payment plus the lender's foreclosure fees and costs. That is, instead of just catching up on the delinquent payments, you have to pay the whole remainder of the mortgage. Since most people don't have enough cash, the most common method of redemption is taking out a new loan to pay off the existing lender (refinancing).

Some states have both a right to redeem and a right to cure. Many states place conditions on using these rights. You will need to check the law in your state. However, even in states which do not allow you to redeem or cure, many lenders will agree to accept redemptions or cures voluntarily.

A handful of states allow you to redeem the property by paying the full amount owed shortly after the foreclosure sale is completed. You will also have to pay any costs of sale. The time period allowed in these states ranges from a few days to a year.

Additionally, you have bankruptcy rights under federal (national) law, rather than state law. You always have a right to redeem and a right to cure in bankruptcy before a foreclosure sale is completed. Your bankruptcy rights trump any limitation on the right to redeem or cure under the law in your state. In fact, as discussed in Chapters Thirteen and Twenty, the bankruptcy right to cure in a chapter 13 case includes a right to pay back any amount in default in installments over a period of time. This can be as long as three to five years. This means that if you are behind, you can use chapter 13 bankruptcy to get caught up over a manageable period of time, even if your state's law would not allow it.

As you can see, these issues can be complicated. Consider seeking out a lawyer or nonprofit foreclosure counselor to help you.

The Foreclosure Sale. Generally, a foreclosure sale is a poorly advertised and poorly attended auction. In many cases, no one attends except the foreclosing lender, who bids no more than the balance of the debt, and maybe significantly less. Depending on state law, the auctioneer might be a sheriff or other court official. In other states, usually where there is "nonjudicial foreclosure," the auction is conducted by a lawyer or an auctioneer hired by the lender. Although you can attend the auction and bid on the property, every state has rules about making a down payment at the auction and paying any balance in a limited period of time.

Once the sale is held, you should ask for information about who bought the property and the price. This will help you determine if you are owed money from the sale or if you are likely to face a deficiency claim. Unless you ask, you may not receive this information.

The Mortgage Deficiency. If the sale does not bring in enough to pay off the lender, in many states the lender can seek a "deficiency." A deficiency is the remainder due on the loan plus costs, minus the amount the lender was paid from the sale proceeds. Some state laws prevent lenders from seeking this deficiency or place certain conditions on lenders before they can seek the deficiency. If lenders can collect a deficiency under your state's law, the deficiency will be an unsecured debt (unless the lender has collateral other than the foreclosed home.) You may be sued in court and you will have the right to defend against the lawsuit. For a discussion of dealing with collection lawsuits, see Chapter Eight.

– 12 –

Mortgage Workouts

- *When You Should and Should Not Negotiate a Workout Agreement*
- *How to Prepare for the Negotiation, How to Start the Process, What to Ask For, And What It will Cost You*
- *What to Do If the Workout Negotiation Is Not Going Well*
- *Tax and Credit Consequences of Workout Plans*

MORTGAGE LENDERS NOW WILLING TO NEGOTIATE

In the past several years it has become easier to negotiate pre-foreclosure "workout" agreements. A workout is any agreement between you and the lender which changes how you pay your mortgage delinquency or otherwise prevents foreclosure.

Many lenders now realize it is better for them to accept what you can afford to pay than to foreclose on your home.

In the past, consumers were often frustrated in attempting to work out a deal with a mortgage lender when they fell behind in their payments. In many cases, it was impossible to determine who in the lender's office to contact to discuss a workout. When a consumer did find the appropriate person, that person generally had little flexibility to consider postponing a foreclosure or arranging reasonable workout terms. While borrowers with huge debts, such as Donald Trump, were getting significant concessions, individual homeowners with small mortgages were generally told that immediate full payment with fees and costs was necessary.

More recently, however, the potential for reasonable agreements with reputable lenders, while still imperfect, has begun to improve. To a large extent, this improvement is because lenders are realizing that large numbers of foreclosures on small properties is not in their self-interest.

After a glut of foreclosures in the late 1980's and early 1990's, lenders were left with the problem of managing large numbers of deteriorating properties. Although some foreclosures were very profitable because of the potential for the lender to resell property bought cheaply at foreclosure at full fair market value, large portfolios of foreclosed property generally lost money. For these reasons, most lenders will now talk to anyone, including owners of small properties, about agreements to avoid foreclosure.

THE IMPORTANCE OF
GETTING HELP

In most cases (as long as the potential pitfalls discussed below are avoided), it can't hurt to try to arrange a workout on your own. If you have a good idea of what you want, an ability to work with numbers, and an aggressive approach, good results are possible.

However, arranging workouts is a tricky business. Too often, the lender will have far more information than you about available options. The lender may push you to choose an option which is not what you want or which is really too expensive for your family to afford. For this reason it is a good idea to try to find a nonprofit counselor or a lawyer who has experience with mortgage workouts to help you through the process. You may be able to find a nearby HUD-approved counseling agency with experience doing mortgage loan workouts by calling HUD at 1-800-569-4287 (TDD 1-800-877-8339). Having an advocate will help you get a fair deal by balancing the bargaining power between you and the lender.

If you do try to arrange a workout on your own, you should read the rest of this chapter to get some tips on how to prepare, on what to ask for, and on how to negotiate with a lender. Even if you decide to get help, you should review this chapter carefully to help you understand the workout process.

SHOULD YOU CONSIDER
A WORKOUT, AND, IF SO,
WHEN SHOULD YOU SEEK IT?

For many homeowners facing foreclosure, negotiating a workout is the best strategy for saving their home. But it is not always the best approach for all homeowners, and, even when it is, care must be taken to start negotiations with the lender at the best time. This section provides guidelines to help you decide whether and when to initiate discussions with the lender about a workout agreement.

You Should Determine if You Have Defenses to Repayment. As discussed in Chapter Thirteen, there are some situations in which you have defenses to repayment of a mortgage. You should never agree to repay money which you do not owe unless you can work out a compromise of the amount in dispute or you obtain an agreement to eliminate the inappropriate charges.

In some cases, you may have potential consumer defenses to collection, such as Truth-in-Lending violations, usury, fraud or unfair and deceptive practices. When appropriate, legal claims can be used as bargaining chips for workouts either before or after legal action begins. You should remember, however, that a lender who took advantage of you in making the original loan also may look for ways to take advantage of you in arranging a workout. You should try to obtain a lawyer for help in this process.

Do Not Initiate a Workout When There Are Other Financial Problems Which Are Equally Pressing. A workout does not make sense if you will lose the home anyway because of another mortgage problem which cannot be worked out. You do not want to throw away money on a mortgage workout if you are going to lose your home anyway.

Sometimes, if you have a large number of pressing financial problems, bankruptcy will be a better option than a workout because the bankruptcy process will allow you to deal with all of your financial problems at the same time.

Do Not Initiate a Workout When It is Too Late to Finish the Process Before the Sale. If your foreclosure sale is very soon, a workout process can be risky. Workout negotiations almost always take at least thirty days to complete. If you are within thirty days of a scheduled sale date, always obtain a *written* agreement to postpone the sale as one of the first steps in the workout process. Without such an agreement, you will be better off exercising your bankruptcy rights since you will get the benefit of an automatic stay of the foreclosure sale by filing bankruptcy.

Start Workout Discussions As Early as Possible. In situations other than those described above, a workout is usually a good approach after you default on a home mortgage. Always begin a workout discussion as early as possible after the default. There are five reasons to do so:

1. It is easier to negotiate a workout before you get too far behind in payments.
2. Starting early avoids the difficulty of negotiating at the last minute with a potential foreclosure sale date pending.
3. You will appear more responsible if you try to prevent the problem from getting out of hand.
4. Beginning early avoids potential foreclosure fees and costs, which can be substantial.
5. It is better to begin negotiations before the lender has turned the matter over to a foreclosure lawyer.

As discussed above, when a foreclosure is pending, careful attention must be given to preventing the sale. A foreclosure sale will cut off your ownership, as well as your ability in most cases to cure the default in bankruptcy, and your right to raise most defenses to the validity of the mortgage.

If you are thinking about bankruptcy, workouts should generally be considered prior to filing. Once bankruptcy is filed, most lenders will not negotiate an agreement which goes beyond the best potential result under the bankruptcy law.

TIPS FOR PREPARING
FOR A WORKOUT

Gather Information Before You Contact the Lender. An important key to success is preparation. This begins with understanding your own financial situation, how much you can afford to pay on the mortgage, and what you will need to make things work in the long and short term. Throughout the process, remember that no proposed solution makes sense if you cannot really afford it because you will only fall behind again.

Prepare a Reasonable Budget for the Future. You will need to provide detailed information about your debts, assets, income and expenses. Realistic income and expense projections are particularly important. You will also need to provide documents such as tax returns which illustrate your financial circumstances.

After gathering this information, you and your family should agree on a strategy before you contact the lender. You should base your strategy on a budget for the future which is as realistic as possible. This budget should detail both your income and expenses. More information about budgeting and sample forms are contained in Chapter Two.

Reexamine the Budget to Determine If You Have Any Way to Increase Your Income or Reduce Your Expenses. Ways to reevaluate your budget in times of financial stress are discussed in more detail in Chapter Two. Careful budgeting is important to the workout process for two reasons. First, you may find that you have more (or less) money that you thought to devote to the mortgage. An accurate forecast is essential to make everything work in the long term. Second, if you are living a luxurious lifestyle, the lender is likely to reject your proposal. Since workout agreements are voluntary alternatives to foreclosure, lenders want to see that the homeowners are doing as much as they can to cut back on expenses to concentrate on making the maximum possible mortgage payments.

In setting up your budget, remember your priorities. You should not spend any money, for example, to pay unsecured debts such as credit cards and medical bills at the expense of making your mortgage payments. Although you will need to tell the lender about your credit card bills and other debts, you should inform the lender that these creditors will not be paid in any month before the mortgage payment is made. Only food, utilities, necessary current medical expenses (not past due debts), property insurance, and essential transportation costs should come ahead of the mortgage. Nonessential costs such as private school expenses, charitable contributions, costs of eating out and entertainment are likely to cause a problem when you are seeking a negotiated agreement from a lender.

At the same time, you should look at all your expenses, even those for necessities, to see if there are ways to reduce them. You should also evaluate your income to see if there are options for increasing it.

Develop a Plan to Deal With Other High-Priority Debt Problems. Workouts on one mortgage will have little benefit when there is no plan in place to deal with other mortgages on the same property or to keep utility services flowing for the residence. Similarly, if you need a car to get to work, you will need a plan to pay those bills as well to prevent repossession. On the other hand, if a creditor can do little to hurt you, (such as credit card debts when you have not been sued), you can plan to pay nothing on those debts until your situation improves.

Prepare a "Hardship" Letter Which Explains Why You Defaulted. One of the things the lender will want is a short letter which explains the reasons why you fell behind in your payments. Sympathetic aspects of your situation should be thoroughly explained. The lender may also want documentation on issues which can be verified. For example, the lender may want proof that you have been laid off and have applied for unemployment compensation. Lender representatives are human beings and they will often go farther to assist you if they feel some sympathy for you based on the reasons you fell behind.

Gather Certain Information About The Property and Its Value. It is also important to obtain information about your property, particularly its condition and its value. You might consider having a broker evaluate it for the purposes of sale. Other potential sources of information about value include what you know about prices of nearby homes that are similar to yours. The lender's willingness to discuss a deal may depend in large part on the real value of the property in the event of foreclosure. Physical problems with the property, including deterioration or liability associated with ownership (such as lead paint liability), make foreclosure a less desirable option for the lender. As discussed below, such information may be an important bargaining chip.

Decide Before You Contact the Lender What You Want and Why You Should Get It. You should know before you contact the lender what type of workout you need to resolve your situation. A variety of options are discussed below. Think about what you realistically need to make things work.

For example, if you are experiencing a temporary lay-off, you may need only a period of temporary help on mortgage payments. However, if you have a permanent income reduction (because of retirement, for example), you may require a complete loan restructuring. You also may see from the beginning that you have little choice other than to sell your home, but need time to arrange a full value sale to obtain the benefit of your accumulated equity.

In general, the rule is to ask for what you need to make things work out, but not for more than what you need. Lenders will be turned off by if you seem too greedy. Where your needs are so unrealistic as to be out of the question for any reasonable lender (if for example, you cannot afford to pay any interest at all), consider the possibility that you need to sell your home before foreclosure rather than lose it involuntarily.

Understand the Details of Your Loan and the Amount of the Default. An understanding of your existing loan terms and the amount of your default is essential to a workout negotiation. A high existing interest rate, for example, might be negotiated down to market rates.

Obtaining a breakdown of the default from the lender between principal, interest, late charges, insurance escrow, tax escrow, foreclosure fees will also help. It is easier to negotiate reduction of late charges than reduction of actual costs like insurance charges paid by the lender.

Additionally, in some cases, a breakdown of the default will reveal that some charges claimed are not proper. For example, the lender may not have credited a payment you know you have made. You may also find that the lender is charging you unreasonable fees and costs associated with default or foreclosure.

HOW TO START
THE WORKOUT PROCESS

You will always need to begin to try to arrange a workout as early as possible in the foreclosure process. For you to understand whom you should contact, and what that individual's role in the foreclosure process, you need to know more about the various parties involved with your mortgage. There may be a mortgage holder, a mortgage servicer, a foreclosure attorney, and a mortgage insurer. In some cases the mortgage holder has a separate servicer for foreclosures.

Usually You Do Not Contact the Mortgage Holder. The mortgage holder is the lender which actually holds your mortgage. The mortgage holder is the person or company that has the right to foreclose. Since many mortgages are transferred after you borrow the money, the mortgage holder is not likely to be the bank or mortgage company which made the loan to you originally.

A high percentage of mortgages are now held by investors, including Fannie Mae (The Federal National Mortgage Association) or Freddie Mac (The Federal Home Loan Mortgage Corporation). Other mortgages are gathered together ("pooled") and sold under trust agreements so that the mortgage holder acts as a trustee for a larger group of investors. As described below, you generally do *not* initially contact the mortgage holder directly unless you cannot otherwise get help.

> You should determine who holds your mortgage,
> who is servicing the mortgage,
> and if there is mortgage insurance.

Usually, You Initially Contact the Mortgage Servicer. Although the mortgage holder has final authority to decide whether to accept a workout, very often some or all of this authority is transferred to one or more companies who are responsible for dealing directly with customers. These companies are called "servicers." The servicer may or may not be the same company as the lender you borrowed from. For example, you may have taken out a mortgage from the Third National Bank, who sold your loan to Fannie Mae. The Third National Bank may continue to service the loan for Fannie Mae, or the loan servicing may have been transferred separately to the Main Street National Bank.

Sometimes a loan is transferred to a special servicer for the purpose of foreclosure. There is often a lot of confusion when servicing is transferred, although the law now requires that you get notice of who is servicing the mortgage.

In many cases, the servicer will be an out-of-state company which processes thousands or hundreds of thousands of mortgages. Fannie Mae,

Freddie Mac and a variety of mortgage holders give their servicers differing amounts of authority to act on their behalf. This authority is spelled out in writing in servicing guides and contracts.

Frequently, the servicer will be the only party with whom you have any contact. Only on investigation will it become apparent that the servicer is acting on another company's behalf. If you request it, the servicer must tell you the name, address and telephone of the mortgage holder. In addition, servicers are required by Freddie Mac to tell you on their own initiative if Freddie Mac is your mortgage holder.

It is almost always appropriate to begin the workout process with the servicer. The servicer should have workout specialists who will tell you what you need to provide, take your application, and provide information on the normal requirements for a workout. Contact the servicer, explain that you are interested in a loan workout and ask to get any available information packages as well as any forms the lender will want you to submit.

You may want to keep a record of contacts with the servicer, including names and phone numbers of the people you speak with, as well as a record of what you are told. Significant communications should be confirmed in writing.

In this chapter, we use the term "lender" to apply mainly to the "servicer" and not the "mortgage holder." That is because you will rarely have any contact with the mortgage holder. The mortgage holder will rely on the servicer to deal with you directly.

If You Are Referred to the Lender's Attorney. The lender's attorney also works for the mortgage holder, although sometimes the attorney is hired by the servicer. Some servicers will ask you to speak only to their attorney once the legal process of foreclosure has begun. When the servicer tells you to do so, you have little practical alternative.

Although some attorneys will readily participate in workout discussions or give you permission to speak with their client directly, others will need to be pushed. Unresponsive attorneys should be reported to the servicer or to the mortgage holder if necessary.

You Should Also Contact Any Mortgage Insurer. Mortgage insurance is increasingly common in residential mortgage transactions. If your down payment was less than twenty percent of the purchase price, private mortgage insurance was probably required. In other cases, mortgages are insured by the

Federal government (FHA, FmHA, RHS, or the Veterans Administration) or by a state housing finance agency.

If you default and your property is sold, the mortgage insurer generally will pay the lender part of your debt not recouped in the foreclosure process. The good news is that mortgage insurers realize they have an interest in preventing foreclosure in many cases. They will sometimes step in to insist that the lender accept proposed workout terms. Alternatively, they may agree to pay a small arrearage (or part of it) or provide other limited relief in order to help you keep your home. They do so in order to prevent a potential larger loss in the event of foreclosure.

If you are paying for private mortgage insurance, it is a good idea to find out the name of the insurer and to send them copies of anything you send to the lender to keep them informed of the progress of workout negotiations. The name of the mortgage insurer should not be kept secret from you; you are the one paying for the mortgage insurance. Check your original mortgage documents or ask the lender. Even if the mortgage insurer is not willing to participate in the workout discussions, keeping it informed will keep the mortgage holder and servicer on their best behavior.

HUD, VA, FmHA, and RHS Guarantee Mortgages. If your mortgage is insured (guaranteed) by a federal or state funded entity, the lender may be subject to special servicing requirements designed to help you avoid foreclosure. Check your loan papers. HUD (FHA insured mortgages), the Veterans Administration (VA), the Farmers Home Administration (FmHA), and the Rural Housing Service (RHS) have substantial programs to avoid foreclosures. These are discussed more fully in Chapter Fourteen. In some cases, these programs may be better than a workout. In others they will be similar to the workout alternatives discussed below.

Make Partial Payments on Your Mortgage If the Lender Will Accept Them. If you can afford to make partial payments on your mortgage and want to try to arrange a workout, you should start submitting partial payments to the lender. You can then try to formalize partial payments under a workout plan. Keep a careful record of any partial payments you send so that you can check later that they have been credited properly.

If the Lender Refuses Partial Payment. The lender has no obligation to accept partial payments and your payments may be returned to you. If payments are returned to you, it is crucial to save this money (as well as to continue to put aside as much as possible) while you are attempting to arrange a workout agreement.

If possible, any funds saved should be placed in a special account. At a minimum, they should be placed in a savings account which earns interest. You should resist the temptation to dip into these funds as other financial problems come up. Once the money is put aside, consider it as if the money has already been spent on the mortgage.

Many lenders will provide much more favorable workout terms if you have a lump sum saved to help you get caught up on the default. Over a period of time, the lender's incentive to agree to a workout may increase based on a lump sum, even if you are actually further behind.

If a workout is arranged, you will pay this savings to the lender to reduce your future obligations on the mortgage. If a workout is not possible, you can use the money to move and start again.

The Workout Application Process. Different lenders have different workout application processes and forms. Every lender will require you to provide financial information about your debts, assets, income, and expenses with appropriate verification. You will also need to submit a hardship letter explaining your reasons for default. Many lenders require, additionally, a property appraisal and/or a credit report. It is usually a good idea to get any necessary forms from the lender and an understanding of what kind of supporting information will be required prior to submitting a workout application. Otherwise you may have to submit an application twice.

Your income is usually verified by pay stubs, unemployment compensation award letters, back-tax forms, and the like. You may have to submit verification of your expenses as well, such as utility bills, tax payments and other fixed costs of home ownership. Since a workout involves giving you a second chance on a defaulted loan, it is not unreasonable for the lender to expect information similar to that required for qualifying for a mortgage. Additionally, it is not unfair for a lender whose collateral is at risk to want an appraisal or, at minimum, a property inspection.

The application form may not have a space to describe what workout terms you are seeking. If it does not, you should include your request in the hardship letter or in a cover letter to the application. You should also explain the reasons you have for making your proposal.

Once the application is made, you may have to follow up with the lender. It is not uncommon for applications to be swallowed up as if by a black hole. It is a good idea to find out who has the application at any given time (as well as the name of that person's supervisor) and to make polite but regular follow-up phone calls. Some give-and-take may be required. Remember that proposals are subject to a negotiation process.

WHAT TO ASK FOR
IN A WORKOUT

General Considerations. The most important part of a workout negotiation may be deciding what terms to request from the lender. There are a variety of workout terms available and lenders use an infinite number of labels to name their workout programs. Try using the names for workouts used here. You may need to offer a further explanation if the lender does not understand the names you have used.

You should always propose workout terms which are sufficient to address the problem which caused your default. There is little value to you or the lender in negotiating terms which, if accepted, will not resolve your problems for both the long and short term. For negotiating purposes, you might consider asking for a little more than you need at the outset in order to get to an agreement you can live with.

The following list includes a variety of different potential workout options. Some lenders may not offer each of these options, while others may offer options which are not listed here. The rule of thumb is to ask for what you want. Do not assume a particular option is not available.

It may also be necessary to use more than one option in combination. For example, if you are currently unemployed, but you have found a lower paying job which will not start for three months, you may need a temporary moratorium on payments, and a permanent interest rate reduction. (All of these options are discussed in more detail below.)

Request a Delay of Any Impending Foreclosure Sale. At the outset, the most important request may be for a delay of the foreclosure sale process long enough to make a workout application. A completed foreclosure sale will generally cut off all workout possibilities (although there are some exceptions).

You should always request a delay when a scheduled sale is less than thirty days away. If the sale is not yet scheduled or if it is more than thirty days away, you usually have time to complete a workout negotiation before the sale is held. Nevertheless, it is important to keep track. When you get inside the thirty day window, ask for a postponement of the sale.

A request for delay is more likely to be granted when preliminary information is provided about your circumstances and your ability to make a reasonable workout proposal. For example, if you have recently returned to work, documentation of employment would usually justify postponing a sale. Similarly, an offer of partial payment may help obtain several months' delay.

Lenders have different approaches to handling requests for delay. Some may not agree to a delay until the sale date is fairly close. One pitfall to avoid is leaving the decision to grant a delay in the lender's hands to the very last minute. The risk is that you will assume that the application is being acted upon even if it is not, and you will lose the opportunity to pursue other strategies prior to sale. When you request a delay well before the foreclosure, try to obtain a response to your request at least seven days before the foreclosure sale date. If not, this is a good indication that the lender is not really serious about negotiating a workout.

**Be careful that your home
is not foreclosed while you are waiting
to finalize your workout agreement.**

When you receive an agreement to delay a sale, you must get it in writing. In most cases, it is sufficient if the lender puts the agreement in a letter to you. But, if the foreclosure sale is a court-supervised process, you should make sure that you meet applicable procedural requirements to delay the sale — including notice to the court. These will vary from state to state. Whatever the process, it is a good idea to verify that the sale is actually canceled.

If there is no sale date or if that date is a long way off when workout negotiations are commenced, it is still important to keep an eye on the sale process. It is not unheard of for a property to be sold while a workout application is pending.

Traditional Payment Agreements. A payment agreement (or "forbearance agreement," "reinstatement agreement," or "deferral agreement") involves curing a default by making regular monthly mortgage payments as they are due, together with partial monthly payment on the arrears. For example, a typical agreement might call for making one-and-a-quarter monthly payments until the default is resolved. Until recently, most lenders limited payment agreements to no more than one year for reinstatement. Agreements up to thirty-six months are now becoming common. This type of agreement is most similar to a cure of arrears in the context of a chapter 13 bankruptcy.

You are most likely to benefit from this traditional payment agreement if you have experienced temporary financial difficulties which are now resolved. You need to have some excess income in your budget to commit to the mortgage beyond the regular monthly payment.

Example of a Payment Agreement

Mr.and Ms. Smith are three months behind on their monthly mortgage payment because Ms. Smith lost her job. Ms. Smith has now returned to work so the family budget is more flexible, but not flexible enough to get caught up by paying a lump sum.

Step 1: How much are the Smiths in the hole?
Their monthly mortgage payment is $1,000
They have missed 3 payments for a total of..$3,000
The lender has foreclosure court costs
(the Smiths may need to check with the lender about costs)...........................$600
Total Amount the Smiths are Behind..**$3,600**

Step 2: How much will it cost each month for the Smiths to get caught up?
Over One Year: Total delinquency ($3600) divided by 12 months.................$300
Over Two Years: Total delinquency ($3600) divided by 24 months...............$150
Over Three Years: Total delinquency ($3600) divided by 36 months............$100

Step 3: What will the Smiths total payment be while they get caught up?
They will need to make their regular payment each month $1000
Together with a payment to cure the delinquency:
One year cure (total payment)..$1300
Two year cure (total payment) $1150
Three Year cure (total payment) $1100

Step 4: The Smiths must return to their budget. To determine which plan can they afford. If the plan they need is longer than one year, they will need to provide information to the lender that establishes that they cannot get caught up over a shorter period.

One pitfall to this type of arrangement is that you may fail to account for the extra initial expenses associated with recovery from temporary financial difficulties. Homeowners often have substantial budgetary pressures for several months after dealing with a temporary financial problem.

Other bills, including utilities, may have fallen into arrears and expenses, such as urgent clothing needs for children, may have been deferred. The agreement must realistically take these expenses into account — perhaps by proposing graduated payments on the delinquency at the beginning of the workout plan.

Temporary Interest Rate Reduction. You may want to seek a temporary interest rate reduction if your financial problems are likely to last for a limited period of time, but you cannot presently meet your mortgage payments. You generally must have a reasonable plan for increasing your income so that you can make full payments by a certain date.

The theory behind a temporary rate reduction is that if you get help by lowering payments in the short term, you will be able to keep from falling further behind while waiting, for example, for a recall from a lay-off. Some lenders want assurance that if you can't return to paying the full rate within a reasonable time, foreclosure will go forward unopposed.

Typically, rates can be reduced fairly easily to the market rate of interest or, with a good reason, below market. Fannie Mae and Freddie Mac may be willing, in appropriate cases, to go as low as 5% for a temporary period. You should make certain that any temporary interest rate reduction agreement does not just lower your payments, but actually lowers the interest rate used to compute the outstanding principal. Otherwise, the lender may add the interest you have been forgiven back into the loan amount you have to eventually repay.

Recasting of Missed Payments. Another form of temporary mortgage relief is known as "recasting" or "deferral." Recasting involves canceling your present obligation to catch up on missed payments, and instead delaying your obligation to make those payments until the end of the loan term. That way you can start making your regular monthly payments again, without having to immediately address the problem of your back-due payments. It is ideal for those whose financial situation has improved enough to start making regular mortgage payments, but not enough to allow them to get caught up on their mortgage default.

This option is becoming increasing rare, because of complications related to computer based accounting systems. When recasting is available, lenders are much more willing to recast payments you have already missed than to recast payments not yet due. In addition, most lenders are unwilling to recast more than six past due monthly payments.

Permanent Modification of Loan Terms. In some cases lenders will agree to permanent changes in loan terms, such as permanent interest rate reduction, extension of the loan's payment period, reamortization, capitalization of arrears, cancellation of principal or some combination of these. An agreement of this type occurs most frequently when you can no longer afford the original loan terms due to a permanent change in your circumstances (for example, your retirement), and it is not in the lender's financial interest to foreclose. These types of agreements are usually called "loan modifications." Some lenders may use the terms "loan refinance" or "note change."

The lender generally does not have a financial interest to foreclose when a forced sale of your home will bring in significantly less than what you owe. This might occur where your property's value has gone down since taking out the mortgage, where lead paint or other hazards may create liabilities for someone foreclosing on the property, where you have a large, senior mortgage with another lender, or where the property is unmarketable for some reason.

A loan modification may also be available if you have counterclaims or other leverage to exchange for the change in loan terms. As discussed briefly below, you also may achieve the same change in loan terms by a complete refinancing with a new lender. There are at least five ways to permanently change the loan terms:

1. *Interest Rate Reductions.* The most common scenario for a permanent interest rate reduction is when the existing rate is above market, and is permanently unaffordable due to financial hardship. In some cases, this may involve converting your variable rate to a fixed rate loan or vice versa. The lender may recognize that if it forecloses on the property and then makes a loan on the property to sell it to someone else, it can obtain no more than the market rate of interest. Some lenders will combine a temporary interest rate reduction below market interest rates with a permanent reduction at some point in the future to a market interest rate. This is sometimes called a "step-up" plan.

2. *Extension of the Loan Payment Period* is a change in loan terms which helps some homeowners by allowing them to repay the principal over a longer term, thereby reducing the monthly payment. For example, an older homeowner who borrowed $100,000 in 1970 on a thirty year mortgage might owe only $20,000 today. Payments might be $750 monthly based on the

original note. By extending the term back to thirty years on the $20,000 balance, monthly payments can be reduced to $175 dollars (even if the interest rate is increased from the market rate in 1970 to the market rate today.) The lender does not lose out as long as the rate is at least as high as the market rate, because the entire current principal will be repaid with the applicable interest.

3. Reamortization/Capitalization of Arrears. If a loan is reamortized, the existing interest rate is applied to the existing principal balance over the remaining loan term as if there is no default. That is, the lender recalculates fixed monthly payments based on the current principal amount.

In most cases in which there has been a default, "capitalization of arrears" will also be necessary in connection with reamortization. When arrears are "capitalized," the amount of the arrears is included in the principal before the interest rate is applied and the payment is recalculated. The theory under which this makes sense is that the arrears are owed anyway. It is easier to repay them over the remaining length of the loan, rather than in a lump sum or even in monthly payments over a few years.

Capitalizing the arrears and reamortizing the loan, even without extending the period or changing the interest rate, may help you because it lets you spread out whatever payments you have missed over the remaining term of the loan while canceling your arrears. If the lender does not agree to adjust the loan rate, period or principal, your monthly payments will go up slightly. If reamortization is combined with an interest rate reduction, an extension of the period of the loan, or a cancellation of principal, your monthly payments may go down significantly, even though your total outstanding balance is higher. See example below.

4. Reduction of Principal Balance may be available in some cases where the loan amount is more than the value of your home because reasons beyond your control have lowered its value. (You may also be able to reduce your principal balance if you have legal claims against your lender.) The lender recognizes that it is better to receive mortgage payments on a lower principal than to foreclose on property worth far less than the amount of the mortgage. Most lenders will require an appraisal of your home before considering an agreement to modify the principal. Once your principal is reduced, if the loan is reamortized, your payments will be lower.

5. Deferred Junior Mortgages. Some lenders will only reduce their principal if they are allowed to keep a "deferred junior mortgage" in the amount that the principal is reduced. For example, if your principal balance is lowered by $20,000, the lender would ask for a second mortgage for $20,000 which you do not have to pay immediately. This junior mortgage protects the lender in the event that the property value later goes up. Deferred junior mortgages typically require you to pay the principal on that mortgage only if you transfer your home to someone else. Your granting the lender such a junior mortgage may be a bargaining chip to obtain a modification involving reduction of principal.

Example of a workout plan that extends the loan term, reamortizes, and capitalizes arrears:

Ms. Jones is five months behind on her mortgage payments after an expensive divorce. She has found a higher paying job, but her income will still be less than the total household pre-divorce income.

Step 1: What is the Current Situation?

Total principal now owed to pay off the debt (based on original balance of $120,000)	$96,000
Back-due interest	$3,400
Foreclosure costs	$600
Total Amount Owed	$100,000
Interest Rate	8%
Current Monthly Payment (without escrow)	$880.50
Total Delinquency (without escrow)	$4,402.50
Months remaining in loan term (out of original 360)	240

Step 2: What would this loan cost if the lender agrees to extend the loan back to 30 years (360 months), reamortize and capitalize the arrears?

New (modified) loan amount (same as Total Amount Owed Above)	$100,000
Months in Modified Loan Term	360
Interest Rate (same as above in this example)	8%
New Monthly Payment (without escrow)	$733.75

The advantage of this plan is that Ms. Jones would save approximately $150.00 each month. She also would not have to arrange to pay the delinquent payments separately, since these amounts are part of the new total loan amount on which interest is calculated.

Step 3: Ms. Jones must return to her budget. She must determine whether she can afford the payments necessary to get caught up in this way. To determine whether the plan is affordable, Ms. Jones will have to budget for the new monthly payment and for any fixed monthly payment (of escrow) to the lender for taxes and insurance. These charges cannot be modified. If taxes and insurance are not paid to the lender under an escrow account, these charges must be listed separately in a monthly budget.

Several websites offer helpful calculators to evaluate this type of plan. For some examples, see the bibliography.

Other Creative Workout Terms. Some lenders will consider other offers of workouts involving temporary or permanent relief, even if they are highly creative. Some examples are making a home equity loan for emergency home repairs (particularly if your failure to make the repairs will reduce the value of your home and thus the lender's mortgage), cancellation of arrears, or substitution or surrender of other property in exchange for a modification. However, some lenders may be uninterested if the proposal is too complicated.

Pre-Sales for More than You Owe the Lender. A pre-sale is a sale or transfer of your home in lieu of a foreclosure. Some lenders also refer to deeds in lieu of foreclosure and refinancings by third party lenders (discussed below), as pre-sales.

In many cases it is in your interest to sell the property rather than to have it foreclosed, since the property is likely to sell for a higher price through a realtor than in the foreclosure process. This is especially true if you have substantial equity and little likelihood of being able to afford reinstatement or modification of your loan.

The biggest potential problem in arranging a pre-sale is time. If you decide it is in your interests to sell the property, you should list it for sale with a realtor immediately. You must complete your pre-sale before the lender holds a foreclosure sale.

In some cases you will want to ask the lender for a short delay in the foreclosure sale process to give you an opportunity to complete a pending sale. This will usually be approved only when you can show the lender that you have made substantial progress toward a sale which will pay off the loan balance in full. Many lenders will not consider a pre-sale arrangement as grounds to postpone a foreclosure sale until you find a buyer and sign a "purchase and sale" agreement.

If you do not need extra time and can sell the property for more than the lender is owed, you need not get the lender's approval to complete a presale. When you have equity in your home because the pre-sale price exceeds the amount owed the lender plus the costs of sale, you get your equity from the sale proceeds after paying off the lender and your costs. But remember, you will have to pay off not only the first mortgage, but also other liens and mortgages, if any, or your sale will not go through.

Short Sales. Some lenders, particularly in a depressed real estate market, will agree to let you sell your home through a realtor rather than a foreclosure sale, even if the sale proceeds will not cover the amount due on the mortgage. This is called a "short" sale. A short sale may help the lender avoid additional foreclosure costs which cannot be recouped in the foreclosure sale process. It allows you to pay as much of the loan as possible by selling your home. It also avoids a foreclosure notation on your credit report.

You will always need to get agreement from the lender if you want to sell your property in a short-sale situation. The lender will want to make sure that you are obtaining the best price possible, because the higher the price, the more of the amount you owe is paid. At the time of an agreement for a short sale, make sure you also get an agreement in writing that the lender will not seek payment on the balance of the debt (cancel any deficiency.) Realtors, particularly those who have experience dealing with a particular lender, may be able to help you convince the lender to agree to a short sale. The realtor's incentive is the commission on the sale.

In some cases, the lender will insist that you make a cash contribution to any deficiency, because it thinks you can afford to do so. This is negotiable. Explain the financial difficulties you are in and the purposes for which you have earmarked any available savings.

A short sale is not a miracle cure. You are losing your home just as you would if a foreclosure was completed. What you get is freedom from worry about being sued to cover the deficiency and perhaps a slightly improved credit record for the future. (Although there will be no foreclosure notation, the fact that you missed monthly payment will probably appear.) In rare cases, if the lender thinks the price is high enough or if you can show hardship, it may agree to let you have between $500 and $2,000 from the sale proceeds to help you move. It can't hurt to ask.

Mortgage Assumptions and Other Transfers. Some mortgages can be assumed (taken over) by a third party. When a mortgage is assumable, the property can be transferred, and the person to whom it is transferred can pick up the payments on the mortgage. If payments were behind when the mortgage was assumed, absent a workout agreement, the person assuming the mortgage will be in default and subject to foreclosure. The advantage may be that the assuming party is in a better position to deal with the default than you.

A mortgage is always assumable if the contract documents say it is or, in most states, if the documents are silent on this issue.

Other mortgages contain a "due on sale" provision which is a clause specifying that transfer of the property creates a default. There are a number of situations in which assumption can take place despite attempts by the lender to enforce a due on sale provision. For example, lenders cannot block a transfer from parent to child or from one spouse to another.

Your lender may let another person assume your mortgage even if your loan documents say otherwise.

Even if a mortgage is not assumable, lenders will sometimes agree to what are usually called "delinquent assumptions" so that they can start getting payments from someone. If you want to transfer the property to someone who can better afford the mortgage payments, it does not hurt to ask the mortgage company for permission.

MODIFICATION FEES, FORECLOSURE FEES AND LATE CHARGES

Many lenders charge a modification fee for handling workout applications. Some want this fee at the beginning of the workout process regardless of the application's outcome. Fees can run as high as $600 or more plus costs. There are a number of approaches you can take in dealing with this request. One approach is simply agreeing to pay the fee, which may be a small price to pay for an agreement to lower the interest rate or to make serious modifications to your mortgage.

Where possible, however, you should try to minimize your modification fees. Request a waiver or a fee reduction to make the modification affordable. Remember that a modification can sometimes save the lender thousands of dollars in foreclosure fees, loss of principal and resale costs after foreclosure. In some cases a mortgage insurer will agree to step in and pay the fee or pressure the lender to waive it.

The lender's out-of-pocket costs to modify your mortgage, such as appraisal fees and credit report charges, probably will not be waived.

However, these fees should be examined to make sure that they are reasonable. If the fees exceed $200-300, they should be reduced. You can also request an agreement to pay some or all of the modification fees in installments or to have the fee lumped together with the loan balance if your workout is a modification involving capitalization.

Related problems arise when the lender has already begun to incur foreclosure fees and costs when you request a workout. These should be scrutinized to make sure that they are legitimate and reasonable. They should be minimized whenever possible. A typical problem arises when you are required to pay for an attorney's retainer for foreclosure and the foreclosure does not take place due to your workout agreement. These fees should then be credited back to your account. To the extent foreclosure fees and costs are valid, they need to be paid or otherwise accounted for in the modification process.

Late charges will often be waived if you ask, especially if it is necessary to the success of a workout agreement. You should push for waiver of late charges whenever possible.

DOCUMENTING
A WORKOUT AGREEMENT

The lender generally has forms which it requires for finalizing a workout agreement. These should be reviewed carefully to make sure they are consistent with the agreement.

Even if there is a delay in signing the forms for the workout, you should make sure that the basic terms of the agreement are spelled out in writing. If a sale needs to be postponed while you are finalizing the agreement, make sure postponement takes place and make sure that you have a record in writing. A trained professional can be very helpful in this part of the process.

Many workout forms include an agreement under which you give up all legal claims which you may have against the lender. You should never sign that type of agreement (which may be labeled "release") until the actual workout agreement is finalized, because if you do not complete a workout agreement, you may want to pursue other legal remedies. Once a workout agreement is reached, it may make sense to give up your legal claims as part of the final agreement, but you should do so knowingly. To complete an agreement, you should make sure all the forms are properly signed by the lender and recorded, if necessary, with the mortgage in the property registry.

IF YOUR WORKOUT NEGOTIATION
IS NOT GOING WELL

Appeals to Higher Ups. If you feel you aren't receiving sufficient cooperation in negotiating a workout agreement, ask to speak to a supervisor. It is also appropriate to go over the head of the loan servicer and complain directly to the mortgage holder or mortgage insurer. Fannie Mae, Freddie Mac and some institutional investors have "loss-mitigation" departments which will intervene, if pushed, to address a proposed workout. The applicable Fannie Mae offices are regional. Freddie Mac's loss mitigation is done on a national basis. If you are having a problem with the servicer, it is a good idea to learn the location of the mortgage holder's office and to find a person in that office to call or write with specific complaints about the servicer's conduct. (It is best to ask to speak with someone in "loss mitigation" or "workouts.")

Who to Contact at Fannie Mae and Freddie Mac. Fannie Mae's home office can be reached at (202) 752-7000. Usually, though you should try to contact the regional office where the mortgage servicer is located (not the regional office near where you live):

FANNIE MAE REGIONAL OFFICES

OFFICE	TELEPHONE	SERVES
The Midwestern Regional Office	(312) 368-6200	Illinois, Indiana, Iowa, Michigan, Minnesota, Nebraska, North Dakota, Ohio, South Dakota, and Wisconsin
The Northeastern Regional Office	(215) 575-1400	Connecticut, Delaware, Maine, Massachusetts, New Hampshire, New Jersey, New York, Pennsylvania, Puerto Rico, Rhode Island, Vermont, and the Virgin Islands
The Southeastern Regional Office	(404) 398-6000	Alabama, D.C., Florida, Georgia, Kentucky, Maryland, Mississippi, North Carolina, South Carolina, Tennessee, Virginia, and West Virginia
The Southwestern Regional Office	(972) 773-HOME	Arizona, Arkansas, Colorado, Kansas, Louisiana, Missouri, New Mexico, Oklahoma, Texas, and Utah
The Western Regional Office	(626) 396-5100	Alaska, California, Guam, Hawaii, Idaho, Montana, Nevada, Oregon, Washington, and Wyoming

To lodge a complaint about a Freddie Mac servicer, it is necessary to call 1-800-FREDDIE and access the customer service representative from the initial menu. Ask the customer service representative for the name and number of someone in the loss mitigation department who can review your workout proposal.

Refinancing With Another Lender. If your existing home mortgage lender will not agree to a reasonable workout, you can consider refinancing your existing mortgage with a new lender. If your existing mortgage is at a high interest rate or if there is just a short term left on your mortgage, refinancing at a lower interest rate and/or with a longer payment period can greatly reduce your monthly payments and bring the payments within reach. Moreover, refinancing a low-interest first mortgage and high-interest second mortgage into a single low-interest first mortgage can also reduce payments.

For example, a family with a 25-year, $10,000 first mortgage at eight percent interest and a 15-year, $30,000 second mortgage at eighteen percent interest has combined monthly payments of $560.31. Refinancing what is left owing on those two mortgages with a 25-year, $30,000 first mortgage at ten percent will result in new monthly payments of $272.61. This is $287.70 per month less.

On the other hand, many refinancing schemes are frauds. Even legitimate refinancing options that look helpful may, on closer inspection, be far more costly than the existing mortgage. Whatever choice you make about refinancing, it is never a good idea to payoff other presently unsecured debts with a debt secured by a mortgage. It is essential that you carefully review Chapter Four to decide whether refinancing makes sense.

If you decide in favor of refinancing, you should make every effort to obtain a loan at a reasonable rate, usually from a savings bank, a commercial bank, a credit union, or a legitimate mortgage company. Most finance companies and certain mortgage companies do not make residential loans at reasonable rates and terms.

You should *not* assume that legitimate lenders with low interest rates will turn you down because you are in financial distress. Only by applying can you determine the availability of a loan from a particular lender. Chapter Seven sets out guidelines that mortgage lenders may utilize in reviewing your credit rating in conjunction with a mortgage application.

When applying for a residential loan you should present your financial problems in the best possible light. The presentation should show how the problems are being solved, and how refinancing will provide substantially lower payments. You should stress your past financial, residential, and employment stability, and indicate your plans for the future. People often refinance when interest rates drop; you should not feel that your application will be considered unusual.

If your application is rejected, you should obtain the reasons for the rejection and determine whether the reasons are legitimate. You should try to cure any problems so that the next application will be successful. Your rights under federal law to be notified as to the reasons for your rejection are detailed in National Consumer Law Center, *Credit Discrimination* (2d ed. 1998).

Some lenders actively solicit financially distressed families for refinancing loans by phone or mail. Usually the terms of their loans are not just unfavorable, but disastrous. In general, avoid such offers unless reviewed by a counselor, lawyer, or accountant you can trust.

Refinancing With a Reverse Mortgage. If you are an older homeowner, and workout negotiations do not seem to be working, another possibility is to consider refinancing with a reverse mortgage. Although a reverse mortgage is not always a good idea because it uses up the equity in your property which might otherwise be a financial resource, in certain situations reverse mortgages make sense. In most reverse mortgage transactions, you do not have to make payments, because the lender will recover the amount you borrow and accrued interest from the property when you no longer live there. Anyone interested in this option should find a qualified reverse mortgage counselor to go over the pros and cons. For more information, see Chapter Two.

Deeds in Lieu of Foreclosure. If a lender will not agree to a workout, it may consider taking your deed "in lieu of foreclosure." That is, you voluntarily turn over your home to the lender as an alternative to foreclosure. (Lenders will not be interested in deeds in lieu if there are junior mortgages or other junior liens on your home, because in that case foreclosure is necessary for the lender to obtain clear title to your home.)

Deeds in lieu are usually, but not always, a bad idea. A deed in lieu of foreclosure will voluntarily terminate your ownership. You should not agree to a deed in lieu unless the lender agrees to something in exchange for the deed in lieu agreement, such as elimination of a negative credit reference, or an extra period of time for you to remain in the property before eviction.

Some lenders will even agree to pay a small amount of cash (under $2,000) for a deed in lieu to help you move. The lender may agree to these terms in order to save the time and expense of foreclosure. If you do decide to give a lender a deed in lieu of foreclosure, be sure to get the agreement in writing, including anything the lender agrees to give you in exchange for the deed.

Deeds in lieu are almost always a poor choice if you have significant equity in the property. The only way to get that equity is through a sale, perhaps even a foreclosure sale. If you give a deed in lieu, you can not get cash back from the lender's sale of the property.

TAX CONSEQUENCES
OF SHORT SALES
AND WORKOUT PLANS

Some workout plans and almost all short sales involve an agreement by the lender to cancel some part of your debt. Cancellation of a debt can have tax consequences. In general, the IRS treats a loan as income to you which is offset by the obligation to repay so that no tax is owed. If you are forgiven from repaying some or all of the debt, the IRS may treat the amount forgiven as taxable income in the year in which the forgiveness takes place.

Certain lenders file a 1099C form with the IRS any time they agree to cancel or forgive a debt. You should get a copy of this form from the lender when it is filed. You should not ignore this 1099C or the IRS will charge you tax on the amount the lender forgave.

You can avoid tax on the amount listed on the 1099C form to the extent you can show the IRS that you were insolvent at the time the debt was forgiven. To establish insolvency, you need to send the IRS a statement concerning the discharged debt listed on the 1099C form together with a list which shows that at the time of forgiveness you had more debts (including the forgiven debt) than assets. All debts and assets must be listed.

If you subtract your debts from your assets and you get a negative number, you were insolvent. If so, subtract the amount by which you were insolvent (converted to a positive number), from the amount of your forgiven debt. If you still get a negative number, then you owe no tax on the forgiven debt at all. If the amount is more than zero, you owe tax on that amount.

Tax issues can be complicated. You may want help from a qualified tax professional.

Calculating tax on forgiven debt. Example:

Mr. and Ms. Brown owed $120,000 on a property worth only $100,000. They sold the property for $100,000 and the bank canceled the balance.

The Brown's have forgiven debt of $20,000

The Brown's total assets upon sale of the home are worth..........................$35,000

They have debts totalling (including the forgiven debt) $50,000

Step One: Subtract debts from assets:

Assets $35,000

Minus Liabilities $50,000

Total ....(15,000)

The Browns are insolvent by $15,000. (If they sold every asset and used the money to pay debts, they would still owe $15,000)

Step Two: Subtract the amount of the insolvency from the amount of the forgiven debt.

Forgiven Debt...$20,000

Minus Amount Insolvent $15,000

Total Amount on which Tax My Be Owed $5,000

The Browns owe tax on $5,000 in forgiven debt. If the total had been less than zero, they would owe no tax on the forgiven debt.

Information to establish the insolvency must be provided to the IRS.

CREDIT CONSEQUENCES
OF FORECLOSURE
AND WORKOUT PLANS

There is no easy way to know how a foreclosure will affect your credit. Your mortgage delinquency is likely to be reported by credit bureaus for seven years. If you cannot avoid a foreclosure sale, the fact of the sale will also be reported for seven years.

There is a great deal of information about credit reporting and how to improve a bad credit report in Chapter Seven. As discussed in that chapter, there are no hard and fast rules about how any individual lender will evaluate a notation on your credit report. Each creditor evaluates credit reports differently. A notation which is fatal to an application for credit with one lender may not preclude credit on reasonable terms from a different lender.

This is some general information about foreclosure and future credit which may be useful if you are worried about your long-term prospects:

1. **Concerns about future credit should rarely influence how you address your current problem.** You cannot control how the credit report is evaluated by those who check credit reports.

Any significant delinquency will usually mean "bad credit risk" to most creditors even if it is paid in full relatively quickly. There are generally more important concerns in the foreclosure avoidance process than the small improvements which will result from one type of workout plan over another.

2. **A completed workout plan of any type is likely to look better on your credit report than a completed foreclosure sale.** Any effort which prevents a foreclosure from being completed will show a creditor that you have made an effort. Repayment plans and loan modifications, if you cure the arrears, will show that you have gotten back on your feet.

3. **A completed foreclosure sale or bankruptcy is usually fatal to applications for new mortgages from reputable lenders for at least two years.** After two years have passed, the completed foreclosure will be an important consideration for most lenders until the notation is deleted from the credit record after seven years. However, after two years, you should qualify if you can show a lender that your financial problems are behind you.

4. **A deed in lieu of foreclosure is not a big improvement over foreclosure.** One myth about credit reporting is that a deed in lieu of foreclosure is going to keep you in good standing on your credit record. A deed in lieu of foreclosure is a strong negative mark on a credit record; it is only slightly less damaging than a foreclosure. A deed in lieu should be considered where appropriate, but it should not be seen as a "miracle cure" for future credit.

5. **It is a good idea to explain the reason for any mortgage delinquency and/or a foreclosure when applying for credit, if you know it appears on the credit record.** Explain why the delinquency or foreclosure occurred if there was a good reason, the efforts you made to deal with it, and the ways in which you are in a better position now to pay your debts. This can be done either with a letter to the credit reporting agency for inclusion with your credit report as discussed in Chapter Seven or by a written explanation directly to lenders who are evaluating your report.

6. **Unsecured credit, such as credit cards, is often available even if you have a recent foreclosure on your credit record.** There is a great deal of competition in the credit card business. Companies even compete for borrowers with bad

credit records. It is a good idea to shop around for reasonable terms, rather than simply accepting the first offer. Lower interest rates and fees may be available. (See Chapter Ten for more information.)

7. **If you are in a high-risk credit group, it is especially important to shop around when you apply for credit.** Many finance companies and other abusive lenders prey on people's beliefs that they have no other potential source of credit. If you are offered credit only at high rates, shop around. You are likely to obtain better terms if lenders know you are shopping. Read the terms of credit carefully when it is offered to you. Use the APR (annual percentage rate) to compare it to other offers you have received. Lower APR's are better, unless there are other terms of credit (such as the type of collateral you must give) which are worse. You can walk away from a deal even at the last minute.

– 13 –

Foreclosure
Defense

- *Giving Yourself Time to Find a Solution*
- *Nailing Down Exactly How Much You Owe*
- *Curing Your Delinquency and Keeping Your Home*

If your home is being foreclosed, you are not powerless, as long as you are realistic in defining your objectives. You often have a good chance of achieving the following three objectives in the legal process of defending a foreclosure:

1. Delaying a sale to give you enough time to find a solution to the foreclosure problem.
2. Finding out the valid amount you owe on the debt so that you are not repaying more than you should.
3. Using legal rights at various stages in the process to cure your default or to redeem your home. You can usually also exercise those rights by filing a chapter 13 bankruptcy.

This chapter focuses on the steps you can take to meet these three objectives, no matter what type of foreclosure is involved. The next chapter sets out additional rights you have to accomplish even more objectives for certain special types of mortgages, such as loans insured by the FHA or VA, or where fraud or oppression is involved. In those specific situations you may be able to keep your home even though you defer payments for a while, or you may even be able to wipe out your mortgage in whole or in part.

The previous chapter discussed saving your home with a workout agreement. Often you are better off first trying to negotiate a workout agreement than defending a foreclosure. A workout may accomplish your goals without resorting to a legal process. However, a foreclosure sale may be so imminent that a workout agreement is not feasible, or the lender may not agree to an acceptable arrangement. In these situations, your only option may be to defend the foreclosure in court.

GET LEGAL ADVICE

Because foreclosure is a harsh legal process, when threatened with foreclosure you should immediately try to obtain legal help. Possible sources of low-cost legal help are the neighborhood legal services office and a bar association panel of pro bono attorneys. A small number of other community lawyers may handle foreclosure defense cases for a fee and many lawyers will handle bankruptcies. You should exercise care in hiring a lawyer to help you with foreclosure defense, just as you would in hiring any professional. Find someone you trust to do what you need them to do, if possible by referral from a friend or relative.

The size of the fee should not be the only consideration. A free legal services lawyer may be the best in town. A costly lawyer may rip you off. The important thing is to find someone you feel comfortable with hiring at a price you can afford (when free help is unavailable).

One thing to avoid is "quick fix" attorneys who may advertise or solicit through the mail from published foreclosure lists. Many times these practitioners will push you to file a bankruptcy prematurely. A bankruptcy may be necessary at some point. But, as with many things, proper timing may be critical.

Another source of help in some cases is nonprofit foreclosure prevention counseling (sometimes called "default counseling"). Contact a local nonprofit housing organization to find out where this service is offered in your community. Try calling 1-800-5694287 (TDD 1-800-877-8339) to find a HUD-approved housing counseling agency near you.

Too often, people postpone getting help until after the time to assert their legal rights has passed. Others prematurely walk away from their homes in frustration, leaving themselves without any equity and vulnerable to deficiency claims. For each foreclosure situation, a counselor or lawyer must carefully evaluate your objectives and interests. It is better to get this help too soon rather than too late.

DELAYING
THE FORECLOSURE
PROCESS

Foreclosure can move very quickly. One advantage of exercising your legal rights is that you can slow down the process. In the short-term, delay can be helpful because it will give you more time to put into place a long-term solution to the problem.

If you succeed in delaying the foreclosure, you should do everything possible during that time to put money aside toward your mortgage to avoid falling further behind. You should also act diligently to try to deal with your underlying financial problems.

While delay can be helpful to you, you cannot properly delay foreclosure just because you need more time. The actions you take must be based on some underlying legal claim which is raised in good faith.

Procedural Defenses May Delay the Process. In most areas of the country, foreclosures are rarely contested, and lenders' attorneys tend to assume that there is no defense to foreclosure. Consequently, lenders may be sloppy in their procedures and sometimes do not comply with preforeclosure requirements. Lender noncompliance can be to your benefit when you are contesting foreclosure, forcing the lender to start over, or, at the very least, forcing the lender to comply with required procedural requirements. This will provide you with additional time to refinance, sell privately, or arrange a workout agreement. (See Chapter Twelve.)

Foreclosure procedures and defenses to foreclosure vary significantly from state to state. Therefore, a lawyer or some other professional will have to determine whether the lender has complied with all the required procedures and whether defenses to foreclosure are available.

Examples of possible defenses include the failure to give you the proper notice, failure to give you a fair chance to correct the default, failure to properly advertise the sale, failure of a lender to introduce the original documents in the foreclosure proceeding, failure to sue all of the proper parties, failure to sue in the name of the real mortgage holder, or discouraging bids at the foreclosure sale.

In states where foreclosure cases are resolved by court action, you can raise defenses in that action. If the creditor can foreclose without a court case, because your state allows nonjudicial foreclosure, then you will have to bring a legal case of your own, and ask the court to stop the foreclosure. Many of the legal remedies discussed here are covered in more detail in National Consumer Law Center, *Repossessions and Foreclosures* (3d ed. 1995 and Supp.).

The Lender's Acceptance of Partial Payments May Be Grounds to Delay a Foreclosure. Late or partial payment on a mortgage generally triggers the lender's right to "accelerate" the loan—to call the full amount of the mortgage due immediately. Failure to pay the full amount then leads to foreclosure.

Nevertheless, many courts refuse to allow foreclosure if the lender surprises you by suddenly calling a loan due when the lender has been lenient in accepting late or partial payments in the past. If a lender habitually accepts late or partial payments, it must warn you that it will no longer continue to accept those payments, before it calls the whole loan due and attempts a foreclosure. Failure to do so may provide you with grounds to stop a foreclosure and give you another opportunity to catch up. The delay can be substantial.

Similarly, if the lender accepts a payment after foreclosure has started, you can argue that there is no longer a default. In some states, this will require the lender to restart the foreclosure process from the beginning.

Asking the Court for More Time. In some states, courts have the power to delay foreclosures for other reasons. Two situations where delays may be granted are serious hardship and if there is substantial amount of equity in the home which protects the lender against losses on its claims.

Filing for bankruptcy will delay a foreclosure, but only some bankruptcies will permanently prevent foreclosure.

Serious hardship claims must be documented and they must involve more than the unfortunate circumstance of homelessness. If a family member has a serious illness, for example, a temporary delay may sometimes be granted. Usually the hardship must be temporary as well. If the hardship will last forever, the judge may feel that now is as good a time as any to allow the foreclosure.

If you have a great deal of equity in your home, a court may allow you a short period of time to sell the home without foreclosure. This will allow you to get the best possible price and to preserve your investment. The lender is not hurt because even if its claim against the property goes up because you are unable to make payments, there is enough value in the property to eventually pay the lender's full claim.

A Chapter 7 Bankruptcy May Create A Temporary Delay. As discussed in more detail in Chapter Twenty, a chapter 7 bankruptcy case cannot address a foreclosure problem in the long term. That is because mortgages and other liens (with a few exceptions) survive chapter 7 bankruptcy without being effected. However your filing a chapter 7 bankruptcy case will delay a foreclosure because the automatic stay in the bankruptcy case will temporarily prevent the foreclosure process from continuing. The lender cannot continue foreclosure without permission of the court (this usually takes at least sixty days) or until the case is over.

Two things are important to keep in mind. First, you cannot file a chapter 7 bankruptcy solely to delay foreclosure. You must have some other legitimate purpose to file bankruptcy. For most homeowners in financial distress, this is hardly a problem because there are lots of other debts outstanding. Second, if you want a more permanent solution to your mortgage problem, you will need to file under chapter 13. This is discussed in more detail below.

OBTAINING A DETERMINATION
OF THE AMOUNT YOU OWE

One silver lining in the dark cloud of foreclosure is that a foreclosure proceeding gives you an opportunity to get a determination of the real amount you owe. It is quite common for a lender to claim more than you believe is owed and foreclosure provides an opportunity to have the balance due accurately determined. As a side benefit, if you have a legitimate basis to claim that the lender is seeking more than it is entitled to receive, the process of deciding the accurate amount of the debt may delay the foreclosure.

Some common disputes about the amount claimed due include:

1. Failure to credit all the payments you made;
2. Crediting payments you made in a way which is inconsistent with the accounting principles required by the contract;
3. Compounding interest when compound interest is not permitted;
4. Failing to properly reduce interest rates as required in a variable rate mortgage;
5. Crediting amounts paid by you in ways which are not permitted by the contract (for example, applying payments to credit insurance which you did not authorize);
6. Failure to properly manage escrow balances, (for example, failing to make timely tax payments and thereby incurring late charges);
7. Charging the mortgage account for things not permitted by the loan contract or for amounts which are not reasonable under the circumstances (for example, excessive inspection fees);
8. Charging excessive attorneys fees or costs for foreclosure (only real costs can be charged to your account — the lender should not be able to profit by padding foreclosure fees);
9. Double counting foreclosure fees and costs by including them in the escrow balance and then also separately breaking them out as individual charges;
10. Charging late charges in amounts which are not permitted by the contract.

Occasionally a lender will have caused the default by making one or more errors in accounting or by otherwise mishandling your money. Problems commonly arise when servicing is transferred from one lender to the other. Payments get lost and accounting can be confused. In some cases you may be able to prove that you aren't delinquent at all.

Using the foreclosure process to determine the real amount of the debt can be very important. It can reduce what you have to pay in order to get caught up. Even if you don't have the financial resources necessary to get caught up, you will want to minimize the amount collected from the proceeds of the foreclosure sale (or any voluntary presale) by the lender. This will increase your potential to recover some of your equity if you cannot get back on track with your payments.

The ability to raise and win any of these issues will often require complicated legal work. You will need to review the lender's records in a process known as "discovery." You will also need to present evidence such as canceled checks which supports your own position. More often than not, a lawyer will be needed in order to effectively raise these issues. One helpful resource on many of these issues is National Consumer Law Center, *The Cost of Credit: Regulation and Legal Challenges* (1995 and Supp.).

In some foreclosures, there will be other significant defenses and counterclaims, usually because the lender has done something seriously wrong. Those issues can also be raised in the foreclosure process. Some of those defenses are discussed in more detail below.

Setting Up a "Tender" Defense. If you have a real dispute with your lender about the amount owed, you may want to set up the defense of "tender." To "tender" means to offer the lender the undisputed amount of the debt. The purpose of tendering is to prevent the lender from being able to argue that even if your defense is accepted, there will still be a default which gives rise to a right to foreclose. Although it is not required that you tender the balance in order to dispute the amount claimed due, your effort to tender will help prevent foreclosure and will make your case more sympathetic to a judge.

If you can afford to do so, tender is usually achieved by mailing the undisputed amount of the debt (by check or money order) to the lender with a letter explaining that you dispute the balance. The letter should also state that the amount you tender is offered in full satisfaction of the dispute.

Most often, your tender will be returned. If it is returned, you have the defense that the money was offered and refused. Keep your letter and the lender's response as proof. Put the money into escrow while the dispute is being resolved. You can add the claim of tender to your defenses in the legal process.

If your tender is accepted, in some states you can then claim that acceptance by the lender settles the dispute in your favor. This defense is usually called "accord and satisfaction."

One disadvantage of tendering is that if the money is kept, and later you cannot afford to keep the property or the dispute is resolved against you, you will not be able to get the money back. Sometimes in foreclosure this can mean that you are further investing in a home which cannot you afford in the future.

Even if you cannot afford to tender, or choose not to do so for other reasons, it is a good idea to put money aside during a dispute. The money can be used to cover as much as possible of the mortgage payments if you lose the dispute or to cover any undisputed portion if you win. In the worst case scenario, if foreclosure goes forward, you can use this money to move.

LEGAL RIGHTS
TO CURE AND REDEEM

Using Foreclosure Legal Process to Cure or Redeem. As discussed above, in many states you have a legal right to cure a default by paying all the back-due payments plus certain fees and costs which the lender is permitted to charge you. In most states you also have the right to redeem before the sale by paying the total amount due on the mortgage. In a few states, you can even redeem after the sale. These rights are usually limited in a variety of ways by state laws.

Although many lenders will accept cures or redemptions even when they have no legal obligation to do so, others will not. Some lenders prefer foreclosure, either because they think foreclosure will be profitable or because they no longer want to deal with a borrower who has had financial problems.

You can usually stop a foreclosure if you are able to pay all past-due mortgage payments plus certain costs.

If you have money to get caught up or to pay off the full balance owed on the mortgage, you can usually use the legal process to force the lender to accept it — even if at first glance it looks like your state's law permits the lender to refuse the money. That is because judges have discretion in most states to impose fair resolutions of disputes. This can include ordering things like cure or redemption.

Most judges will not want to allow a family to be put on the street when the family has money to pay the arrears or the full balance owed. Even in states where judges do not have this power, offering a cure or redemption to the lender in court in front of a judge, will sometimes embarrass the lender into accepting.

Filing a Chapter 13 Bankruptcy May Stop a Foreclosure Permanently If You Make Required Payments. You should carefully consider filing a bankruptcy case if you are in financial distress and about to lose your home. This can stop the foreclosure process and allow you time to regroup and try to work out a plan to keep your home. Chapter 13 of the bankruptcy law always requires lenders to accept cures and redemptions even when state law says otherwise. In fact, in chapter 13 bankruptcy, you can cure or redeem in installment payments over time rather than have to come up with a lump sum.

Bankruptcy is covered in detail in this book's Chapter Twenty and in even more depth in National Consumer Law Center, *Consumer Bankruptcy Law and Practice* (5th ed. 1996 and Supp.). Only some of the most important impacts of the bankruptcy process on foreclosure will be discussed here.

The bankruptcy option may not be effective unless carefully planned and timed. For example, a premature bankruptcy filing may eliminate your right to receive special state assistance or may prevent the lender from discussing more favorable workout options. If you file too late, your ability to cure or redeem may have been lost. You will almost always have to file before the foreclosure sale in order to cure or redeem.

The Automatic Stay. The first reason why bankruptcy is a powerful method of dealing with a foreclosure is the "automatic stay." The filing of your petition in bankruptcy automatically stops most creditor actions against you and your property, including foreclosure, foreclosure sales, and the filing of liens against your property.

The lender cannot proceed without first asking for the bankruptcy judge's permission to do so. The bankruptcy judge will often *not* give the lender permission to proceed — especially if you have proposed a plan in chapter 13 to cure or redeem the debt on the mortgage.

Curing Delinquent Payments and Reinstating the Mortgage. The automatic stay gives you time to take advantage of other aspects of the bankruptcy law. In a chapter 13 bankruptcy filing, called a "debt adjustment" case, you can "cure" (pay back) the delinquent payments gradually over a period of years so long as you can also keep up on future mortgage payments as they come due each month. In a chapter 13 case, you normally have three years to pay back-due mortgage payments, but that can be extended to five years if there is a good reason.

The following example of a cure in a five year chapter 13 case shows how helpful a bankruptcy filing can be. Assume you are six months behind on $500 monthly mortgage payments, so that your total arrears is $3000. In a five year chapter 13 case, you can cure by making future $500 payments as they come due, and catching up on the past due $3000 in sixty monthly payments of $50 each.

You may also have to pay interest on the $3000 while you cure the default and a commission to the bankruptcy trustee for handling your payments. This will add about $16.00 a month to your obligation. Although a few courts require that you get caught up in less than five years, most presently will allow a five year payment plan if it will take you that long to get caught up.

You can cure delinquent payments in a chapter 13 bankruptcy case even if a lender has already accelerated payments so that the full loan amount is due or even if the lender has obtained a foreclosure judgment. You can also pay off a mortgage in bankruptcy even if the last payment has already become due or if it will be due during the bankruptcy case itself.

Another important issue when using the bankruptcy law to cure a mortgage delinquency is the extent to which lenders can collect attorney's fees and costs as part of the amount needed to cure. The lender is only entitled to attorney's fees and costs if the credit agreement clearly provides for collection of such charges. Even then, many state laws either place significant limitations on fee arrangements or prohibit them entirely.

When fees are appropriate, they should be assessed only if they are reasonable, necessary, and actually paid. A lender whose litigation is unsuccessful or unnecessary should not be allowed to collect fees.

Redemption (keeping your home by paying off the full debt) is another option in a chapter 13 bankruptcy. If you redeem, you can do so over the full three or five year term of the chapter 13 plan, and, in some parts of the country, you can reduce the interest rate on your loan principal from the rate originally specified in the loan to interest rates prevailing in your community today for similar loans. This can be a big savings.

Raising Disputes in Bankruptcy. The bankruptcy process gives you another opportunity to raise defenses to the lenders' claim (if they have not already been raised and rejected by another court). You do not lose your right to raise disputes about how much you owe or about fraud or unfairness when you walk into bankruptcy court. These defenses and others can be raised as "objections to claims" as part of determining how much you have to pay under your chapter 13 bankruptcy plan.

Sale of a Home in a Chapter 13 Bankruptcy. If you can no longer afford your mortgage payments, you will not benefit from the ability to cure past delinquencies. However, you can use the bankruptcy process to sell the home on your own in an orderly fashion, thereby keeping your equity and avoiding the problems of a foreclosure sale. This strategy is probably only available to you if you will earn enough from the sale of the property to pay both your secured and unsecured creditors from the sale proceeds.

If you want to sell your home after filing bankruptcy, you usually have to request that the court approve your realtor. When a sale is arranged, you will also have to file with the bankruptcy court a "Complaint to Sell Property Free of Liens" and obtain an order from the bankruptcy court approving the sale and allowing the property to be sold free of liens. (Many title insurance companies require this order for the sale to go through.)

This section provides only a brief overview of your options in bankruptcy. If you want to use bankruptcy to help prevent a foreclosure, you should also read Chapter Twenty.

IF YOU DECIDE
TO GO TO COURT

If you decide to go to court for one of the reasons discussed in this chapter, keep in mind that there are strict time deadlines to do so. At the very latest, any defenses you have must be raised before the foreclosure sale process is completed. And in many states defenses are cut off even earlier.

When evaluating how to raise claims in court in your state, keep in mind that there are significant differences between states that have a court process for foreclosure (often called "judicial" foreclosure) and states that do not (often called "nonjudicial" foreclosure.) Some of these differences are discussed in Chapter Eleven.

In a judicial foreclosure state, you should receive notice that the lender started a court case. You will then have a short period of time to file an "answer" to the foreclosure case or to file motions to raise procedural issues. Sometimes, this deadline can be extended if you make a request. If you miss this deadline, it may be more difficult to raise defenses. At the least, you will have to explain in your court papers why you missed the deadline. If a court order has been entered in the case (usually called a "judgment"), you will have an even greater obligation to show why you did not file your response on time.

In nonjudicial foreclosure states, time restrictions until the date of sale may be less severe. However, raising your defenses is substantially more complicated because there is no court process in which to do so. This means that you have to begin your own case in court to prevent the foreclosure. You may have to pay court fees and other court costs to do so.

Access to the bankruptcy court is discussed in more detail in Chapter Twenty. More discussion about court procedures is contained in Chapter Eight.

Foreclosures Which Create Special Consumer Rights

- *FHA, HUD, VA, and RHS Mortgages and Special State Mortgage Programs*
- *Mortgages Not Used to Buy Your Home, Abusive Home Improvement Loans, and Unfair or Deceptive Loan Terms*
- *Condominiums, Mobile Homes, and Judicial Liens*

The prior chapter examined your right to defend against a foreclosure of your home. That chapter is generally applicable to all foreclosures. In addition, you have special rights if your mortgage falls within one or more of the following ten categories:

- Your mortgage is insured by FHA or HUD;
- Your mortgage is insured by the VA;
- Your mortgage is insured by the Rural Housing Service (formerly FmHA);
- Your state has a mortgage assistance program or a foreclosure moratorium;
- The mortgage is a second mortgage or a first mortgage not used to purchase the home (so that you may have Truth in Lending rescission rights);
- The lien or mortgage results from a home improvement scam;
- The loan agreement has unfair or abusive provisions;
- Your home is a condominium;
- Your home is a mobile home; or

- The creditor has no mortgage, but is foreclosing based on a court judgment.

The discussion of each of these ten topics will reference other sources of information. For all of these topics, if you need more information, you can see National Consumer Law Center, *Repossessions and Foreclosures* Ch. 13 (3d ed. 1995 and Supp.).

FORECLOSURE OF FHA/HUD-INSURED MORTGAGES

For More Information. At present, families with mortgages insured by the Federal Housing Administration (FHA) and the United States Department of Housing and Urban Development (HUD) have some rights not available to families with conventional loans. (We will refer to all of the FHA and HUD loan programs as "HUD mortgages.") Help with your rights under a HUD mortgage can be found by asking your HUD regional office for information about how to obtain HUD-funded foreclosure prevention counseling. You can also get help through HUD's automated phone line. It will identify HUD-approved housing counselors that are close to your community. Call 1-800-569-4287 (TDD 1-800-877-8339). You can also try calling a local housing or credit counseling organization that you identify on your own.

How to Tell If You Have an FHA or HUD Mortgage. If you have an FHA or HUD mortgage you are likely to be paying government insurance premiums with your mortgage payment. If you don't know whether this is the case, look at your original mortgage or loan documents. (Since some lenders use the HUD forms for all mortgages, you cannot assume that if your forms say FHA or HUD at the top or bottom, you have a HUD mortgage.) Look to see whether your payment includes a government mortgage insurance premium. You can also check whether there is a box marked "FHA insured" that is checked off on your settlement statement.

If you have any doubt, call and ask your lender. Their records should be clear on this issue because the existence of the insurance is a benefit to them.

YOUR HUD
MORTGAGE RIGHTS
IN A NUTSHELL

Notice Of Default. Lenders must give you notice of your default no later than the end of the second month of your delinquency. This notice must explain what you must do to get reinstated.

Face-to-Face Interviews. Lenders must make reasonable efforts to arrange face-to-face interviews with you before three full monthly installments are overdue. Telephone reviews are also possible. These interviews give you an opportunity to talk to the lender about a loan workout or other alternative to foreclosure.

Foreclosure Limits. Lenders cannot begin legal foreclosure proceedings until you are at least three monthly payments overdue. Lenders also cannot foreclose if your only default is an inability to pay an escrow shortage in a lump sum.

Special Forbearance Workout Plans. If you have defaulted on a HUD loan, you are eligible for a special forbearance plan if you have recently experienced a reduction in income or an increase in living expenses for reasons beyond your control. You must show the lender that you have a reasonable ability to pay in the future under the terms of such a forbearance agreement.

If you qualify for a special forbearance plan, reduced or suspended payments may apply for up to eighteen months from the date of the oldest unpaid payment. The amount of your payment in that period can be based on your budget. However, the total amount of the forbearance cannot exceed the equivalent of twelve monthly payments over the eighteen month period. This means that you can get reduction of your payments for at least twelve months, but no more than eighteen months — depending on the amount of any partial payments you can make.

At the end of the eighteen months, you must begin paying at least the full amount of the monthly mortgage payment due under the mortgage. You must also agree to a repayment plan to catch up on any amounts that you have fallen behind. These payments on the arrears can be made in small installments over any part of the remaining period of your loan.

You can negotiate a special forbearance agreement even if foreclosure proceedings have started. In that case, the lender may first require that you pay foreclosure costs.

Negotiating a special forbearance agreement can be a difficult process. Many lenders resist following the rules that HUD sets for special forbearance. Help is available from HUD's Servicing and Loss Mitigation Division in Oklahoma City at 888-297-8685.

HUD provides special options
for homeowners who need help getting
caught up on their mortgage payments.
One option, special forbearance, may allow you
to make reduced payments for up to 18 months
so that you can get back on your feet.

Partial Claims. In some cases, HUD will pay your lender to get your loan payments caught up to date. Lenders may make a claim to HUD on your mortgage insurance in the amount of no more than the equivalent of twelve monthly mortgage payments. If HUD approves the claim, the money is applied to your account to cover payments you have missed.

To be eligible for a partial claim, you must be at least four months, but no more than twelve months behind. You must be able to resume making full monthly mortgage payments and you must not be able to afford a special forbearance agreement (described above).

If lender applies and HUD agrees, HUD will pay the lender directly to get your loan payments caught up. You must agree to give HUD an interest-free mortgage in the amount of HUD's payment on your behalf. You will not need to pay this mortgage, unless you choose to do so, until you sell or transfer ownership of the property or pay off the original mortgage.

Mortgage Modification. HUD will allow some homeowners to modify their mortgages, usually to change the loan term and lower the monthly payment. For the most part, this option is the same as the mortgage modification options discussed in Chapter Eleven.

Short Sales and Deeds in Lieu of Foreclosure. A lender may also agree to accept a solution to your problem in which you sell or give up your property voluntarily. These options are discussed in Chapter Eleven. If you can show need, HUD may also allow you a small amount of money to help you move.

If the Lender Fails to Meet HUD Requirements. A lender's failure to meet HUD's servicing requirements can be a defense to foreclosure. Before raising a defense, you may wish to get help from a HUD-approved counselor as discussed above. Sometimes a counselor can pre a lender to give you a second chance.

HUD also has an office in Oklahoma City whose responsibilities include helping you if you are facing foreclosure on a HUD mortgage. At the time this book was being written, the telephone number for that office is 888-297-8685. Stay on the line until a HUD field officer picks up.

Unfortunately, even if you ask for special help as discussed in this section, either the lender or HUD may reject your application for special assistance if it does not think your plan is realistic. As a last resort, a lawyer may be willing to raise the failure of a HUD-insured lender to comply with the governing law as a reason to stop a foreclosure. More often than not, this will delay rather than permanently prevent foreclosure. Once the lender has given you the options discussed here, the foreclosure can proceed.

FORECLOSURE OF VA-GUARANTEED MORTGAGES

If your mortgage is insured by the Veterans' Administration (VA), you have rights that are not available to homeowners with private conventional mortgages. To tell whether you have a VA mortgage, look for the VA logo on the top corner of the mortgage or other loan documents. If you are unsure, call and ask the lender.

Restrictions on Lender's Right to Foreclose on a VA Mortgage. Families with VA mortgages have certain protections against foreclosure. The lender cannot foreclose unless you fail to make three full monthly payments. The lender must give the VA thirty days warning of its intent to foreclose, and must make all reasonable efforts at forbearance before actually foreclosing on the property. In addition, the VA may assist you if you are an active member of the service and if a job transfer requires relocation, and you lack time to adequately market your home.

The lender must consider temporary suspension of payments, extension of the loan, and acceptance of partial payments. If the lender still intends to foreclose, you can stop the foreclosure by paying all delinquent payments, late charges and any of the lender's foreclosure expenses to date.

The lender's failure to meet its obligations in this area can be a defense to foreclosure. If you hope to use this defense it is a good idea to send a letter to the lender which asks the lender to consider one or more of these foreclosure avoidance strategies. The lender's failure to respond appropriately would then be evidence of its failure to meet its responsibilities.

In recent years, the Veterans Administration has devoted more resources to helping homeowners with workout plans. Contact a local VA office and ask to speak to an employee that deals with the VA's mortgage guarantee program. It is helpful to be ready to explain the reasons for your default and what you foresee as the best plan for getting your mortgage payments back on track.

FORECLOSURE OF RURAL HOUSING SERVICE MORTGAGES

The Rural Housing Service (RHS) (formerly known as the Farmer's Home Administration or FmHA) also runs programs designed to help you avoid foreclosure. To tell whether your mortgage is RHS insured or guaranteed, look at the mortgage papers or loan documents or call the lender. Older loans may refer to FmHA insurance or guarantees. You also may find a reference to the "section 502 Single-Family Housing Program."

Traditionally, loan servicing at RHS was handled at the local level through Rural Development field offices. Since September 1997, however, all servicing has been handled through the RHS's Centralized Servicing Center in St. Louis, Missouri. As this book is being written, that office can be reached at 1-800-793-8861. It is easier to get assistance if you have your account number handy.

RHS Assistance Programs. When a financial setback interferes with your ability to make payments, RHS has special servicing programs designed to assist you. These include "payment moratoriums," "delinquency workout agreements," and "protective advances." In addition, if you have an Interest Credit Payment Assistance subsidy, RHS can increase your subsidy within certain limits to make your payment more affordable.

Payment Moratorium. A payment moratorium is available when you can show that due to circumstances beyond your control, you are unable to continue making full payments without substantially impairing your standard of living. Under the moratorium program, your scheduled monthly payments may be reduced, based on need, for up to two years. At the end of two years (or earlier if RHS determines that you no longer need moratorium assistance), your monthly payments will be recalculated based on the existing balance at that time. If you are unable to afford the payments after they are recalculated, some or all of the interest that came due during moratorium may be canceled. Eligibility for the moratorium program is reviewed every six months, and you should be provided with sixty days notice before the moratorium is terminated.

Other RHS Options. A Delinquency Workout Agreement (DWA) allows you to make a delinquent account current, either by making a single lump-sum payment or by paying the delinquent amount, in addition to your scheduled mortgage payment, over a period of no more than two years. This works like a payment agreement as discussed in Chapter Eleven.

A "protective advance" occurs when RHS advances money to pay for taxes or insurance, and then recalculates the loan balance and payments. When the loan is recalculated, if the payment period is extended, your loan payments may go down. This is illustrated with an example in Chapter Eleven.

Many RHS loans come with interest rate subsidies to make the payments affordable. If you are experiencing financial problems, the subsidy may be increased for a period of time while you get back on your feet.

You Must Apply Quickly When These Options Are Offered. RHS will not initiate these special servicing options until you are at least two months delinquent. You should apply for special servicing options very quickly, because foreclosure can proceed just a month later if you are not prepared to go forward.

Appeals. If a request for special servicing is denied, you can appeal to a higher RHS official. If your application and your appeal are improperly denied, it may be possible to challenge the lender's decision to foreclose on your home.

SPECIAL PROTECTIONS AVAILABLE IN CERTAIN STATES

Homeowners in a few states have special protections from foreclosure. These protections may involve a state program to provide temporary payments to help pay mortgages or state laws that prohibit foreclosures in certain situations. These protections are relatively rare, but states are more likely to reinstitute such programs during financial recessions or after natural disasters.

State Mortgage Assistance Programs. Pennsylvania presently has a special mortgage assistance program that provides loans from state funds to homeowners who are threatened with foreclosure to help them get caught up on delinquent payments and make some future payments. Similar programs in Maryland, Connecticut and New Jersey may be temporarily or permanently closed due to lack of funds.

If you receive a notice about the availability of special assistance with foreclosure, you should apply if you think you have any chance at all of meeting the program's requirements. These programs have early deadlines which you must meet. Failing to meet the deadlines will disqualify you.

Private Programs. There are also a variety of private programs for financial assistance with mortgage payments in different parts of the country. To find out about these programs, you should contact a local nonprofit housing counselor or other specialist.

One pitfall, however, is that some scam artists have learned to design their rip-offs to look like assistance offered by a nonprofit. Before getting into a deal too deeply, investigate to make sure the program is legitimate. Never sign away rights to your home in order to get help.

State Bans On Foreclosure. During the economic depression of the 1930s, many states enacted moratorium laws postponing foreclosure sales of homes and farms. Where still in effect, these laws sometimes prevent foreclosures by requiring lenders to accept smaller payments during moratorium periods. For example, the Iowa foreclosure law provides general relief in cases of natural disasters and both Iowa and Minnesota provide relief when the governor declares an economic emergency.

Occasionally, a state will declare a temporary local emergency and allow foreclosure relief in areas where plant closings have created widespread distress and depressed housing markets. This gives dislocated workers time to put their affairs in order. Similarly, during a plant closing crisis in the early 1980s in Pennsylvania, local judges and sheriffs postponed home foreclosures against dislocated workers without resorting to a moratorium law. Massachusetts had a temporary moratorium in 1991 on foreclosures. The legislature was responding to widespread instances of home improvement fraud and other second mortgage scams.

When there is a state ban on foreclosures, you will be temporarily protected for a period of time. This will give you an opportunity to get back on your feet.

Disaster Assistance. If the default on your mortgage was caused by a natural disaster (either because it affected your income or required unusual expenses for repairs), you may be able to obtain state or federal disaster relief. Check with your local government or a local Federal Emergency Management Assistance (FEMA) office.

Lender Funded Counseling Programs. Some lenders have established programs to provide special counseling assistance to homeowners facing foreclosure — usually through local nonprofit organizations. These programs are generally free.

Counselors in these programs will guide you through the process of presenting an application to the lender for a loan workout or temporary delay of foreclosure. In many cases, counselors will have access to programs and lender personnel that you cannot reach yourself directly. It can't hurt to ask the lender if it has a program for homeowner assistance in your community.

Free foreclosure counseling assistance is especially common for homeowners that bought their homes with the help of first-time homeowner education programs. If you received prepurchase education about homeownership, contact the organization that provided your classes to find out if they also provide foreclosure prevention assistance.

Finally, even if the lender is not offering free homeowner assistance, there may be nonprofit organizations in your community that can help. Contact your local government housing office or a community group that addresses housing and homeownership.

MORTGAGES NOT USED
TO PURCHASE YOUR HOME

Truth in Lending Rescission Provides Potent Relief in Certain Circumstances. Federal law provides you with an extraordinarily effective means of stopping a foreclosure in certain special situations. Instead of giving you more time to make reduced payments, this federal remedy allows you to permanently *cancel* your mortgage and significantly reduce the amount of the debt you owe the lender. Once the mortgage is canceled, there can be no foreclosure.

If you can legally rescind your loan

under Truth in Lending, you, not the lender,

will be in the driver's seat.

This remedy, called Truth in Lending rescission, is not available to cancel a mortgage used to purchase or build your home. But it may be available to cancel other types of mortgages, such as second mortgages, first mortgages not used to purchase your home, refinanced mortgages, debt consolidation loans involving mortgages, and home equity lines of credit.

Experience has shown that Truth in Lending rescission is most effective when dealing with credit contracts imposed by home improvement contractors, finance companies, and mortgage companies that prey on families in financial distress. In fact, in 1994, Congress added to the law for just this purpose. High-interest rate loans and loans with high up-front costs now carry special rescission rights.

While Truth in Lending rescission sounds almost too good to be true, there are three catches. First, Truth in Lending rescission does not apply to certain types of loans. Second, the lender must have made one of a list of basic mistakes when providing information to you about your mortgage. Third, you must usually go to court to convince the lender to honor your Truth in Lending rescission rights.

Obviously, a lawyer or other highly specialized professional will be necessary if you are to successfully utilize Truth in Lending rescission. Contact your local bar association referral service, your local legal services office, or seek a recommendation from a local nonprofit. You may want to ask for a specialist in consumer law. If your case is successful, the home will be free from the mortgage, your indebtedness may be reduced by thousands of dollars, and the lender may have to pay for your attorney.

This section is not a detailed analysis of Truth in Lending rescission, which can be quite technical. This section does help you identify when Truth in Lending rescission is definitely not available and when it may be, thus telling you whether it is worth contacting an attorney to discuss your rescission rights. More detailed information is available in National Consumer Law Center, *Truth in Lending* (3d ed. 1995 and Supp.). Besides a detailed analysis of all aspects of the law, the volume reprints the key sources of Truth in Lending law — the Truth in Lending Act (TILA), the federal TILA regulations, and the official federal TILA interpretations, as well as sample letters and pleadings.

When Does Truth in Lending Rescission Apply? Truth in Lending rescission applies to most home mortgages except the ones taken when you buy or build a home. When more than one person has the right to rescind a transaction (such as husband and wife), any one of the individuals can exercise the right and cancel the transaction on behalf of all.

TILA rescission applies unless:

- The mortgage loan was used to purchase or build the home;
- The mortgage loan was not for consumer purposes, but was for business or agricultural purposes;
- The lender was only involved in a very few loans within the last year;
- The mortgage is on investment property, a vacation house, or other property *not* your principal residence at the time the loan was extended. (A mobile home, condominium, cooperative, two or three-family home, trailer, even a

houseboat *can* be a principal residence);
- You no longer own the home that the mortgage relates to;
- The mortgage is a refinancing of an existing loan where no new money is borrowed and the same property stays mortgaged;
- The mortgage is more than three years old (although there may be extensions of this time period in some states).

When Can You Rescind a Mortgage? There are three different situations where you can use TILA rescission to cancel your mortgage. You can rescind for any reason within three days after taking out a loan that uses your home as collateral. This obviously will have little relevance in most foreclosure situations, but is very useful when dealing with high-pressure lenders and home improvement sellers.

You can also cancel a mortgage loan if you did not receive proper notice that you could rescind the loan. Lenders must deliver two copies of the notice of the right to rescind. The notice must be on a separate document that identifies the transaction, discloses that the lender has a mortgage on specified property of yours, and that you and joint owners have a right to rescind. The notice must also give directions on how to rescind, with a form for that purpose, with the appropriate addresses, the effects of rescission, and how long you have to rescind. Failure to include all this information or failure to give you this notice are grounds for you to cancel the loan.

The third basis for canceling the loan is if the lender makes a mistake in its disclosure of certain important terms of the loan. If the disclosure is improper, you can rescind the loan unless you are given a corrected disclosure. In practice, since lenders rarely correct mistakes, you can cancel just before the foreclosure unless the loan is more than three years old. Some courts allow rescission even for loans older than three years if you are trying to prevent a foreclosure.

For many loans, the key issue will be whether the lender has made a mistake on the disclosure form sufficient to allow you to cancel. This issue can be quite complicated. However, errors are often made in important calculations, especially when there are a variety of costs and charges in connection with the loan. In 1995, Congress tried to make it harder for homeowners to rescind mortgages by increasing the limit for permissible errors; however, most of the changes do not apply when you are using the law to defend against a foreclosure.

Uncovering Truth in Lending Errors. Any decision to pursue Truth in Lending rescission should be made with the assistance of an attorney or other professional experienced with financial calculations and Truth in Lending issues. In fact, the analysis necessary to uncover lender mistakes may be intimidating for many. Nevertheless, there are several steps that you or your counselor can take to explore whether your home can be saved through Truth in Lending rescission:

- *Check the numbers.* Based on the payment schedule, is the total of payments accurate? Is the annual percentage rate calculation correct? Does the amount financed and finance charge add up to the total of payments? The National Consumer Law Center's *Truth in Lending* manual explains what mathematical errors to look for and how to show that the lender made a mistake.
- *Review the calculation of the amount financed.* See what happened to the "amount financed," that is the money you borrowed, by reviewing the contract and any itemization you received. Be suspicious if large portions of the amount financed does not go to you or for your benefit. When a loan is loaded with broker's fees, points, insurance, assorted fees, and the like, it may pay to ask a lawyer familiar with Truth in Lending law to scrutinize the contract. The National Consumer Law Center's *Truth in Lending* gives a step by step analysis as to whether the existence of these charges in the amount financed will allow a homeowner to rescind.
- *Prohibited terms in some loans.* If you have a recent high-interest rate loan or a loan with high fees and costs (paid from the loan), the lender is subject to extensive additional regulation. Additional disclosures are required. Many unfair terms are prohibited in those loans including most balloon payments, negative amortization, and most prepayment penalties. Failing to make necessary special disclosures or including a prohibited term in these loans is a ground for you to rescind.
- *Did you receive information about your right to cancel?* If not, the loan is rescindable. For home improvement contracts, did the contractor begin working before the three day period elapsed?

How to Cancel. If three days have not yet passed since the loan papers were signed you need not find any errors in the loan terms in order to cancel. Simply return the cancellation form provided by the lender. Make sure to do this by the deadline, and be sure to keep a copy for yourself.

If you think you may have a right to cancel but more than three days have passed, you should check with an experienced consumer lawyer. You will need to send a notice of rescission to the lender, but the requirements for doing so after the three day period has expired are somewhat technical. Several sample forms related to cancellation are included in National Consumer Law Center, *Truth in Lending* (3d ed. 1995 and Supp.).

The Effect of Cancellation. Sending the rescission notice automatically voids the mortgage. As long as the rescission was proper, the lender no longer has the right to foreclose on your home. Within twenty calendar days after the lender receives the notice of rescission, the lender must cancel the mortgage and file that release on the public record. Although you may later have to return to the lender the amount borrowed (not including interest and other charges), you need not do so at the outset. The mortgage is still void and the home is out of danger.

Of course, a lender receiving a cancellation notice but no loan payments will not be happy. Typically, the lender will ignore the notice and pursue the mortgage foreclosure. What this means is that you will have to retain an attorney to fight for enforcement of the right to rescind. Your lawyer can raise the Truth in Lending rescission as a defense to the foreclosure.

There is much misunderstanding, even by lawyers, as to a consumer's financial responsibility after rescinding a loan. It is true that rescinding a loan does not mean that you necessarily get to keep all the loan proceeds. On the other hand, many people mistakenly believe that the consumer, when rescinding, must immediately tender the full amount of the loan. Obviously, this usually would be impossible.

The exact answer as to when and if you must pay the loan back after rescission will depend on many factors. The bottom line is that you should not have to pay anything back before the mortgage is voided, meaning that the home will be safe from foreclosure.

The amount you do pay back will often be significantly less than the amount borrowed. If your rescission is proper, you will not have to repay interest, most fees, closing costs, points, insurance payments and other charges. Any payments you have made will be credited to the principal.

For a home improvement contract, you may just have to return the value of the work done, which is often much less than what you paid for it. Furthermore, the lender's violation of Truth in Lending law will usually mean that you can knock off at least another $2000 from the amount owed, and perhaps significantly more.

You will probably need to go to court for a decision about whether your cancellation was proper. In such a case, you should also raise whatever other legal claims are available, such as breach of warranty, deception, and the like as additional reasons why the amount owed should be further reduced.

If you still have to return a sizeable amount to the lender, you may not be able to do so. But there may not be much the lender can do about that. The amount might become an unsecured debt, depending on the situation. Unlike the canceled debt, your home would no longer be collateral for the loan. Alternatively, you can seek to refinance the amount owed (which should be much less than the original loan amount) with a different lender and at lower interest rates. This may well result in affordable payments.

MORTGAGES RESULTING FROM A HOME IMPROVEMENT SCAM

A widespread and vicious scam is to pressure you into a home improvement contract — aluminum siding, basement waterproofing, replacement windows, roofing, etc. — and then have you sign up for very unfavorable financing and a mortgage on your home. If the home improvement contractor never completes the work or the work is shoddy or wildly overpriced, you then have resulting legal claims against the home improvement contractor. A different company, often a finance company or a mortgage company, will nevertheless try to collect on the loan and foreclose when you refuse to pay or get behind.

In almost all such situations, you can fight the foreclosure based on the misconduct of the home improvement contractor. That is, even though the contractor and lender are not the same company, there is enough connection between the two so that you can raise the contractor's misconduct as a reason why you need not repay the loan.

While raising the conduct of a contractor or salesperson is a very effective defense to a foreclosure, it is best to obtain legal representation to make sure that the defense is raised correctly. More detailed information (than what is presented below) about raising the contractor's misconduct as a defense to a foreclosure is found in another National Consumer Law Center manual, *Unfair and Deceptive Acts and Practices* (4th ed. 1997 and Supp.) You also may wish to look at National Consumer Law Center, *Consumer Warranty Law* (1997 and Supp.) for a description of many defenses you have against the home improvement contractor in these sorts of transactions.

If a contractor ripped you off, you may not have to repay a loan that the contractor arranged for you to pay for the work.

When Is Your Lender Responsible for Your Contractor's Misconduct?

You can almost always defend a foreclosure based on the home improvement contractor's misconduct. In most cases the loan documents will say that any holder of the loan is subject to all claims and defenses that you have against the seller. In other words, the very loan the lender is trying to enforce will say that you can raise the contractor's misconduct as a defense.

Where this provision is not in the loan documents, you still may be able to raise the contractor's misconduct as a defense. First, distinguish between loans where the contractor was the original lender and loans where the contractor arranged for a different party to be the original lender.

In the first situation, the contractor's name will be on the loan as the lender, and the contractor will then have sold the loan to another lender. In that situation, the law allows you to raise against the second lender all defenses that you could have raised against the home improvement contractor.

The situation is not so clear-cut when another lender (not the contractor) was the original lender. About half the states have laws that say that the lender is responsible for what a closely related seller did. So if the home improvement contractor referred the lender to you, the lender is responsible for what the contractor did. In the other half of the states, there are various arguments that a lawyer can make as to why you can still raise what the contractor did as a defense to the foreclosure.

Defending a Foreclosure Based on Contractor Misconduct. If the contractor never did any work, failed to complete required work, or did the work in a very sloppy or inadequate way, that should be sufficient to stop a foreclosure. These situations create warranty or deceptive practices claims.

It is also possible to have a partial defense based on a warranty or deceptive practice which would reduce the amount you owe to prevent foreclosure. On the other hand, small errors or minor problems with the work probably will not suffice as foreclosure defense. In some cases, these problems can be fixed by calling the contractor.

Similarly, door-to-door sellers (including contractors who go door to door) have to give you a three day cancellation right, either under Truth in Lending law or under door-to-door sales laws or both. If this right to cancel was never given, or if work began before the three day period ended, you may be able to cancel the home improvement contract. A canceled sales contract would be a complete defense on the loan.

You may have claims against the contractor, which are smaller in amount than the total amount you owe on the loan. The loan will still be a binding obligation even though you have a defense to repayment of part of it.

If you are in default, the lender may be able to foreclose because of your obligation to pay part of the loan. Nevertheless, some courts will delay the foreclosure until the amount owed is established. You can often negotiate so that you need only keep current on smaller payments based on the new loan amount. Alternatively, you can consider refinancing with a reputable company for the amount which is still owed.

MORTGAGES BASED ON
UNFAIR AND OPPRESSIVE LOANS

Some lenders engage in outrageous loan conduct, and victimized borrowers should defend the foreclosure based on the lender's misconduct. Especially suspect are high-interest loans from home improvement contractors, finance companies, and mortgage companies. There are many types of lender practices that may provide you with a defense on a foreclosure.

Conduct That May Void Your Loan. Look for the following, which may eliminate your obligation to repay the loan and thus stop the foreclosure:

- The lender misrepresented the nature of the document you signed, for example, saying — "this is just an application;"
- The lender made false statements about the basic loan terms, orally or in writing;
- The interest rate exceeds the state maximum;
- The lender is not licensed to do business in your state;
- Illegal terms are included in the loan documents;
- The lender coerced you into signing the loan;
- The person who signed the mortgage was not the real owner of the mortgaged property (usually this involves forgery);
- The person who signed for the loan was not legally competent to do so (for example, children below a certain age or people who are mentally infirm).

Where these defenses are available, you can have the loan declared void. Often you will need the help of a lawyer to do so.

Other Types of Lender Misconduct. Other lender conduct may not nullify your loan, but may influence a court in a foreclosure proceeding to give you more time and lower the amount you owe. Generally speaking, anything that the lender does that is unfair, unconscionable or deceptive can be the basis for a claim.

Similarly, the lender's failure to accurately disclose important information, such as the disadvantageous nature of an unusual loan provision, creates a legal claim. If the lender's misrepresentation was intentional, the lender may even be liable for punitive damages in addition to your actual injury from the misrepresentation.

You may have a defense if the lender knew you could not afford the loan payments, or arranged a variable rate loan knowing that your income was fixed. You should also consider challenging consolidation loans if the monthly payments are higher than the total payments of the loans being consolidated.

Lenders also should not refinance low or no interest debts, such as medical or utility bills or low-rate first mortgages, into a high-interest loan. Continually re-obligating consumers with new refinanced loans may be unfair if prepayment or rebate penalties apply with each new loan. Also, consider seeking legal advice if the lender gave you a loan amount substantially larger loan you applied for but you didn't get additional cash.

A loan may also violate one of a number of credit laws, such as a state usury law or the federal Truth in Lending law. Usually it takes a professional well versed in these areas to identify such violations. Substantial additional information on identifying these types of claims and how to pursue them is contained in National Consumer Law Center, *Unfair and Deceptive Acts and Practices* (4th ed. 1997 and Supp.).

CONDOMINIUM FEES

If you are having trouble paying the mortgage on your condominium, you are probably also behind on your condominium fees. It is important for you to understand the implications to you of your delinquent condo fees.

Condominium owners own their unit, but the building, the land on which it sits, and the other "common areas" are owned by the association of unit owners. Each unit owner has a percentage interest in the common areas, and the condominium association collects a fee (usually monthly) from each unit owner to pay for upkeep of the common areas and for certain other services (e.g. landscaping, snow and trash removal, etc.).

The condominium association will have collection remedies for failure to pay your condominium fees and may pursue them aggressively. State laws vary in terms of how associations may go about collecting the debt.

A recent trend in some states has been to give condominium associations a priority lien for the payment of fees. A priority lien means that the condominium association may foreclose and collect a certain amount of its fees through the sale of your unit. This means that you can lose your condominium unless you pay your fees or reach some type of agreement to get caught up over time.

When condominium association liens are put on your property records, they may complicate the process of arranging a workout with your other mortgage lenders. That is because the mortgage may be at risk if there is a foreclosure on the condominium liens. For this reason, when pursuing a workout agreement in a state that allows associations a lien, you will need to pay off your fees or negotiate with the condominium association at the same time as you deal with your other lenders.

Another common way for an association to get its fees is through legal action. The association's trustees may file suit and then seek to enforce the court's judgment if they win. If your unit is rented, they may also be able to collect rent from your tenants until the arrears are paid. If your condo association pursues this remedy, the lawsuit will be just like any other lawsuit to collect a debt. Your options for dealing with debt collection lawsuits in general are discussed in Chapter Eight.

It is important to communicate with the association's trustees or property manager if you are unable to pay your condominium fees. Let them know the reason you fell behind and try to arrange an agreement which will address the problem based on your financial circumstances. Remind them that you have to make your mortgage, food, and utility payments first and then you can apply funds toward the condominium fees. Since the other owners are your neighbors, they may be willing to work out an agreement with you that will help you through difficult times.

MOBILE HOMES

Is a Mobile Home Realty or Personal Property? Mobile home owners face some unique issues when dealing with a threatened foreclosure. The first question is whether the mobile home is real estate (similar to a home) or personal property (similar to a vehicle). In states that treat mobile homes as realty, the lender who wants to foreclose will have to use real estate foreclosure procedures. If your state treats mobile homes as personal property, the lender may be able to repossess the mobile home through a judicial procedure, commonly known as replevin or through self-help repossession.

Whether a mobile home will be treated as real property or personal property depends on your state's laws. You will need to get information about your state's approach to this question. In some states there is no clear answer, because the treatment of a mobile home depends on a variety of factors, including where the mobile home was when the mortgage was signed. Was it on the dealer's lot or attached semi-permanently to land? If it was attached to land, was it your own land or was it in a mobile home park?

It is important to know that the law in some states may treat your mobile home as personal property in some circumstances and as real property in others. You may need legal help to answer this important question.

You should consider discussing the possibility of a workout agreement with the lender if you are behind on payments whether your mobile home is real estate or personal property. A variety of options for workouts are discussed at Chapter Twelve.

If a workout is not possible and your mobile home is treated as real estate under your state's law, then your legal rights will be consistent with the legal rights of other homeowners, as discussed in this and the previous chapter. If your state treats your mobile home as personal property, then your legal rights will conform more closely to the rights of automobile owners facing repossession. These rights are discussed in Chapter Seventeen.

Special Rights for Mobile Home Owners. Mobile home owners may have certain rights not available to other homeowners. Federal protections apply to certain mobile home first mortgages. You have thirty days to get caught up on a default after notice of the default is provided.

A lender does not have to provide this federal protection, but the federal government offers certain incentives for lenders to do so, and many choose to do so. If so, the lender must send you a notice of default by certified mail, return receipt requested. The notice must state the nature of the default, what you must do to cure the default, the lender's intended actions if you fail to cure, and your right to redeem the property under state law. The lender may not repossess your mobile home or call the rest of the note due until thirty days after the notice is mailed. To cure, you must pay the delinquent amounts due plus any late or deferral charges.

Since issues related to mobile home foreclosures and repossession vary significantly from state to state, it is recommended that you also consult with someone who is knowledgeable about the laws in your state. Pamphlets may also be available from your state's attorney general or at a local counseling agency or legal services office.

Mobile Home Lot Rent. If you rent the land on which your mobile home sits, failure to make your lot payments can result in eviction. Typically, the mobile home park or other landowner that owns the lot will have to bring a legal action to evict you. In some states this legal action will be similar to other landlord and tenant actions, as discussed in Chapter Fifteen. About half the states have special legislation dealing with mobile home park evictions, and that procedure will apply instead.

If the owner of the lot evicts you after a court action for failing to pay rent, at a minimum you will have to move the mobile home. Sometimes this presents practical problems because the home is not really movable, is expensive to move, or because you may have nowhere else to put it.

Equally importantly, in many states, the lot owner has special remedies allowing it to take action to repossess the mobile home in the event you fail to pay your lot rent. In many states, this process is the same as for any other creditor with a claim against you. The lot owner can seek a money judgment and then use that judgment as a lien on your mobile home. These issues are discussed in Chapter Eight. In other states, however, special laws give the lot owner the right to an automatic lien and special repossession rights ahead of other creditors.

It is just as important to pay your lot rent as your mobile home mortgage.

You will need to check with a specialist who is knowledgeable about these issues in your state. You can also ask a mobile home park tenant's association or mobile homeowner's association for advice. But it is important to deal with your lot rent as a priority debt just as high as your mobile home mortgage payment.

Consumer Issues Associated With Mobile Homes. Mobile homes are the source of a variety of abuses. It is not uncommon for mobile homes to be defective, for loans used to purchase mobile homes to be made on unfair terms, or for mobile home park owners to exercise abusive collection tactics. These practices may give rise to defenses against foreclosure or eviction. They may also create legal claims for which you have the right to recover money.

If you think you have a defense to foreclosure or eviction or an affirmative claim for damages, it is a good idea to check with a lawyer or mobile home park association sooner rather than later. Delay can cost you your legal rights. In some locations, local legal service organizations will advise you about your rights or represent you for free.

Mobile home-related debts raise unique issues which can be very complicated. Further information can be found in National Consumer Law Center, *Repossessions and Foreclosures* (3d ed. 1995 and Supp.). Other useful publications include National Consumer Law Center, *Unfair and Deceptive Acts and Practices* (4th ed. 1997 and Supp.) and *Manufactured Housing Park Tenants: Shifting the Balance of Power* (AARP 1991).

FORECLOSURES BASED ON
A JUDGMENT LIEN

Most foreclosures are based on your nonpayment of a mortgage, a tax lien, or a workman's lien. Creditors without a mortgage or lien can also try to seize your home, but you have important protections. First of all, the creditor has to go to court to sue on the debt. (See Chapter Eight for tips on defending such lawsuits to collect a debt.)

After a hearing, if the judge rules for the creditor, a lien, called a "judgment lien," may be placed on your home. The creditor can later "execute" that judgment by asking a court to sell your home and use the proceeds to satisfy the amount of the judgment lien.

Even then, state homestead laws usually prevent such a sale. Additionally bankruptcy is likely to give you the opportunity to remove the lien if you do not have substantial equity in your home. Further discussion of these and other protections available against judgment liens is contained in Chapter Eight.

Evictions and Other Disputes With Landlords

- *Advice on Getting Out of Your Lease*
- *Preventing Eviction*
- *Coping With Problems at a New Rental Unit*

If you cannot afford your rent payments, you are likely to be facing one of three significant problems: 1) you want to move out, but the landlord wants you to pay for breaking the lease; 2) you want to stay in the residence, but your landlord is seeking to evict you; or 3) you have moved, but are experiencing problems with the new, less expensive rental unit. This chapter provides advice on the best way to deal with each of these problems.

GETTING OUT OF A LEASE

Getting Out of Your Lease as an Alternative to Eviction. Affordable rents can quickly become unaffordable when you lose your job or when, for some other reason, your financial situation worsens. Moving to a less costly apartment or house may be your best option, at least until your situation improves. This is usually better than being evicted and then being forced to find another residence under severe time pressure.

If you break a lease, you may owe your landlord rent not just for those months you are in the apartment, but for some number of months after you leave. Nevertheless, switching apartments on your own time schedule, even with this penalty, may still be a better choice than waiting to be evicted.

Eviction can be a devastating and disruptive experience. Eviction makes the financial hardships you already have even worse because it puts extra costs and pressures on you. The speed of the eviction process may force you into unwanted choices, extra expenses, and acceptance of far from satisfactory alternative living arrangements. Frequently, the only other housing available is more expensive than that from which your family was evicted.

You can avoid most of these problems by moving out on your own. This is almost always better than an eviction. While you may owe your landlord a penalty for breaking the lease, there are steps you can take to lessen this amount, as set out below.

Read the Lease. The first step in terminating a lease is to read the rental agreement carefully. If the agreement provides that either party can terminate the lease by giving advance notice, you need only give the notice specified in the lease. Then you may move without responsibility for additional payments.

Check to see if the lease is for a specified amount of time, usually one year, or if it is a month-to-month lease. If you have lived in the apartment for a long time, the lease might have started out as a one year lease, but may have turned into a month-to-month lease after that year ended. State landlord-tenant law will establish the rules for terminating those agreements. In most states you must give thirty days written notice before moving, unless something is seriously wrong with the property, making it unsafe to remain there.

Landlords will often forgive
back-rent payments or reduce the penalty
for terminating the lease early
in exchange for agreement to move.

Negotiate With Your Landlord to Reduce What You Owe. If the lease requires you to pay for all rent due until the end of your lease, try to get a better deal from the landlord. If you want to try to stay in the apartment, start by asking for a rent reduction, explaining why the rent is no longer affordable. Lowering the rent may be less costly for the landlord than going to the expense of evicting you and finding a new tenant. This is less likely if you live in an area where it is very easy to find new tenants. Still, even if the landlord will not reduce the rent permanently, he might do so for a few months until you get back on your feet.

Landlords may also allow you to break the lease without penalty so that they can rent to others who are better able to pay. You can even try to get the landlord to agree not to charge you for back-rent if you move out by a certain date. Landlords will often do this to get you out of the apartment more quickly and avoid expensive court costs. Be sure to get in writing any deal you make with the landlord! This will protect you if the landlord breaks his or her word.

Find Someone Else to Take Over the Apartment. There are two different ways that someone else can take over your apartment and the rent payments for you. One way is a sublease, where someone else takes over your apartment and pays the rent. In a sublease, you are still obligated to pay the landlord for any rent your subtenant fails to pay. The other way is for someone else to take over not only the apartment, but the whole lease, called assuming the lease. If you can find someone to assume the lease, you will be able to wash your hands of the lease forever even if the new tenant does not pay the rent.

Look at the language in your lease to see if subleasing or lease assumption are allowed, and whether the landlord must approve the new tenant. Whatever the wording of the lease, the landlord may let you move out early with no penalty, if you have arranged for responsible tenants to sublet or assume the lease. Even when a lease permits subletting or assumption, landlords should be consulted before you begin looking for new occupants. Landlords are more likely to cooperate with a sublease or an assumption if you let them know what you are trying to do.

Breaking the Lease. If it is impossible to negotiate a friendly early termination, assumption, or sublease, you should evaluate the financial cost of breaking the lease. Although there may be financial consequences of breaking a lease, the alternative of eviction, or of continuing to pay rent for an apartment you can't afford, is usually worse.

When a lease is broken, the amount you will owe the landlord is limited in most states. The landlord must try to find a new tenant for the unit right away. If the landlord does not try, this may provide you a defense to the landlord trying to collect additional rent from you.

If you have a month-to-month lease and you give proper advance notice that you are leaving, you have no financial liability to the landlord. If you have a one year lease, you can only be obligated to pay rent until the end of the one year lease period although you may have to give notice that you are not renewing.

If there are still a number of months left on your lease and there are no state laws that limit how much you owe, breaking your lease may mean that you will owe the monthly rent for the remainder of the lease or until the landlord finds a new tenant plus any costs associated with the landlord finding a new tenant (whichever is less).

You can only be forced to pay, however, if the landlord goes to court. Landlords who take their cases to court may sometimes also be awarded court costs or attorneys' fees, if such fees are allowed by the lease agreement and state law. If a new tenant is found who will pay rent in an amount lower than you would have paid, you may be responsible for the difference.

If your landlord does sue you for rent owed, you might not make payments a high priority because the debt to the landlord is an unsecured debt. This means that it can only be collected by a lawsuit. Even after the landlord obtains a judgment against you, he must find non-exempt property to satisfy the judgment. A bankruptcy may also eliminate the landlord's right to collect on the judgment. (See Chapter Eight for more information about protecting your property from judgments.)

If the landlord does not sue, your loss will be limited to the security deposit, last month's rent, or other money held by the landlord (together with anything you agree to pay voluntarily).

Having a judgment on your record may cause you problems in looking for a new apartment. Some landlords subscribe to "tenant screening services" which gather information from court records and sell this information to landlords who want to find out more about prospective tenants. If you live in an area where landlords frequently use these services, it is even more important to try to reach an agreement with your landlord before you move out. It is also important to try to get a copy of your credit report to make corrections if necessary.

Other Things to Do If You Decide to Break the Lease. If you decide to break the lease, here are some steps to take to minimize your liability for damages:

- You should give the landlord plenty of notice, preferably thirty to sixty days, so the landlord will have time to advertise for new tenants.
- You should consider advertising the apartment yourself, either by word of mouth or through newspaper classified advertisements. Even if a sublease or lease assumption is not permitted, offering a suitable substitute tenant will make it hard for the landlord to argue that no other tenants were available.
- The premises should be cleaned thoroughly and left in good condition when you move so that there are no claims of damages against your security deposit. It is also to your advantage that there be minimal delay before the next tenant moves in. You should request that the landlord go over the property after you clean it to prevent any dispute over damages. You may also want to have a neutral party review the condition of the property before you move in case you need a witness later. You can also take pictures or video of the clean apartment to use in the event of a dispute.
- Check newspaper ads to verify that the landlord is making an effort to find new renters.
- After you move, you may also want to go by the rental unit from time to time for signs of new occupants.

The bottom line is that if you break a lease, you will probably lose your security deposit. However, if you plan carefully, making sure that the landlord suffers no loss of rent and has no unplanned expenses, you may recover some or all of the deposit.

State landlord-tenant laws provide specific procedures for recovering your security deposit if the landlord does not voluntarily return it. These state laws usually specify the number of days or weeks after you move out during which the landlord must return the deposit. If they do not return your entire deposit, most laws require landlords to send you an itemization of costs that were deducted from the original deposit. Check this itemization over carefully as landlords will very commonly try to charge you for damage to the apartment that was not your fault. In most states, you can recover damages in a court case if the deposit is wrongfully withheld.

RESPONDING TO
A LANDLORD'S
EVICTION ATTEMPTS

Sadly, if you are unable to pay your full rent on a regular, ongoing basis, you almost inevitably will have to move. Although some defenses to eviction are available, landlords can nearly always remove you eventually for nonpayment of rent. The best potential outcome to an eviction proceeding is generally to ensure that your family has enough time to find alternate housing that is both affordable and adequate with minimal disruption to your lives.

Be wary of attorneys or other professionals who claim that they can keep you in an apartment indefinitely. These services are often rip-offs. Some will take your money and never file any papers on your behalf. Others will file inadequate defenses or improper bankruptcy petitions. Even though you may feel desperate to stay in your apartment, your best strategy is to determine on your own, or with the assistance of a reliable attorney or counselor, whether you have real challenges to your landlord's eviction action. Possible defenses are discussed below.

If you don't have any defenses and your problem is that you simply can't afford where you are living, you should avoid getting yourself into more trouble by paying money to a bogus eviction defense service that is just trying to profit from your desperation.

If You Are Sued for Eviction, You Have the Right to a Fair Trial. The legal steps for an eviction vary from state to state, so you must become familiar with local rules. Most eviction proceedings take place very quickly. The entire process may be completed in as little as two weeks. In some states, the process can take considerably longer, particularly if you have reasons to argue that you should not be evicted. Appeals are also possible if you lose.

If you lose an eviction case, the court will usually order that you move out immediately. If you do not move out, court officials or the sheriff will come to put you out. How long that takes depends on your state. It may be days, weeks, or even months. The local legal services office or the court clerk should be able to tell you how long you usually have. Remember that court officials and sheriffs rarely take breaks for holidays or weekends. You should assume that you will have the least amount of time.

Here are some general rules about the eviction process:

The Notice to Quit Is a Warning. In most states, the first step in an eviction is a notice telling you that you must move within a short time. This is usually called a "notice to quit" or a "notice to vacate." If you have not paid your rent, the notice usually instructs you either to pay rent or to get out.

A "Notice to Quit" does *not* mean you have to leave — it is just a warning.

This notice does not, by itself, require that you move. Instead, landlords that want to put legal teeth behind the notice must first go to court after the time allowed in the notice has expired. (In a few states this notice is not required and the landlord may go directly to court.) A notice to quit should be seen as a warning, not a final notice.

Generally, the notice will give you a specified number of days in which to vacate the premises. In many states, the notice must also give you the right to stay in the apartment by "curing," that is, paying a specified dollar amount of back-rent within a specified number of days. State law usually requires landlords to accept rent during this "cure" period if you offer them the full amount.

Sometimes the landlord will also claim other violations of the lease, such as damage to the premises or keeping a pet forbidden by the lease. These violations may also be cured by taking care of the underlying problem.

Negotiating With the Landlord. Even after receiving a notice to move out, you should consider talking to the landlord about a mutual agreement which would resolve the problem. For example, if you are having trouble paying your monthly rent in a lump sum, some landlords agree to accept weekly or biweekly installments. Landlords sometimes also agree to lower the rent, at least temporarily. Whether a landlord will agree to work something out depends upon the landlord and your relationship with the landlord in the past. Remember that landlords are not required to work things out with you if you are behind on your rent.

At the very least you can suggest that the landlord exchange lower rent for your agreeing to move in a certain number of months. This would let you leave on your terms without the threat of an immediate eviction.

Landlords who know that their tenants will definitely move, usually allow them some extra time. This saves the landlord the expense of eviction.

Temporary and Permanent Rent Assistance. You may also want to look into various sources of temporary rent assistance that can buy you some time. Emergency rental assistance is available in some states, usually through the local welfare office. In other places, you may want to call local community action agencies.

Welfare programs also can help tenants. Most programs provide housing payments to needy individuals in certain circumstances, at least for short periods. In addition, church groups and private charitable organizations are potential sources of financial assistance. Some programs will help you pay back-rent. Others will help by giving or loaning you moving expenses and money for a new security deposit.

Tenants who do not already receive a government housing subsidy can also apply for various kinds of government housing assistance, including special rental assistance, state or nonprofit housing programs, and traditional public housing. Waiting lists are quite long. Urgent circumstances, such as homelessness, illness, or small children, sometimes move applicants higher on waiting lists.

Priorities for assistance and the length of waiting time vary from program to program and from community to community. Needy individuals should promptly apply for any assistance for which they may be eligible. The first place to contact for more information is your local or regional housing authority.

Responding to the Eviction Case. If you have not paid the full back-rent and have not moved out by the time specified in the notice to vacate, the landlord can file an eviction action in court. This is sometimes called a forcible entry, detainer or ejectment action. (We refer here to all these actions as "eviction actions.")

Eviction actions are usually scheduled for a hearing right away. State laws require that you be given the landlord's complaint and a summons to appear in court — generally by a process server or a local official. State law also specifies a minimum number of days, often as few as five, between when you are served and when the hearing takes place. Therefore, you should promptly take steps to respond, or consult a lawyer.

If you disagree with a landlord's complaint, or if you have any defenses, you should immediately contact the court and file an answer or counterclaim. Some common defenses and counterclaims are discussed briefly below.

Many landlord-tenant cases are held in less-formal housing courts or state district courts. This should make it easier for you to file your own answers or counterclaims without using sophisticated legal terminology. Some courts charge a fee for filing papers — but the fee should be waivable if you can show that you cannot pay it.

Attending the Eviction Hearing. If you have been served with notice of an eviction proceeding, you should always attend — whether or not you have already moved out. Even if you believe you have no defenses, you should attend the eviction hearing to make sure you know what is going on. You want to be certain, for example, that the landlord does not misstate the amount of rent you owe or ask that you be put out by a quicker than normal process.

Even if you have no defenses, you can request that the judge give you additional time before moving if there are special circumstances. Some examples might be illness of a family member, a lease for a new apartment which is not yet ready to move into, or unavailability of emergency shelter. The judge will be more likely to grant additional time if you are able to offer at least partial rent, or if other housing has been arranged. Judges are also more inclined to grant delays for compelling circumstances, such as for families with many small children or the elderly.

At the hearing, you will need to be prepared to present your defenses, if any, to the eviction. This should include relevant documents and witnesses, if any. Preparing a case for court is discussed in Chapter Eight. Some defenses which may be available in an eviction case are discussed below.

Raising Defenses. Tenants with defenses to an eviction must raise those defenses at the eviction hearing (or in some states earlier by filing required papers — usually called an "answer" or an "appearance"). Defenses will always be lost if you do not appear at the hearing.

Most courts require that an evicting landlord strictly comply with all the technical requirements of the eviction law, including the content, timing, and service of all required notices and court documents. Any mistake in complying with these requirements, including misstatement of the amount of rent owed, if it is pointed out to the court, may cause a landlord's petition to be dismissed. The landlord will then be required to begin the procedure over again. Remember that if you don't have any other defenses to the eviction, the landlord will usually be able to correct the technical problem and still end up evicting you in a relatively short period of time.

State law sometimes allows other defenses or claims that might defeat or delay an eviction. For example, some states recognize a defense called "peaceable possession." This defense states that if a landlord fails to file an eviction action promptly after the expiration of a notice to vacate time period, the landlord has consented to continued occupancy. Peaceable possession may result in dismissal of the eviction, although the landlord can send a new notice to vacate.

Another possible defense is that the landlord habitually accepted late or partial payments, and then suddenly, without warning, started eviction proceedings based on late payment or nonpayment of rent. The eviction is then improper, because it was started even though the tenant was no later in payments than usual.

Other issues may be present when a landlord is subject to federal housing laws, such as HUD or FmHA regulations. In addition to state laws, these laws provide specific requirements for a landlord's eviction case.

Legal advice may be necessary to understand specific procedural requirements for the landlord's action and your potential responses. In many communities eviction clinics or legal pamphlets on tenants' rights are offered by the local legal services office, the bar association, or the court clerk.

Substandard Housing Condition as a Defense; Retaliatory Evictions.

In most states, courts will recognize defenses or counterclaims based upon the property not being "habitable" (in livable condition) or if the property is not properly maintained. These claims are based on the landlord breaching the rental agreement by not keeping the property in good repair. Other defenses available in many states are "retaliatory evictions" if you can show that an eviction action is in retaliation for your exercise of legal rights.

The availability of defenses and counterclaims based on the condition of the apartment varies widely from state to state. Almost everywhere, you will have a defense if the apartment has been cited for housing code violations. If there are serious problems with the apartment, you may want to call the housing inspector to come out and look at the conditions. If a citation is issued, you should make sure to get a copy to take with you to court. A "certified" copy may be required in some courts. Ask the housing inspector how to get a certified copy of the report.

Even if there are no housing code violations, problems with the apartment can still partially or fully offset your obligation to pay rent. In some cases, you may be able to afford the lower amount. In others, you may still end up getting evicted, but the court may lower the amount of back-rent you owe because the apartment was never in proper condition. Take pictures or videos of any problems, if possible. In the alternative, for problems like lack of adequate heat, a disinterested witness may testify.

Many states require prior notice to the landlord of the bad conditions before the conditions can be used as a defense to eviction. The notice requirement is designed to give the landlord an opportunity to correct the problem. It is always a good idea to provide notice in writing with a copy for your records. This notice should be sent by certified mail if you have a history of disputes with your landlord. You should bring several copies with you to court in order to prove that you have complied with the law.

Some evictions are brought by landlords in order to punish tenants for enforcing their rights. The classic example is an eviction case which is brought because one tenant has organized other tenants in the building and submitted joint complaints to the landlord. Similarly, some landlords routinely evict tenants who contact housing inspectors because of problems with the property.

Retaliatory eviction cases are hard to prove — especially when there is also a back-rent issue. This is because you will have to show that the landlord is really evicting you because you stood up for your rights and not because you didn't pay rent. Among the important questions will be the timing of the eviction and its relation to your actions, any statements or threats made by the landlord, and whether the underlying problems about the property had merit. If a retaliatory eviction has occurred, it is a good idea to consult a lawyer.

Appeals. If you lose an eviction case and the court orders an eviction, one possibility is to appeal the case to a higher court. This may buy you more time to move in a more orderly fashion. The threat of an appeal may also allow you to negotiate more time with the landlord.

An appeal may require that you pay certain filing fees or other charges. Sometimes these fees can be waived if you can show you cannot afford to pay. However, you should only consider an appeal if you honestly believe you have a case. Frivolous appeals can result in fines or other sanctions against you.

Other Responses to a Court's Eviction Order. You should respond to a court order of eviction by making arrangements to move before you are forced out into the street. It is always a mistake to just ignore the eviction order.

In some states, but not all, you will get notice of an actual eviction date. You may want to consult the sheriff, a court clerk, or your local legal services office about how long you are likely to have. Often, you will have only a very short opportunity to move before you are put out.

In some cases, arrangements to move by a certain date can be made directly with the landlord or by the court with a judge's approval. Sometimes, you can get assistance with moving costs from the welfare department in your community or from a charity.

If you have not vacated by the time specified in a court eviction order, a sheriff or a similar official may move your belongings onto the sidewalk, or place them in storage. You will then have to pay moving and storage costs.

In some states, landlords can place a lien on your furniture and other possessions to cover moving and storage charges. Until you pay those charges, you cannot get your property back. It is better to avoid this problem entirely by moving voluntarily.

Seizures of Personal Property and Unauthorized Lockouts. As described above, seizures of your personal property as part of a court-ordered eviction process may be legal. On the other hand, in most states, it is illegal for a landlord to seize your personal property without court permission.

There are a few states that do give landlords the right, if you are behind in paying rent, to seize all or part of your belongings on the property without first obtaining court permission. You may then be forced to go to court to seek return of the property, and you may have to pay money (or post a bond) to obtain its release.

A tenant whose property has been seized should seek legal advice. Even in those states that allow such seizures, certain property will be listed as exempt from seizure. There may even be grounds for a constitutional challenge to the procedure itself.

Lockouts, utility shut-offs and eviction-related harassment are illegal in all states. When landlords take these actions, they are generally known as "self-help evictions." If you are locked out, or if your landlord is harassing you to get you to move out (including the common practice of shutting down utility service to your property), you are likely to be entitled to get back into the property and to have the harassment ended by a court. You also may be entitled to damages. Legal assistance for a case of this type is a good idea.

Without permission from a court, landlords cannot padlock your apartment, shut off your utilities or otherwise force you to leave.

When you are locked out, or if your utilities are shut off, your landlord may claim that you have abandoned the apartment. You may want to let the landlord know in writing that this is not the case. If the landlord does not let you back in or turn on the utilities, a copy of the letter will serve as proof that the landlord knew that you had not moved out. Remember that even if you are not able to pay your rent, landlords are not allowed to try to put you out without court approval. Landlords must go through the legal process and allow you to have your day in court if that's what you want.

The Landlord's Suit for Back-Rent. Landlords sometimes sue for back-rent or property damage after a tenant moves or is evicted. As part of that suit, a landlord may also ask that the tenant be required to pay the landlord's attorney fees.

A case for back-rent may or may not be included with the eviction. If you are sued for back-rent, it should be treated just like a suit for money by any other creditor. A discussion of ways to address lawsuits generally is included in Chapters Eight and Nine. In addition, some special considerations apply.

Some of the claims that you may raise in evictions are also potential defenses or counterclaims in suits for back-rent. Common defenses include: substandard housing conditions; miscalculation of the amount owed; illegal attempts by landlords to seize your property; a landlord's attempt to lock you out; or a shut-off of utility service. Landlords, collection agencies, management companies and their lawyers are also potentially responsible for debt collection harassment. For any of these claims, you should consider consulting a lawyer.

DEALING WITH PROBLEMS
IN A NEW RENTAL UNIT

The two most common problems faced by those moving into new residences are: the condition of the property and problems hooking up utility service. Tips on hooking up utility service at a new address are found at Chapter Sixteen. This section explains your rights if the new apartment has substandard conditions.

To protect against substandard conditions, the law in most states requires that a dwelling meet minimum standards of habitability. Rental property must meet local housing, health, fire, and building ordinances. Heat and hot water must be available. Appliances must be safe and in working order. Usually the property must be free of insect and rodent infestation. When housing is not habitable, you can take several steps.

Written Requests that the Landlord Make Repairs. When substandard conditions are present, the first step toward correcting them is to request that the landlord make the desired repairs. Because repair disputes tend to arise frequently, the request should be made in writing. Any oral request should be confirmed in writing.

Reporting Code Violations to a Housing Inspector. If a direct request to the landlord does not bring results, then city or county ordinances, available at a city hall or public library, should be checked for possible housing code violations. You can also call the housing inspector's office directly to ask about the applicable regulations. If you think there are violations of the housing code, you can complain to the local housing inspector. Again, this complaint should be in writing and copies retained. The resulting enforcement action against the landlord should be designed to get the problem fixed.

Resist Retaliatory Evictions. Some landlords react badly to tenants' complaints and to inspectors' reports, and attempt to evict complaining tenants. However, many state landlord-tenant laws protect tenants from retaliatory evictions. It is important to get legal advice from a neighborhood legal services office, pro bono attorney, or other source when a retaliatory eviction is threatened, so that you can properly bring a legal defense consistent with the state law.

Forcing the Landlord to Make Repairs; Rent Withholding. If your requests and inspector reports bring no results, you may decide to go to court. Courts can order landlords to make repairs, to refund your rent, or to pay for your damages. A landlord's refusal to make necessary repairs also gives you the right to terminate your rental agreement and move elsewhere. Sometimes, if conditions become so bad that you are forced to move, a landlord may be required to reimburse you for the cost of temporary substitute housing.

Depending upon the circumstances, some state laws permit you to withhold rent to pay for necessary repairs. Sometimes these laws require you to follow specific steps in withholding your rent, and it will be important to follow these rules.

None of these strategies should be considered without first consulting a lawyer, a tenant counselor, or a clerk at a local housing court. Legal education pamphlets published by bar associations, community legal services programs, and public interest groups explain the rules for withholding rent, for court injunctions, and for lease terminations. These laws should be carefully followed, or your rights may be affected.

– 16 –

Utility Terminations

- *Choices in Utility Service Providers*
- *Ways to Reduce Your Utility Bills*
- *Your Rights When a Utility Threatens Termination of Service*
- *Getting Your Utility Service Turned Back On*

We all know how important it is to maintain necessary utility service — we need electricity to light our homes and run the furnace; we need water to drink and bathe and clean with; we need gas or other fuel to heat our home; and we need telephone service to make and receive essential calls.

Utility providers have a powerful method of forcing their customers to pay their bills. Unlike other creditors, utility providers can impose the drastic remedy of terminating service to force payment of back-bills. So when faced with a large utility bill, you may feel that you have no where to turn — pay an unaffordable bill or lose essential service. This chapter explains that you have tools to help you manage these debts.

CHOICES IN UTILITY SERVICE PROVIDERS

More and more, competition and consumer choice is coming to utility service. In the past, customers had no choice about which company to use for local or long distance telephone service, electric and gas service, or water service.

Now, all households in America can choose their provider of long distance telephone services, and some even can choose their provider of local telephone service. In many states, consumers also have choices about their providers of electric or gas service. Making decisions about which providers are best for you can be tricky.

Often, the choice of your utility provider will not only determine the price you will be charged, but also the protections you have from termination of service, assistance with bill payments, eligibility for assistance for weatherization and conservation efforts, as well as the amount of basic information that you will receive about your rights and obligations. When choosing between utility service providers, especially gas and electric providers, ask questions about the company's policies regarding late payments, protections from shut-off, and special programs for elderly, disabled or low-income homeowners. This chapter explains many rights and benefits that are available to utility customers. If you have a choice in the provider of your utility service, find out from the different providers which rights and benefits each has to offer you.

WAYS TO REDUCE
YOUR UTILITY BILLS

Even if your most pressing concern is getting *past-due* utility bills paid to maintain service, you should still be interested in reducing your *future* bills, to avoid falling behind on your payments in the future. This section will provide specific ideas on how to reduce the bills, by

- Reducing the amount you are charged for the utility service you do use;
- Changing the type of service you receive;
- Changing the way you are billed to make the bills easier to pay;
- Reducing *usage* of the utility service through weatherization; and
- Obtaining cash assistance in paying your bills.

You May Be Eligible for a Discount Plan. Often utilities have special programs which will allow you to reduce the *charges* for the utility service that you receive. It only takes some investigation to see what the different utilities have to offer and whether you are eligible for the program.

Discounted Rates for Financially Distressed Households. Many utilities around the nation have special programs for low-income households to help them pay their utility bills. Many of these programs are automatically available to households which are receiving some sort of public assistance or energy assistance payments. Some of these programs reduce the bills by a set amount each month; others provide discounts based on the amount of the bill. Check with your utility to see what is available.

PIPS or Energy Assurance Programs. Additionally, a growing number of utilities have plans by which families pay a certain percentage of their income for utility service if it is less than their normal utility bills. This results in lower bills. Typically, your consistent payment of the lower amount is rewarded by gradual forgiveness of old unpaid bills. So you get two benefits in one.

These plans are sometimes called Percentage of Income Plans (PIPs) or Energy Assurance Plans (EAPs), but each utility seems to have its own unique name for the program. The best way to determine if a utility has such a program is to contact the utility or the public utility commission in your state capitol.

Telephone Discounts. There are special programs for discounts on local telephone rates for low-income households. In most states, households in financial distress can obtain a significant discount on telephone monthly charges under the "Lifeline" program run by your local phone company. Contact the public utility commission or the local telephone company for details.

Eligibility. Eligibility for each of these programs varies considerably. Some simply look at household income, others look for receipt of, or eligibility for, governmental benefits such as Social Security, SSI, welfare assistance, Food Stamps, or the Low Income Home Energy Assistance Program (LIHEAP). Check with your utility company to see if you are eligible.

Changing the Type of Service Can Reduce Your Bill. You may be receiving some utility services which you could do without. While the charges for each of these individual services may not seem like a lot, together they can add up to quite a few dollars each month. A careful review of your bills and a discussion with each utility company may yield some real savings.

Electric Service. Sometimes you can save considerably by going to a "time of use" type of service with your electric supplier. Whether you actually save money is entirely dependent on the type of program that your electric supplier has and your household's actual electric use patterns. A "time of use" type of service means that you are charged less for using electricity at some times of the day — generally during the evening and night hours and the weekend, and more for electricity used during the daytime. These programs often work well for households where no one is home during most of the work day. Check with your electric company to see if this program is available and would be beneficial to your family.

Cable TV Service. Are there cable TV services that you can drop? During your period of financial difficulty, can you return to using an antenna for your television, and eliminate the entire bill?

Local Telephone Service. Examine your telephone bill. Are you paying for call waiting, call forwarding, call answer and other high-tech services? Could you do without these services to save $6 to $15 a month? Are you paying for extended area service (local rates for calls to an area which otherwise would be long distance)? How much is this costing you, and do you really call to the extended area enough to justify the extra cost each month? Another question is whether you are paying a lot for local measured service — which is when you are billed separately for each local call. Contact the telephone company and see if they have different programs that might save you money.

Long Distance Telephone Calls. How much does your long distance service cost? Shop around with the different long distance carriers. Their various deals are often complicated, but can result in significant savings depending upon your calling patterns. Some programs have less expensive calls during the day, others at night. Look for the long distance service which best fits your actual calling patterns.

Be cautious of those programs that require you to pay a flat monthly charge regardless of how many calls you actually make, and then charge what seems to be a low per minute amount. Generally, these plans only benefit very heavy long distance users.

Sometimes, your long distance bill includes calls you did not make. If you are billed for calls that you did not make, or do not feel you owe the full long distance bill, ask the long distance company to delete these charges from your bill.

To prevent bills for unauthorized calls from occurring in the future, you may want to investigate a blocking service. Every local telephone company must provide a service to its customers which will block long distance calls from being made unless a password or some other device is used. The local telephone company can charge for these blocking services. Keep in mind that blocking is not foolproof. A creative and sneaky relative or friend can figure out a way around the long distance blocking, and you will still be charged for the calls. So be careful who you let use your telephone.

Phone Cards for Long Distance Calling. Often consumers purchase phone cards or calling cards, and thus "prepay" for their long distance calls. When you are concerned about minimizing your household's long distance calling, using these cards can sometimes help you reduce your usage. You should be cautious to purchase the cards only from reputable merchants. In this way, if the phone card does not work, or more time is deducted from the card than you actually used, or the long distance provider went bankrupt, you can go back to the merchant from whom you purchased the card and get a refund.

Other Telephone Charges. Are you being billed high amounts for 900 calls or other "audio text services" that you didn't make or didn't authorize? **Every local telephone company is prohibited from terminating your *local* telephone service for nonpayment of these "pay per call" services.** Further, you can put a block on your telephone so that these calls can no longer be billed to your telephone. Unlike the block for long distance service, this block should be free, and should be foolproof.

REDUCING YOUR BILL BY CHANGING YOUR BILLING PATTERNS

Level Payment Plans. If you are able to pay your *average* utility bill, but have difficulty meeting your heating bills in the coldest months of winter or your electric bills in the hottest months of summer (because of air conditioning), a level payment plan might make sense for you. A level payment plan allows you to avoid running up debts during high-usage months by averaging your expected bills so that you can pay the same amount each month. Many states require their regulated utilities to provide these plans.

Changing your payment schedule may make your utility bills more affordable

---

In a level payment plan, your projected yearly bill is divided into equal monthly installments. Monthly bills reflect this amount, rather than each month's actual use. For example, a customer whose total gas bill for a year is $1200, would pay $100 each month instead of $200 to $300 a month in the winter, and $30 to $40 a month in the summer.

Dealing with Quarterly or Bi-Monthly Bills. In some areas, utility services are billed quarterly or every other month. If this applies and financial problems cause you to live month to month temporarily, you may find it difficult to deal with large quarterly or bi-monthly bills, particularly when those bills represent significant portions of your monthly income. Contact your local utility company and explain the difficulty. Ask them to bill you on a monthly basis. In the alternative, ask them to accept monthly payments from you, even if they won't send you a separate bill each month.

If you make this choice, ask about "service charges" or "finance charges." This is the cost of paying over time. If the cost is too high, this type of payment plan may not be the best solution for you.

Avoiding Late Payment Charges by Changing the Date Your Bill Is Due. If your main source of income arrives in the mail on the fifth of the month, but your utility bill is due to be paid on the fourth, it is obviously going to be very difficult for you to pay your utility bill on time. The result may be that you not only have the high utility bill to contend with, but also you will have to pay additional interest or late charges. Generally, utility companies will help you deal with this, if you explain the situation. Although they may insist that you pay the late charges that have already been billed to your account, the utility company should agree to change the date your bill is due each month so that late charges don't keep accruing. By avoiding the late charges, you may reduce your bill by $5 to $15 each month.

REDUCING YOUR BILL BY
REDUCING YOUR UTILITY USAGE

Utility Company Sponsored Weatherization or Conservation Programs. Many utilities have programs that provide free, or low-cost weatherization or conservation services. Sometimes these programs are available to all households, sometimes they are limited to the elderly, or homes with disabled persons and/or children. In other areas, eligibility for the program may be based on your household's income or eligibility for a government program such as Energy Assistance (also called Low Income Home Energy Assistance Program or LIHEAP) or the Weatherization Assistance Program.

Different utility companies offer very different types of programs. These programs run the gamut. In the best programs, the utility sends someone who conducts a full energy audit of your home and provides extensive weatherization services. Other programs simply provide hints on how you can reduce usage, or they supply conservation products such as special energy efficient light bulbs, insulating hot water tanks, and "low flow" efficient faucets, or other conservation products. Even the less ambitious programs which provide only some conservation advice should be helpful to you. Investigate by calling your local energy and water providers and finding out what programs they have available.

You should be very cautious before investing more than a few dollars of your own money in any weatherization or conservation efforts with a contractor, however. While it might make sense in the long run for households with extra cash, it is often not the wisest use of funds for households which are strapped to pay for rent and food. To know whether an energy conservation investment is a good use of money, you must analyze the cost of the investment against how long you expect to live in this residence and your anticipated energy savings. This type of analysis should be done by an expert.

Government Sponsored Weatherization Programs. Several programs are designed to provide weatherization assistance for owner-occupied housing as well as rental units. The primary program is the Weatherization Assistance Program. Households that qualify generally receive over $1000 in actual weatherization benefits which are provided at no cost.

Additionally, many states have state weatherization programs. Cities also have Community Development Block Grant money which is often used to help low-income households weatherize their homes. Although there may be a long waiting list for all of these programs, the benefits are often so great, that it is worthwhile to add your name.

Self-Help Weatherization. If you are unable to find or qualify for any of programs through your utility or the government, there are still a number of practices which may help reduce your usage. In some situations, people are surprised how much these relatively inexpensive procedures reduce energy bills.

Check for leaks of air or water. If you are a tenant, try to get the landlord to fix these leaks properly. If the landlord does not fix the problems, or you own your own home, try a number of homespun fix ups. For example, use heavy tape for air leaks around windows. For leaks around doors, leave a rolled up towel next to the bottom of the door. If necessary to stop leaks around the top and sides of doors, tack up a blanket or large towel. If there are holes in the walls, try to plug them up. You will be surprised how much warmer a house or apartment can be without the heat loss from cracks between openings and walls. If you have a fireplace, make sure the flue is tightly closed. As the home warms up, you can consider turning down the heat.

Remember that your sewer bill is generally determined by how much water you consume. So that by saving water you are saving twice—on your water and your sewer bill. Putting a brick in your toilet tank may seem silly, but it will actually cut down on the amount of water consumed each time you flush. Turn off the water while you are brushing your teeth. If you have water leaks that you cannot afford to fix, call your water company. Many water companies have programs that assist homeowners with plumbing problems.

Turn off lights and heat or cooling when not at home. Also close the door for any rooms you are not using, and don't try to heat or cool them.

Reducing Your Bill Through Government Assistance. If you have a low income and high utility bills, you are probably eligible for one or more of several sources of assistance with your utility bills. These programs vary a great deal. Some types of aid are available only certain times of the year, others are available only if you have a certain type of fuel. Some programs only help you if you are facing a termination of utility service; other programs only help you if you are not facing a termination. All programs have eligibility requirements, but they differ considerably in their specific terms.

The Federal Low Income Home Energy Assistance Program (LIHEAP), which is run by the states, helps low-income families pay their utility bills. All states provide this assistance for winter heating bills; some states also use LIHEAP funds to assist families with summer cooling expenses. LIHEAP benefits are also provided to some renters and public and subsidized housing tenants, with the energy assistance payments going directly to the landlord's fuel supplier and the amount being credited against the family's rent.

Guidelines for LIHEAP eligibility vary by state, but most states require that family income over the past three or twelve months be below 150% of the federal poverty guidelines. (In some states, income must be even less.) The size of a family's LIHEAP benefits generally depends on the family's income and the number of household members, and may also depend on housing type, fuel type, fuel prices, weather conditions, or actual energy consumption.

To apply for LIHEAP benefits, a household should contact the local agency in the community administering the program. This is usually a nonprofit agency, such as the local community action program (CAP), or a county department of social services office. Benefits are sometimes paid directly to the utility company or fuel vendor, and the family's utility or fuel obligation is reduced accordingly. Other times, joint checks are made out to the customer and the utility. In a few states fuel assistance checks are provided solely to the customer.

YOUR RIGHTS WHEN THE UTILITY THREATENS TO TERMINATE YOUR SERVICE

Utilities Must Follow Rules Before Terminating Your Service. In most states there are laws which provide a variety of significant protections when utility companies threaten termination of your utility service. Many of the larger utilities are regulated by commissions called public utility commissions, or public service commissions. Utility companies can only shut off your service if they have followed the requirements set out by these commissions.

You can use a utility's violation

of shut-off rules

to stop termination of your service.

Utility termination rules generally have the following basic requirements:

- Notice of the proposed termination;
- A right to a hearing;
- A limit on circumstances permitting termination;
- The right to a deferred payment plan;
- Protection from terminations during the winter months;
- No terminations if there is serious illness in the household;
- The right to information about places to go for assistance with paying the utility bill;

- Protections for tenants from termination of service by landlords;
- Prohibitions on termination of local telephone service for bills for other services.

Some states also have a temporary limit on termination of utility service when there is a factory closing.

The utility's failure to follow these termination rules typically allows you to demand that the termination process start all over. Utility service must be maintained throughout the process. If your utilities were wrongfully terminated, you might also have a claim for damages. An attorney can often get a special court order (an injunction) to stop termination or to have service restored when the utility has failed to follow the rules on termination procedures.

Often utility representatives refuse to negotiate a payment plan, or fail to give notice of all your important rights, such as the opportunity for appeal or the right to participate in a payment plan. Because your only information provider is generally a company representative, you should not hesitate to contact a local legal services attorney or the consumer services division of the state public utilities commission to find out whether the utility has complied with the termination rules. Public utility commissions generally have dispute resolution authority, and a call to the appropriate person can often stall or prevent a termination altogether.

The state public utility commissions offer consumers other protections. Commissions typically have a legal division (or general counsel's office), a consumer complaint division, and separate divisions to handle problems with particular types of service, such as electric, gas, and telephones. Individual customers can often obtain help with utility disputes directly from the staff of the state commission. Look for an "800" toll free number to call for consumer assistance.

In addition, you have certain rights to stop a termination when you file for bankruptcy. Finally, you may be eligible for certain emergency funds you can use to stop the shut-off.

The following is a more detailed explanation of your rights concerning a threatened utility termination:

Notice. Prior to termination of your utility service, you must be given notice that the service is subject to termination, and of the various rights that you have to prevent termination. Often this requirement repeats written notices. Face-to-face notice may also be required in certain parts of the country.

Limit on Circumstances Warranting Termination. Regulations typically permit disconnection for nonpayment, but often prohibit disconnections for very small amounts, or for amounts which have been owed for less than a certain number of months. Further, if you dispute that you owe the bill which the utility says must be paid, the utility is generally prohibited from terminating service until the dispute is resolved. If you dispute part of the bill, you must pay the undisputed amount to preserve your rights.

Right to a Hearing. Before or after termination, you have a right to appeal to both the utility and to an independent third party such as the Public Utility Commission. In many states, informal appeals can be made by telephone prior to termination and often utility service will be maintained or reconnected during the appeals process.

A utility commission's consumer division responds to phone calls, letters, and visits by residential customers. Many of these complaints are resolved informally, by consultation between the consumer division and the utility. Consumer divisions also hold hearings on complaints that cannot be resolved informally. In large states, several hundred of these hearings are held each year.

Consumers generally have a legal right to a hearing whenever they have grounds to contest a utility termination. Simply request the utility commission to provide a hearing before service is terminated. (If you dispute only part of a back-bill, you will usually have to pay the undisputed part to keep your service on while the dispute is being decided). While city-owned utilities are generally not regulated by the utility commission, customers of municipal utilities also have a constitutional right to a hearing before termination.

You do not need the services of a lawyer at the hearing. However, it may be helpful to have a paralegal or experienced utility counselor assist with the hearing. To support the claim, it is important for you to bring all relevant documents, such as a physician's affidavit or past bills. It may also be helpful to have witnesses such as friends and neighbors present.

Right to a Deferred Payment Plan. Before utility service is shut off, most states require that you be informed about the option to pay all overdue bills over a period of some months through a reasonable installment plan. Often this payment plan has a six month or a one year limit for bringing the account up-to-date.

The plan may be designed so that you pay current usage, and slowly catch up on the amount you are behind. However, if your financial circumstances require, sometimes you can negotiate a better plan whereby the monthly payments do not even completely cover current bills, and do nothing to catch up on arrears.

To make a successful payment plan, develop a simple budget that you can reasonably meet, and be assertive with the utility company employee who negotiates the agreement. Payment plans need not require the same each month. For example, seasonal workers may want to pay less toward arrears in the winter and more in the summer, or vice versa.

The utility company may want a payment plan that requires larger payments than you can afford. Large payments are in the company's short-term interest, because it recovers past debts more quickly. Too many customers, believing they have no choice, agree to these payments.

It is usually a bad idea to agree to a payment plan which you know you cannot afford. This will only make things worse in the long run. It is better to explain your financial circumstances and push for an affordable agreement from the beginning.

Unrealistic plans harm both you and the utility company in the long term. You may not be able to make the payments, and may lose the service, and the company does not collect its debt. In some states, utilities are not required to enter into a second payment plan with consumers who have defaulted on a first payment plan. If a company refuses to agree to a reasonable payment plan, help can be obtained from the consumer division of the utility commission.

Winter Moratorium on Terminations. In most northern states, heat-related utilities are prohibited from terminating any residential customer between November 1 and March 31st. In other states, there is usually a limited moratorium to prevent utility terminations for households with elderly or disabled residents, and occasionally for households with infants. Generally, financial hardship must be shown. Some of these rules require that before a household be considered for the moratorium, all efforts to obtain state energy assistance must have been pursued.

Note that a moratorium only prevents disconnection of service. Your bill will still be charged and you will be responsible to pay for service used during the moratorium period. For this reason you should pay, if you can, even if your service is not subject to being disconnected.

No Termination If There Is Serious Illness. Similarly, state law or public utility commission regulations often restrict termination of service for households whose members face a serious illness, are threatened with serious illness, or depend upon life support systems. Often, the illness must be certified by a doctor. A family with very young children or a pregnant woman may also be able to use the health risk to the children as grounds to stop utility termination.

Information About Sources of Assistance. Utility companies often must provide consumers, before a disconnection, with information about the existence of energy assistance programs, such as LIHEAP or local crisis intervention programs. (See the discussion below concerning these sources of emergency assistance.)

Tenants Protected from Termination of Service for Landlord's Failure to Pay. When a landlord is responsible for providing utility service, it is all too common, particularly in difficult economic times, for a landlord to fail to pay for that service. This puts tenants at risk of losing their utility service. Tenants in this situation sometimes have special protections. In some states, tenants must receive a special shut-off notice if the landlord is delinquent. Then, tenants make utility payments directly to the utility, and deduct those payments from their rent.

Tenants Protected from Shut Off by Landlord. It is illegal in almost every state for a landlord to cut off your utility service as a way of making you move or pay your rent. Landlords must go through the courts to evict tenants. They cannot make the residence uninhabitable by terminating the heat or water service to force the tenant to move. Generally, a tenant not only can stop a "self-help" eviction when the landlord tries this, but also the tenant is entitled to recover damages for the landlord's wrongful actions. See Chapter Fifteen for more information.

No Termination of Local Telephone Service for Bills for Other Services. Some states prohibit the local telephone company from terminating your service for nonpayment of long distance service, but the majority of states do not yet have these protections. Also, every local telephone company is prohibited from terminating your local telephone service for nonpayment of 900 calls or "audio text" services.

A Moratorium Linked to a Plant Closing. Sometimes a utility or utility commission will impose a temporary prohibition against termination of utility service for customers or neighborhoods particularly hard hit by a recent factory closing. If such a moratorium is not in effect, it may be possible for families affected by a plant closing or their unions to negotiate one. A moratorium does not erase financial liability for utility service used before or during the moratorium period. The moratorium only prevents the utility company from terminating service if bills incurred during the moratorium period are not paid. When the moratorium period expires, the utility can then start the termination process for amounts not paid during the moratorium. Most utilities encourage their customers to pay what they can afford during a moratorium.

Bankruptcy Protections. Although it is rarely a good idea to file bankruptcy solely for utility bills, you may consider bankruptcy due to other financial problems. When you file a bankruptcy petition there is an automatic requirement that the utility company must restore service or stop a threatened termination. The bankruptcy filing starts a twenty day period during which you are entitled to service from all applicable utilities. The utility can only terminate service after that twenty day period if you fail to pay bills arising *after* the bankruptcy is filed. Then, if you successfully complete your bankruptcy case, you never have to pay the past due arrears. The utility, though, can also require that you provide adequate assurance that *future* bills will be paid, such as providing a new security deposit. Bankruptcy is explained in more detail in Chapter Twenty. The process can be complicated. Professional advice is a good idea.

Sources of Emergency Assistance. There are several sources of emergency assistance that may provide you with funds to prevent a utility termination. The following sources should be pursued:

- *LIHEAP Crisis Assistance.* Contact your local CAP agency (community action program) or the county department of social services to find out who provides these funds in your area.
- *Emergency Assistance for Families with Children.* If you have

children and you are about to lose essential utility services (water, heat in the winter months, etc.) contact your county department of social services to see if special emergency funds are available to help you.

- *State Emergency Assistance.* Some states have special funds to help prevent utility terminations. Also many counties have "homeless prevention" funds which can be used to prevent utility terminations. Contact your local CAP agency or the county department of social services.

- *Utility Fuel Funds.* Many utilities collect money from their customers and their shareholders to go into a special fund to help people pay their utility bills. Contact both the utility which is threatening to shut off your service, and any other utility from which you receive service, to see if they have a fund which might be of some assistance to you. You should not assume that because they haven't told you about it that they don't have such a fund, or that you are not eligible.

- *Salvation Army, Local Churches.* The Salvation Army and other local religious and charitable organizations often have money that is available to help needy people in the community with emergency bills such as utilities. Check around, ask the utility company, the public utility commission, or the department of social services. Many churches that have these funds do not limit them to their own members.

WAYS TO GET YOUR UTILITY SERVICE TURNED BACK ON

Everyone has the right to receive utility service from the provider in their area. Establishing new service after a move or after previous service has been terminated can be difficult and expensive. However, utilities are prohibited from discriminating in service, and required to establish *reasonable* rules for customers to follow.

If you have had your prior utility service terminated for nonpayment, it may be difficult to establish renewed service. You will generally have to pay the old bill plus late charges, a reconnection fee, and often a deposit. However, there are a number of things you can try to reduce the amount of money you have to pay to obtain new utility service.

Dealing With an Old Bill. If the bill is *very* old, such as more than three or four years, it is possible that the utility can not legally require you to pay it before providing you with new service. Check with the utility commission or a local attorney, if you have a very old bill.

The best method to deal with back-bills which must be paid may be to request the utility to allow you to pay the old bill off in installments over a period of six to twelve months or longer. So long as you maintain your payments on the new service you will be receiving, there is no reason for the utility to refuse to provide you service under this arrangement. After all, a utility provider is generally permitted to terminate utility service only as a way of avoiding future losses. If you are ready and willing to pay for future service as it is provided, and to pay for the old service, over time, the utility does not have reasonable grounds to deny you this new service.

Late Charges. Generally a utility will charge late fees for paying a utility bill after it is due. There are usually specific rules on how much these late charges can be, and state law and regulations generally limit the late charges to reasonable amounts. The purposes of the late charges are to compensate the utility for its extra costs in collecting the overdue bill, and to discourage you from missing payments.

If the late charges are so high as to be unreasonable, try contacting the consumer services division of your state public utility commission to challenge the amount. Otherwise, try to negotiate with the local utility about the amount. If you lost your job, went through a separation or divorce, or suffered an illness in the family which caused you to be late on your payments before, you can show that this was a temporary difficulty which has now passed — so you do not need the *lesson* that late charges are meant to provide. Bargain with the utility; in many cases they will reduce all or part of the late charges, especially if you had a good reason for missing payments.

Reconnection Fee. This is a fee which may be imposed on a household after it has its service terminated for nonpayment. The purpose of this fee is similar to late charges. Try the same type of arguments and negotiation.

Deposits. Before establishing new or renewed service, many utility companies ask households with poor payment histories to pay a deposit, usually equal to the average bill for one or two months. Utilities are prohibited from discriminating against certain types of customers in setting the deposit requirements. Customers who believe that a deposit is being requested unreasonably, or that a requested deposit is too large, should not hesitate to complain to the public utility commission's consumer division.

If the issue is not reasonableness, but affordability, some of the sources of assistance listed earlier in this chapter may be available to help pay deposits. Later, when you have established a good payment record, or when you decide to terminate service, request that the utility return the deposit, with interest. This should always happen if you did not fall behind again after the deposit was made.

Instead of a deposit, some utilities accept the signature of a cosigner or guarantor, who agrees to be responsible for payments you fail to make. In some states, the cosigner is responsible for all payments you fail to make. In other states, the cosigner's responsibility is limited to several months' worth of unpaid bills.

Failure to Pay Bills From Prior Address as Grounds for Denying Service.
Utility companies often require customers to pay outstanding bills from a previous address before connecting service at a new address. An unpaid bill is the most common reason for refusing new service. But in many states it is not always legal for a utility to do this. Check with a local legal services attorney or the public service commission. If you are given no choice, and you must pay the bill from the previous address in order to obtain new service, you should be able to pay for the old service under an installment agreement.

You Can Not Be Forced To Pay Someone Else's Bills. Even in those states where the utility is permitted to require customers to pay for their outstanding bills from other addresses, a utility generally can not insist that one customer's payment of another customer's bill. For example, you are not obligated to pay the delinquent bills of the prior tenant of your new residence, or bills that your old landlord was obligated to pay. Similarly, you may not have to pay an old bill where the old service was in someone else's name (for example, an old roommate or former spouse). Another example applies when service is now in your name, and one of your current household members has an old delinquent bill.

When you are obligated to pay an old bill before service will be connected, one option is to file for bankruptcy. The old obligation will likely be discharged in the bankruptcy. The utility will have to provide new service as long as you provide a reasonable assurance, such as a deposit, of the ability to make *future* payment. The filing of the bankruptcy will immediately entitle you to service at the new address.

Failure to Provide Information as Grounds for Denying Service. Sometimes companies refuse to hook up service because you have not provided requested forms of identification or proof of residence. The company will use this information for various reasons, including to make sure that you do not owe money for service received at a previous address. This is generally not an unreasonable request unless the company carries it to extremes, such as demanding a birth certificate, or information about all previous residences.

When a utility refuses
to provide service in your name,
look for a rental that comes with utility service,
or have another household member
sign the lease and apply for utility service.

Avoiding Utility Company Restrictions on New Service. When you cannot pay a prior bill with the utility or afford the security deposit, there are still ways to obtain utility service. Look for a house or apartment that includes utilities in the rent. Another option is to establish utility service in the name of someone else with a good payment history. However, since that individual becomes responsible for any unpaid bills, this approach must be considered carefully, with full disclosure of the risks to the individual assuming responsibility for the bills.

Special Telephone Link Up Program. In most states, households in financial distress can obtain steep discounts on new service installation charges under the link-up program run by the local phone company. You may also be eligible for a significant discount on telephone monthly charges under the "Lifeline" program. Contact the public utility commission or telephone company for details.

17

Automobile Repossessions

- *When Your Car Can Be Repossessed and How Repossession Works*
- *Strategies to Prevent Repossession*
- *What to Do If a Repossession Has Just Occurred*
- *Creditor's Collection of the Balance Due After the Repossession*

WHEN TO WORRY ABOUT REPOSSESSION

When you buy a car on credit, you are almost always required to put up the car as collateral on the loan. Some consumers also put up their car as collateral on a loan unrelated to the purchase of the car. This means that if you get behind on your payments at any point, you risk the immediate loss of your car. A repossessor may legally break into your car one night and simply drive or tow it away.

The car may be repossessed only by a leasing company or by a lender that has specifically taken the car as collateral.

For example, if you do not pay a credit card bill, the credit card company cannot repossess the car. All the credit card company can do is sue you, obtain a court judgment, and if the car is not protected by a state law exemption, ask the sheriff to seize the car. This rarely happens in practice, and if it does, it might occur a year or more after default. The situation is very different for car loans and car leases. Miss one or two payments and the car may be gone.

Losing your car may be particularly disastrous if you are recently laid-off and looking for work. The loss of your car makes it much harder to look for and get a new job. But that is only the beginning of your problems after a car repossession. After the creditor repossesses your car, it will then sell it for much less than it is worth, and your equity in the car will be wiped out. On top of all that, you may find yourself being sued for thousands of dollars that the creditor claims is the difference between the amount owed on your loan and the price for which the car was sold.

This chapter provides advice on how to avoid repossession and what to do if a car is repossessed — how to get the car back or avoid the worst consequences after repossession. While repossession law varies somewhat from state to state, this advice is generally applicable nationwide. Most of the advice here is also applicable to motorcycles and trucks, including trucks that you use for business purposes.

HOW TO TELL IF A CAR CAN BE REPOSSESSED

A car can be repossessed only if you have put up the car as collateral on a loan or if you have leased the car. Usually this is easy to check. Look at the loan documents used to purchase the car. Examine the front page of the loan or on a separate one-page disclosure statement and see if the car is listed under "security." Sometimes the loan will clearly state that it is a lease, in which case the car is also subject to repossession.

Next, examine the car's certificate of title. The title will usually list the names of creditors who have rights to the car. If the title is not in your name, but in the name of a company, you are probably leasing the car.

It is possible, but not likely, that a creditor will take a car as collateral and not indicate this on the certificate of title. The only way to discover this is to look at all the loans you have taken out and examine the "security" provisions to see if the car is listed.

HOW SELF-HELP REPOSSESSION WORKS

Self-help repossession is a very real and dangerous threat whenever you fall behind on even one car payment. Creditors in most states have the right to seize the car even when you are only a few weeks late in making payments, and in some cases even if the creditor just thinks you will not make payments when due.

The process is called "self-help" because the creditor is not required to get court permission to repossess the car. The creditor can have one of its own employees or a hired "repo man" seize the car. In most states, the creditor does not even have to notify you that a repossession is about to take place. As long as the seizure does not "breach the peace" (discussed below), it is perfectly legal.

There are important exceptions to a creditor's right to use "self-help" repossession (these exceptions prevent a creditor from seizing a car you own, but may not prevent a lessor from repossessing a leased car):

- The creditor must have taken the car as collateral.
- In some states, the creditor must first give you notice of the right to catch up on delinquent payments. See "Right to Cure" below.
- Self-help repossession is generally illegal in Louisiana and Wisconsin and on certain Indian reservations. Self-help repossession is allowed in Maryland only if the credit agreement allows it.
- A creditor cannot repossess a car owned by military personnel or their dependents if the debt was incurred *before* the individual entered the military.

STRATEGIES TO PREVENT YOUR CAR FROM BEING REPOSSESSED

Keeping Current on Car Payments. Do not pay credit card debts, doctor bills or other low priority debts ahead of car payments. You will not lose any property if you skip payments on low priority debts for several months. Skip one or two car payments, and you risk losing the car. (Keep your car's damage insurance payments current as well, or the creditor will buy insurance for you that is *much* more expensive than your own for *much* less protection for you.)

Curing a Default. Many states give consumers a second chance to make up late payments before repossession. This is called a right to cure. The information about how much you need to pay to cure the default will be in a notice the creditor is required to send you. You can prevent repossession by paying just for the months you are past due and some late charges. (Rights to cure auto *leases* are also available in some states.)

In other states making all back-payments may *not* prevent a repossession. Creditors generally insert into their agreements the right to call the whole loan due if you miss a payment. This is called "accelerating" a loan and means that the entire amount borrowed must be repaid immediately.

In these states, paying just the delinquent payments will not stop a repossession unless the creditor agrees in writing to accept the back-due payments and reinstate the loan. That agreement should specify that the lender will not repossess the car unless you fail to make future payments. Otherwise, the creditor may pocket the back-due payments and still repossess the car.

Negotiate a Work-Out. Many creditors are willing to negotiate a work-out arrangement, where your monthly payments are lowered, and where the lender agrees not to seize the car. Particularly where the loan amount is higher than the car's worth, a work-out may ultimately be less expensive for the lender. The work-out can be a good deal for you as well if you want to keep the car.

Carefully evaluate any work-out proposal before taking it to a creditor. You should balance the importance of keeping your car against the cost of doing so. Consider how much you have already paid, the risk of a deficiency if the car is repossessed (see below), and the importance of keeping the car. For example, a well-running car worth $3500, with only $1300 still owed on the car loan, is worth trying to save. The same may not be true of a $17,000 car with $18,000 still owed where the car loan and insurance payments are beyond what you can hope to afford.

Work-out arrangements should also take into consideration whether you have any claims or defenses relating to the car loan or to the car purchase. Was the car a lemon? Were promised repairs made? Were illegal debt collection contacts made? See Chapter Nine for more information on raising your car complaints as a defense to loan repayment. An attorney representing you may be able to raise these claims and defenses more effectively than if you do so yourself.

Sell the Car. It may be that you simply cannot afford car and insurance payments and maintenance costs necessary to keep a car, or you cannot afford a car as expensive as the car you own. One option is to sell the car yourself. When you sell the car yourself, you will get a *much* higher price than what a buyer would pay at a repossession sale. Just as important, you avoid repossession, storage, selling, and other expenses which the creditor would otherwise eventually charge back to you. You also get a rebate on car insurance when the coverage is canceled early.

Before trying to sell your car, make certain whether you own it or are merely leasing it. Since you do not own a leased car, you cannot sell it. If you do own the car, you must still obtain the creditor's permission to sell it. If you do not, you might get into trouble for an illegal sale.

It is critical that you coordinate the car's sale with the creditor. The creditor is unlikely to allow a new purchaser to assume the car loan and may require you to pay off the car loan in full to give the new purchaser clear title.

If you cannot sell the car for as much as is owed on the loan, the lender is unlikely to cancel the lien. It will hold out for payment in full. Point out to the creditor that this is not in its own self-interest because it will actually get less money if it repossesses the car and sells the car itself.

If a creditor still refuses to go along with the sale, make sure you have a written record of the offer for the car. If the creditor eventually seizes the car, the creditor may have difficulty justifying a sale price significantly lower than the bid you received.

Avoid anyone who offers to broker a sale or lease. In many states car brokerage is illegal. A widespread scam is for con artists to take money from both you and the new "purchaser," but not complete the paperwork for a real transfer in ownership. Instead, you will still owe the creditor or lessor the full amount. These brokers do not get the lessor's permission or release a creditor's lien on the car. The broker may not even forward monthly payments to the lessor or creditor.

Turn the Car In to the Creditor, But Make Sure You Get a Fair Deal.

This strategy is similar to selling the car, only you let the lender sell the car. Although generally not a good idea (because the lender will do such a bad job selling the car), the strategy is acceptable if you get a *written agreement* from the lender that you do not owe anything else on the loan.

Make sure the agreement is in writing. You can also try to negotiate an agreement that the lender will not report the default to a credit reporting agency.

Your agreement to turn the car in voluntarily is attractive to the lender because then it does not need to go to the expense of seizing the car possibly followed by a legal battle to justify the repossession. The creditor will particularly not mind giving up the right to collect additional money if your assets are protected from seizure, meaning that you are "judgment proof." (See Chapter Eight).

Too often consumers voluntarily surrender the collateral without trying to negotiate fair terms. Passive, voluntary surrender of collateral requires less effort, sometimes creates good will with the creditor, and generates fewer expenses (for towing, attorney's fees, and the like) than self-help repossession.

However, voluntary surrender has serious disadvantages. Voluntary surrender will not prevent the creditor from seeking a deficiency claim (the amount of the debt less the re-sale price of the car). The creditor will normally sell the car for a low price and then come after you for the difference. In addition, a surrender can mean that you unintentionally waive some of your claims or defenses.

The situation is similar when you turn in a leased car. It is a common mistake to believe that you will have no further obligation on the loan agreement after you return the car. You will have no further obligation only if you turn the car in at *scheduled* termination of the lease. Your liability at *early* termination may be thousands of dollars, or even as high as $10,000 in some cases. Before turning in a leased car, negotiate with the lessor to reduce or eliminate your early termination liability.

Resisting the Repossession. This strategy is possible, but risky and may be only a temporary solution. Repossessors are required by law to listen to you if you resist their efforts to take your car. They are only allowed to seize your car if they can do so without "breaching the peace."

Breach of the peace is a technical term, and the laws set out strict rules as to when repossessor conduct breaches the peace:

- The repossessor cannot use bodily force or threats. Physical contact is prohibited.
- The repossessor can seize the car from the street or even a driveway, but cannot break open a locked garage door to get at a car.
- The repossessor cannot take property over your oral objections.
- The repossessor cannot be accompanied by a government official, such as the police, unless the official has a court order.
- Courts are divided over whether a repossessor can use trickery to seize the car, such as agreeing to make free repairs as a pretext for seizing the car.

In practice, this means that the repossessor cannot take a car if you or your family is present at the repossession and objects to the seizure just *before* the seizure takes place. Your objection should *not* involve force. You do not even have to scream. Just politely and firmly tell the repossessor not to take the car. You should definitely decline to turn over the keys when requested to do so. Do not be swayed by any legal advice offered by the repossessor or by any "legal documents" the repossessor may wave in front of you. You have an absolute right to object to the repossession.

You can stop a repossession

by politely objecting —

as long as you are there when the car is seized —

or by storing the car in a locked garage.

Never resort to force. Never meet force with force. Never use force to object. Never use force to impede a government official. If the repossessor uses force or threats, or otherwise breaches the peace, call the police. Do not take matters into your own hands. After the fact, consult an attorney. There are significant legal remedies available to challenge an illegal repossession.

To avoid consumers objecting to the seizure, repossessors tend to take cars away in the middle of the night. This is perfectly legal, even if the car is parked in your driveway or in a company parking lot. On the other hand, repossessors cannot break open a garage door lock and force themselves into your garage.

Even though you should never resist government officials in the performance of their duties, it is appropriate to verify the identity of any alleged government official appearing at a repossession and the basis for the official's presence. Government officials should only operate pursuant to written court orders and should not assist self-help repossessions.

Remember that people in uniforms are not necessarily government officials. If the "official" does not provide proper identity, politely object to the seizure — but do so orally, not physically.

Obviously, repossessors cannot seize a car they cannot find. There are ways you can try to hide the car, but you should know that some state statutes make it a criminal offense to conceal collateral (such as your car) or to move it out of state.

If you do not want your car repossessed, you should never turn it over for repairs to the dealer or anyone else the creditor would know. Do not drive the car to the creditor's place of business to discuss a work-out agreement. You may have to walk home if you fail to reach a satisfactory arrangement.

Minimize the Loss of Personal Property Inside the Car. Property left in a car has a way of disappearing after the car is seized. To avoid this problem, you should remove personal property such as tools, tapes and tape deck, clothes, and sporting equipment from your car. You can remove other items like child seats or even spare tires when the car is not being used, and return them if you need them when you use the car.

Before the repossession, ask friends to verify the items left in the car and their condition. You should also make a written inventory or take pictures or video of the car's interior. The creditor has no right to keep personal property that was left in the car at the time of repossession. You can ask the creditor to pay for items not returned, and, if the items are valuable enough to justify the costs, you can file a lawsuit.

File for Bankruptcy Protection. It may not make sense to file for bankruptcy solely to stop a car repossession, but you may have other reasons to file for bankruptcy. In that case, you should know how bankruptcy can deal with the threatened repossession.

Filing several simple forms with a bankruptcy court (with the rest of the forms to be filed later) starts the bankruptcy case and automatically triggers what is known as "the automatic stay." Under the automatic stay, no one, including car repossessors, can take any action against your property. Although a lender can later ask the bankruptcy court for permission to take the car, any attempt to repossess before such court permission is illegal.

In practice, most creditors are careful not to seize cars after you file bankruptcy, particularly after you let them know about the bankruptcy filing. If your car has already been repossessed but not yet resold, bankruptcy can help you get it back. This is discussed in more detail below.

Once the automatic stay freezes everything, you can take several steps to try to permanently prevent the loss of your car (discussed below). See also Chapter Twenty for a more detailed discussion of your bankruptcy rights.

WHAT TO DO *AFTER*
THE CAR IS REPOSSESSED

Get Back Personal Property Left in the Car. Creditors cannot keep property left in your car when it is repossessed. The lender can only keep the car itself. As soon as possible, demand any property left in the car.

A lender's failure to promptly return the property is illegal. (A grey area is whether certain improvements to a car have become so much a part of the car that you do not have a right to their return, such as a tape deck or radio semi-permanently installed.)

Put the request in writing and specify everything left in the car and do so *quickly*. Some credit contracts require (probably illegally) that you request return of your property within a certain number of days.

You Can Reinstate the Contract in Some States. Reinstating the contract allows you to recover the repossessed car and pay only the back-due payments, not the full amount of the note. You must act quickly. In most states, you only have a few weeks to reinstate after repossession.

You Can Redeem the Car. In every state, after a repossession, you can redeem the car assuming you owned the car and did not lease it. The creditor must send you written notice of the date of the car's sale or a date after which the car will be sold. You can redeem the car up until the very moment before the car is sold.

To redeem the car, you must pay off the whole note in one lump sum, plus reasonable repossession and storage charges. Be sure to get a breakdown from the lender of how much you owe. The breakdown should include a refund for unearned interest and insurance charges that are not owed because the note has been paid off early.

Redeeming the car will rarely be a practical solution. Most owners of repossessed cars could not afford the monthly payments, never mind paying off the whole note in one lump sum. But where the car is important to you and worth more than the loan, consider whether you can borrow from another source, including friends or relatives. It is rarely a good idea to mortgage the house to get the car back because defaulting on that loan may result in your losing your home.

Try to Negotiate With the Creditor. If your car has just been repossessed, you might be able to negotiate to get the car back. The creditor might agree to reinstate the original payment schedule or even agree to a new schedule. The same considerations apply as when negotiating a work-out arrangement prior to repossession.

You are in a particularly strong position if you have significant claims or defenses relating to the car, its credit terms, or its repossession. If a car has minimal resale value, the creditor should also prefer a work-out agreement to a worthless asset.

If you do not want the car back, it is still worthwhile trying to get the creditor to permit you to sell the property privately. If you can't sell it yourself, learn whether the creditor intends to sell the car at wholesale or retail, and encourage retail sale, which will produce a price about forty percent higher than wholesale.

Get the Car Back by Filing Bankruptcy. Even after a car is "lost" through repossession, you can get it back in most states by filing bankruptcy. If the loss of the car is your only problem, a bankruptcy filing may not be justified. But if you have other financial problems, a bankruptcy may be justified and you should know how bankruptcy can help to get your car back.

You will have to file for bankruptcy before the lender resells the car. The lender should return the car voluntarily. If not, then you may be able to obtain a court order directing the creditor to "turn over" or return repossessed property. Once you get the car back, you will need to pay for it if you want to keep it for the long-term. If you file a straight bankruptcy (known as a chapter 7 bankruptcy), you can keep the car by "redeeming" it. Redeeming a car in bankruptcy is different than redeeming a car outside of bankruptcy. Outside of bankruptcy, you would have to pay the full balance of the loan plus all the lender's costs. In bankruptcy, you merely pay the car's value.

Although this value often is less than the amount of the loan, most consumers will not be able to come up with the cash. Some creditors will let you redeem in installments. Additionally, since other debts are wiped out by the bankruptcy filing, you can take any cash you get to keep after bankruptcy and apply that to redeem the car. Of course, you may have more pressing needs for your cash, such as to pay rent or utilities.

Another way to keep a car in the long-term is to file a chapter 13 bankruptcy, sometimes known as a "reorganization." In a chapter 13, you have several ways of keeping the car. Probably the best one is to set up a plan to pay off the car loan in monthly installments over a period as long as five years.

The interest rate charged in this plan can in some instances be lower than what you are paying on the car loan. You may even reduce the amount owed to the current value of the car if the car's value is less then the amount you owe. The bottom line is you get to keep the car and significantly lower the car payments. See Chapter Twenty for a more detailed discussion of your bankruptcy rights.

Where the Repossession Was Wrongful. Sometimes cars are seized even though the creditor has no right to seize the car or no right to take the car at that time. Other times, the repossession company will not follow proper procedure in seizing the car.

In each of these situations, you have a right to get the car back and be paid money damages. As a practical matter, enforcement of your rights will usually require a lawyer or someone who understands repossession law. The first four items in the next section provide an overview of this law. Items five and six deal with situations where the creditor or lessor has already sold the car.

CREDITORS' COLLECTION EFFORTS *AFTER* THE REPOSSESSION SALE

After repossession, the creditor will sell your car and apply the sale price (after deducting all repossession and sale expenses) against the amount you owe. Creditors then sometimes come after you for any remaining amount due on the debt. This is called a deficiency action. (When a lessor repossesses a leased vehicle, the result is the same. The car is sold and the lessor seeks a further amount under the lease, called an early termination charge.)

Many consumers feel especially victimized in this situation. They have already lost their car and now the creditor is trying to get more money. You should realize two things about the creditor's claim for a deficiency that might make you feel better. First, the obligation is no longer backed up by any collateral, but is just an unsecured debt. The creditor can take no immediate steps if you do not pay. The deficiency debt is just like a hospital bill or a credit card debt. You should not pay this unsecured debt ahead of more pressing obligations, such as rent or utility bills. (For more on collection of "unsecured debts," see Chapter Six.)

Second, many defenses are available to you when a creditor attempts to collect this deficiency amount. Creditors who repossess cars are required to follow strict technical requirements.

**A creditor tripping up
on even one small repossession requirement
is enough to wipe out any balance due
and may even require the creditor
to pay cash to you.**

If the creditor trips up on even one technical requirement, the deficiency action may be thrown out or the creditor may even end up owing *you* money. Because creditors frequently make mistakes, it is always a good idea to get legal advice before agreeing to pay any deficiency. This section provides an overview of six types of defenses you may have when the creditor seeks a deficiency. It also reviews claims relating to other aspects of the sale and repossession that can often be raised as counterclaims when you are being sued for a deficiency.

1. Claims Concerning the Car or the Credit Terms. In many cases you can fight a deficiency claim by showing the car was a lemon, the dealer misrepresented the quality of a used car, the credit terms were illegal or not disclosed accurately, or the creditor engaged in debt collection harassment. These type of defenses are summarized in Chapter Eight.

The mere threat that you will raise these claims is helpful in negotiating a resolution of the deficiency claim. Depending upon the value of your defenses, a work-out can even lead to a "wash-out," so called because both parties agree to call the debt even, or a "wash," and release each other from liability for further payments.

2. Is the Car Collateral on the Loan? Sometimes the creditor trips up on a technical requirement to make the car collateral for a loan. If the creditor has not taken the car as collateral, it cannot repossess the car, even if you defaulted on a loan used to purchase the car.

Your agreement to put up the car as collateral must be in writing and signed by you. The agreement must also correctly identify your car, and the car's title must be in your own name. Otherwise, the lender has no right to seize the car.

For example, if a wife alone signs a loan and security agreement, but puts the car in the husband's name, the creditor may not have a valid security interest in the car. A repossession may also be illegal if the lender explicitly took the car as collateral only on an earlier loan, but not on the loan at issue.

Another common dealer tactic is to try to get you to buy a car "on the spot" before the financing arrangements are completed. This practice is called "spot delivery." Dealers will allow you to take the car home while they supposedly try to find a good financing deal for you. Often, the financing never comes through, and the dealer will then try to repossess the car. A claim you might have in this situation is that the dealer never properly took the car as collateral because the financing arrangements were never final, or that you are not in default (see item #3).

For more analysis as to whether a creditor has properly taken a car as collateral, see National Consumer Law Center's *Repossessions and Foreclosures* Ch. 3 (3d ed. 1995 and Supp.).

3. Were You in "Default" When the Car Was Seized? Creditors can repossess your car only if you are in default on the car loan. Being late on payments does not necessarily place you "in default."

For example, if a creditor routinely accepts your late payments, the creditor cannot surprise you and seize the car just because a payment is late. You sometimes can also avoid a default by giving the lender notice that you are withholding payments because the car is a lemon.

Moreover, if state law gives you the right to cure the default, the creditor cannot repossess the car before the right to cure has expired. More detail on when a consumer is actually in default can be found in National Consumer Law Center's *Repossessions and Foreclosures* Ch. 4 (3d ed. 1995).

4. Did the Car's Repossession Breach the Peace? Whether a seizure breaches the peace has already been discussed earlier in this chapter at "Strategies to Prevent a Car's Being Repossessed, Resisting Repossession." See also "How Self-Help Repossession Works," above, for situations where self-help repossession is not permitted at all. When a seizure is wrongful, the creditor generally should not keep the car or collect a deficiency. The creditor may owe you money instead.

5. Improper Repossession Sale or Miscalculation of the Deficiency.
Creditors must either keep the cars they repossess or sell them. If it keeps a car, which is rare and allowed only in certain circumstances, the creditor cannot seek any more money from you.

Creditors usually sell a car after repossessing it. The law is very strict on the exact procedure the creditor must use in selling a repossessed car. You can challenge the creditor's attempt to collect a deficiency simply by showing that the creditor did not take the correct steps in selling the car. Tripping up on one technical requirement is usually enough to stop a deficiency. While these technical requirements are very briefly summarized below, see National Consumer Law Center's *Repossessions and Foreclosures* Ch. 10 (3d ed. 1995 and Supp.) for more details.

Failure to meet these requirements may prevent collection of a deficiency if they are raised in court:

- After a repossession or if you turned the car in voluntarily, you must be sent advance notice of the creditor's intention to sell the repossessed car. The notice must include the time and place of a public auction or the date after which the car will be sold privately. The creditor must make reasonable efforts so that you receive a fair warning of the sale date. This notice is very important, and many consumers have prevented a deficiency merely by showing errors in the notice of sale.
- The sale cannot be too rushed and it cannot be overly delayed. On the one hand, there must be time for you to receive the notice of sale and for others to read advertising about the sale. On the other hand, the creditor cannot wait too long to sell the car, or the car's value will depreciate.
- *Every* aspect of the sale, including the manner, the time, the place, and the terms must make business sense, and must be "commercially reasonable." Particularly if the sale price was unreasonably low, look at every aspect of the sale, including the decision to sell at retail or wholesale, and to use an auction or to sell the car off a lot. Advertising for the sale must be sufficient, an auction must use competitive bidding, and the car should be available for advance inspection. At a private sale, usually neither the creditor nor the original dealer can

purchase the car. This helps prevent hidden agreements to dispose of the car at a below market price.

- Check to see if the creditor correctly calculated the amount of its claimed deficiency. Were you given proper credit for all payments? Were the late charges correctly calculated and unearned finance charges and insurance premiums properly rebated? Were you credited with the car's actual sale price and not the car's "estimated" cash value? Were the creditor's expenses (repossession, reconditioning, sale, attorney's fees) reasonable and accurate?

6. Auto leases. Special laws and rules apply where you leased the repossessed car instead of buying the car on credit. The lease will specify the formula used to calculate how much you owe upon default or early termination. The formula is usually quite complex and difficult to understand, and may be unreasonable or not properly applied by the lessor. Federal and state law provide you with powerful remedies when lessors apply unreasonable formulas or do not clearly disclose the formulas they use.

Aggressive attorneys can usually force lessors to settle for a "wash." That is, although it is not uncommon for a lessor to demand $5,000 to $10,000 at early termination of a car lease, proper legal advocacy can often get car leasing companies to drop the whole claim. For more detail on challenging auto lease early termination penalties, see National Consumer Law Center's *Truth in Lending* Ch. 9 (3d ed. 1995 and Supp.).

YOUR RIGHTS WHEN THE CREDITOR MAKES A MISTAKE

The penalties are severe when creditors trip up in repossessing cars. In many states, any mistake will lead to the creditor being barred from seeking any deficiency.

Moreover, if the creditor trips up on one of the requirements, it may have to pay you as a penalty ten percent of the car's original purchase price plus the whole finance charge on the car loan. This penalty can run into many thousands of dollars.

If repossessor conduct is seriously improper, you may also be able to recover punitive damages running into many thousands of dollars. Sometimes, the creditor will even have to pay your attorney fees. Legal representation is often essential to recover any of these penalties.

FOR MORE INFORMATION

To learn more about consumer repossession rights, the best legal practice manual is the National Consumer Law Center's *Repossessions and Foreclosures* (3d ed. 1995 and Supplement), which is the source of much of the information in this chapter. The manual covers all the federal and state laws governing consumer repossessions. *Repossessions and Foreclosures* includes step-by-step checklists for different types of repossession situations, and samples of different documents a lawyer will have to prepare in a repossession case. The manual covers both car loans and leases.

18

Seizure of
Household Goods

- *Limited Situations Where Creditor Can Seize Your Household Goods*
- *Different Types of Liens Which May Affect Personal Property*
- *Nine Strategies to Stop Household Goods Seizures*

UNDERSTANDING CREDITOR THREATS
TO SEIZE HOUSEHOLD GOODS

One of the most frightening creditor practices is the threat to seize your household goods, such as your television, wedding rings, bedroom furniture and the like. These threats can be effective because of these items' special personal significance, even if they have minimal resale value.

In most cases, you should not take such threats seriously. The goods' limited economic value means the creditor has no financial incentive to follow through with the threat. Additionally, federal and state laws limit the types of household goods a creditor can take, and how it can seize those goods.

This chapter explains the limited situations in which a creditor can legally seize your household goods, how it must conduct the seizure, and what steps you can take to prevent such seizures. There are only four situations in which a creditor can try to seize your household goods:

1. When you take out a loan specifically to purchase certain household goods, and agree to have those goods serve as collateral for the loan, the creditor has a "purchase money security interest" in those household goods. For example, if you buy a dining room

set on credit offered by the furniture dealer, the dining room set is likely to be collateral for the loan. Similarly, some types of store credit cards are secured by household goods you buy. (Non-store cards such as Visa, Mastercard, Discover or American Express typically are not.) If you default on a loan with personal property collateral, the creditor can seize those goods, but only if it goes to the expense of a court procedure or if you make the mistake of letting repossessors into your home.

2. When a loan is *not* used to purchase household goods, but the creditor insists that you put up household goods as collateral for the loan, the creditor has a "non-purchase money security interest." Federal law gives you special protections from the seizure of such goods which are helpful but not universally applicable. More discussion of this issue is found below.

Unless property is specifically listed as collateral for the debt, creditors can only seize goods *after* they have sued you and *after* they obtain a court judgment. Even then, state exemption law usually protects personal property from seizure.

---

3. When you do not put household goods up as collateral for a loan, creditors can ask a sheriff or other official to seize these goods only *after* obtaining a court judgment on the debt. The creditor uses that judgment to try to "execute" on the household goods. Even then, state law generally protects most of your household goods from such executions.

4. When you rent goods with the option to purchase them after all payments are made, this is called a "rent-to-own" or RTO transaction. Although the RTO merchant has the right to take the goods back if you get behind on payments, the merchant does

not have the right to enter your home without your permission to take the goods.

These are the *only* four situations where creditors have *any* legal right to follow through on their threat to seize household goods. Outside these four situations, the creditor has *no* right to seize the goods.

You can usually determine if one of these four situations apply by looking at the loan documents. The credit agreement indicates if household goods are taken as collateral, and if the loan was used to purchase those goods. Sales agreements will also indicate if they are rent-to-own transactions.

DESCRIPTION OF DIFFERENT TYPES OF LIENS WHICH MAY AFFECT HOUSEHOLD GOODS

Although you have many protections in each situation, there are important differences between "purchase money security interests," "non-purchase money security interests," and "judgment liens." Each is a type of "security interest" which may apply to your personal property. You should understand these differences before reading the next section since your legal rights depend on which type of security interest applies.

Purchase Money Security Interests. A "purchase money security interest" arises when you agree to allow a lender to take as collateral the property you are purchasing with the loan. A common example is a car loan, although repossession issues for car loans are discussed in Chapter Seventeen. Some stores which have their own credit cards take a purchase money security interest in property you buy at their store with their card. This would be reflected in your credit card agreement and on your charge slips.

Non-purchase Money Security Interests. A non-purchase money security interest arises when you agree to give a lender collateral which was not purchased with money from that loan (property you already own). For example, a finance company may insist that you give a lawn-mower or living room set as collateral for a loan you take out to pay for car repairs. A non-purchase money security interest would be reflected in your loan papers and in your disclosure statement concerning the cost of the loan.

Judgment Liens. Sometimes a creditor obtains collateral which is not related to any agreement at all. Court judgments in most states can be attached as a lien on certain items of personal property. That lien can be used to seize the property according to rules which apply in your state.

Ways to deal with each of these potential threats to your personal property are discussed below.

NINE STRATEGIES TO PROTECT YOUR HOUSEHOLD GOODS

This section lists nine strategies that can help you keep your household goods when a creditor threatens to seize them. For more details, see the National Consumer Law Center's *Repossessions and Foreclosures* (3d ed. 1995 and Supp.).

1. Do Not Panic; Determine If the Threat Is False. The first thing to realize is that a creditor threatening seizure is usually bluffing. The value of most household goods after deducting repossession, storage, and selling expenses, is negligible. The creditor has no economic interest in the goods and therefore is unlikely to pursue repossession.

The creditor is using the threat of repossession to frighten you into paying off that creditor's debt first, even though it is in your overall best interest to pay off other debts instead. Sometimes creditors also make these threats to build up their reputation as being tough on defaulters.

Several factors help tip you off that a threat to seize your goods is false. A threat to seize household goods is false if the debt does not fall within any of the four categories of allowable seizures listed at the beginning of this chapter.

Even if one of these four situations apply, the threat is still usually false. This is particularly the case where the creditor is threatening to execute on household goods under a court judgment, since state laws usually protect most common household goods from execution.

Beyond that, evaluating a threat will often depend on the value of the collateral, the difficulty of seizing it, and the nature and reputation of the creditor. For example, a consumer electronics store is more likely to seize

$2000 worth of the stereo and video equipment it sold you a few months ago than a loan company is to seize the family photo album or the five year old refrigerator.

If the threat is false, obviously you should not worry about it. False threats are illegal, and you may be able to recover as much as $1000 plus your attorney fees even if you are not injured. See Chapter Six.

As outlined below, even if the threat is not false, you have a series of strategies to protect the goods or make it very expensive for the creditor to seize them. In protecting your household goods, you have the upper hand in dealing with the creditor; do not be frightened into doing something you will regret.

2. Determine if the Creditor Can Take the Household Goods as Collateral. Federal law prohibits creditors from taking "non-purchase money security interests" in most household goods. This rule is particularly important in dealing with finance companies, but usually not helpful in dealing with furniture or appliance dealers that are seeking to seize the goods you purchased from them.

A creditor *can* take household goods as collateral if you use the loan *to purchase those particular goods,* although it may not choose to do so. The only way to tell is to check your credit agreement to see if the lender is claiming a security interest in the goods purchased.

Under federal law, a creditor *cannot* take the following household goods as collateral for a loan which is *not* used to purchase the goods: clothing, furniture, appliances, one radio, one television, linens, china, crockery, kitchenware, and other personal effects such as your wedding rings and photographs. The law probably allows the following types of goods to be taken as collateral, even if the loan is not used to purchase these items: art, lawn equipment, tools, audio systems, a second television or radio, cameras, boats, sporting goods, typewriters, firearms, bicycles, musical instruments or jewelry (other than wedding your rings).

No creditor can claim a security interest in all of your household goods or all items located at your residence, because this will include many types of prohibited collateral. In addition, creditors cannot take as collateral goods which you do not yet own at the time of the loan, but will own in the future. As a consequence, a creditor, for example, cannot take a security interest in all tools or audio systems you will ever own, only in identified items you own at the time of the loan.

Sears, Circuit City, and other merchants sometimes try to take a security interest in all goods you purchase in their store with their credit card. (This applies to the stores' own cards, but not to other cards accepted by the stores, such as Visa or MasterCard.)

A store may or may not be successful in taking purchased items as collateral, depending on how they comply with various technical requirements as to signatures, contract language, and record-keeping. You will have to ask an attorney whether the security interest is valid.

3. Do Not Consent to the Creditor Coming Into Your Home. This strategy pertains *only* if the person coming to your home works for the creditor or a collection agency. See the next item if a sheriff or other government official comes to your home.

No creditor, collector, or hired repossessing agent may come into your home without your express permission in order to repossess property. You can easily stop them by politely, but firmly, refusing permission to enter.

Repeat your objection to entry each time a repossession threat or effort is made, and instruct landlords, spouses, children, and/or roommates *not* to consent to repossessors entering your residence. This protection also applies to a locked garage on your premises. If you have property outdoors, consider bringing it inside or placing it in your locked garage.

You can stop a creditor's self-help repossession by refusing to allow the repossessor to enter your home. The creditor has no right to enter unless invited by you.

Do not physically resist the entry, just politely and firmly object to the entry. Even walking uninvited through an open door makes the repossession illegal. If repossessors do force themselves in or break a lock to gain entry, your first concern should be for the safety of individuals in the house. After the repossession, contact the police and an attorney, because the repossessor's action was an illegal breach of the peace. Witnesses, of course, are helpful. Other evidence, such as a broken lock, should be retained.

4. *Do* Cooperate with the Sheriff. In rare cases, it will not be the creditor who is seizing the goods, but a government official, the sheriff or constable. This situation is unusual because the creditor would have had first to obtain a court order to arrange for the sheriff to come. Obtaining a court order is likely to cost more than the goods are worth. If it is the sheriff (and not the creditor claiming to be the sheriff), ask for identification and then comply with any order the sheriff makes.

5. Claim that the Household Goods Are Exempt. When a sheriff is seizing the goods, it is important to determine which creditor has asked for the seizure, a creditor who has taken the property to be seized as collateral or some other creditor. Furniture and appliance stores are the most likely creditors to obtain a court order sending a sheriff to seize collateral.

If the creditor had not previously obtained your agreement that the goods will be collateral, but is attempting to seize the goods after obtaining a court judgment, you have important rights under state law. Almost all states protect certain household goods from seizure to satisfy a court judgment.

The state laws offering this protection are usually called exemption laws. They may provide blanket protection for all household goods, for household goods under a certain dollar figure, or for certain types of household goods. It is important to know the exemption law for your state. Ask a legal services office or other attorney, or a credit counseling agency. Often the information is available in pamphlet form.

In addition, property in your residence owned by someone else should not be seized to satisfy a judgment against you. This even applies to property owned by other family members.

If property is exempt or owned by someone else, this should be pointed out to the sheriff, or, even better, to the court before the sheriff comes. Usually, there is a form which will be sent to you before the seizure. It should be returned as soon as possible, and definitely *before* the scheduled date for the seizure.

If the sheriff still takes the goods, *quickly* go to court after the sheriff takes the goods to explain that the household goods are exempt under state law or belong to someone else. The court clerk's office or sheriff's office may have a form to fill out to help you with your claim.

6. Challenge the Creditor in Court If You Have Defenses. Some sheriff seizures are not to enforce a judgment on a debt, but a creditor's right to recover its collateral. If you gave a creditor a security interest in certain goods, the creditor can go to court (sometimes without even telling you) and claim that you are behind on your payments and that the sheriff should seize the collateral. (Depending on what state you are in, this proceeding may be called "replevin," "sequestration," "detinue," "claim and delivery," or "bail." State law generally does *not* exempt any of your property from seizure by a creditor if you have given it as collateral to that creditor.)

Sometimes you will be given notice and the opportunity to contest this seizure before it happens, and sometimes you can only do so after it happens. (If your hearing is not until after the seizure, the creditor will not obtain permanent custody of the property until *after* your hearing.) In either case, just as in other types of lawsuits, the creditor is not expecting you to contest the matter or to be represented by an attorney. Raising a serious defense, such as that the goods which the creditor seeks to repossess are not the same goods which serve as collateral for the loan, may be enough for the creditor to drop the suit, allowing you to retain or recover your property.

7. Negotiate an Agreement. Since the goods the creditor is seeking are likely to have very little value if seized, the creditor may be willing to agree to very fair terms to facilitate your voluntary repayment. You should approach this negotiation based on what you can reasonably afford, and with a thorough understanding of what you can do to prevent repossession if the creditor does not accept your offer. You should never agree to make voluntary payments in an amount larger than you can afford or if you have other higher priority debts which will remain unpaid.

8. Preventing RTO Repossessions. Rent-to-own (RTO) contracts give you ownership of rented goods after you make all the payments. If you stop making payments, the RTO company has the right to take the rented property. But most states prohibit the RTO company from repossessing over your objection or entering your home without permission. This result is not changed even if you gave permission in the small print of the sales agreement to the repossession or entry into your home. Be careful of the "switch out" technique whereby the RTO company claims it is taking a item in for repair, maintenance, or upgrading, when it is actually repossessing it.

RTO companies may also threaten criminal action if you do not return rented goods. But failure to let RTO personnel into your home is not a crime, and the RTO company usually has no intent to pursue a criminal action.

Nevertheless, unless you have made substantial payments on a rent-to-own contract, it is usually a good idea to return the goods and stop paying. There will be no liability except for back due payments. And typically the rented item is significantly overpriced. You will have paid for the goods many times over before you own them.

9. File for Bankruptcy. The cost and other complications of filing bankruptcy may not make sense just to protect certain household goods. But a bankruptcy filing also offers you benefits in dealing with other debts, so that bankruptcy may make sense for other reasons. It is thus important to know how bankruptcy can protect your household goods.

Filing for bankruptcy provides immediate relief by automatically stopping *any* threatened seizure of the household goods. This applies to seizures of collateral and even to rented items.

Bankruptcy can usually protect your household goods in the long run as well. If the household goods are exempt under applicable law, then bankruptcy permanently prevents their seizure to satisfy a court judgment.

Many non-purchase money security interests in household goods can also be canceled in bankruptcy if the goods are exempt under the bankruptcy law. Even if the creditor has a purchase money security interest, that interest may be eliminated in certain situations if the creditor has since refinanced the original loan used to purchase the goods.

Even if a security interest in certain household goods cannot be cancelled in bankruptcy, you may be able to keep the property after a bankruptcy filing by paying the creditor only what the property is worth. This is called "redemption." Used household goods may be worth far less than the outstanding debt.

In an RTO transaction, if you want to keep the goods after filing bankruptcy, you can pay any delinquent payments over time and keep current on future rent payments. In certain states you can categorize the RTO transaction as a sale, and this will give you additional strategies in bankruptcy, including the possibility of redemption for the goods' real value. For more on bankruptcy, see Chapter Twenty.

Student Loan and Federal Income Tax Collections

- *How to Postpone Your Student Loan Payments When You Are In Financial Trouble*
- *Coping With Collection on Seriously Overdue Student Loans*
- *Your Rights If the School Ripped You Off*
- *What to Do If You Owe the IRS*

STUDENT LOANS

Why You Should Pay Particular Attention to Your Student Loans. The government has special powers to collect on your student loan—including seizure of your tax refunds, denying you new student loans and grants, seizing up to ten percent of your wages without a court order, and charging you very large collection fees.

On the other hand, you can sometimes keep the government from using these special collection powers by choosing from a variety of excellent options that are available when you cannot afford to pay your student loan. Unfortunately, you cannot sit back and wait for the government to offer these choices to you. *You must know about and request these options on your own.* Requesting one of these options may allow you to skip payments for a while, reduce your payments, stop collection efforts against you, and in certain cases involving a school closure or school misconduct, may even allow you to cancel out the loan and receive a refund!

Identify What Kind of Loans You Have and To Whom You Owe Them.
There are three major types of student loans, and a number of different
lenders to whom you might owe repayment. Your rights and best strategies
will vary depending on what type of loan you have.

From about 1980 to 1995, the most common type of student loan was
a Stafford or Guaranteed Student Loan (GSL). GSLs come in two types:
subsidized (where the government pays part of the interest costs) and
unsubsidized.

Related to GSLs are unsubsidized GSLs and PLUS loans taken out by
students' parents. Generally, the rules concerning GSL loans also apply
to these loans. Subsidized and unsubsidized GSLs, SLS and PLUS loans
are all called Federal Family Education Loans, or FFELs. GSL loans are
very confusing, and it is often hard to figure out who to talk to about
payment problems.

Even though the school might have helped you fill out the loan papers,
the loan was actually from a bank. That bank may have sold the loan to
another lender, such as the Student Loan Marketing Association (Sallie
Mae). Whoever is holding the loan might hire another company to "service" the loan. Loan servicers receive your payments and correspond with
you. If you stopped making payments on that loan, the loan was then
turned over to a guaranty agency. For certain older loans, it was eventually
passed on to the U.S. Department of Education.

Starting in about 1994, certain schools started offering a new type of
loan called a Federal Direct Student Loan, often called an FDSL or a Direct
Loan. These loans work differently than GSLs and others because the
school, not the bank, arranges for a loan between the United States
Department of Education and the student. Payments are made directly to
the United States Department of Education.

A third type of loan is a Perkins Loan, formerly called a National Direct
Student Loan or NDSL. This loan is made directly from the school you
attended, and you repay the amount to the school. If you stop paying the
school, the loan is eventually turned over to the U.S. Department of
Education.

Try to figure out what type of loan you have because your options are
somewhat different for different types of loans. The first place to look is the
loan application and promissory note. You can also ask the lender or collector you are dealing with.

What to Do If Your Loan Is Not Yet Seriously Delinquent. If you are not yet too far behind in your loan payments, you may be able to obtain relief that will last several years, but you must apply for this help, and you must do so quickly.

The best option is to obtain a loan deferment from the creditor to whom you make your loan payments. A loan deferment means that you delay repaying your loan, usually for a year. The deferment may then be renewed for one or two or sometimes even three additional years. If the loan is a subsidized GSL, the government makes interest payments for you during the deferment period, but eventually you will have to pay the full loan principal. You can also get a deferment of an unsubsidized GSL or PLUS loan but you will later be obligated to pay back the interest that accrued during the deferment period.

You have a legal right to a loan deferment under specified conditions: if you have gone back to school, have lost your job, or are experiencing certain other specified financial hardships. The exact grounds for deferment vary with the type of loan involved and when you took out the loan. For example, deferment rules for GSLs vary dramatically depending on whether you took out the loan before or after July 1, 1993. If you are having financial difficulties, ask your lender whether you can qualify for a deferment.

If you get too far behind on your payments, you will no longer qualify for a deferment. This means that it is essential to apply for a deferment as early as possible.

If you cannot qualify for a deferment, an alternative is to request loan "forbearance." Forbearance means that you do not have to pay for a while, and no adverse action will be taken against you during the forbearance period. (If you want, you can arrange to make small payments instead during the forbearance period.) Unlike a deferment on a subsidized GSL, the government does not pay interest for you. You will eventually have to repay the full loan amount and all accrued interest.

In some circumstances, you will have a legal right to a forbearance. For example, you have a right to forbear a GSL payment that exceeds twenty percent of your income, even if you are many months delinquent, as long as a guaranty agency has not yet taken over the loan. Even if you don't have a right to a forbearance, lenders have the option to grant you one especially if you are having health problems or other personal problems that affect your ability to make your monthly payments.

Another option is to consolidate, that is exchange, the type of student loans you have with one new loan. Loan consolidation is often the best strategy when you are in default, and is discussed in more detail later in this chapter.

**You can delay loan repayment
if you are having financial problems,
but only if you take the initiative
to ask for assistance.**

The common feature of all of these approaches — deferments, forbearance, or loan consolidation — is that you must apply for them. If you just sit back and wait, your situation can get worse.

What to Expect If You Have Not Paid Your Student Loan For Several Years. The main method the government uses to collect on defaulted student loans is seizure of federal income tax refunds. This includes any earned income tax credit you are owed. The only safe way to avoid this collection method is not to have a tax refund due by decreasing your withholding or lowering any estimated tax payments you make. Other strategies to deal with tax intercepts are detailed later in this chapter.

If you are seriously behind on your student loan, you also can expect the following:

- You will be denied new federally-backed student loans and grants;
- Your default will stay on your credit record for seven years;
- The guaranty agency or the Department of Education may order your employer to pay up to 10% of your wages to them;
- A large portion of anything you pay to a collection agency on the loan will go to collection agency fees and not to pay off your loan.

On the other hand, the odds of your being sued are relatively low, so that you need not worry about losing personal property or your home because of a defaulted student loan.

What to Do If You Have Not Paid Your Student Loan For Several Years. If you have not paid on your student loan for a number of years, you will be in default on the loan, and your loan will have been turned over to a guaranty agency or the United States Department of Education. At this point, you are generally not eligible for forbearance or deferment. The holder of your student loan can try to collect the money from you using the various collection tactics described above.

It may be that you do not have sufficient wages to be garnished, no tax refunds to intercept, no special concern for your credit rating, and no interest in applying for new student loans and grants. In that case, you may decide to do nothing, and instead use what income you have to pay your rent, mortgage, utility payments or other priority debts.

There are still a number of good strategies to pursue if you are worried about these collection tactics. One approach is to contact the party collecting on the loan, and state that you want to renew your eligibility for a new loan and want a reasonable and affordable repayment plan.

You have a legal right to a reasonable and affordable payment plan. Payments in this type of plan can be as low as $5 a month, depending on your income. Generally, it is best to pay at least as much as your monthly accrued interest, if possible. But federal law states that you should not be required to pay more than you can afford.

Make sure you say words similar to "I want a reasonable and affordable payment plan so that I can renew my eligibility for new loans." These are the magic words collectors usually need to hear before they will offer you the plan. You may have other claims against collectors who tell you that there's no such thing as a "reasonable and affordable" payment plan or who refuse to set one up for you. (See Chapter Six).

If you get a reasonable and affordable plan, it is important that you stay on it and make all payments on time. If you do not, you will not get another chance at a low payment plan.

The advantages of a reasonable and affordable payment plan are that you should not experience debt collection harassment, tax intercepts or wage garnishment. Also, if you make six consecutive monthly payments, you will re-establish your eligibility for new student loans and grants.

Despite these advantages, your credit rating will still list the loan in default, a portion of what you pay may be going toward collection costs, interest charges will continue to mount, and you must continue to make monthly payments in order to remain eligible for new student loans and grants.

After twelve monthly payments, you may get out of default status by requesting "loan rehabilitation." After receiving this request, the loan holder will attempt to sell your defaulted loan to a lender. If your loan is purchased, you are no longer in default, the default is removed from your credit record and a ten year repayment schedule is established. Usually, the schedule will require you to make larger payments than what you were paying under the reasonable and affordable payment plan. But you will no longer be considered in default and will be eligible once again for deferrals and forbearance.

**After losing her job,
Jane Doe stopped paying on her Stafford Loan,
and faced severe collection efforts.
Her loan amount kept going up by addition
of interest charges and collection fees.
She solved her problem by converting
her loan to a Direct Consolidation Loan.
Because her income was low,
her monthly payments were zero.
Then she received an unemployment deferment,
so that no interest charges were added
to her loan for up to three years.**

Another alternative is to "consolidate" your loans into either a new Direct Loan with "income contingent repayments" or a new FFEL loan with "income sensitive repayments." You can do this even if you are in default, even if you only have one loan, and even if that loan is very small. The advantage of this option is it requires only that you pay an amount that is related to your income and you will no longer be in default.

There should be no efforts made to collect from you as long as you keep the new loan current. You will also be eligible for new loans and grants, you will have a credit record showing a past delinquency but no current default, and what you owe for collection fees will be reduced. Perhaps most importantly, you can then apply for a deferment based on your returning to school, unemployment or economic hardship.

If you are in default on your old loan, you can obtain a Direct Consolidation Loan immediately, and a FFEL Consolidation Loan after making three payments that the guaranty agency specifies as reasonable and affordable. A sample (not for actual use) form to request a Direct Consolidation Loan application is reproduced in Appendix Two but you must obtain an official form from the Department of Education for actual use. (Information on existing loans can be obtained from your lender.) You can also apply electronically through the consolidation website at http://www.ed.gov/directloan. Make sure to fill in all the requested information.

You can also obtain estimates of what your monthly payments would be under different repayment plans through the calculator website at http://ed.gov/DirectLoan/calc.html.

If You Feel The School Ripped You Off. Special rights apply if the school you attended (particularly a for-profit trade or vocational school) ripped you off. If you received a school loan after January 1, 1986, you can cancel your loan, get all of your payments back, and clean up your credit record if the school closed while you were still enrolled or within ninety days of your leaving the school. Ask whomever is holding your loan for an application for a closed school discharge.

You can also apply for loan cancellation if you were "falsely certified as eligible," which is defined in the regulations as any one of three types of fraud:

1. At the time of enrollment, there was a state law that would have disqualified you from getting a job in the area for which you were being trained (for example, the school enrolled you in a truck driving school even though you had a physical handicap that prevents you from obtaining a truck-driving license).
2. If you did not have a high school diploma when you went to the school, the school had the responsibility to make sure you could benefit from the educational program, usually by

giving you an exam. You can receive a loan discharge if your exam score was falsified in some way. For example, if a school employee took the test for you or gave you the answers.

3. The school forged your name on the loan papers or check endorsements, and you never went to school for the times covered by the forgery.

If you were victimized by one of these types of fraud, you should seek a loan cancellation by requesting an application from whomever is holding your loan. Be prepared to meet resistance and delay. You will have to insist on your rights. Because it usually takes a long time to process discharge applications, it is a good idea to request a forbearance so that collection activities will stop while your application is pending.

In addition, the fact that the school defrauded you may be a defense to loan repayment. Stafford (GSL) loans after January 1, 1994 state that you can raise this defense where the for-profit trade school referred you to the lender. You can also raise the school's fraud as a defense on any Direct loan or Perkins (NDSL) loan. For GSLs before 1994, you will have to consult a lawyer.

Other Ways to Wipe Out a Student Loan. There are a few other important grounds for canceling a student loan. That the loan is very old is *not* such a ground. However, the student's death or permanent disability are grounds for canceling the loan permanently. You also have a right to a cancellation of at least part of what you owe if you did not complete your education and the school failed to give you a refund that they owed you.

It is generally difficult to discharge a student loan in bankruptcy. The only basis for doing this is to convince the bankruptcy judge that it will be a significant hardship for the foreseeable future to repay the loan. It is usually better to ask the bankruptcy court to make this determination at the time of the bankruptcy filing, but if you fail to do so, the bankruptcy court or a state court can later make that determination when collection attempts on the student loan are renewed. The type of hardship required usually involves serious economic problems which are likely to persist for reasons beyond your control.

Dealing With Tax Intercepts. Seizure of tax refunds is the most common way the government collects on defaulted student loans. There are several steps you can take to deal with this seizure. If your joint tax refund is seized to pay for your student loan, your spouse can recover some of the amount seized by filling in a simple IRS form.

You should also be notified before any actual interception. This notice gives you the right to fight the intercept. Check whatever boxes are appropriate on the form (e.g. the school closed, false certification, or the school defrauded you) and return it immediately, asking for a hearing. Send the form back return receipt requested as proof you sent it in. (There are widespread stories of the government failing to process requests for hearings.) You will have to do this every year you get a notice.

You should also be notified after any seizure. You should complain to the Department of Education if you did not have a chance to raise your defenses before your refund was seized.

Responding to a Wage Garnishment. Student loan collectors have the right to garnish a certain amount of your wages *without first obtaining a court judgment.* Student loan collectors often threaten to do this, but less frequently actually follow through. Those collectors who do follow through with garnishments rarely let you know that you have a right to challenge the seizure of your wages.

There are four ways you can stop such a wage garnishment to repay your student loan:

1. You can ask for a repayment agreement instead of the garnishment.
2. You can stop a wage seizure if you lost your old job against your wishes and you have not been continuously employed in your new job for a full year.
3. You can stop seizure of your first $154.50 a week in take-home pay.
4. You should receive a notice about your right to a hearing. Request a hearing and explain any reason why you think you need not repay the loan.

FEDERAL INCOME TAXES

When your debt burden is overwhelming, you may find yourself behind on your taxes. Most people have a variety of tax obligations, the most common three being property taxes and federal and state income taxes. Some advice on property taxes is found at Chapter Two. This section concentrates on back due federal income taxes. Some of the information here also applies to state income taxes.

You must give special consideration to your federal income tax obligations for two reasons. First, the IRS has special powers to collect back taxes that make it important for you to pay these taxes ahead of many other types of debt. Second, the IRS sets out specific procedures and protections that you should know about if you are behind on your tax obligation.

File the Return on Time Even if You Do Not Pay the Taxes Owed.
One of the worst things you can do if you cannot afford to pay your taxes is not to file your tax return. You must file an income tax return, in general, if you are a U.S. citizen or resident alien whose taxable income exceeds certain amounts. (For 1999 this amount is $7050 for individuals and $12,700 for joint filers. These dollar amounts will go up each year.)

April 15th is the deadline for most people to file individual income tax returns and pay any taxes owed. Extensions may not be available unless you pay any taxes you are likely to owe.

If you fail to file your tax returns by April 15 and you owed tax, you may be (although usually you will not be) prosecuted for a misdemeanor crime. More likely, the government will assess a fine. If you owe tax and are late sixty days or less in filing, the combined late-filing and late-payment penalty is five percent of the tax owed each month or part of a month that your return is late, up to twenty-five percent. If your return is over sixty days late, the minimum penalty is the smaller of $100 or 100% of the tax owed.

**Always file your tax return
even if you do not send in your tax payment —
the penalties will be *much* smaller.**

It is best to avoid these additional penalties, because they increase your debt. Failure to pay is not, by itself, a crime. Instead you will merely be behind on a debt. The penalty for late payment is only a fraction of the larger penalty for not filing a return—it starts at only one half of one percent of the tax owed per month up to a maximum of twenty-five percent, plus interest.

Getting an extension to file is also not the solution it might seem to be. Although the IRS will automatically give you a four month extension if you request it with payment of the taxes you are likely to owe, keep in mind that this is only an extension of time to *file*. It does not give you more time to *pay* taxes you owe and you will be charged both interest and probably a late payment penalty during the time of the extension. As noted above, if you can't pay the taxes due, it is a better idea to file the return, pay as much as you can if anything, and then consider negotiating with the IRS (discussed below).

Negotiating With the IRS. When you file a return, but cannot afford to pay the taxes due, one option is to ask the IRS to put the tax obligation on your credit card (if you still have a card that works). The credit card interest will generally be less than IRS interest and penalties, and you can develop a plan to pay down the credit card debt at a later time.

You should only put amounts on your credit card you believe you can repay. But if your circumstances change, and you cannot repay the debt as soon as you are required, it may be easier to deal with the credit card company than the IRS.

Another option is to ask the IRS to let you pay the amount due in monthly installments over a period of up to three years. The IRS will generally allow this. Sometimes you can even get the IRS to drop penalties. (The IRS will only drop interest if the IRS made an error that resulted in the tax liability.)

You can attach an IRS form, "Installment Agreement Request" to your return or attach your own written request for a payment plan. Be sure to document the severe financial hardship you are undergoing, and why this was caused by factors outside your control. Also make sure that any installment payment plan or reduction in the amount owed is in writing.

The IRS will sometimes settle with you and allow you to pay an amount less than what they claim you owe. This is called an "offer-in-compromise" and is generally granted only when you have evidence that you do not owe the taxes, or when there is doubt that the taxes can be collected in full. You may appeal if your offer-in-compromise is rejected by the IRS.

In some cases your responsibility to pay a tax may be cancelled when the tax is owed entirely by your spouse or ex-spouse. This is true even if you filed a joint return. Help from a tax professional is recommended.

Steps the IRS Can Take to Force Payment. If you do not set up a payment plan or obtain an agreement on an offer-in-compromise, the IRS will force payment. If you have not filed a return in which you calculate the amount due, the IRS will send you a series of several letters asking for payment of the amount it claims is due. The last letter gives you a period of time to file a petition with the tax court disputing the amount owed. (If the taxes owed are less than $50,000, you will be eligible for special informal tax court procedures.) A tax court petition is the last opportunity you have to protest the tax without paying it first.

If you do not respond, or if you have already filed a return admitting the amount owed, the IRS will send an assessment notice saying that it is placing a tax lien on all your property. This will give the IRS the authority to seize any of your property, with the exception of certain exempt types of income and possessions. In practice, the IRS will wait awhile and then go after bank accounts, paychecks, and even homes.

About $150 a week in wages (depending on your personal exemption and standard deduction), unemployment and workers' compensation, public assistance, job training benefits, income needed to pay court-ordered child support, and certain federal retirement and disability benefits are exempt from seizure. Other exempt property will be certain amounts of clothing, furniture, personal effects and job-related tools. A state homestead exemption will *not* protect your home from an IRS tax lien or seizure.

Unless most of your assets and all of your income are exempt from seizure, it makes sense to negotiate a payment schedule with the IRS to avoid seizure of personal property and income. Make sure any agreement is in writing.

A good source for information about taxes is the IRS web site at: www.irs.ustreas.gov.

Bankruptcy. Bankruptcy is not as effective a remedy when dealing with taxes as with other debts. In general, most taxes cannot be discharged in a chapter 7 bankruptcy. Some exceptions apply when the taxes are more than three years delinquent if you properly filed the tax return for the year in question. Existing tax liens are likely to remain on your property even after the bankruptcy. In a chapter 13 reorganization, the full amount of the taxes owed can be paid in installments over a three to five year period.

Bankruptcy

- *Ten Factors in Deciding Whether to File Bankruptcy*
- *What Bankruptcy Can and Cannot Do for You*
- *How to Choose What Type of Bankruptcy, and When to File*
- *The Basic Steps to Chapter 7 and 13 Bankruptcies*
- *How To Get Help With Your Bankruptcy Filing*

IS BANKRUPTCY THE RIGHT CHOICE FOR YOU? 10 IMPORTANT CONSIDERATIONS

1. Bankruptcy may be the easiest and fastest way to deal with all types of debt problems. Bankruptcy is a process under federal law designed to help people and businesses get protection from their creditors. Bankruptcy can be the right choice if you have no better way to deal with your debts. Although you may want to try other options first, you should not wait until the last minute to think about bankruptcy because some important bankruptcy rights may be lost by delay.

2. Most bankruptcy cases are complicated. You should consider getting professional help. Bankruptcy is a legal proceeding with complicated rules and paperwork. You may want to get professional legal help, especially if you hope to use bankruptcy to prevent foreclosure or repossession. Most bankruptcy professionals will provide a free consultation to help you decide whether bankruptcy is the right choice.

3. Bankruptcy temporarily stops almost all creditors from taking any steps against you except through the bankruptcy process. This assistance is provided by the "automatic stay" that arises as soon as you file the necessary paperwork at the beginning of a bankruptcy case. Foreclosures, repossessions, utility shut-offs, lawsuits, and other creditor actions will be immediately (but perhaps only temporarily) stopped.

4. Bankruptcy can permanently wipe out your legal obligation to pay back many of your debts. This benefit arises because of the bankruptcy "discharge" that you get for successfully completing a bankruptcy case. Certain debts may not be discharged, such as most student loans, liens associated with many secured debts, alimony, child support, and debts you incurred after the bankruptcy case was started. After bankruptcy, you will continue to owe those debts. In the long term, for those debts, you may have to fall back on strategies which are discussed in other parts of this book.

5. When bankruptcy does not wipe out a debt, a chapter 13 bankruptcy (a "reorganization") gives you an opportunity to catch up on that debt. For example, bankruptcy will not allow you to discharge home mortgages or car loans without repayment. If you want to deal with debts of that type in the bankruptcy process, you will need to propose a chapter 13 repayment plan. That requires affordable payments from your income over a period of three to five years.

6. In most cases you will *not* lose property by filing for bankruptcy. Most of your property is likely to be protected from sale in the bankruptcy process by bankruptcy "exemptions." However, if you have certain types of very valuable property, the bankruptcy law may not allow you to keep it unless you pay its value to your creditors over a number of years in a chapter 13 plan.

7. The initial fee for bankruptcy is presently $160 dollars under chapter 13 and $175 under chapter 7. That fee is likely to go up in the future. The fee is not usually waivable, but it can be paid in installments over a period up to 120 days (and 180 days with court permission). In addition to the initial fee, a variety of papers concerning your financial situation must be provided to the court.

8. If you file bankruptcy, you usually do *not* need to go to court. You will have to attend one meeting with the bankruptcy trustee (not with a judge). Creditors are invited to that meeting, but rarely attend. You will not usually have to go to court for your bankruptcy case unless something out of the ordinary occurs. If you do receive a notice to go to court, it is important that you go.

9. Bankruptcy will usually not make your credit record any worse. Most people filing bankruptcy already are behind on their bills and already have a tarnished credit record. It is unlikely that bankruptcy will make a bad credit record worse. Some creditors may be *more* wiling to lend you money than if you have a number of debts remaining in default. However, the fact that you filed bankruptcy can remain on your credit record for ten years, while your defaults may stay on your record for only seven years.

10. Watch out for bankruptcy related scams. There are many people and companies which advertise bankruptcy related services in order to take advantage of vulnerable, financially distressed consumers. Some of these enterprises charge enormous fees. Others make promises which they cannot possibly keep. Do not pay money for debt counseling or bankruptcy without being sure you are dealing with a reputable business.

GENERAL INFORMATION
ABOUT BANKRUPTCY

The right to file bankruptcy is an important tool which society provides for people with debt problems. In the short term, bankruptcy prevents continued efforts by creditors to collect debts. In the long term, bankruptcy can completely eliminate repayment obligations so that you can get a fresh financial start.

It is often stated that bankruptcy should be considered as a "last resort" for financially troubled consumers. This advice is oversimplified. In some cases legal rights can be lost by delay. You should be especially careful to get early advice about bankruptcy if you are hoping to use the bankruptcy process to help save your home or your car. (For example, bankruptcy cannot help you keep a home after a foreclosure sale has already occurred.)

This chapter will provide you with an overview about bankruptcy. It is not a complete bankruptcy guide. If you are interested in filing bankruptcy, you should seek the services of a professional specializing in bankruptcy.

If you want a more detailed discussion about bankruptcy, several published books focus on bankruptcy exclusively. The National Consumer Law Center publishes *Consumer Bankruptcy Law and Practice* (5th ed. 1996 and Supp.) which is a detailed analysis of bankruptcy for lawyers and others specializing in bankruptcy.

WHAT BANKRUPTCY CAN
AND CANNOT DO FOR YOU

Bankruptcy may make it possible for you to:

- Eliminate legal responsibility for many of your debts and get a fresh start. This is called a "discharge." When a debt is discharged at the close of a successful bankruptcy case, you will have no further legal obligation to pay that debt.
- Stop foreclosure on your house or mobile home and allow you an opportunity to catch up on missed payments.
- Prevent repossession of your car or other property, or force the creditor to return property even after it has been repossessed.
- Stop wage garnishment, debt collection harassment, and other similar collection activities and give you some breathing room.
- Prevent termination of utility service or restore service if it has already been terminated.
- Lower the monthly payments on some debts, including some secured debts such as car loans.
- Allow you an opportunity to challenge the claims of certain creditors who have committed fraud or who are otherwise seeking to collect more than they are legally entitled to.

Bankruptcy, however, cannot cure every financial problem, nor is it an appropriate step for every individual. In bankruptcy, it is usually *not* possible to:

- Eliminate certain rights of "secured" creditors. A "secured" creditor has taken some form of lien on your property as collateral for a debt. Common examples are car loans and home mortgages. Although you can force secured creditors to take payments over time in the bankruptcy process, you generally cannot keep the collateral unless you continue to pay the debt.

- Discharge types of debts singled out by the federal bankruptcy law for special treatment, such as child support, alimony, most student loans, court restitution orders, criminal fines, and some taxes.
- Protect all cosigners on their debts. When a relative or friend has cosigned a loan, and you discharge the loan in bankruptcy, the cosigner may still have an obligation to repay all or part of the loan.
- Discharge debts that are incurred after bankruptcy has been filed.

POSSIBLE ADVANTAGES
OF BANKRUPTCY

The Automatic Stay of Foreclosures, Evictions, Repossession, Utility Shutoffs, and Other Creditor Actions. Your bankruptcy filing will automatically, without any further legal proceedings, stop most creditor actions against you and your property.

Your request for bankruptcy protection creates an "automatic stay" which will prevent commencement or continuation of repossessions, garnishments, attachments, utility shut-offs, foreclosures, evictions and debt collection harassment. The automatic stay will offer you a breathing spell, providing time to sort things out and to solve your financial problems.

Filing bankruptcy will automatically,
without further action,
stop almost all creditor attempts
to collect from you.

If you file bankruptcy, a creditor cannot take any further action against you or your property without permission from the bankruptcy court.

Sometimes creditors will seek such permission immediately, and sometimes they will never seek permission.

Permission to continue collection activity is rarely, if ever, granted to unsecured creditors. It is common for secured creditors to get relief from the stay in a *chapter 7* case to continue foreclosure or repossession of their collateral. (As described below, a chapter 7 bankruptcy has minimal impact on a secured creditor's collateral.) On the other hand, an automatic stay will almost always continue in effect to protect you in a *chapter 13* bankruptcy case as long as payments are being made on the secured debt.

If the creditor takes action against you despite the automatic stay, the creditor can be held in violation of the stay and may have to pay you money damages and attorney's fees. If necessary, the creditor's actions against you can also be reversed. For example, a foreclosure sale which is held in violation of the automatic stay can be set aside.

Discharge of Most Debts. The principal goal of most bankruptcies is quite simple. It is to achieve a discharge, which eliminates your obligation to repay many unsecured debts. Bankruptcy is thus a relatively easy way, though not the only way, to permanently end creditor harassment, and the hardship, anxiety and stress associated with excessive debt. (See Chapter Six for other strategies to stop debt harassment).

On the other hand, a creditor's collateral is not affected by your bankruptcy filing unless you pay off those debts being secured by the collateral. A bankruptcy discharge does offer some protection for these secured debts. After you obtain a discharge, a secured creditor has no right to seek a deficiency judgment or to collect money from you in any way other than by selling the collateral.

This means that after bankruptcy, the creditor can seize its collateral if you don't pay, but cannot otherwise try to collect the debt. For example, if you do not pay a car loan, the creditor can seize your car and sell it. But it cannot sue you for the deficiency between what you owe and the amount for which the car was sold.

Protection Against Wage Garnishment and Enforcement of Judgment Liens. After you file a bankruptcy petition, creditors are prohibited from garnishing your wages or other income. Bankruptcy even stops government agencies from recouping Social Security or other public benefit overpayments, so long as your receipt of the overpayment was not deliberate.

Bankruptcy is also an effective tool to deal with some types of legal judgments against you. If a creditor's judgment for money against you does not create a lien against any of your property, that creditor is unsecured and the debt can be discharged in bankruptcy as if no judgment ever existed. If the judgment does create a lien on your property, you may ask the bankruptcy court to remove the lien if it affects exempt property.

Which items of property are exempt, and protected from a court judgment, is discussed in more detail in Chapter Eight. Bankruptcy offers two extra protections for this exempt property. First, bankruptcy can wipe out a lien entirely, while state exemption laws only prevent the creditor from seizing certain property. Without a bankruptcy filing, if your assets increase in the future, a lien may then allow the creditor to seize some of your property. A second extra protection offered by bankruptcy is that in some states you may use national exemption amounts if those provide better protections for you than those offered by your state law.

Added Flexibility in Dealing with Secured Creditors. Bankruptcy can be helpful in dealing with creditors who have taken items of your property as collateral for their loans. Usually, you still have to make payments on your secured debts if you want to keep the collateral. However, bankruptcy does provide added flexibility in dealing with these debts.

First, in some situations, bankruptcy can stop secured creditors from seizing collateral by "avoiding" (meaning removing or eliminating) the creditor's lien. This makes the debt unsecured.

For example, when you file bankruptcy, you can avoid liens on most household goods when you did not use money from that creditor to purchase those goods. To the extent that household goods are exempt — and most families' household goods will be completely exempt — you can request the bankruptcy court to eliminate the creditor's ability to seize that collateral.

Second, bankruptcy allows you to keep collateral by redeeming it, that is paying the creditor not the amount of the loan, but the value of the collateral. For example, if a car is only worth $1000, even though the car loan is $3000, you can keep the car by paying the creditor only the $1000.

The greatest flexibility in dealing with secured creditors is available when a chapter 13 bankruptcy is filed. For example, if you are six months delinquent on a mortgage, filing a chapter 13 bankruptcy will stop a threatened foreclosure and allow you to gradually catch up on the back payments, perhaps over as long a period as several years. In some cases a chapter 13 filing may also allow you to revise a loan schedule by extending the repayment period or lowering the interest rate to make lower monthly payments.

Utility Terminations. A bankruptcy filing will not only stop a threatened utility termination, but will also restore terminated utility service, at least for twenty days. To keep utility service beyond twenty days after the bankruptcy filing, you must provide a security deposit or other security for future payments, and keep current on the new utility charges. To keep service, you need not pay bills incurred *before* the bankruptcy was filed.

Driver Licenses. A driver's license can be critical to keep a job or to find a new job. In some states a driver's license can be revoked because you have not paid a court judgment arising from an automobile accident. In that situation, bankruptcy is sometimes the only possible way for you to keep or regain the license. Normally, bankruptcy can be used to discharge the obligation to pay the court judgment, and you then have a right to regain or retain the driver's license.

OTHER BANKRUPTCY CONSIDERATIONS, INCLUDING POSSIBLE DISADVANTAGES

You will get to keep
some of your property in bankruptcy,
and most bankruptcy filers
get to keep all of their property.

In Most Cases You Will Lose Little or None of Your Property. Some people believe that a bankruptcy filing results in the loss of most of their property. This belief is wrong. Everyone who files bankruptcy gets to keep some of their possessions. In fact, most people get to keep all of them.

Whether you get to keep *all* your possessions depends on a number of factors. These factors include whether you file a chapter 7 or a chapter 13 bankruptcy, whether certain debts are secured or unsecured, and how much of your property is exempt.

Generally, you will keep all or virtually all your property in a bankruptcy, except property which is very valuable or which is subject to a lien which you cannot avoid or afford to pay. In most circumstances, bankruptcy should be seen as a method of preventing loss of property rather than causing the loss of property.

In a chapter 7 bankruptcy, all of your equity in property is divided into two categories — exempt and nonexempt. (Equity equals the value of your home minus what you owe. The longer you have lived in the house and paid off your mortgage, the less you owe and therefore the more equity you have). State law or in some cases the federal bankruptcy law will specify which property is exempt. Usually, at least a certain amount of equity in your home, car, clothes, jewelry, appliances and furniture will be exempt.

In valuing property for the purposes of bankruptcy, the question is not the property's original cost, but rather what the property could be sold for at the time of filing. It is often useful to imagine a hypothetical yard sale to try to estimate what the value of particular items will be. Remember also that exemption laws vary widely from state to state. It is important to check what exemptions are available in the state where you live.

It is also important to understand how the concept of equity relates to exemption laws. If an exemption law protects a $2000 motor vehicle, this applies to $2000 of your equity in the car, not to the total value of the car. For example, if you have a $7000 car with a $5000 car loan balance, you have only $2000 in equity. You can thus fully protect the $7000 car with the $2000 exemption. You will still have to repay the car loan, but you won't lose the car.

If you have significant *non*-exempt assets, a chapter 13 bankruptcy may be a good way to keep all of your possessions. In a chapter 13 bankruptcy, you keep your possessions (unless you choose to sell them) and instead pay their value over time from future income under a plan approved by the bankruptcy court.

The Effect of Bankruptcy on Your Credit Record. A bankruptcy can remain part of your credit history for ten years. The effect of a bankruptcy on your credit record is unpredictable, but of understandable concern.

For most people, this concern alone should not be considered a disadvantage of bankruptcy. If you are seriously delinquent on a number of debts, this information will already appear on your credit record. A bankruptcy is unlikely to make your credit worse. In fact, there is some evidence that the bankruptcy will make it *easier* to obtain future credit, because new creditors will see that old obligations have been discharged and that the new creditor will therefore be first in line for payment from your income. Also, once a discharge is received, many new creditors recognize that you cannot then receive a new chapter 7 discharge for the next six years.

If you do not yet have problem credit, the impact of a bankruptcy on your ability to obtain credit is more difficult to answer. Research on the effects of bankruptcy on future credit is inconclusive. It seems fair to say that most credit decisions depend upon the judgment of individual lenders. Most lenders seem to look at a potential customer's income and income stability more than anything else.

After bankruptcy, some lenders may demand collateral as security, ask for a cosigner, or want to know why bankruptcy was filed. Other creditors, such as some local retailers, do not check credit reports or inquire about bankruptcy on credit applications at all.

The Effect of Bankruptcy on Your Reputation in the Community. If you file bankruptcy, what happens to your reputation among friends, neighbors and coworkers? Most people find their reputations suffer no perceptible harm.

Bankruptcies are not generally announced in newspapers, although they are a matter of public record. It is unlikely that your friends and neighbors will know that you filed bankruptcy unless you choose to tell them.

However, in a small town, where debts are owed to local people, some difficulties connected with filing bankruptcy may still be present. Embarrassment and damage to reputation must be personally evaluated and weighed against bankruptcy's potential advantages. If you believe that this is a problem, you may choose to voluntarily pay selected debts after bankruptcy. Voluntary payment of discharged debts is specifically allowed by the bankruptcy law, but you cannot leave certain creditors out of the bankruptcy process entirely.

Feelings of Moral Obligation. For some people, a feeling of moral obligation creates a hesitation about filing bankruptcy. Most people do want to pay their debts and make every effort to do so if payment is possible.

However, if bankruptcy is the right solution for your financial problems, you should balance your feelings of moral obligation with other considerations. Remember that a provision concerning bankruptcy is contained in the United States Constitution. Big corporations like TWA, A.H. Robbins, Johns Manville, Macy's and Penn Central, and famous people like Toni Braxton, Kim Basinger, Tammy Wynette and Mickey Rooney, have all chosen to file bankruptcy.

You may find comfort in the fact that the Bible mentions the need for a process which is like bankruptcy. The book of Deuteronomy states:

> At the end of every seven years thou shalt make a release. And this is the manner of the release: every creditor shall release that which he has lent unto his neighbor and his brother; because the Lord's release hath been proclaimed. (Deut. 15:1-2.)

There is no good reason to feel embarrassed about filing bankruptcy if it is the best solution to your financial problems.

Most importantly, whatever its negative connotations, bankruptcy should be considered in relation to the hardships it can avoid. During hard times, bankruptcy may be the only way to provide your family with food, clothing, and shelter. This book does explore alternatives to bankruptcy, and these should be considered carefully. But it may be that bankruptcy is your best or only realistic alternative.

Potential Discrimination after Bankruptcy. The bankruptcy law offers you some protection against discrimination by creditors and others. Government agencies, such as housing authorities and licensing departments, cannot deny you benefits because of a previous bankruptcy discharge of your debts to those agencies.

Employers are also not permitted to discriminate against you for filing bankruptcy. However, for some sensitive jobs which involve money or security, your bankruptcy may be considered evidence of financial problems which could be detrimental to your work. Also, the bankruptcy law does not prevent discrimination by others, including private creditors deciding whether to grant new loans.

Cost of Filing a Bankruptcy Petition. There are several expenses related to filing bankruptcy. First, there may be costs associated with hiring an attorney to handle the bankruptcy. Hiring an attorney and the advisability of alternatives are discussed later in this chapter.

In addition to an attorney's fee, a bankruptcy petition presently requires a $160 filing fee under chapter 13 and a $175 filing fee for chapter 7. This filing fee cannot be waived, but can be paid in installments.

In a chapter 13 reorganization case, the trustee is usually entitled to a commission of about ten percent of the payments made through the plan. These payments must be included with the amount that you pay the trustee under a plan.

In addition, utility companies may be entitled to collect a security deposit following a bankruptcy (usually equal to approximately twice the average monthly bill) just as if you were a new customer. Some, but not all utility companies take advantage of this right. In most areas, you can request up to sixty days to make this payment.

Ability to File Another Bankruptcy If You Have More Financial Problems. One consideration about filing bankruptcy is whether you will have the opportunity to file again if a new financial problem arises. The answer depends on what type of bankruptcy you file.

The different types of bankruptcy are discussed immediately below. For simplicity, you can think of a chapter 7 as an immediate discharge of many of your debts with the liquidation of any of your assets that are not exempt. A chapter 13 is a reorganization of your debt where you pay your creditors some or all of what they are owed over a period of years, but where you generally lose none of your property.

You can receive only one discharge under chapter 7 every six years. That means that if you choose to file bankruptcy under chapter 7 now, you may not be able to do so again for a period of time. For this reason it is usually best to wait until other options have been explored before filing a chapter 7 case.

However, if you have filed under chapter 7, you may still be able to file again under chapter 13 (or another chapter), before six years have expired. Similarly, you can file more than one case under chapter 13 in a six year period as long as you meet the requirements under that chapter when you file.

Other issues can arise if your case is unsuccessful for some reason. (It is rare to have an unsuccessful chapter 7 case, but chapter 13 cases frequently fail because the consumer cannot afford the necessary payments.) If your case is dismissed, that dismissal may bar a new case from being filed for 180 days.

WHEN BANKRUPTCY MAY BE
THE WRONG SOLUTION

For some individuals bankruptcy is the wrong solution. There are five situations in which bankruptcy may be a bad option:

1. You have only a few debts and strong defenses for each. Instead of filing for bankruptcy, you can raise these defenses vigorously. Usually the disputes can be settled out of court in an acceptable way. If they are not settled, you can use bankruptcy later. (You can also raise claims and defenses in the bankruptcy court if they have not been decided in other courts.)
2. The debts at issue are secured by your property — such as home mortgages or car loans — and you do not have sufficient income to keep up payments and also catch up on past due amounts. Bankruptcy may not help you when the long-term expense of keeping your home or car exceeds your long-term income.
3. You have valuable assets that are not exempt in the bankruptcy process and you do not want to lose these assets. (Note that a chapter 13 filing may still help if you can afford the necessary payments.)
4. Because of a prior bankruptcy, you cannot receive a discharge in a chapter 7 bankruptcy. However, in most cases a chapter 13 petition can still be filed.
5. You can afford to pay all of your current debts without hardship.

There is also a situation in which bankruptcy is not the wrong choice, but in which it is not necessary or urgent. Where state exemption laws are generous, you may be totally "judgment-proof" at the time you are thinking about bankruptcy. (See Chapter Eight for more information about exemptions and about what it means to be "judgment proof.") If that is the case, creditors can do virtually nothing to harm you. There is no action they can take which will affect your property or your wages.

When there is no urgency for you to file for bankruptcy, it often makes sense not to file immediately. If you wait, additional debts may arise which can also be included and discharged in the bankruptcy case. For a more detailed analysis of the advantages and disadvantages of a bankruptcy filing, see the National Consumer Law Center's *Consumer Bankruptcy Law and Practice* Ch. 6 (5th ed. 1996 and Supp.).

CHOOSING THE TYPE
OF BANKRUPTCY TO FILE

The Two Common Types of Bankruptcy for Consumers. The bankruptcy law provides for two main types of consumer cases: chapter 7 and chapter 13. If you file bankruptcy, you will need to decide which is the better chapter for you.

DESCRIPTION OF CHAPTER 7
(LIQUIDATION)

A case under chapter 7 of the bankruptcy laws is often called a "liquidation." In a liquidation case, your assets are examined by a court appointed trustee to determine if anything is available to be sold for the benefit of creditors. Certain property cannot be sold, and instead you keep it despite the bankruptcy. This property is called "exempt."

The trustee may sell only property which is either not exempt or which has value which exceeds the exemption limits. In most consumer bankruptcies, virtually all, if not all, of the assets are exempt; therefore, little or no property is taken away and sold. If property is partly exempt and partly non-exempt, the trustee may sell it and pay you the value of your exemption in cash. Or, if you have the money, you may pay the trustee the amount of the non-exempt value and keep the property.

Exemption laws vary from state to state and may be fairly complicated. You cannot make a final choice about bankruptcy without understanding the exemption laws for your particular state.

The best way to do this is to ask for a listing from a neighborhood legal services office, a private attorney, or pro bono bar organization. Another approach is to see if there is an accurate and up-to-date listing in a legal publication for your state. See Chapter Eight for more detail on state exemption laws.

In deciding what can be sold, the trustee will only look to your *equity* in property. If you owe money on a mortgage or other lien on a home, that mortgage or lien reduces your equity in the home. The trustee will not sell property if your equity in the property is fully exempt.

In a chapter 7 bankruptcy, you get to keep all of your exempt assets, which usually include your home and your car.

For example, if the applicable state exemption for your home is $50,000, the home's value is $150,000, and you have a $100,000 mortgage, all of your $50,000 equity in the home is exempt. The trustee will *not* sell the home in a chapter 7 liquidation. (The trustee also is unlikely to sell your home if there is a small amount of non-exempt equity. That is because the equity would not cover the costs of sale including realtor's fees and taxes. In the above example, the trustee is unlikely to sell the home even if it could be sold for $160,000.)

At the end of a chapter 7 case, you obtain a discharge of most unsecured debts. This means that you will no longer have a legal obligation to pay those debts. Generally the discharge will include credit card debts, medical bills, utility arrearages, and other similar debts for which the creditor does not have collateral.

Some unsecured debts, such as most student loans, debts based on fraud or malicious conduct, drunk driving debts, most tax debts, government fines, alimony, and child support are not likely to be discharged.

Chapter 7 bankruptcies rarely help with large secured debts, such as home mortgages, because the creditor retains its rights in the collateral. While bankruptcy discharges most personal debts, it does not prevent secured creditors from recovering their collateral if a debt is not repaid. This means that a chapter 7 case will not affect, except temporarily, the rights of a bank to foreclose on a home or repossess a car that is loan collateral. However, if you have received a chapter 7 discharge, and a creditor later sells its collateral, the creditor may not sue you for any balance still owed.

ANSWERS TO
SOME BASIC QUESTIONS
ABOUT CHAPTER 7

Chapter 7 bankruptcy cases are usually straightforward. Occasionally, complications arise if creditors take aggressive action, if the trustee thinks you are hiding assets, or if you wish to challenge creditors' claims. Those potential complications are not covered in detail here.

Who can file? Any individual who lives in the United States or has property or a business in the United States can file a chapter 7 bankruptcy. There are no preconditions to a bankruptcy filing, such as insolvency, although a judge can dismiss your chapter 7 case if you engage in an abuse of the bankruptcy system. This is rare, but may occur if you are using bankruptcy for an improper purpose (such as to harass creditors) or if you have substantial income to pay your debts. If you received a bankruptcy discharge within the past six years you are disqualified from receiving a discharge in chapter 7.

What are the first steps? The first step in a chapter 7 bankruptcy is completion of certain basic forms. These include a two page initial "petition." A number of other forms must also be filed either at the same time as the petition or shortly afterwards. These include your statement of financial affairs, statement of intentions with respect to certain debts, and a set of schedules — listing all your debts, property, income and expenses.

At the beginning of the case you will also need to file a mailing list including all of your creditors. All of these forms must meet certain specifications required by the court. You should check with a bankruptcy specialist or your local bankruptcy court for a full list of filing requirements.

What will happen after filing? Filing the petition triggers the automatic stay. With few exceptions, this stops any creditor from taking collection action or pursuing a court case against you, or seizing your property based on debts that arose before you filed your bankruptcy petition. If you are worried about a creditor action like a foreclosure or repossession, you should make a special effort to notify that creditor so that the action is stopped before it occurs.

If a creditor does take action against you other than in the bankruptcy court, including collection calls or letters, you should politely inform the creditor about the bankruptcy. The creditor action may violate the automatic stay. If you have an attorney, you should also tell your attorney about the contact. You may start a process to obtain damages for certain violations of the stay.

Within a few weeks after filing, the bankruptcy court or the trustee mails a notice of the stay and of the date and place for a "meeting of creditors." This notice will be mailed to all creditors, to you, and to your attorney, if you have one.

What is a bankruptcy trustee? After you file bankruptcy, a trustee is appointed to represent the interests of creditors. In a chapter 7 bankruptcy, the trustee collects any property that can be sold, handles the sale, distributes the property to creditors with valid claims, and makes a final accounting to the court.

What is the meeting of creditors? The meeting of creditors is conducted by the trustee, usually at a place outside the courthouse. The meeting of creditors gives the trustee and others a chance to examine your financial affairs.

Despite the name, few creditors appear at the meeting of creditors in a consumer bankruptcy. You, however, must attend. The meeting consists of a series of routine questions by the trustee and lasts from two minutes to half an hour. Usually, the best thing you can do to prepare for this meeting is review the papers you or your attorney have filed with the court.

What happens after the meeting of creditors? Unless there is an objection to the exemptions you have claimed, after the meeting of creditors, you keep the property listed as exempt in your schedules. Property that is mostly, but not totally, exempt is usually abandoned by the trustee, which means that you get to keep it.

If larger non-exempt assets remain, they are turned over to the trustee. You will usually be offered the option of paying the non-exempt value of the assets to the trustee in cash instead of turning over those assets. The trustee then sells any property collected, converts it to cash, and distributes it among the creditors.

The trustee must give notice of intent to sell the property. Any party, including you, can object (within specified time limits) to the proposed sale, which is either private or by public auction.

During a chapter 7 bankruptcy, you take one of several steps to deal with your secured debts. You can surrender the collateral to the secured creditor if that is your intention, or you can keep the collateral outright by paying the creditor the value of the collateral. You also have the option of "reaffirming" the debt to protect the collateral. This option is discussed in more detail below.

What is reaffirmation and when should I consider it? Reaffirmation is your agreement during bankruptcy to remain legally obligated on some or all of a debt which you could have otherwise eliminated. You should always approach reaffirmation agreements with a great deal of caution. By signing a reaffirmation agreement, you give the creditor rights to collect from you which it did not otherwise have.

You should never agree to reaffirm if:

- The debt is totally unsecured by collateral;
- The creditor cannot provide paperwork show you that the debt is secured;
- The debt is secured and you have no interest in keeping the collateral;
- The debt is secured, and you are hopelessly behind on payments, so that the property will be repossessed in any event; or
- The debt is secured and you are up to date on payments, but your bankruptcy court is one which allows you to keep up your payments and keep the property without reaffirmation (check with a bankruptcy professional).

You might consider reaffirmation if:

- The creditor gives you something valuable in return, such as an agreement to let you get caught up on a default in a manageable way or a reduction in a secured debt to the value of the property;

- You want to keep property used as collateral for a secured debt and your bankruptcy court will not allow you to keep it without reaffirming (and you cannot afford the better alternative of paying the creditor the value of the property in a lump sum); and
- You can easily afford the payments which will be required after bankruptcy.

Reaffirmation is an agreement you make to repay debts despite your bankruptcy. It is unwise to reaffirm except in very limited situations.

Two important points about reaffirmation:

1. If a creditor asks you to reaffirm, you can say no. You can also negotiate the terms on which you agree to reaffirm.
2. Never reaffirm a debt just because a creditor offers to advance you some new credit or to keep your account in good standing. There are easier ways to obtain new credit than to agree to the expense of repaying a debt which bankruptcy can eliminate.

How do I get my bankruptcy discharge? The final step in most chapter 7 bankruptcy cases is the discharge. In most places, if no one objects to your discharge, the court enters the discharge without a hearing. You get the discharge order in the mail.

What will my chapter 7 discharge cover? The discharge in chapter 7 covers all unsecured debts including most credit cards, medical bills and back utility debts. Your discharge may *not* include:

- Certain taxes;
- Debts not listed in your schedules;

- Most debts for alimony, child support, and property settlements;
- Most fines and penalties owed to government agencies;
- Most student loans;
- Debts incurred by driving while intoxicated;
- Debts incurred to pay taxes which cannot be discharged;
- Debts you have formally agreed to repay despite the bankruptcy (by "reaffirming" your obligation to pay); and
- Many debts with collateral.

In addition, a court may find some other debts nondischargeable, but only if the particular creditor seeks determination of nondischargeability within a strict time limit after the meeting of creditors. These types of debts include:

- Debts incurred by certain types of fraud;
- Debts incurred while acting as a trustee for someone else's property; and
- Debts for purposely causing injuries.

What should I do if a creditor tries to collect a debt which has been discharged? Collection of discharged debts is illegal. You should contact your lawyer if you had one during your bankruptcy case. You may bring a legal action to have the discharge enforced and to recover any damages which the collection efforts caused you.

DESCRIPTION OF CHAPTER 13 (REORGANIZATION)

A case under chapter 13 of the bankruptcy laws is often called a "reorganization." Reorganization cases under chapter 13 work very differently from chapter 7 liquidations. In a chapter 13 case, you submit a plan (meeting the rules set out in the bankruptcy law) to repay your creditors over time, usually from future income.

Most consumer reorganization cases take place under chapter 13 of the bankruptcy law. However, some debtors with large amounts of debt may be required (or prefer) to proceed under chapter 11. Family farmers can also proceed under chapter 12.

In certain circumstances, there are advantages to filing a chapter 13 case rather than a chapter 7. Most importantly, in a chapter 13 case, you are allowed to get caught up on mortgages or car loans over a period of time.

For example, most mortgages and car loans allow the bank to call the whole loan due when you miss a payment or two. Although the bank may let you work out an agreement to catch up over time on back payments (and you should call to find out if this is possible), the bank usually is not legally required to let you catch up. Where the bank or any creditor is uncooperative, a chapter 13 bankruptcy may be the only way to force it to let you keep the property while you make the back payments over a period of years.

Chapter 13 cases also allow you to keep both exempt property (which would be protected in chapter 7) and non-exempt property (which would be sold in chapter 7). You can keep the non-exempt property by paying its value to creditors under a court approved plan, usually over a period from three to five years.

The heart of a chapter 13 case is your bankruptcy plan. This is a simple document outlining how you propose to make payments to various creditors while the plan is in effect.

The law places certain limits on what you may do under a plan. Nevertheless, there are substantial opportunities for reorganizing your debt payments and protecting your property from creditors, including mortgage and other lien holders, as long as appropriate payments are made.

In a chapter 13 bankruptcy, you may have as long as five years to catch up with overdue payments on secured debts, and you may be able to keep all of your property.

A chapter 13 bankruptcy plan normally requires monthly payments to the bankruptcy trustee over a period of three years. However, plans can last for as long as five years with court approval. In most jurisdictions, bankruptcy courts will routinely approve requests to have the monthly payments to the trustee paid automatically by wage deduction.

Once your payments are completed under the plan, you are entitled to a discharge just as in a chapter 7 bankruptcy. The discharge available in chapter 13 covers more debts than a discharge under chapter 7. If you have caught up on any mortgage debt or other secured loan, the loan will be reinstated and the law requires the creditor to treat you as if you never fell behind.

Reorganization cases can be quite complicated. Working out the best possible bankruptcy plan is frequently difficult. If you are considering a reorganization in bankruptcy, consult with an attorney specializing in bankruptcy as quickly as possible. Your delay may allow a foreclosure or repossession to proceed to the point where bankruptcy can no longer help.

ANSWERS TO SOME BASIC QUESTIONS ABOUT CHAPTER 13

Most of the initial steps in a chapter 13 case are quite similar to those in chapter 7. The major difference is that in chapter 13, you must file a chapter 13 reorganization plan. You must begin making payments under that plan within thirty days after filing.

The following material is intended to point out some of the other significant differences in the procedure for chapter 13.

Who can file? Chapter 13 is available to "individuals with regular income" who live in the United States, or have a place of business or property in the United States. An "individual with regular income" includes not only wage earners, but also recipients of government benefits, alimony or support payments, or any other regular type of income.

A chapter 13 discharge can even be obtained by a debtor who has received a chapter 7 discharge within six years before filing, or who would not be granted a discharge because of some other provision in chapter 7.

There are limits to the amount of debt which you may have as a chapter 13 filer. Since these limits are quite high (exceeding one million in total), they do not affect most consumer cases.

What are the initial forms and first steps? As with chapter 7, a chapter 13 bankruptcy begins with a two-page petition. The filing fee is $160, which can be paid in installments if you have not already paid the fee to an attorney. The additional schedules must also be filed either with your petition or shortly after. A chapter 13 plan must be filed with your schedules. This is your description of when creditors will be paid, how they will be paid, and how much they will be paid.

As with chapter 7, filing a petition sets the bankruptcy process in motion. The filing immediately establishes the automatic stay, which prevents any further creditor acts against you or your property. Filing a chapter 13 petition also puts into effect a prohibition that prevents creditors from taking any action against any codebtors (cosigners) who have not filed bankruptcy.

A trustee is appointed and the a meeting of creditors is held. At a meeting of creditors in chapter 13, the focus is usually on whether your plan meets the requirements of the law and on whether you can afford to make the payments which are required in the chapter 13 process.

What will I have to pay? You must begin making plan payments within thirty days after filing the plan, unless the court orders otherwise. These payments are held by the chapter 13 trustee and not paid out to creditors until your chapter 13 plan is approved by the court. If the court does not approve your chapter 13 plan, the payments are returned to you after deduction of administrative costs.

Your payments will be based on the debts you intend to pay, the rules of chapter 13, and your ability to pay based on your budget. This means that after paying for necessary living expenses, you will need to pay the balance of your income to the trustee while your bankruptcy proceeds. If you so choose, this can occur automatically by wage deduction.

Once your plan is in place, if you fail to make payments, your case is likely to be dismissed. Dismissal will put you back to the situation you were in prior to bankruptcy. In some cases you can avoid dismissal even if you cannot afford payments, by converting your chapter 13 case to a case under chapter 7 or by seeking a "hardship discharge" from the court.

What does a trustee do in chapter 13? The chapter 13 trustee has more to do than the chapter 7 trustee. In addition to the duties of a chapter 7 trustee, the chapter 13 trustee must collect your payments and distribute that money to creditors. The trustee will ask the court to dismiss your case, if you fail to make the plan payments.

Depending upon the type of case or the matter involved, and in some cases the trustee's personality, a chapter 13 trustee is either your friend or foe. The trustee's opinion is not necessarily the last word on any matter. You have the right to raise any appropriate issue with the bankruptcy judge. Trustees are not judges and have no power to rule on disputes between creditors and debtors.

How does my plan get approved? The court will evaluate your plan at a "confirmation hearing." This occurs either on the same day as the first meeting of creditors, or some time within the next several months, depending upon local practice. The court will inquire into whether the requirements of chapter 13 have been met, and hear any objections to approval of your chapter 13 plan raised by creditors or the trustee.

In many courts there is no formal hearing at the time of confirmation unless there is an objection to your plan. Also, in many cases, if the plan is uncontested, you will be advised that you do not need to come to court.

For various reasons, you may want to modify your original plan after it is filed. Before confirmation, a plan can be modified freely, so long as the modified plan meets the chapter 13 requirements. After confirmation, plans can still be modified, subject to court approval. Creditors or the trustee may object.

What if I fail to complete my plan? Some people are unable to complete their chapter 13 plans by making payments as proposed, usually because of loss of income. When this occurs, four options are normally available, each having somewhat different consequences:

- *Hardship Discharge.* The bankruptcy law provides for a hardship discharge of debts if problems are caused by circumstances for which you are not responsible, such as serious deterioration of your financial circumstances.
- *Modification.* It is possible to modify a plan to address new problems, but creditors have a right to object to the modification, and, if so, the court will decide whether to allow the modification.
- *Conversion.* You have the right to convert a chapter 13 case to chapter 7. After the conversion, nonexempt property is liquidated and you receive a chapter 7 discharge.

- *Dismissal.* Occasionally, dismissal is preferable to any of the other options. You have the right to dismiss your chapter 13 case unless the case was previously converted from chapter 7.

What debts are discharged in chapter 13? The final step in a successfully completed chapter 13 case is the discharge. The chapter 13 discharge includes all debts provided for by the plan, except for most support and alimony payments and for long-term debts with final payments due after the completion of the plan. Other exceptions to discharge in chapter 13 are most student loans, drunk driving debts and criminal restitution debts. A chapter 13 discharge can eliminate legal responsibility on many debts which are not dischargeable in a chapter 7 case, including debts incurred through fraud or false pretenses, and claims for injuries purposely caused by you.

The chapter 13 discharge can be enforced in the same way as the chapter 7 discharge discussed above. Under current law, your chapter 13 discharge stays on your credit record for ten years from the date your case is over.

CHOOSING THE RIGHT
TYPE OF BANKRUPTCY

Advantages of a Chapter 7 Bankruptcy. If a chapter 7 bankruptcy will accomplish your goals, it is generally the best choice because it is simpler and quicker than a chapter 13 bankruptcy. Once the papers are filed, unless unusual issues are raised, you will receive a discharge within six months. A chapter 7 bankruptcy will generally meet your goals if it will discharge most of your debts and not result in the loss of any of your property.

Generally, chapter 7 is the best option when two factors are present:

- All or nearly all of your property is exempt; and
- The debts which are causing problems for you are unsecured and dischargeable in chapter 7.

Even if some of your property is not exempt, a chapter 7 bankruptcy may be the right choice for you because you can exchange small amounts of non-exempt property for exempt property.

Even where there are secured debts, a chapter 13 filing may not be necessary. This is particularly true if you are current on your mortgage, car loan and other secured debt payments. If you can keep current on secured debt payments, you can keep your home or other collateral, if it is exempt, even while going through a chapter 7 bankruptcy. (A chapter 13 filing is generally preferable if you are delinquent on a secured debt and want to cure this default over time.)

Some Considerations Favoring Chapter 13 Bankruptcies. Probably the most common reason for filing a chapter 13 petition is that one or more secured creditors cannot be dealt with satisfactorily in any other way. Few legal procedures create opportunities to deal with foreclosures and repossessions as quickly and effectively as a chapter 13 petition and plan.

Another reason to file a chapter 13 bankruptcy is to protect non-exempt assets, which would be sold in a chapter 7 case. However, the current value of the non-exempt property usually has to be paid over the course of the plan.

Other important reasons favoring a chapter 13 filing include:

- As discussed above, some debts that are not dischargeable in chapter 7 can be discharged in chapter 13.
- Some creditors consider a chapter 13 filing, compared to a chapter 7 filing, to be less harmful to your credit rating and reputation.
- If you obtained a chapter 7 discharge within the previous six years, a new chapter 7 filing is not an option; only chapter 13 is available.

The type of bankruptcy you choose is not irreversible. It is easy to convert a case (at least once) from chapter 7 to chapter 13 or vice versa.

Should You File With Your Spouse? If you and your spouse are living together, it is usually preferable for you to file bankruptcy jointly. The filing fee is the same whether you file jointly or alone. If you file together, you will both get the advantages of a bankruptcy discharge. Since most married couples are jointly responsible for their debts, a spouse who does not file remains liable as a codebtor, and may be pursued by creditors.

There is no requirement that you file together with your spouse. Therefore, if you want to file and your spouse does not (or vice versa), or if you and your spouse are separated, there is nothing to prevent a married individual from filing alone. However, the consequences of not filing jointly should be considered carefully.

Unmarried partners do not have the option of filing together. However, separate cases can be filed and administered by the court together.

THE TIMING OF YOUR BANKRUPTCY FILING

The Emergency Bankruptcy. You may have no choice other than to file immediately to prevent a foreclosure, repossession, eviction, execution sale, or utility shut-off. Bankruptcies in an emergency can be filed with as little as ten minutes preparation. A good discussion of how to do this is set out in the National Consumer Law Center's *Consumer Bankruptcy Law and Practice* §7.2.2 (5th ed. 1996), "The Emergency Bankruptcy Case, or How to Prepare a Bankruptcy Case in Under Ten Minutes."

Delaying Bankruptcy in Anticipation of Further Debt. If you are not facing immediate loss of property and anticipate further unavoidable debts, such as new medical, utility or unpaid rent bills, a bankruptcy filing should be delayed until after these debts occur. That way you will gain the maximum benefit from the discharge.

Debts incurred after the bankruptcy filing are *not* discharged in that bankruptcy case — you will still be obligated to repay them. As a general rule, bankruptcy should not be filed until your debts have peaked.

If you decide to wait to file bankruptcy, you must avoid the temptation to obtain goods or services on credit which you do not intend to pay for. In a chapter 7 bankruptcy, debts incurred in this way can be declared nondischargeable. Debts for prebankruptcy vacation trips and credit card shopping-sprees have frequently been found nondischargeable. Expenses for medical bills and other essentials are rarely challenged.

Exemption Planning. You can legally take a number of steps to improve your legal position prior to filing bankruptcy. These steps are generally called exemption planning. Basically, exemption planning means arranging your affairs so that a maximum amount of property can be claimed under exemption provisions, and a minimum amount is lost to creditors.

It is similar to making arrangements to take maximum advantage of tax laws, and, if done reasonably, is perfectly legal. However, excessive transfer of property to create exempt assets can sometimes be found to be in bad faith.

Also, you cannot simply give away nonexempt property or sell it at nominal cost. Any transfer of property within a year of filing must be disclosed. Improper transfers of property to third parties can be recovered and may be grounds for denying a discharge.

HOW TO GET
HELP WITH YOUR
BANKRUPTCY FILING

Hiring a Bankruptcy Attorney. Generally, the best course of action if you are considering bankruptcy is to obtain the services of an attorney who is expert in the field of bankruptcy. Hiring an attorney to handle any legal case is a difficult process. This is especially true in hiring a bankruptcy attorney.

As with any area of the law, it is important to carefully select an attorney who will be responsive to your personal situation. The attorney should not be too busy to meet with you individually and to answer your questions. You should take care before hiring an attorney to meet the attorney personally and to be comfortable with the attorney's style. At all points in the case, your attorney should take time to answer questions either directly or through an office paralegal. If an attorney does not respond to your telephone calls, you should keep trying and demand an answer. If you have a dispute with your attorney, you can file a complaint with the court or the bar association.

The best way to find a trustworthy bankruptcy attorney is to seek recommendations from family, friends or other members of the community. Retainers and other documents should be read carefully. An attorney retainer is a contract under which you hire the attorney. It governs what the attorney proposes to do for you and the fees for the proposed work. Make sure you understand the terms about what the attorney agrees to do if unusual issues come up during your case. Remember that the lawyer advertising the cheapest rate is not necessarily the best.

Avoid For-Profit Debt Counseling. For-profit bankruptcy counseling is rarely a good idea. Unfortunately, there are many people who offer counseling and credit repair to people with debt problems in order to rip them off. If you are going to pay for debt counseling, you should be careful to avoid scams and offers of high-rate debt consolidation loans as a way out of debt. Most of these deals will only make your situation worse. If a deal seems too good to be true or if a solution to your problems seems too easy, it probably is.

**It is very easy to get ripped off
by a for-profit debt or bankruptcy counselor
or to get into trouble using
a bankruptcy document preparation service.**

There is little that a for-profit debt counselor can offer concerning bankruptcy other than a recommendation about whether bankruptcy is appropriate. When bankruptcy is the right choice, they will simply recommend a lawyer. There is no good reason to pay someone for this service.

A reputable attorney will offer advice on whether bankruptcy is appropriate. This avoids the double charge of having to pay a counselor and then an attorney. If bankruptcy is not appropriate, a good attorney will offer a range of other strategies which you can pursue independently.

In most communities, there are *nonprofit* counselors who may be able to help you deal with your debts. However, they are not always easy to find. Try to get a referral, if possible, from local officials, from a friend or neighbor, or from a legal services office. If someone approaches you by mail or telephone because they read a foreclosure notice or announcement of a court proceeding against you, think twice before paying them for assistance.

Problems With Document Preparation Services. Document preparation services have recently generated a large number of consumer complaints. These services involve non-lawyers who offer to prepare the initial bankruptcy forms for a fee.

There are several reasons for consumer dissatisfaction with these services. Non-lawyers cannot offer legal advice on bankruptcy cases. Document preparation services also offer no services after a bankruptcy case is started.

This means that if issues arise after your forms are filed, you will have nowhere to turn for help. Often, the actual case will involve complications or even simple problems which you may not be prepared to meet. For these reasons, document preparation services are rarely a good place to get help with bankruptcy.

Preparing to Meet With a Bankruptcy Specialist. You should be prepared when first meeting a bankruptcy specialist to answer the following questions:

- What types of debt are causing you the most trouble?
- What are your significant assets?
- How were the debts incurred and are they secured by your property?
- Has any creditor started a process to collect any debt, or to foreclose or repossess property? You should be prepared to report on the status of any pending lawsuits or foreclosures.

The answers to these general questions will reveal not only whether bankruptcy is likely to help you, but also the dimensions of your financial problems—their cause, scope, and likelihood of recurring. Whenever possible, it is helpful to take written information about these issues to the bankruptcy specialist, particularly copies of your bills. This will help the specialist understand how much is owed and to whom. It will also provide necessary information such as account numbers and addresses of creditors.

Complete information is essential to an effective bankruptcy. If information is not complete, you may lose your rights in whole or in part. Expected tax refunds might be lost, major debts might turn out to be nondischargeable, and property might unexpectedly be considered non-exempt.

At the same time, every possible debt should be unearthed so that the opportunity to discharge your legal liability can be used to its fullest. Debts not listed in the bankruptcy may not be discharged.

Try to review the full extent of your debts, including situations in which payments have not been recently demanded. Remember that any legal claim against you is a debt, if you are the one being sued. If you have recently obtained a credit report, a bankruptcy specialist can use that report to remind you about debts you may have forgotten.

In the worst case scenario, failure to provide complete and accurate information to your attorney or to the court can lead to big trouble. If a judge thinks that your failure to fill this obligation is significant and deliberate, you can be charged with criminal fraud. This happens rarely, but is very painful when it does occur. More commonly (but still infrequently), you can be denied your bankruptcy discharge.

TAX CONSEQUENCES
OF BANKRUPTCY

Unpaid debt usually has tax consequences. This is because the IRS views owing money in the same way it views borrowing money with one important difference. Borrowed money is income. However, because you have to repay a loan, when you borrow money, the IRS does not tax the money you borrowed. When you cancel a debt, you do not repay the amount you "borrowed." Therefore, a canceled debt is not only income, but taxable income.

Bankruptcy is one exception to this rule. If debt is discharged in the bankruptcy process, you do not owe taxes on the unpaid amount of the debt.

You may receive a 1099C form from one or more creditors listing the amount you discharged in bankruptcy as canceled debt (even though creditors are not required to file this form unless they have reason to think the loan was for business or investment purposes). Since this form also goes to the IRS, you should treat this amount as income which is exempt from taxes. You should attach an explanation to your tax form which includes your bankruptcy case number and the date of the discharge.

The tax laws are complicated. When in doubt, you should seek the advice of a qualified tax professional.

Getting Back on Your Feet: A Checklist

This book has focused on the importance of making wise decisions during periods of financial distress. Many of the choices you must make to resolve urgent debt problems are temporary and can be reversed when your financial circumstances improve. For example, you may cut clothing purchases out of your budget so that more money is available to pay the mortgage. When the mortgage is caught up, you will need to start buying necessary clothing again.

Once you start resolving your financial problems, it is important to make choices for the future which avoid renewing past problems. This checklist is intended to help you think about your financial life and your use of credit once your current debt problems are resolved.

I. YOUR BUDGET

The process of resolving your debt problems undoubtedly taught you the importance of making and sticking to a reasonable budget. Pulling yourself out of a debt crisis should not be your final goal. Do not give up your budget entirely simply because you are no longer facing a crisis situation. However, because your financial situation has changed, your budget should be reexamined.

When faced with a financial crisis, you learned what your family can do without. In reexamining your budget keep in mind what your family's true needs are. Here are some suggestions about issues to consider:

• Can you start saving to rebuild your savings account? Savings

is an important part of getting back on your feet. Your savings
account can help to protect you against new financial problems
if they arise.

- Do you have deferred home maintenance or other necessities
  which should be viewed as priorities now that your crisis has
  passed?
- Did you cut back in areas like auto maintenance, that require
  special attention in order to prevent future problems?
- Have you forgotten about any low-priority debts which you
  now wish to address?
- Did you reduce or eliminate contributions to a retirement
  plan, or borrow against that plan? Do you need to resume
  contributions or repay a retirement plan loan in order to
  provide for a stable retirement?
- Did you reduce insurance or medical coverages to save money
  temporarily? Is it necessary to restore the original coverage?

II. YOUR CREDIT CARD CHOICES

You are likely to continue to get offers for credit cards despite your recent
financial problems. While access to some credit can be necessary, you want
to avoid getting back in over your head.

- Have you reduced your reliance on credit card spending?
  Can you start to pay your balance in full each month to avoid
  new problems?
- Do you have the cheapest available credit card? Do you
  understand all of its terms? (See Chapter Ten.)
- Have you checked your credit limits recently to make sure
  that you don't have more than you need? Are you avoiding
  making minimum payments which run up the balances?
- Have you resolved any disputes you have about how much
  is due?
- Are you unnecessarily using a secured credit card, when an
  unsecured card at a similar rate is available?

III. PROTECTING YOUR HOME OR APARTMENT

To make sure that you can keep your home for the long term, here are some things to consider:

- If you have caught up on home mortgage or lease payments, have you reviewed your recent bills to make sure that your mortgage company or landlord thinks you are caught up as well? Has the lender or landlord properly credited all necessary payments? Have all court cases related to foreclosure or eviction been dropped?
- Is your current savings plan sufficient to protect you if urgent home repair needs arise in the future? Is your savings plan sufficient to help you get through any new period of financial difficulties?
- If you find that you are continuing to struggle financially, have you thought about moving to a cheaper residence? Would it relieve pressure for your family if you spend less on housing?
- Have you implemented utility conservation measures which will make your home less expensive to maintain in the long-term?
- Have you shopped around for home insurance at the best possible rate? Have you applied for any real estate tax abatement you may be entitled to?
- Have you received a larger than expected escrow payment increase from your mortgage company? (If you are caught up on back-payments, this may be in error. Some mortgage companies are careless about escrow accounting. If you can't get the issue resolved quickly, you may want to see a lawyer.)

IV. IF YOU FILED FOR BANKRUPTCY

A bankruptcy case may have gone a long way toward helping you resolve financial problems. Some follow-up actions which may be necessary:

- Did you receive a copy of your bankruptcy discharge and have you put it away in a safe place?
- Do you know what debts you still have to pay because they

were not covered by your bankruptcy discharge? (If not check
with your lawyer or review Chapter Twenty.)

- Are you still hearing from collection agencies or others about
  debts you thought were eliminated in bankruptcy? (If so,
  check with your lawyer.)
- If you successfully completed a chapter 13 bankruptcy case,
  are you still getting correspondence which indicates that
  your home or auto lender thinks you are behind? (If so, see
  your lawyer.)
- Have you dealt with the problems which caused you to file
  bankruptcy in the first place? Will you be able to avoid filing
  again in the future?

V. CREDIT REPAIR

As discussed in Chapter Seven, if you have had financial problems, there are
likely to be some things on your credit report which won't easily go away.
However, there are some things you can do which may make things easier
for you in the future.

- Have you checked your credit report to make sure it is accurate? (Although there may be many things on your credit
  report which you can do little about, you may have legal
  remedies under the Fair Credit Reporting Act if there are
  errors. For more information including how to order a
  report, see Chapter Seven.)
- Have you resolved any disputes about your credit report or
  sent the reporting agencies an explanatory letter to include
  when it distributes your report? (See Chapter Seven.)
- Are you establishing better credit habits which will show new
  creditors that you are responsible? Have you tried borrowing a
  small amount of money and repaying it immediately to show
  potential lenders that you can manage your debts?
- Have you canceled unnecessary credit cards and lines of credit
  which may make new creditors concerned about your potential to become overextended?
- Are you still getting credit card solicitations in the mail? Have

you limited yourself to one unsecured credit card on the best terms offered?

- Are you still shopping around for credit on fair terms? (If not, you may be making a mistake. Don't assume that because one creditor tells you that you are a poor credit risk, others will tell you that as well.)
- When you apply for credit for big ticket items like a home or car, are you providing a good explanation for your financial problems together with evidence showing that they have been resolved?
- Are you worrying about your credit record unnecessarily? Having resolved your financial problems, can you make a decision to reduce your reliance on credit for several years so that you don't have the pressure of new difficulties?

VI. AVOIDING SCAMS

Consumer scams are often targeted against people that have had recent financial problems. A company may get your name from bankruptcy court records, foreclosure records, or by buying lists from debt collectors. Some of these companies assume that you will be desperate enough to make bad decisions about credit. Here are some scams to avoid:

- **Paying for credit repair.** No credit repair agency can clean up your credit record if you have been behind on many debts. Promises to do so are lies designed to get you to pay for something that can't really help you. The self-help strategies discussed above and in Chapter Seven are much more likely to help you get back on your feet.
- **Taking high-rate loans to tide you over.** Some lenders offer high-rate loans to help you get back into the market for credit. The worst of these are high-interest rate loans secured by your home. These lenders are counting on your belief that you cannot get credit on better terms elsewhere. They also may make false promises that the rate can be reduced if you establish a year or more of timely payments. Lenders offering high-rate credit in these circumstances are only trying to rip you off.

- **Don't immediately accept a lender's statement that you are a "sub-prime" borrower who must pay very high interest rates to get credit.** You should always shop around rather than accept a higher than normal rate loan. You may have perfectly good credit in the eyes of another lender. Even if you are considered a high risk "sub-prime" borrower by every lender you contact, there are many types of sub-prime loans. You should shop among the different sub-prime loans until you find a reasonable rate and reasonable terms.
- **Beware of people or companies that market their services as "loan brokers."** Although some loan brokers are perfectly honest, there are other that will find a loan for you on the worst terms possible because high-rate lenders will pay them the biggest commissions. Brokers that advertise to people with a history of financial problems are among the most likely to be unscrupulous.
- **Beware of companies that advertise with claims such as "no credit check" or "bad credit no problem."** These companies are either loan brokers or lenders that are looking for borrowers that consider themselves too risky to pass a credit check. Companies that pretend they do not care about your credit record, say so in order to find borrowers willing to sign up for high rates. Remember that you can't evaluate your own credit. You may discover that when reputable lenders evaluate your credit record, they will find that you are a better credit risk than you might think.

SOME FINAL THOUGHTS

The first hurdle for many people coming out of a financial crisis is to get over feeling ashamed about past problems. The reality is that nearly everyone in this country experiences some type of financial difficulties at one time or another. It is nothing to be embarrassed about. It is important to be up-front with new creditors or lenders and not be afraid to acknowledge that you have had problems. Emphasize that you are back on your feet and financially stable.

Feelings of embarrassment might lead you to try to wipe the slate clean too quickly. This can be a mistake. It is important to realize that even though not all past problems can be erased or covered up, most creditors and lenders understand that people fall on hard times, and are usually willing to help you if you can prove that you are no longer facing financial problems.

Before you try to repair your record, make sure that your past financial problems are fully fixed. Don't be too eager to take on substantial new debt. The most critical step in rebuilding is not necessarily the number of new credit cards that you have, but rather evidence of your ongoing ability to repay loans or credit. Perhaps the worst thing you can do for your credit record is to take on too much new credit too soon and fail a second time.

Rebuild your credit history by focusing on stabilizing your income and keeping your debt burden low. Creditors know that virtually all delinquencies occur because consumers are unable to pay their debts and not because they are trying to avoid legitimate obligations. Many creditors will be more concerned about whether you have the present and future ability to repay a debt, than about your past problems.

— Appendix 1—

Budget Charts

INCOME BUDGET				
SOURCE OF INCOME	LAST MONTH ACTUAL (1)	THIS MONTH EXPECTED (2)	THIS MONTH ACTUAL (3)	ADJUSTED MONTHLY (4)
Employment (5)	$	$	$	$
Overtime				
Child Support/Alimony (7)				
Pension				
Interest				
Public Benefits (8)				
Dividends				
Trust Payments				
Royalties				
Rents Received				
Other (List) (9)				
TOTAL (MONTHLY)	$	$	$	$

NOTES

(1) This should be based on your income records for the past month.

(2) This column should include your best projections of your regular monthly income for coming months.

(3) After making your initial budget, keep careful records for the next month. Then fill in your actual income from each source. This will help you determine if your actual income meets your budget projections.

(4) After keeping records of your actual income for at least a month, go back and fill in this column based on your experience. Although this column will be a projection for the future, it should be more accurate than the projection you made when you started the budgeting process, because it will be based on actual monthly income for one month or more.

(5) Include the income of all household members who will be contributing to the family budget.

(6) You can list either your take home pay or your total employment income. If you use the total, remember to list all of your payroll deductions as expenses in the expense budget. If you use your take home pay, remember to check your pay stub to make sure that there are no unnecessary deductions.

(7) Include only the amounts you are actually expecting to receive, if any.

(8) This should include all money received from public benefits each month including food stamps, welfare, social security, disability, unemployment compensation, worker's compensation etc. If you are receiving more than one type of income, then you may want to use as box labeled "other" at the bottom of the budget.

(9) If you need more space, combine two or more other sources of income on a separate sheet and then list them together as one line in your budget.

EXPENSE BUDGET				
TYPE OF EXPENSE (10)	LAST MONTH ACTUAL (11)	THIS MONTH EXPECTED (12)	THIS MONTH ACTUAL (13)	ADJUSTED MONTH (14)
Payroll Deduction (15)				
Income Tax Withheld				
Social Security				
FICA				
Wage Garnishments (16)				
Credit Union (17)				
Other				
Home Related Expenses (18)				
Mortgage or Rent (19)				
Second Mortgage				
Third Mortgage				
Real Estate Taxes (20)				
Insurance (21)				
Condo Fees &				
Mobile Home Lot Rent				
Home Maintenance/Upkeep				
Utilities (22)				
Gas				
Electric				
Oil				
Water/Sewer				
Telephone				
Other (23)				
Food				
Clothing				
Laundry and Cleaning				
Medical (24)				
Current Needs				
Prescriptions				
Dental				
Other				
SUBTOTAL PAGE 1				

Transportation				
Auto Payments				
Car Insurance				
Gas and Maintenance				
Public Transportation				
Life Insurance				
Alimony or Support Paid				
Student Loan Payments (25)				
Amounts Owed on Debts (26)				
Credit Card (27)				
Credit Card				
Credit Card				
Medical Bill (28)				
Medical Bill				
Other Back Bills (List)(29)				
Cosigned Debts (30)				
Business Debts (List)(31)				
Other Expenses (List)(32)				
Miscellaneous (33)				
TOTAL				

INCOME AND EXPENSE TOTALS				
	LAST MONTH ACTUAL	THIS MONTH EXPECTED	THIS MONTH ACTUAL	ADJUSTED EXPECTED
A. TOTAL PROJECTED MONTHLY INCOME (34)				
B. TOTAL PROJECTED MONTHLY EXPENSES (35)				
EXCESS INCOME OR SHORTFALL (A MINUS B)				

NOTES

(10) Include the total expenses of everyone in your household who shares expenses.

(11) This should be based, as closely as possible, on your experience in the most recent month. Estimate items for which you have not kept complete records.

(12) This column should include your best projections of your monthly expenses for coming months.

(13) After making your initial budget, keep careful records for the next month. Then fill in your actual expenses for each item. This will help you determine if your actual expenses meet the budgeted amount.

(14) After keeping records of your actual expenses for at least a month, go back and fill in this column based on your experience. Although this column will be a projection for the future, it should be more accurate than the projection you made when you started the budgeting process, because it will be based on actual monthly expenses for one month or more.

(15) Do *not* fill this section out if you have used your take home pay in your income budget. However, you should check your pay stub to make sure that there are no unnecessary deductions from your pay. *Do fill this section out if you used your gross employment income budget or if you are self employed.*

(16) Bankruptcy can eliminate many types of wage garnishments. See Chapter Twenty.

(17) These payments can usually be eliminated during a period of financial hardship.

(18) Ways to keep your home during periods of financial crisis are discussed in Chapters Eleven through Fourteen if you own, and in Chapter Fifteen if you are a renter.

(19) Include amounts here only for your primary home. If you have a vacation home or a time share, include that separately below under "other expenses". This will help you determine whether you can make ends meet by giving up your second home or time share.

(20) Include your real estate taxes only if these amounts are not included with your escrow payment on your mortgage.

(21) Include your home insurance payments if these amounts are for renter's insurance or if they are not included with your escrow payment on your mortgage.

(22) Many options for reducing these amounts are discussed in Chapter Fourteen.

(23) For example, propane and cable television subscriptions are discussed in Chapter Sixteen.

(24) This should not include your back bills. Back medical bills are unsecured debts which should be handled differently in your budget and listed below under "Amounts Owed on Debts". Generally, they should only be paid in times of financial hardship if you can afford to pay. Strategies for dealing with back medical bills and other unsecured debts are covered in Chapter One.

(25) Many options for dealing with or reducing student loan obligations are discussed in Chapter Nineteen.

(26) List here the monthly payments you plan to make on your unsecured debts like credit cards and medical bills. These are low priority debts as discussed in Chapter One. You may plan to pay little or nothing if you are trying to deal with other more important expenses on a limited income. It does not make sense to make even "minimum" payments on these debts unless you can afford to do so after paying for your necessities and higher priority bills. A variety of choices for dealing with these debts and with collection activities by creditors are discussed in Chapter One and Chapter Six. Dealing with lawsuits on unsecured debts is discussed in Chapter Eight. Using bankruptcy to address unsecured debts is discussed in Chapter Twenty.

(27) In most cases you should list the minimum required payment unless you can afford to pay more. This can be costly however, since with credit card bills, interest will mount up very quickly if you pay only the minimum. If you cannot afford even the minimum monthly payment, then list zero and look into your other options for dealing with these debts as discussed in the prior note.

(28) List your back bills here. Current anticipated medical expenses should be listed separately above as a higher priority expense. Old bills can generally be dealt with like other low priority unsecured debts.

(29) Some examples might include other debts owed to professionals such as lawyers or accountants, personal loans, bills owed to prior landlords, deficiency claims on prior foreclosures or repossessions and any other debt for which the creditor has no collateral.

(30) You need to treat debts on which you are a cosigner as a high priority debt if you have given your property as collateral for the debt. Cosigned debts are a lower priority if your property does not serve as collateral. See Chapter One.

(31) Your obligations on business related debts can be complicated and depends on the type of business. You may want to get special legal assistance on whether payment on these debts should be included in your budget as a high priority.

(32) Everyone has a different situation. You should think about any other source of regular household expenses and list them here. Some frequently overlooked items include cigarettes, diapers, pet related expenses, children's allowances, lay-away payments, rent-to-own, etc. Some of these items can be quite costly and will throw your budget out of whack if they are not accounted for.

(33) You may want to include a small sum here for the miscellaneous small expenses or for emergencies which are unaccounted for elsewhere.

(34) Take this amount from your income budget above.

(35) Take this amount from your expense budget above.

(36) If you have excess income — congratulations. However, make sure that your budget actually works by trying it out for a few months. You may want to use your excess income to pay down any back debts which are carrying interest — particularly credit cards. If you have a shortfall, you should consider limiting or ending any discretionary items in your budget, terminating payment on your credit cards in order to maintain your necessities and reading the rest of this book for strategies to use to help you survive your debt while you are getting back on your feet.

— Appendix 2—

Direct Loans
William D. Ford Federal Direct Loan Program

Federal Direct Consolidation Loan
Application and Promissory Note

Warning: Any person who knowingly makes a false statement or misrepresentation on this form shall be subject to penalties which may include fines, imprisonment, or both, under the U.S. Criminal Code and 20 U.S.C. 1097.

OMB No. 1840-0693
Form Approved
Exp. Date 3/31/99

BEFORE YOU BEGIN

This form should be printed in blue or black ink or typewritten and must be signed and dated by the applicant(s).
If you cross out anything and write in new information, put your initials beside the change.

SECTION A: BORROWER INFORMATION

1. Last Name   First Name   Middle Initial   2. Social Security Number

3. Permanent Street Address (if P.O. box, see instructions)   4. Home Area Code/Telephone Number ( )

City   State   Zip Code   5. Fax Number (Optional) ( )

6. Former Name(s)   7. Date of Birth   8. Driver's License Number (put state abbreviation first) ( )

9. Employer's Name   10. Employer's Address

11. Employer's Area Code/Telephone Number   City   State   Zip Code
( )

12. If you are married, does your spouse have an eligible loan(s) (see instructions) that you want to consolidate with your loan(s)?   Yes ☐

    No ☐   If yes, complete Section C, include your spouse's loan(s) in Section D, and have your spouse sign and date
    Item 30 in Section F.

SECTION B: REFERENCE INFORMATION

13. References: Enter the requested information for two relatives or acquaintances who do not live with you and who have known you for at least three years. References may not live outside the United States.

Name   1 _____   2. _____

Permanent Address   _____   _____

City, State, Zip Code   _____   _____

Area Code/Telephone Number   ( ) _____   ( ) _____

SECTION C: SPOUSE INFORMATION   To be completed only if you responded Yes to Item 12.

14. Last Name   First Name   Middle Initial   15. Social Security Number

16. Date of Birth   17. Driver's License Number (put state abbreviation first) ( )

18. Former Name(s)   19. Fax Number (Optional) ( )

20. Employer's Name   21. Employer's Address

22. Employer's Area Code and Telephone Number   City   State   Zip Code
( )

Borrower's Name_____

Borrower's Social Security Number_____

EDUCATION LOAN INDEBTEDNESS (See instructions before completing this section.)

23. Loan Holder/Servicer's Name Address, and Area code/Telephone Number	24. Loan Type	25. B=Borrower S=Spouse J=Joint	26. Account Number	27. Current Balance	28. To be Consolidated? Yes	No

Borrower's Name_____

Borrower's Social Security Number_____

SECTION E: REPAYMENT PLAN SELECTION

Carefully read the repayment plan information in "Direct Consolidation Loans" that accompanies this application and promissory note to understand your repayment plan options. Then, complete this section to select your repayment plan. Remember—

- All student loans must be repaid under the same repayment plan. Parent PLUS loans may be repaid under a different repayment plan.
- If you select the Income Contingent Repayment Plan, you must complete the "Repayment Plan Selection" and "Income Contingent Repayment Plan Consent to Disclosure of Tax Information" forms that accompany this application and promissory note. Your selection cannot be processed without these forms.
- **If you want to consolidate a defaulted student loan(s) and you have not made a satisfactory repayment arrangement with your current holder(s), you must select the Income Contingent Repayment Plan.**

29. Place an "X" in the box that corresponds to your repayment plan selection for each loan type. Note that Direct PLUS Consolidation Loans cannot be repaid under the Income Contingent Repayment Plan.

	Income Contingent	Standard	Extended	Graduated
STUDENT LOANS *Direct Subsidized and Unsubsidized Consolidation Loans*	☐	☐	☐	☐
PARENT LOANS *Direct PLUS Consolidation Loans*	Available		☐	☐

SECTION F: PROMISSORY NOTE — To be completed and signed by borrower and spouse, if applicable.

Promise to Pay:

I promise to pay to the U.S. Department of Education (ED) all sums (hereafter "loan" or "loans") disbursed under the terms of this Promissory Note (note) to discharge my prior loan obligations, plus interest, and other fees that may become due as provided in this note. If I fail to make payments on this note when due, I will also pay collection costs including but not limited to attorney's fees and court costs. If ED accepts my application, I understand that ED will on my behalf send funds to the holder(s) of the loan(s) selected for consolidation in order to pay off this loan(s). I further understand that the amount of this loan will equal the sum of the amount(s) that the holder(s) of the loan(s) verified as the payoff balance(s) on that loan(s) selected for consolidation. My signature on this note will serve as my authorization to pay off the balance(s) of the loan(s) selected for consolidation as provided by the holder(s) of such loan(s).

This amount may be more or less than the estimated total balance I have indicated in Section D. Further, I understand that if any collection costs are owed on the loans selected for consolidation, these costs may be added to the principal balance of the consolidation loan.

I understand that this is a Promissory Note. I will not sign this note before reading it, including the text on the reverse side, even if I am advised not to read the

note. I am entitled to an exact copy of this note and a statement of the Borrower's Rights and Responsibilities. My signature certifies that I have read, understand, and agree, to the terms and conditions of this note, including the Borrower Certification and Authorization printed on the reverse side and the accompanying Borrower's Rights and Responsibilities.

If consolidating jointly with my spouse, we agree to the same terms and conditions contained in the Borrower Certification and Authorization. In addition, we confirm that we are legally married to each other and understand and agree that we are and will continue to be held jointly and severally liable for the entire amount of the debt represented by the Federal Direct Consolidation Loan without regard to the amounts of our individual loan obligations that are consolidated and without regard to any change that may occur in our marital status. We understand that this means that one of us may be required to pay the entire amount due if the other is unable or refuses to pay. We understand that the Federal Direct Consolidation Loan we are applying for will be cancelled only if both of us qualify for cancellation. We further understand that we may postpone repayment of the loan only if we provide ED with written requests that confirm Federal Direct Consolidation Loan Program deferment or forbearance eligibility for both of us at the same time.

I UNDERSTAND THAT THIS IS A FEDERAL LOAN THAT I MUST REPAY.

30. Signature of Borrower _____ Date _____

31. Signature of Spouse (if consolidating jointly) _____ Date _____

Bibliography

NCLC PUBLICATIONS

*All National Consumer Law Publications can be ordered
from Publications, National Consumer Law Center,
18 Tremont Street, Boston, MA 02108, 617-523-8089
Website:www.consumerlaw.org*

Access to Utility Service (1996 and Supp.) covers all aspects of utility service issues — termination protections, terminations relating to service in landlord's name, concerns of mobile home park tenants, erroneous billing, impact of bankruptcy, federal energy assistance benefits, weatherization programs, and more.

Automobile Fraud (1998) explains consumers' remedies when they purchase used cars with tampered odometers or other problems such as cars that were lemons or salvage vehicles.

Consumer Bankruptcy Law and Practice (5th ed. 1996 and Supp.). The best resource available on all aspects of consumer bankruptcy filings, including hundreds of model forms.

Consumer Class Actions: A Practical Litigation Guide (3d ed. 1995) explains how even a small law firm can mount a consumer class action, thus obtaining widespread relief for victims of a consumer scam.

Consumer Law Pleadings with Disk, Numbers One, Two Three and Four (1994, 1995, 1997, 1998) presents sample pleadings for use in consumer law cases — sample complaints, interrogatories, other discovery, motions, settlements, and more.

Consumer Warranty Law (1997 and Supp.) is a detailed manual on all aspects of consumer warranty law and the rights of consumer purchasers of goods and services.

The Cost of Credit (1995 and Supp.) is a unique legal resource, covering federal and state law regulating interest rates and other credit terms for consumer loans and credit sales.

Credit Discrimination (2d ed. 1998) covers consumers' rights when they are denied credit, including a thorough analysis of the federal Equal Credit Opportunity Act.

Fair Credit Reporting Act (4th ed. 1998) explains a consumer's rights in dealing with credit reporting agencies, including extensive treatment of the federal Fair Credit Reporting Act.

Fair Debt Collection (3d ed. 1996 and Supp.), the definitive treatise on consumer remedies to fight debt collection harassment, including extensive treatment of the federal Fair Debt Collection Practices Act.

Repossessions and Foreclosures (3d ed. 1995 and Supp.) covers all aspects of consumer repossession and foreclosure law, including seizure of homes, automobiles, mobile homes, and household goods.

Truth in Lending (3d ed. 1995 and Supp.) is the essential guide for anyone handling a Truth in Lending case, either to obtain statutory damages or to cancel a loan. Also included is a detailed analysis of the federal Consumer Leasing Act.

Unfair and Deceptive Acts and Practices (4th ed. 1997 and Supplement) is a unique resource covering all types of unfair and deceptive conduct in the marketplace, including special sections on student loans, the federal racketeering statute, other consumer remedies, and insurance issues.

NCLC Energy & Utility Update (National Consumer Law Center), a bimonthly newsletter that keeps readers current on low income utility issues, such as utility terminations, low income payment plans, the federal fuel assistance program, low income weatherization, and telephone and water issues.

NCLC REPORTS (National Consumer Law Center) covers the latest developments in all major areas of low income consumer law. Twenty-four issues a year are divided into four different editions each published bimonthly: Bankruptcy & Foreclosures Edition; Debt Collection & Repossessions Edition; Consumer Credit & Usury Edition; and Deceptive Practices & Warranties Edition.

Consumer Brochures on many topics are also available.

BOOKS

Caher, James P. and John M. Caher, *Debt Free!* (1996) is a guide to personal bankruptcy. Reviews basic bankruptcy terms and concepts and gives information on "life after bankruptcy."

Center on Budget and Policy Priorities, *EITC Community Outreach Kit* is a particularly helpful resource on the earned income tax credit. It is designed for organizations and counselors to help them inform low-income families about their potential eligibility for tax refunds. The kit contains a fact sheet, eligibility guidelines, campaign posters, flyers printed in English and Spanish, and a summary of effective outreach strategies. To receive the kit, write to the EITC Campaign, Center on Budget and Policy Priorities, 777 N. Capitol St., Suite 705, Washington D.C. 20002, 202-408-1080.

Elias, Leonard, & Renauer, *How to File for Bankruptcy*, is a guide for those attempting to file bankruptcy on their own. Available from the Nolo Press, 950 Parker Street, Berkeley, California 94710, 1-800-846-9455. http://www.nolo.com.

Evans, James, *Law on the Net*, is a helpful resource for those who want to do legal research using the internet. There is a lot of information in this book including research sites for case law, statutes and for particular legal topics. Available from the Nolo Press, 950 Parker Street, Berkeley, California 94710, 1-800-846-9455. http://www. nolo.com.

Federal Home Mortgage Association, *Sellers' and Servicers' Guide* contains the guidelines all Freddie Mac lenders must utilize in foreclosing on a home and negotiating repayment schedules. The cost is $275, which includes a one year update service. Available from Freddie Mac, Attn: Subscription Services, 8200 Jones Branch Drive, McLean VA 22102.

Federal National Mortgage Association, *Servicing Guide* contains the guidelines all Fannie Mae lenders must utilize in foreclosing on a home and negotiating repayment schedules. The cost is $300, which includes a continual upkeep service. Available from Fannie Mae, 510 Walnut St., 16th Floor, Philadelphia, Pennsylvania 19106 and from other Fannie Mae regional offices.

Food Research Action Center, *Guide to the Food Stamp Program* (9th ed. 1994 and 1997 Supp.) is an excellent resource on the federal food stamp program and is available for $22 directly from the Food Research Action Center, 1875 Connecticut Ave. NW, Suite 540, Washington. D.C. 20009-5728, 202-986-2200. http://www.frac.org.

Leonard, Robin, *Money Troubles: Legal Strategies to Cope With Your Debts* is a good consumer self-help manual for certain types of less serious consumer debt problems, such as straightening out a credit report or dealing with billing errors. Available from the Nolo Press, 950 Parker Street, Berkeley, California 94710, 1-800-846-9455. http://www.nolo.com.

Leonard, Robin and Shae Irving, *Take Control of Your Student Loans* is a good introduction to student loan issues including federal, state and private loans. Available from the Nolo pres, 950 Parker Street, Berkeley, California 94710, 1-800-846-9455. http://www.nolo.com.

National Health Law Program, *Advocates' Guide to the Medicaid Program* (1993) is an excellent source for information on Medicaid benefits. It is available for $50 from NHELP, 2639 S. La Cienega Blvd., Los Angeles, California 90034, 310-204-6010. http://www.healthlaw.org.

Sommer, Henry J., *Consumer Bankruptcy* (1994) is a guide to consumer bankruptcy suitable for a sophisticated non-lawyer. It is based on National Consumer Law Center, *Consumer Bankruptcy Law and Practice* (5th ed. 1996 and Supp.).

Strong, Howard, *What Every Credit Card User Needs to Know,* (1999) includes almost everything you want to know about selecting and using credit cards. Includes numerous sample complaint letters as well as an in-depth look at the ins and outs of the credit card industry.

PERIODICALS

Clearinghouse Review (National Clearinghouse for Legal Services) is a monthly magazine covering recent developments in all areas of poverty law, including government assistance, rights of consumer debtors, housing issues, health law, and special issues relating to the elderly, migrant workers, immigrants, and veterans. Annual subscription is available from the National Clearinghouse for Legal Services, 205 W. Monroe Street, Second Floor, Chicago, Illinois 60606, 312-263-3830. http://www.nclsplp.org.

The Health Advocate (National Health Law Program), a quarterly publication concentrating on Medicaid benefits and other low income health law issues. It is available from NHELP, 2639 S. La Cienega Blvd., Los Angeles, California 90034, 310-204-6010. http://www.healthlaw.org.

Washington Weekly (National Senior Citizens Law Center), a weekly publication focusing on issues of interest to seniors including Social Security, Medicare and other health issues. It is available from NSCLC, 1101 14th St., NW Suite 400, Washington, D.C. 20005, 202-289-6976. http://www.nsclc.org.

HELPFUL WEB SITES

Car Information

- *www.autosite.com*: Good collection of resources regarding cars, including fact sheets, reports on used and new cars, and information on repairs and financing.
- *www.carwizard.com*: Car pricing and safety information for used and new cars.
- *Kelly Blue Book: www.kbb.com*: Information on new and used automobile prices and other automobile information.
- *www.carprices.com/lemon_law.html*: State by state lemon law summaries.

Credit Bureaus (and to order credit reports)

- *Equifax*: www.equifax.com
- *Experian* (formerly TRW): www.experian.com
- *Transunion*: www.transunion.com

General Consumer and Legal Sites

- *American Bankruptcy Institute*: www.abi.org
  This website provides bankruptcy information for consumers and lawyers.
- *Better Business Bureau*: www.bbb.org
  You can check on a businesses' complaint record or file a complaint on-line.
- *Center on Budget and Policy Priorities*: www.cbpp.org
  Nonpartisan research organization and policy institute that analyzes government policies and programs, particularly those affecting low and moderate-income people.
- *Consumer World*: www.consumerworld.org
  General consumer site offering links to hundreds of other sites providing information to consumers.
- *Laypeople's Law Lounge*: www.lectlaw.com/lay.html
  A user-friendly resource on all types of legal topics presented with good humor.
- *National Association of Consumer Advocates*: www.naca.net
  Provides a listing of consumer attorney members throughout the country, divided by practice area. Also includes updated

information on hot consumer topics and other events.

- *National Consumer Law Center.* www.consumerlaw.org
Updated to include information on key developments in
consumer law. Also includes information on how to order
NCLC publications, including books, periodicals and
consumer education materials.

- *National Senior Citizens Law Center.* www.nsclc.org
A very helpful web site for the latest information on issues of
particular interest to seniors. The focus is on Social Security,
Medicare and other health issues.

- *Nolo Press.* www.nolo.com
Well-known and respected national publisher of self-help legal
manuals. The web site contains information about how to
order Nolo publications as well as helpful legal tips.

Government Sites

- *Federal Trade Commission.* www.ftc.gov/bcp/menu-credit.htm
FTC publications on consumer credit rights.

- *Internal Revenue Service.* www.irs.ustreas.gov
An IRS site that is helpful in answering basic tax filing and
other questions.

- *Government Services Agency.* www.pueblo.gsa.gov
The government's consumer information center. Contains
direct links to federal indexes and agencies, consumer-help
organizations, community nets and freenets and other sites
providing helpful consumer information.

- *National Highway Traffic Safety Administration.*
ww.nhtsa.dot.gov/cars/problems.
Information about vehicle recalls, service bulletins, consumer
complaints and safety investigations.

Glossary

Words in italics are separately defined in this glossary.

Acceleration. When a *creditor* claims the total balance of a loan as due immediately. This cannot usually occur unless you have fallen behind on payments. In the case of a home mortgage, receipt of a letter stating that a loan has been "accelerated" is normally an important warning sign of foreclosure. See Chapter 11.

Accord and Satisfaction. This is the legal term which applies when you make clear that you consider your payment the full and final resolution of a disputed debt. If the creditor accepts the payment, the law treats that acceptance as the final payment of the debt. See Chapter 9.

Amount Financed. The amount of money you are getting in a loan, calculated under rules required by federal law. This is the amount of money you are borrowing after deduction of certain loan charges that the *Truth in Lending Act* defines as *finance charges*. You should think of the amount financed as the real amount you are borrowing. You will find the amount financed for a loan on the *disclosure statement* that is given to you when the loan papers are signed. See Chapter 4.

Annual Percentage Rate. The interest rate on a loan expressed under rules required by federal law. It is more accurate to look at the annual percentage rate (as opposed to the stated interest rate) to determine the true cost of a loan, because it tells you the full cost of the loan including many of the lender's fees. You will find the annual percentage rate for a loan on the *disclosure statement* that is given to you when the loan papers are signed. See Chapter 4.

Answer. In a lawsuit, this is a legal document that the *defendant* must file to respond to the claims being raised. There are often short time deadlines to file an answer. Failure to file an answer can result in a *default judgment*. See Chapter 8.

Arrears. The total amount you are behind on a debt. Usually the amount of all back payments plus any collection costs.

Attachment. A legal process that allows a creditor to "attach" a *lien* to property that you own. Depending on state law, almost any kind of property may be subject to attachment, including your home, automobile, bank accounts and wages. Once a *lien* is attached to the property, you may face further collection action on that property, including *execution, garnishment* or *foreclosure*. See Chapters 8 and 18.

Automatic Stay. A bankruptcy case automatically prevents continuation of creditor collection activity. Filing bankruptcy is the only way to get this protection. See Chapter 20.

Balloon Payment. A large lump sum *payment* that is due as the last payment on a loan. Often used by lenders as a way to make monthly payments artificially low.

Bankruptcy. A legal process available in all states that allows you to address your debt problems according to a set of special rules, while getting protection from continued collection activity. See Chapter 20.

Bond. Amounts required by a court order to protect a party to a lawsuit while the case proceeds. A bond may be required in some circumstances to pursue an appeal. See Chapter 8.

Capitalization. Capitalization occurs when items owed on a loan are treated as part of a new principal balance. When *arrears* are "capitalized," the amount of the arrears is included in the principal before the interest rate is applied. Often, capitalization and *reamortization* go hand in hand. If the arrears are "capitalized" and the loan is "reamortized," your lender will recalculate your payment using the existing interest rate and the new principal balance.

Collateral. Property put up to secure a loan. If you have given a creditor collateral, that creditor can normally take and sell the collateral if you are not able to repay the loan. A creditor with collateral is normally known as a "*secured creditor.*" See Chapter 1.

Complaint. A document commencing a lawsuit. A complaint normally includes a statement of all of the claims being raised by the person bringing the lawsuit. See Chapter 8.

Cosign. Agreeing to be responsible for someone else's debt. A "cosigner" is normally responsible to pay back a debt just as if he or she had received the money.

Counterclaim. A response to a lawsuit in which the person being sued raises legal claims against the person (or business) which started the case. For example, if you are sued by an automobile seller who claims you did not pay for a car, you might counterclaim that the car was a "lemon." See Chapter 9.

Credit Bureau, also called consumer reporting agency or credit reporting agency. This is a company that receives information about a consumer's credit history and keeps records that are available to those seeking data about that consumer. See Chapter 7.

Credit Record, also called a consumer report or a credit report, is the information about a consumer that a credit bureau has on file that it can report to others. See Chapter 7.

Creditor. Any person or business to whom you owe money.

Cure a Default. If you have defaulted on a debt, this is a process for correcting the *default.* Most often, a "cure" refers to getting caught up on missed payments (paying the *arrears*). A cure may also be called *reinstatement.*

Debt Collector. The most common use of this term applies to anyone who collects debts. However, under the federal *Fair Debt Collection Practices Act* "FDCPA," the term "debt collector" only applies to collection agencies and lawyers (or their employees) that are collecting debts for others. For this reason the FDCPA only applies to an independent debt collection agency or a lawyer hired by a *creditor* to collect its debts. State laws may cover other types of collectors.

Debtor. Any person who owes money to another. In *bankruptcy*, the term "debtor" refers to the person who begins a bankruptcy case.

Debtor's Examination, also known as "post-judgment process," "asset examination" and "supplementary process." This is normally a court ordered proceeding in which a debtor must appear in court or in an attorney's office to answer questions about current income and assets from which a *judgment* may be collected. In many states, failure to appear at a debtor's examination can result in an arrest warrant. See Chapter 8.

Deed in Lieu. This is an agreement to turn real estate over to a lender as an alternative to *foreclosure*. See Chapter 11.

Deed of Trust. In some states, this is the term used for a pledge of real estate as *collateral*. It is similar to a *mortgage*.

Default. Failing to meet the requirements of an agreement. Most defaults involve failure to make required payments. However, other types of defaults are possible, including failure to maintain necessary insurance and failure to keep *collateral* in proper condition.

Default Judgment. A *judgment* in a lawsuit against a party who did not meet legal requirements in connection with the case. The most common reason for a default judgment is failing to file an *answer* or other necessary papers before deadlines specified by law. See Chapter 8.

Defendant. In a lawsuit, this is the person or business that is being sued. See Chapter 8.

Defense. A legal reason why a court should not award any or all of what is requested in a lawsuit. For example, a statement that the money is not owed is a defense to a collection lawsuit. See Chapter 8.

Deficiency. The amount a debtor owes a creditor on a debt after the creditor seizes and sells the *collateral*. A deficiency arises when the collateral is sold for less than the amount of the debt. Normally a creditor must bring a lawsuit to collect a deficiency. See Chapters 8, 11, and 17.

Deposition. A proceeding in a legal case in which a person is asked questions about relevant facts (usually in a lawyer's office) and gives sworn answers under oath. Your deposition may be required if you start a lawsuit or if one is filed against you. Your lawyer may require depositions of others. Depositions are a normal part of the *discovery* process used to prepare for a court trial.

Discharge. A document that ends a debtor's legally enforceable obligation to pay a debt. It is common to get a discharge of a mortgage debt after the mortgage is fully paid off. In addition, most bankruptcies result in a discharge at the end of the case that applies to many debts. See Chapters 11 and 20.

Disclosure Statement. This term is commonly used to refer to the document that explains loan terms according to the *Truth in Lending Act*. This Act requires most lenders to provide a disclosure statement in connection with any loan to a consumer. The consumer may have a *defense* to repaying a loan where the loan disclosures were not properly made. See Chapters 9 and 14.

Discovery. This term covers a variety of legal processes by which the parties to a lawsuit obtain information from each other and documents related to the case. The discovery process allows you and your lawyers to prepare a case.

Equity. Your equity in property is the amount of cash you would keep if you sold property and paid off all of the liens on that property. For example, if you own a house worth $100,000, but you owe $60,000 on your original mortgage and $10,000 on a second mortgage, you have $30,000 in equity. The same principle applies to cars and other types of property.

Escrow. Amounts set aside for a particular purpose. A formal escrow usually requires a legal agreement that covers permissible usage of the escrow and how and where the money is to be kept. One type of escrow is money you pay to your mortgage company to cover taxes and insurance. Another use of escrow is in circumstances in which you have a dispute with a creditor. You may choose to set up an escrow to pay the debt in the event you lose the dispute.

Eviction. A legal process terminating the right to occupy a home, apartment or business property. State law eviction proceedings are a prerequisite to putting someone out. See Chapter 15.

Execution. The process of enforcing a court judgment by taking property from the *defendant*. Execution of a judgment of *eviction*, for example, involves the sheriff or a public official putting the tenants out. Execution of a *judgment lien* involves seizing and selling the property subject to the lien. See Chapter 8.

Exempt Property. This is property that the law allows you to keep when you are being faced with collection on an *unsecured debt*. In *bankruptcy*, exempt property is protected from sale to satisfy the claims of creditors. Your exemption applies to your *equity* in the property after deduction for the amounts you owe to pay *liens* on that property. See Chapters 8, 18 and 20.

Exemptions. These are laws that give you the right to maintain your *exempt property*.

Fair Credit Reporting Act. A federal (national) law that governs the conduct of *credit bureaus* and that regulates use of credit reports. See Chapter 7.

Fair Debt Collection Practices Act. A federal (national) law that governs the conduct of debt collectors and that prevents many abusive collection tactics. See Chapter 6.

Federal Law. A law of the United states that applies throughout the country. The *bankruptcy* law is an example of a federal law.

Finance Charge. The amount of money a loan will cost you expressed as a dollar figure. The finance charge includes the interest together with certain other loan charges specified by the *Truth in Lending Act*. You will find the loan's finance charge on the *disclosure statement* given to you when you sign the loan papers. See Chapters 4 and 14.

Foreclosure. This is a legal process to terminate your ownership of real estate that is *collateral* for a debt, based on a *mortgage* or *deed of trust*. In some states, foreclosure involves a court proceeding ("judicial foreclosure"), while in others foreclosure occurs by creditor action alone ("non-judicial foreclosure"). See Chapters 11-14.

Fraudulent Transfer. Giving away property to keep it out of the hands of creditors. The law allows *creditors* to sue to get the property back. See Chapter 3.

Garnishment. A *creditor's* seizure, to satisfy a debt, of property belonging to the *debtor* that is in the possession of a third party. Usually a court has to authorize the seizure in advance. An example would be seizure of money in your bank account to repay a court judgment. Wages owed to you can also be garnished in many states. See Chapter 8.

Guarantor. A person who agrees to pay another person's debt in the event that he or she does not pay. The term guarantor is often used interchangeably with *cosigner*, even though there are some minor legal distinctions in the collection process.

Home Ownership and Equity Protection Act "HOEPA." This is a federal (national) law that provides special protection to homeowners when they obtain home mortgage loans at high interest rates or with fees exceeding 8% of the loan amount.

Homestead Exemption. The right, available in most states and in the *bankruptcy* process, to treat your residence as *exempt property* that cannot be sold to satisfy the claims of *unsecured creditors*. In most states, the homestead exemption covers a certain dollar amount of your equity in your residence. A home cannot normally be sold to pay claims of your creditors unless your equity in the home exceeds the amount of the exemption. A homestead exemption will not normally protect you from *foreclosure* when you have voluntarily pledged your home as *collateral*. See Chapters 8 and 14.

Insolvent. A person or business that does not have sufficient assets to pay its debts.

Judgment. A determination by a court as to the outcome of a lawsuit, including any amounts owed.

Judgment Lien. A *lien* that attaches to property as the result of a *judgment*. For example, if you lose a collection lawsuit, the creditor normally has the right to an *attachment* on any real estate that you own. Once a judgment lien is placed on the property, the creditor may be entitled to *execution* by a forced sale of the property. Judgment liens can attach to property other than real estate.

Judgment-Proof. This term is applied to people or businesses with property of minimal value, which can be entirely protected by *exemptions*. If you are judgment-proof, it is difficult or sometimes impossible for any creditor to force you to pay a debt. See Chapter 1.

Lemon Law. This is a state law that gives you protection if you purchase an automobile that does not work properly and cannot easily be fixed. Most lemon laws only apply to new cars, but some also apply to used cars. See Chapters 9 and 17.

Levy. A process, in some states, for *attachment* of a *judgment lien* and/or *execution* of that *lien*.

Lien. Also called a "security interest," is a legal interest taken by creditors in your property to secure repayment of a debt. A lien can be created voluntarily in connection with a loan, such as when you pledge real estate by giving a creditor a *mortgage* or *deed of trust*. A lien can also be created without your consent by *attachment* based on a court order. A creditor with a lien is called a *secured creditor*.

Liquidation. Sale of property to pay creditors. The term is also used as a shorthand name for the chapter 7 bankruptcy process, even though property is not always sold in that bankruptcy process. See Chapter 20.

Mortgage. An agreement in which a property owner grants a *creditor* the right to satisfy a debt by selling the property in the event of a *default*. See Chapters 9-14.

Mortgage Servicer. A bank, mortgage company, or a similar business that communicates with property owners concerning their *mortgage* loans. The servicer usually works for another company that owns the mortgage. It may accept and record payments, negotiate *workouts*, and supervise the *foreclosure* process in the event of a *default*. See Chapters 11 and 12.

Negative Amortization. In some loan situations, your payments do not even cover the amount of interest due for that payment period. For example, if you have a $50,000 loan at 10% interest for 15 years and make monthly payments of $400 a month, that loan will negatively amortize. At the end of the 15 years, even if you make all of your payments, you will owe more than $50,000. Negative amortization is usually associated with a large *balloon payment* due in the last month of the loan.

Negative Equity. Negative *equity* arises when the value of an item of property you own is less than the sum total you owe on all the liens on that property. For example, if you own a home worth $100,000 and borrow $125,000 to consolidate debts, you have negative equity of $25,000.

Non-Purchase Money Security Interest. A non-purchase money security interest arises when you agree to give a lender collateral that was not purchased with money from that loan (property you already own). For example, a finance company may insist that you give a lawn-mower or living room set as collateral for a loan you take out to pay for car repairs. See Chapter 18.

Note. This term is commonly used as a name for a contract involving the loan of money.

Notice of Right to Cancel. This document explains your right to cancel a loan in some circumstances. You should receive such a notice in connection with most door-to-door sales and for *mortgage* loans that are not used to buy your residence. Cancellation rights are discussed in Chapters 4 and 14.

Notice to Quit. In most states, this is a notice given by an owner of property (usually a landlord) demanding that a tenant leave within a specified period of time or face eviction proceedings. See Chapter 15.

Personal Property. Property other than real estate.

Plaintiff. This is a person or business that begins a lawsuit.

Pre-Sale. Sale of property in anticipation of *foreclosure* or *repossession,* usually with the lender's consent. A pre-sale is likely to lead to a higher sale price than foreclosure or repossession. See Chapters 12 and 17.

Pro Se (also called "pro per"). Representing yourself (without an attorney) in a legal case or bankruptcy proceeding.

Purchase Money Security Interest. A lien on property that arises when you agree to allow a lender to take as collateral the property you are purchasing with the loan. See Chapter 18.

Punitive Damages. Special damages that are sometimes awarded in court to punish a party which is responsible for serious misconduct.

Reaffirmation. An agreement in the *bankruptcy* process to pay back a debt that would otherwise be *discharged* in bankruptcy. Most reaffirmation agreements are a bad idea. See Chapter 20.

Reamortization. When a loan is reamortized, your payment is recalculated based on loan terms that are different from the original terms. For example, if you have paid for five years on a ten year loan, your lender might consider starting the ten year period again and recalculating your payments. This will lower your payments as discussed in Chapter 12. Similarly, your *arrears* may be *capitalized* (included in the principal) and your loan reamortized to reflect the higher principal balance on which interest is accruing. This will always increase your payments if the period you have to repay is not lengthened, but may nevertheless be helpful if your payments after reamortization are cheaper than other plans to get caught up on arrears. See Chapter 12.

Redeem. Recovering *collateral* from a *creditor* by paying the entire amount you owe (whether past due or not). In *bankruptcy*, property can be redeemed in some situations by paying the collateral's value even if that amount is less than the entire amount owed.

Refinancing. The process of paying back old debts by borrowing new money either from an existing *creditor* or a new creditor. Many of the pitfalls to refinancing an existing debt when you are having financial problems are discussed in Chapter 4.

Reinstatement. The process of remedying a *default* so that the lender will treat you as if you had never fallen behind. See definition of *curing a default*.

Rent-to-Own. A process in which you rent property until you have paid enough to qualify for ownership. Most rent-to-own deals are very expensive and a bad idea for the consumer. See Chapter 3.

Reorganization (Chapter 13 Bankruptcy). This is a bankruptcy process to get relief from debts by making court-supervised payments over a period of time. The alternative is usually *liquidation* under chapter 7. See Chapter 20.

Replevin. The legal process in which a creditor seeks to recover *personal property* on which it claims a *lien.* Replevin is often threatened, but rarely occurs. See Chapter 18.

Repossession (often called "self-help repossession"). Seizure by the creditor of *collateral* after the debtor's *default,* usually without court supervision or permission. Repossession is most common in connection with car loans. See Chapters 17 and 18.

Rescission. This is a right under some laws to cancel a contract or loan. The most common example of rescission arises in home equity loan transactions. You have the right to rescind that loan for the first three business days after the loan is signed. In some cases, if the *creditor* has violated the law, your right to rescind may continue after the three day period is up.

Retaliatory Eviction. An *eviction* where a landlord seeks to punish a tenant for exercising his or her legal rights (such as complaining to the building inspector or forming a tenant's organization). While retaliatory evictions are generally illegal, they may be hard to prove. See Chapter 15.

Reverse Mortgage. A *refinancing* option usually available only to older homeowners who have built up substantial equity in their property. In a reverse mortgage, money is drawn based on the value of the property without an immediate repayment obligation, because the lender expects repayment by sale of the property at some point in the future. See Chapter 4.

Satisfaction. This is a legal document that states that a debt has been fully paid or that partial payment has been accepted as payment in full. A satisfaction is a type of *discharge.*

Secured Credit Cards. A credit card for which the card issuer requires that the card holder place a certain amount of money in a bank account with the card issuer. If the debtor does not repay the credit card, the card issuer can seize the money in the bank account. See Chapter 7.

Secured Creditor. Any *creditor* that has *collateral* for a debt.

Secured Debt. A debt for which the *creditor* has *collateral* in the form of a *mortgage, lien*, or *security interest* in certain items of property. The creditor can seize the property (collateral) if the *debtor defaults* in repayment of the debt.

Security Interest. See "*Lien*," above.

Self-help Repossession. This is a process by which a *creditor* that has taken property as *collateral* can *repossess* the property without first getting court permission. See Chapters 17 and 18.

Servicer. See "*Mortgage Servicer*," above.

Short Sale. A type of *pre-sale* in which the *creditor* agrees to let you sell property (usually real estate) for less than the full amount owed and to accept the proceeds of the sale as full *satisfaction* of the debt. See Chapter 12.

State Law. A law passed by an individual state that only applies to transactions in that state.

Subpoena. A document that normally is issued by a court in connection with a lawsuit, and that directs your attendance in a court or law office at a particular time. A subpoena may require production of documents related to the case.

Summons (also called "original notice" or "notice of suit"). This is a document that is provided at the beginning of the lawsuit to tell the *defendant* what is being requested and what must be done to respond to the *complaint*. The term summons is also sometimes used interchangeably with *subpoena* for other legal papers that direct a person to be at a particular place at a particular time.

Tax Refund Anticipation Loan. A loan to the *debtor* to be repaid out of the debtor's tax refund. The refund is often then sent directly to the lender. These loans can be very expensive. See Chapter 3.

Trustee. A trustee is a person or business that is responsible for managing assets for others. In *bankruptcy*, the trustee is a person appointed to administer the bankruptcy case and its assets to maximize the recovery for unsecured creditors. The trustee in bankruptcy is not a court official and cannot make decisions without final approval by the bankruptcy court.

Truth in Lending Act. A federal (national) law that requires that most lenders, when they make a loan, provide standard form disclosures of the cost and payment terms of the loan. Always review and retain these disclosures whenever they are provided to you. See Chapters 4 and 14.

Unsecured Creditor. A *creditor* that has no *collateral* for the debt owed. See Chapter 1.

Unsecured Debt. A debt that does not involve *collateral.*

Variable Rate Mortgage. This is a mortgage loan on which the interest rate can change over time. The changes can affect the amount of your monthly payments. See Chapter 4.

Wage Assignment. An agreement to have wages paid to a person other than yourself. For example, some people assign a portion of their wages to be paid directly to cover a credit union bill. When experiencing financial problems, you should reevaluate any voluntary wage assignments you have made. See Chapter 1.

Wage Garnishment. *Garnishment* of the *debtor's* wages from the debtor's employer. See Chapter 8.

Warranty. Goods or services you purchase contain explicit and/or implicit promises (called warranties) that the goods or services sold will meet certain standards. Sellers may try to disavow these warranties, but failure to live up to warranties often can be a *defense* to repayment of the debt created by the sale contract. See Chapter 9.

Workout. This term covers a variety of negotiated agreements you might arrange with *creditors* to address a debt you are having trouble paying. Most commonly, the term is used with respect to agreements with a *mortgage* lender to restructure a loan to avoid *foreclosure*. See Chapter 12.

Index

To Order

To order *Surviving Debt*, contact your local bookstore, or order directly from National Consumer Law Center by sending $17 (shipping and handling included) for each copy. Please call (617) 523-8089 for MasterCard/Visa orders and for bulk discount orders of five or more.

Send your check to:
National Consumer Law Center
18 Tremont Street, Suite 400
Boston, MA 02108

(617) 523-8089
Fax (617) 523-7398
email: publications@nclc.org

Visit National Consumer Law Center on the web:
www.consumerlaw.org